VOICES
from the
EDGE

**CONVERSATIONS WITH
JERRY GARCIA, RAM DASS, ANNIE SPRINKLE,
MATTHEW FOX, JARON LANIER & OTHERS
INTERVIEWS BY DAVID JAY BROWN AND REBECCA McCLEN NOVICK
CO-AUTHORS OF *MAVERICKS OF THE MIND***

THE CROSSING PRESS
FREEDOM, CA 95019

Library of Congress Cataloging-in-Publication Data

Voices from the edge : conversations with Jerry Garcia, Ram Dass,
    Annie Sprinkle, Matthew Fox, Jaron Lanier, and others / co-authored
    by David Jay Brown and Rebecca McClen Novick.
        p. cm.
    ISBN 0-89594-732-3
    1. Consciousness. 2. Mind and body. 3. New age persons-
-Interviews. I. Brown, David Jay. II. Novick, Rebecca McClen.
BF311.V57 1995
081--dc20   95-20302
                                                    CIP

Acknowledgments

Putting this collection together was a great deal of fun and a wonderful learning experience, with more than a few epiphanies along the way. It was also a lot of work, taking about two years to complete. Many people helped make it possible. We would like to extend extra special thanks to Nina Graboi and Carolyn Mary Kleefeld for their endless support and belief in our work over the years. For their essential help with the book, we are also extremely grateful to Randy Baker, Marie Devlin, Denise Dufault, Patricia Gaul, Alex Grey, Laura Huxley, Oscar Janiger, Fonda Joyce, Dennis McNally, Marlene Rhoeder, Dale Robbins, Tango Parish Snyder, Rasa Julie Thies, and Jonathan Young and Carolyn Radlo at the Pacifica Graduate Institute.

In addition, we would like to express our sincere appreciation to Gabrielle Alberici, Phil Baily, Peter Bartczak, Debra Berger, Faustin Bray, Brummbaer, Kutira Decosterd and Raphael, Sue Espanosa, Robert Forte, Lauran Freebody, Liane Gabora, Peter Gorman, Dieter Hagenbach, Deborah Harlow, Krystle James, Robin Kay, Barbara Clarke-Lilly, Jeff Mandel and Steen, Arleen Margulis, Jimmy Mastalski, Fumiko Takagi, Jerry Snider, Victoria Sulski, S. Mark Taper, Silvia Utiger, Brian Wallace, and Nur Wesley for their help and contributions.

We would also like to thank our farsighted publishers, John and Elaine Gill, as well as our publicist, Dena Taylor.

Most of all, we would like to express our deepest appreciation to all the remarkable men and women we interviewed for sharing their extraordinary lives with us.

Previously published excerpts from interviews:

Marija Gimbutas—*Magical Blend*, Summer 1993, 12–20.
Jerry Garcia—*Magical Blend*, Fall 1993, 32–40, 88–89 and *Relix*, Summer 1995.
Alexander and Ann Shulgin—*High Times*, August 1994, 50–53.
John Robbins—*High Times*, February 1995, 58–61.
Ram Dass—*High Times*, March 1995.
Matthew Fox—*The Sun*, April 1995.

To our significant sentient others,
Wendy and Ronny

Table of Contents

Preface

"You're going to have to explain what these people are doing in a book together," said a close friend, looking at me with loving sternness. "What *do* they have in common, anyway?" On the surface, there does seem to be the need to justify why an ex-porn star and a Catholic priest are rubbing shoulders (or anything else, for that matter) in a collection of interviews, not to mention a chemist, a musician, and an archaeologist. But it seems to me that in this world of ongoing cultural meiosis, it is far more necessary to justify *similarity* than to justify diversity. Loving the alien—or at the very least, accepting the alien—is not just an amusing psychological pastime anymore; it's a survival imperative.

Exclusivity breaks down communication—between neighbors, between cultures, between races, between countries—so that the farmer pollutes the upstream river, giving no thought to the farmer downstream. When we define ourselves as something more than merely a product of a culture, race, sex, or religious group, we realize how our separateness has limited us, and we begin work on what Jean Houston refers to as the "orchestration of our many selves." Appreciation of diversity keeps us supple, stops our minds from crusting over, and allows us to keep reinventing ourselves.

Everyone in this book is used to being judged. Snobbery lurks in the most unlikely places, even in the most decent and open of minds. If you look down your nose you will only see your feet. But to look out and across the apparent barriers that separate you from the Other (a homeless drunk gives you directions to your hotel; a toddler corrects you about the number of Jupiter's moons) is like coming up for air and taking a gulp of the mystery once more. You take a second look—except this time, you look a little harder.

Step into a virtual reality scenario in cyberspace, and imagine that this book is actually the stage for an exotic and eclectic cocktail party. The interior decoration is an odd mix of the titillatingly bizarre, the no-holds-barred holy, and the tongue-in-check academic. Nothing seems to match, but nothing clashes. The guests are an animated and effervescent bunch, their eyes twinkling with inner stars. Laughter of all ranges and sizes fills the room. You feel curiously at home.

Over in the corner, spiritual teacher Ram Dass and VR pioneer Jaron Lanier seem to be having a heated but friendly discussion on the virtues and dangers of technological highs. Fakir Musafar, decorated in nipple rings, tattoos and nose quills, is at the snack table with archaeologist Marija Gimbutas, exchanging insights into the Western mortification of the body. In the kitchen, musician Jerry Garcia and radio host Elizabeth Gips are involved in a conversation ostensibly about rye bread, but stick a Babel-fish in your ear and you hear they're really discussing the ever-expanding mystery of the universe. And out on the porch, chemist Alexander Shulgin and ecologist John Robbins are pondering the alchemical potentials of the human body. Is this a great party or what?

We chose to interview the people who move us—move us to wonder, to contemplation, to inspiration, to action. They are all works in progress, receiving at least as much as they transmit, their commentaries barometer readings of the weather changes at large in this wild and woolly world of ours. Ritual lovemaking, sticking spears in your skin, listening to music, sitting with your eyes closed, taking drugs, hooking your brain up to a machine—the methods for raising the curtains of consciousness vary, but to get hung up on the validity of any one is to miss the boat to spiritual independence. There are so many ways to get high, but once you're up there, everyone gets to share the view, the view of a dynamic universe within which we are all engaged in the most interactive process imagin-able.

As you meander through the pages of this book you begin to sense an ambiance, a link between these seemingly disparate individuals: a com-mon ground of unfettered creativity, deep compassion, personal courage, childlike curiosity, and more than a standard dose of chutzpah. It is that common ground from which these interviews grew and upon which, we hope, a few forbidden fruits will fall.

Rebecca McClen Novick

Introduction

We are currently witnessing an extraordinary shift in the evolutionary winds of history. Poised on a bridge between worlds, our species swings between crisis and renaissance. Never before in the human adventure have there been so many reasons to rejoice and celebrate, yet also, paradoxically, so many reasons to re-evaluate and re-navigate. Wonderful advances in science and the interface between high technology and the creative imagination have spawned forms of artistic expression with a sensory richness inconceivable to previous generations. The imagination has never been more tangible. And yet, sad to say, never before has our own extinction—via our own ignorance—hovered so close.

Within the pages of this book, through conversations with some of the most far-reaching cultural innovators of our day, we explore a variety of exciting new options made available by the cultural renaissance that is upon us and examine some possible solutions to our impending global crisis. When Rebecca McClen Novick and I finished the first volume of *Mavericks of the Mind*, there still remained many extraordinary individuals whom we had wished to include. In addition, friends flooded us with recommendations for potential interviewees. If that were not enough, every time we did a lecture or book-signing, we would meet people who had yet more recommendations. A number of individuals whom I did not even know called me and recommended themselves as candidates. Upon consideration of all this, we decided to do an additional collection, which you now hold in your hands. And a third volume is in the works.

In 1988, Christian theologian Matthew Fox, the Dominican priest we interviewed for this volume, was silenced for a year by the Vatican. Instead of preaching about our Original Sin, he was doing this rap on our "Original Blessing." After a full revolution around the sun, during which he supposedly contemplated his sins in silence, the very first words that he uttered were, "As I was saying . . . " It is in *that* spirit that this book begins. As with our first volume, the people we chose to interview represent the mavericks of their fields, the engineers of evolution, the messengers of our future—those remarkable and brave individuals who stand at the frontline of the cultural frontier, taking the storms of change full in the face. However overlooked, misunderstood, ridiculed, or punished they may have been by society at large, these men and women have persevered to the point where they are now viewed as revolutionary leaders in their fields.

When putting this book together, we operated under the premise that most cultural advance is accomplished by a certain type of individual: those who resist adherence to any particular group or belief system and have an interdisciplinary approach to their work. These were the people we sought out to discuss the basic philosophical issues of life, to ponder the Big Questions: *How did we get here? Why are we here? Where are we going?* But while our previous collection approached these questions primarily from a decidedly scientific viewpoint (with several notable exceptions), our new collection gathers a perspective from a wider cultural arena. And though our pool of interviewees has broadened, the theme of the new volume remains the same: exploring the evolution of consciousness. Also, our approach matured. Rebecca and I became bolder in our interviewing style, and we are perhaps a little less naive than when we set out to do the original collection.

Although the collection spans a diverse spectrum, there are many areas where boundaries overlap. From the emerging gestalt, a vision of our future begins to take form, perhaps providing us with a glimpse into the twenty-first century. We discuss possible solutions to the hunger and ecological crises gripping our planet, new computer and multimedia technologies as vehicles for enhanced communication and artistic expression, future directions of psychedelic drug research, the reclamation of our bodies and our connection to the divine through more expansive forms of sexual expression, the revival of the Goddess, and the reformation of religion. These and other spiritual issues are pondered in depth, always with thoughtfulness, often with humor.

After the publication of the first volume of *Mavericks*, when Rebecca and I hosted a series of events at UC Santa Cruz and UCLA, we brought together individuals from the book and encouraged them to discuss and debate various controversial issues, such as the relationship between technology and the mind. As we sat there on stage, surrounded by all these great minds and their often conflicting perspectives, we realized repeatedly just how relative truth really is. No one has the answer, yet everyone makes a point and contributes a perspective to help create a more encompassing whole.

One of the topics we explore in this book is the mystery of what happens to consciousness after the death of the body. When I posed the question to environmentalist John Robbins, he replied without pause, "I think it celebrates." Ironically, Jerry Garcia of the Grateful Dead told us he thinks "it probably dies with the body." Cultural historian William Irwin Thompson said he thinks we move into "subtle bodies," which "are woven into this larger angelic formation." There is perhaps no greater mystery than death, and infinite mystery will spawn infinite theories.

This is not the first time that crisis and opportunity have danced together arm in arm, and as we evolve through time, this dynamic will most likely be encountered again and again. This is part of the Great Mystery at the center of existence, which inspires art, science, philosophy, and the spiritual quest. Stating the obvious here is powerful. There is simply no escape. Life is mostly mystery, and the mystery only deepens with time and "understanding." A moment's reflection will confront us with the fact that the foundation of every belief rests upon an assumption made in faith. Life is a journey through our own dream fabric.

When I was in graduate school I was amazed to discover that the majority of my professors thought that science had solved about 99 percent of the fundamental mysteries of the universe and that it would not be long before we would have the other 1 percent figured out. I was completely dumbfounded by this, and by the fact that much of the world appeared to follow suit with my professors. As a consequence of my commitment to the exploration of consciousness, my world view was the reverse: 99 percent mystery, 1 percent (or less) figured out.

The universe is an infinitely mysterious place, where consciousness and physical phenomena interact in largely unknown ways to form the adventure of our existence. Because of this fundamental truth, Matthew Fox suggested that we adopt the perspective that "mystery is not something you're ever going to *solve*, it's something you *live!*" John Allen poetically reminded us that "beauty attracts, but mystery . . . lures." After contemplating the nature of God and other timeless philosophical questions with us, Ram Dass asked about our "relationship with the mystery? Are you defending yourself from it? Are you making love to it? Are you living in it?" How we respond to these questions is significant. One of the few things we can state with any certainty about this grand and ambiguous universe we inhabit is that although the phenomena of the physical world will come and go, the mystery lurking at the heart of existence is forever here to stay.

David Jay Brown
Ben Lomond, California

Marija Gimbutas

"Through an understanding of what the Goddess was,
we can better understand nature and we can build
our ideologies so that it it will be easier for us to live."

Learning the Language of the Goddess
with Marija Gimbutas

Marija Gimbutas is largely responsible for the resurgence of interest in Goddess-oriented religions. Her discoveries were the foundation for Riane Eisler's (whom we interviewed in our first volume) highly influential book, The Chalice and the Blade. *For fifteen years, Marija was involved with excavations in southeastern Europe and the Mediterranean, which revealed the existence of a prehistoric Goddess-oriented culture. For at least 25,000 years this peaceful civilization seemingly practiced complete equal rights between the sexes—socially, politically, and spiritually. As Riane Eisler pointed out, the full implications of this discovery have yet to be fully realized by the scientific community, or by society at large.*

Born in Lithuania during a time when 50 percent of the population was still pagan, Gimbutas fled to Austria because of the war. In Vilnius, Lithuania, and later in Vienna, Innsbruck, and Tubingen, she studied linguistics, archaeology, and Indo-European cultures, obtaining her doctorate in Tubingen, Germany in 1946. In 1950, as an expert in eastern European archaeology, she became a research fellow at Harvard, where she remained for twelve years. In 1963 she came to UCLA, where she served as emeritus professor of European archaeology for many years. She is the author of more than twenty books, including well-known works such as The Language of the Goddess, The Civilization of the Goddess, *and* Goddesses and Gods of Old Europe.

We interviewed Marija at her beautiful mountain home—which overflowed with big-breasted, wide-hipped goddess figurines and other archaeological artifacts—in Topanga Canyon, California on October 3, 1992. When Marija died on February 2, 1994, we felt very sad but also fortunate to have had the opportunity to spend time with her before she departed. Even though she battled lymphatic cancer for many years, Marija was vitally alive and active right up until the very end. On June 27, 1993, the Frauen Museum in Wiesbaden, Germany dedicated to her an extensive exhibit, "The Language of the Goddess," and she was there to receive the honor.

After spending much of her life in relative academic obscurity, Marija seemed to be genuinely surprised to discover how popular she had be-

come. For all her accomplishments, she was always humble and gracious. Marija had an incredibly warm, spritelike spirit, lively eyes, and a way of making you feel very comfortable around her. She appeared delicate and graceful, yet filled with strength. There was something timeless about Marija, for she was a woman of many times and places, and the Goddess seemed to shine right through her.

DJB

DAVID: What was it that originally inspired your interest in the archaeological and mythological dimensions of the Goddess-oriented religions of Old Europe?

MARIJA: It has to do with the whole of my life, I think. I was always a black sheep. I did what I saw with my own eyes, and still do—to this day, in fact. I was very independent. My mother was also very independent. She was a student of medicine in Switzerland and Germany when there were no other girls studying.

I was born in Lithuania when it was still 50 percent pagan. I had quite a lot of direct connections to the goddesses. They were around me in my childhood. The Goddess Laima was there; she could call at night and look through the windows. When a woman is giving birth, she appears. The grandmother is there organizing things; she has gifts for the Goddess. Towels and woven materials are laid for her, because she weaves life; she is the spinner. She may be on the way to disappearance, but fifty years ago she was still there.

> *I was born in Lithuania when it was still 50 percent pagan.*

REBECCA: When you say "pagans," you mean people living in the countryside, close to nature?

MARIJA: Yes, well, Lithuania was Christianized only in the fourteenth century, and even then it didn't mean much because it was done by missionaries who didn't understand the language. The countryside remained pagan for at least two or three centuries. Then came the Jesuits, who started to convert people in the sixteenth century.

In some areas, up to the nineteenth and twentieth centuries, there were still beliefs alive in goddesses and all kinds of beings. So in my childhood, I was exposed to many things that were almost prehistoric, I would say. When I studied archaeology, it was easier for me to grasp what these sculptures mean than for an archaeologist born in New York, who doesn't know anything about life in the countryside in Europe.

I first studied linguistics, ethnology, and folklore. I collected folklore myself when I was in high school. And there was always a question: What is my own culture? I heard a lot about the Indo-Europeans and how our language, Lithuanian, was a very old, conservative Indo-European language. I was interested in that. I studied the Indo-European language and comparative Indo-European studies. At that time, there was no question about what was *before* the Indo-Europeans. It was good enough to know that the Indo-Europeans were already there. (*laughter*) The question of what was before came much later.

Then, because of the war, I had to flee from Lithuania. I studied in Austria, in Vienna, then I got my Ph.D. in Germany. I still continued to be interested in my own ancient Lithuanian culture, and I did some things in addition to my official studies. I was doing research in symbolism, collecting materials from libraries. So that is one trend in my interest: ancient religion, pagan religion and symbolism. My dissertation was also connected with this; it was about the burial rites and beliefs in an afterlife. It was published in Germany in 1946.

Then I came to the United States and had the opportunity to begin studies in eastern European archaeology. In 1950 I became a research fellow at Harvard, and I was there for twelve years. I had to learn from scratch, because there was nobody in the whole United States who was really knowledgeable about what was in Russia or the Soviet Union in prehistoric times. So they invited me to write a book on eastern European prehistory, and I spent about fifteen years doing this. So that was my background of learning.

REBECCA: Did you anticipate the incredible interest that this research would fuel?

MARIJA: No. At that time I was just an archaeologist doing my work, studying everything that I could. And after that came the Bronze Age studies, which gave me another aspect on this Indo-European culture. In my first book, I wrote about eastern European archaeology. I started my hypothesis on the Indo-European origins in Europe, and this hypothesis still works and hasn't changed much.

REBECCA: Could you describe your hypothesis?

MARIJA: These proto-Indo-European people came from South Russia to Europe and introduced the Indo-European culture. So European culture was hybridized. It was the old culture mixed with the new elements—the steppe, pastoral and patriarchal elements. So even thirty years ago I sensed that there was in Europe something else before the Indo-Europeans. But I still didn't do anything about the Goddess, about sculptures or art or painted pottery. I knew that it existed, but I didn't really have the chance to dive into the field.

The occasion appeared when I came to UCLA in 1963. In 1967 I started excavations in southeast Europe, Yugoslavia, Greece, and Italy, and I did that for fifteen years. When I was traveling in Europe and visiting museums, I was already building some understanding of what this culture was like before the Indo-Europeans, before the patriarchy.

It was always a big question mark to me: What could it be? It is so different. Painted pottery, for instance, beautiful pottery—and then the sculptures. Nobody was really writing about this. There were so many of them, wherever you went you found hundreds and hundreds. I was just putting in my head what I saw. So then I started my own excavations, and I discovered at least five hundred sculptures myself.

REBECCA: How deep did you have to dig?

MARIJA: It depended. Sometimes at a site of 5000 BC they were on top. You could walk through the houses of 7,000 years ago! Other times you'd have to dig deep. Usually you excavate sites that are already exposed, and where people are finding objects of great interest. Many things have been destroyed in this way. Some interesting excavations were made, especially in Greece, and I started to understand more and more about sculptures. I don't know how it happened, at what moment, but I started to distinguish certain types and their repetitions. For

> *You could walk through the houses of 7,000 years ago!*

instance, the bird and snake goddesses which are the easiest to distinguish.

So I slowly added more and more information. The first book was called *Goddesses and Gods of Old Europe.* Actually the first edition was

> *... the first edition was called* **Gods and Goddesses of Old Europe,** *because I was not allowed to use "goddesses" first.*

called *Gods and Goddesses of Old Europe*, because I was not allowed to use "goddesses" first.

DAVID: According to whom? Was it the publisher?

MARIJA: Yes. The publisher didn't allow me. In eight years, a second edition appeared with the original title, *Goddesses and Gods of Old Europe.*

REBECCA: That first edition could be very valuable one day. (*laughter*) Your work appeals to a very broad audience, and even people who don't have an academic background often feel they have an intuitive sense of what you're saying.

MARIJA: The intuitive people are always the first to say that. Then eventually academia catches up, because these are the least intuitive. (*laughter*)

REBECCA: Could you briefly describe to us the major differences between the old European Goddess traditions and the Indo-European patriarchy that came to dominate? What aspects of the patriarchal culture caused it to want to control the matrifocal one?

MARIJA: The symbolic systems are very different. All this reflects the social structure. The Indo-European social structure is patriarchal, patrilineal, and the psyche is the warrior. Every god is also a warrior. The three main Indo-European gods are the god of the shining sky, the god of the underworld, and the thunder god. The female goddesses are just brides, wives, or maidens, without any power or creativity. They're just there: they're beauties, they're Venuses, like the dawn or sun maiden.

> *I call it* **matristic, *not*** **matriarchal,** *because* **matriarchal** *always arouses ideas of dominance . . .*

So the system is totally different from what existed in the European matristic culture before the Indo-Europeans. I call it *matristic*, not *matriarchal*, because *matriarchal* always arouses ideas of dominance and is compared with the patriarchy. But it was a balanced society. It was not that women were really so powerful that they usurped everything that was masculine.

Men were in their rightful position. They were doing their own work; they had their duties, and they also had their own power. This is reflected in their symbols, where you find not only goddesses but also gods. The goddesses were creatrixes—creating from themselves. From symbols and sculptures, we can see that as far back as 35,000 BC the parts of the female body were creative parts: breasts, belly, and buttocks. It was a different view from ours—it had nothing to do with pornography.

The vulva, for instance, is one of the earliest engraved symbols, and it is symbolically related to growth, to the seed. Sometimes next to it is a branch or plant motif, or within the vulva you find something like a seed or a plant. And that sort of symbol is very long-lasting—it continues for 20,000 years at least. Even now, in some countries, the vulva is a symbol that offers a security of creativity, of continuity and fertility.

REBECCA: Why did the patriarchal culture choose to dominate?

MARIJA: This is in the culture itself. They had weapons and horses. The horse appeared only with the invaders who began coming from South Russia. In old Europe, there were no weapons—no daggers, no swords. There were just weapons for hunting. Habitations were very different. The invaders were seminomadic people, but the Old Europeans were agriculturalists, living in one area for a very long time, mostly in the most beautiful places. When these warriors arrived, they established themselves high in the hills, sometimes in places that had very difficult access. So in each aspect of culture I see an opposition, and therefore I am of the opinion that this local, Old European culture could not develop into a patriarchal warrior culture, because this would be too sudden. We have archaeological evidence that this was a clash. And then, of course, who starts to dominate? The ones who have horses, who have weapons, who have small families, and who are more mobile.

REBECCA: What do you think daily life was like for the people living in the matrifocal society?

MARIJA: Religion played an enormous role, and the temple was sort of a focus of life. The most beautiful artifacts were produced for the temple. The people were very grateful for what they had. They had to thank the Goddess always, give to her, appreciate her. The high priestess and queen were one and the same person, and there was a sort of a hierarchy of priestesses

DAVID: Was the Goddess religion basically monotheistic?

MARIJA: This is a very difficult question to answer. Was it or was it not monotheistic? Was there one goddess or many? The time will come when we shall know more, but at this time we cannot reach deep in prehistory. What I see is that from very early on, from the Upper Paleolithic times, we already have different types of goddesses. So the question is, are these different goddesses or different aspects of one Goddess?

Before 35,000 or 40,000 BC there is hardly any art. But the type of the Goddess with large breasts and buttocks and belly existed very early in the Upper Paleolithic. The snake and bird goddesses are also Upper Paleolithic, so at least three main types were there. But in later times—for instance, in the Minoan culture in Crete—you have a goddess that tends to be more one Goddess than several. Even the snake goddesses that exist in Crete are very much linked with the main Goddess, who is shown sitting on a throne or is worshipped in these underground crypts.

Perhaps, even in much earlier times, there was also a very close inter-relationship between the different types represented. So maybe, after all, we shall come to the conclusion that this was already a monotheistic religion, even as we tend now to call it: the Goddess religion. We just have to remember there were many different types of goddesses.

REBECCA: Do you see remnants of the Goddess religion in different religions throughout the world today?

MARIJA: Yes, very much so. The Virgin Mary is still extremely important. She is the inheritor of many types of goddesses, actually. She represents the one who is giving life. She is the regenerator and earth mother together. We can trace this earth mother quite deep into prehistory. She is the pregnant type and continues for maybe 20,000 years. She is very well preserved in practically every area of Europe, and in other parts of the world.

> *[The Virgin Mary] is the inheritor of many types of goddesses . . .*

DAVID: Do you see the Gaia hypothesis as being a resurgence of the original Goddess religion?

MARIJA: I think there is some connection, perhaps in a Jungian sense. This culture existed so deep and for so long that it cannot be uninfluential to our thinking.

REBECCA: It must have conditioned our minds for a long time. How do you respond to criticism that the Goddess religion was just a fertility rite?

> *This culture existed so deep and for so long that it cannot be uninfluential to our thinking.*

MARIJA: How do I respond to all these silly criticisms? (*laughter*) People who say that are usually not knowledgeable and have never studied the question. Fertility was important to continuity of life on earth, but the religion was about life, death, and regeneration. Our ancestors were not primitive.

DAVID: Did you experience a lot of resistance from the academic community about your interpretations?

MARIJA: I wouldn't say a lot, but some, yes. It's natural. For decades, archaeologists rarely touched the problem of religion.

REBECCA: Was it because they couldn't accept such a level of religious sophistication so far back in time?

MARIJA: Well, they probably accepted the existence of the Upper Paleolithic and Neolitithic religion, but the training was such that the students had no occasion to be exposed to these questions. Sixty or seventy years ago there was no teaching about prehistoric religion except in a few places, like at Oxford University, where Professor James was teaching a course on the Goddess. Nobody at that time was resisting. Now we have more resistance because of the feminist movement, and some people are automatically not accepting.

This kind of criticism is meaningless to me. What is true is true, and what is true will remain. Maybe I made some mistakes in deciphering the symbols, but I was continually trying to understand more. At this time I know more than when I was writing thirty years ago. My first book was not complete; therefore I had to produce another book and another book to say more. It's a long process.

REBECCA: Wasn't it incredibly difficult to find written sources and references for your research?

MARIJA: There was so little, it was amazing! There were some good books in the 1950s. In 1955, a book was published on the Mother Goddess by a Jungian psychologist, Eric Neumann. Then there were very good works on symbolism by Mircea Eliade.

REBECCA: When I tried to get hold of some of your books from the library, they were all checked out. The librarian said that this was normally the case. It seems that works on this subject are definitely in demand now.

MARIJA: I never dreamed of that. I always thought that archaeology books are not generally read, and that you just write for your own colleagues.

DAVID: Were you surprised, in yours and others' excavations, by the advanced designs of the habitats and the settlements of the Goddess religion?

MARIJA: Yes, I was. This was a revelation, to see that the later culture is much less advanced than the earlier one. The art is incomparably lower than what was before, and [the earlier culture] was a civilization of 3,000 years, more or less, before it was destroyed. For thirty years now we've been able to date items using carbon dating. When I started to do my research, chronology was so unclear, and we were working so hard to understand what period the object belonged to.

> *This was a revelation, to see that the later culture is much less advanced than the earlier one.*

Then, in the 1960s, it became so much easier. I spent a lot of time doing chronology, which is very technical work.

That gave us a perspective on how long-lasting these cultures were, and in the architecture and the building of temples you could see a beautiful development from the more simple to the really sophisticated. Some houses and temples were two stories high and had painted walls. Catal Huyuk in Anatolia was such a great discovery. The wall paintings there were only published in 1989, twenty-five years after Myler's excavation. One hundred forty wall paintings—archeologists don't believe him because it's so sophisticated. And this is from the seventh millennium!

REBECCA: Do you think the matrifocal society could have sustained cities, or do you think that the nature of the religion and the lifestyle kept settlements small?

MARIJA: Yes, it would have sustained cities. It did start to develop into an urban culture, especially in one area of the Cucuteni civilization, which is presently Romania and the western part of the Ukraine. There we have cities of 10,000 to 15,000 inhabitants in around 4000 BC. So urban development did begin, but it was truncated.

REBECCA: You have said that you think the meaning of prehistoric art and religion can be deciphered and that we need to analyze the evidence from the point of view of ideology. Do you think that we can honestly do this without being unduly biased by our own modern ideologies?

MARIJA: That's always difficult. Most archaeologists have great difficulty in accepting that the life was so different. For instance, an excavator publishes a plan of a village. This is a circular village, in a concentric circle of houses, and there is also a house in the center. The immediate explanation is that here is a chieftain's house and around him is his retinue and then the last ring of houses around that is everyone else.

But when you analyze the material, it is totally the reverse. The outer ring of houses were the most important ones, the largest houses with the best floors and so on. The smaller houses are in the middle. So you can write anecdotes about the interpretation, because we see only through the twentieth-century prism.

DAVID: What does your research indicate about the social status of women in pre-Indo-European culture?

MARIJA: Women were equal beings, that is very clear. And perhaps they were more honored, because they had more influence in the religious life. The temple was run by women.

REBECCA: What about the political life?

MARIJA: It's all hypothesis; you cannot reconstruct easily, but we can judge from what remains in later times and what still exists in mythology, because this again reflects the social structure. My findings suggest that the political life was structured by the avuncular system. The rulers of the country were the queen, who is also the high priestess, and her brother or uncle. The system is therefore called "avuncular," which is from the word "uncle." The man, the brother or uncle, was very important in society, and probably men and women were quite equal. In mythology, we encounter the sister-brother couples of female goddesses and male gods. It is wrong to say that this is just a woman's culture, that there was just a Goddess and there were no gods. In art the male is less represented, that's true, but that the male gods existed, there's no question. In all mythologies in Europe—whether Germanic or Celtic or Baltic—you will find the earth mother, or earth Goddess, with her male companion or counterpart next to her.

> *It is wrong to say that this is just a woman's culture . . .*

Also, there are other couples, like the goddess of nature, the regenerator, who appears in the spring and gives life to all earth animals, humans and plants. She is Artemis in Greek mythology. She is called "Mistress of Animals," and there are also male counterparts of the same kind called "Master of Animals." His representations appear in Catal Huyuk in the seventh millennium BC, and they are there throughout prehistory. So we shouldn't neglect that aspect. There is a balance between the sexes throughout, in religion and in life.

DAVID: Is there any evidence that the takeover of the matristic society was violent? And how much did the people try to defend themselves?

MARIJA: It was violent, but how much they defended themselves is difficult to tell. But they were losers, that is clear. There was evidence of immigration and escape from these violent happenings, and a lot of confusion involving a lot of population shifts. People started to flee to places like islands and forests and hilly areas. In the settlements, you have evidence of murder.

REBECCA: What about the invading culture—was it always patriarchal? When do you think the patriarchy began?

MARIJA: This is a very serious question that archaeologists cannot yet answer. But we can see for sure that the patriarchy was already there around 5000 BC, and the horse was domesticated not later than that.

REBECCA: Do you think the patriarchy came out of a previously matristic society?

MARIJA: It must have been so. But the trouble is that in South Russia, where it is critical to know, we don't have evidence. We have no extensive excavations in that area from before 5000 BC.

REBECCA: Did the sacred script that you translated from the Goddess culture ever develop into sentences or phrases?

MARIJA: Again, that's for the future to decide. It is possible that it was a syllabic script, and it would have probably developed into something if it were not for the culture's destruction. The script is lost in most of Europe, and it is in eastern and central Europe that we have most signs preserved. In the Bronze Age, in Cyprus and in Crete, the script that persisted is much related to an earlier one, from the fifth millennium BC. Some is preserved, but we do not have very clear links yet because of this culture change.

Scholars are looking into this question, and I hope it will be deciphered somehow. The difficulty is that this pre-Indo-European language is studied very little. People study substrates of languages in Greece and Italy, but mostly what they can reconstruct are place names like Knossos, which is a pre-Indo-European name. The word for *apple*, for instance, is pre-Indo-European, and so linguists, little by little, word by word, discover which words are not Indo-European. Names for seeds, various trees, plants, animals—they're easily reconstructed. And also there exist several pre-Indo-European names for the same thing—like for the pig—and both are used. Some languages use pre-Indo-European; some languages use Indo-European names, or both.

This is a field of research that should be further developed in the future, and I think I am creating an influence in this area. It's extremely important to have interdisciplinary research. For a long time in the universities, there was a department for this, a department for that, and no connection between them. Archaeology was especially so, with no connection to linguistic studies and no connection with mythology and folklore.

REBECCA: You've talked about the need for a field of archaeomythology.

MARIJA: Yes, because when you don't ignore the other disciplines, you start seeing many more things. It is such a revelation, to see in mythology really ancient elements that you can apply to archaeology. To some archaeologists

> *. . . when you don't ignore the other disciplines, you start seeing many more things.*

this is not science. Well, all right, let it not be science! It doesn't matter what you call it. (*laughter*)

REBECCA: The traditional belief has been that language began with men in the hunt, but now people are leaning toward the idea that it began in the home with the interaction of women and children. When and how do you think language first developed?

MARIJA: Early, very early—Lower Paleolithic. And it developed in the family. Some linguists are doing research in the earliest known words, and some formations show that certain words are very, very old, and they exist all over the world.

DAVID: You've collected a lot of European folktales. As creation myths are found in almost every culture in the world, have you come across any that relate to this theme?

MARIJA: Yes. For example, the myth of the water bird and the cosmic egg. The world starts with an egg, which the water bird brings. Then the egg splits, and one part of it becomes earth and the other part becomes sky.

DAVID: Have you found any Lithuanian folktales to correlate with the story of Adam and Eve?

MARIJA: No. But it's interesting that Adam's first wife was Lilith. And who was Lilith? She was a bird of prey, the vulture goddess of death and regeneration. She was the one who later became the witch, so she was very powerful. Lilith flew away from Adam, and he could not control her. Then the second wife, Eve, was made from his rib, so she was naturally obedient and stayed with him. (*laughter*)

REBECCA: In mythology and folklore there are so many transmutations of the Goddess developing from a positive image into a negative one. Do you see this as a conscious attempt to distort the feminine?

MARIJA: Yes, it is. This is really Christianity's doing, because they felt the danger to their world view. They demonized the one who was the most powerful, the one who could perform many things, who was connected with the atmospheric happenings, with rains and storms. This is the Goddess who rules over death and regeneration, the one who was turned into the witch. She was very powerful, and in the days of the Inquisition she is described as really dangerous.

From various descriptions, you can sense that there was fear. She could control male sexuality, for instance. She could cut the moon and stop it growing; she was the balancer of the life powers. She could do a lot of damage, this Goddess. But you must understand *why* she was doing this. She could not allow things to grow forever. She caused death in order to renew the cycle from the beginning. She is the main regenerator of the whole world, and of all nature.

REBECCA: So the patriarchal culture had to make people afraid of the Goddess, so they would abandon her?

MARIJA: Yes. In the fifteenth and sixteenth centuries, which are critical for this change, the Goddess was depicted as an evil monster. This image is still with us. In each country, she is more or less preserved. In the Basque country, she is still very much alive. She is a vulture who lives in caves. Sometimes shepherds arrange Christian crosses above caves to remove the vultures.

> *In the fifteenth and sixteenth centuries ... the Goddess was depicted as an evil monster.*

DAVID: You have been largely responsible for the re-emergence of Goddess consciousness in the Western hemisphere. How do you feel about the way that this perspective is being interpreted socially and politically?

MARIJA: The interpretation of the Goddess is in some cases overdone a little bit. I cannot see that the Goddess as she was can be reconstructed and returned to our lives. But we have to take the best that we can seize. The best understanding is of divinity itself. The Christian God punishes and is angry and does not fit into our times at all. We need something better, we need something closer, we need something that we can touch, and we need some compassion, some love, and also a return to the nature of things.

Through an understanding of what the Goddess was, we can better understand nature, and we can build our ideologies so that it will be easier for us to live. We have to be grateful for what we have, for all the beauty, and the Goddess expresses exactly that. The Goddess is nature itself. So I think this should be returned to humanity. I don't think that Christianity will continue for a very long time, but it's just like patriarchy—it's not easy to get rid of. (*laughter*) But somehow, from the bottom up, something else is coming.

REBECCA: The patriarchy has been around for about 5,000 years, but the Goddess culture existed for maybe a quarter of a million years. Why did it endure for so long?

MARIJA: Because of what I've been talking about. It was natural to have this kind of divinity, and it is absolutely unnatural to create a punishing God and warriors who are stimulating our bad instincts.

DAVID: A lot of the major themes you discuss—the renewing of the eternal earth, death and regeneration, energy unfolding—are well-known, archetypal themes that occur during a psychedelic experience. I'm curious about whether you think that the Goddess-oriented cultures incorporated the use of mushrooms or some kind of psychoactive plant into their rituals. Do you take seriously Terence McKenna's notion that the use of psychedelics was the secret that was lost at Catal Huyuk?

MARIJA: I'm sure they had it. This knowledge still exists in rituals like Eleusis in Greece, where now it's clear that psychedelics were used. From the depiction of mushrooms, maybe you can judge that this was sacred. But this was perhaps not the most important. From Minoan engravings on seals, for instance, you have poppies very frequently indicated. Also, poppy seeds are found in Neolithic settlements, so they were conscious about that. They were collecting, they were using, and maybe growing poppies like other domestic plants.

DAVID: Do you see it influencing the culture?

MARIJA: Yes. From Dionysian rituals in Greece, which can go back to much earlier times, you get all this dancing and excitement. It's always at the edge and taken to a frenzy, almost to craziness. That existed even in the Paleolithic times, I would guess. But what they used is difficult to reconstruct. We have the poppy seeds. Mushrooms? Maybe. But what else? The hard evidence is not preserved by archaeological record. It's disappeared.

REBECCA: What do you think are the signifying differences between a culture that views time as cyclical, and a culture like ours, which sees time as linear and progressing toward some waiting future?

MARIJA: It's much easier to live when you think in terms of a cyclicity. I think it's crazy to think in terms of a linear development, as in the European beliefs in life after death: if you're a king, you will stay a king, and if you're a hero, you'll stay a hero.

REBECCA: That aspect of the Goddess culture, the idea that things travel in cycles—do you think this made them more philosophical about death?

MARIJA: Much more philosophical. And it's a very good philosophy. What else can you think? This is the best. And the whole of evolution is based so much upon this thinking, on the regeneration of life and stimulation of life powers. This is the main thing that we're interested in—to preserve life powers, to awaken them each spring, to see that they continue and that life thrives and flourishes.

DAVID: What relevance do you think understanding our ancient past has to dealing with the problems facing the world today?

MARIJA: Well, it's time to be more peaceful, to calm down. (*laughter*) And this philosophy is pacifying somehow, bringing us to some harmony with nature, where we can learn to value things. And knowing that there were cultures that existed for a long time without wars is important, because most twentieth-century people think that wars were always there.

> *. . . most twentieth-century people think that wars were always there.*

There are books still stressing this fact and suggesting crazy ideas, such as that agriculture and war started at the same time. They say that when villages started to grow, the property had to be defended. But that is nonsense! There was property, but it was communal property. Actually, it was a sort of communism, in the best sense of the word. It could not exist in the twentieth century. And also they believed that in death you are equal. I like this idea very much. You don't have to be queen or a king once your bones are collected and mixed together with other bones. (*laughter*)

DAVID: As rebirth is one of the major themes of your work, what do you personally feel happens to human consciousness after death?

MARIJA: Maybe the same way the Old Europeans thought: individual forms disappear, but the life-energy continues to a certain degree; it does not disappear.

DAVID: Do you think part of your individuality perseveres?

MARIJA: Well, that's what I leave around me now, my influence, what I've said in my books—this will continue for some time. So it does not completely die out.

REBECCA: Are you optimistic that a partnership society can be achieved once again?

MARIJA: I don't know if I'm optimistic. In a way I think I am, otherwise it would be difficult to live—you have to have hope. But that the development will be slow, is clear. It very much depends on who is in the government. Our spiritual life is so full of war images. Children, from the very beginning, are taught about shooting and killing. So the education has to change, television programs have to change. There are signs of that; there are voices appearing.

DAVID: Marija, if you could condense your life's work into a basic message, what would that message be?

MARIJA: Well, maybe the reconstruction of the meaning and functions of the Goddess is my major contribution. It happened to be me and not somebody else. I think it was just fate—Laima—that led me.

Photo: James Stiles Montage: Jim Chandler

Annie Sprinkle

"Let there be pleasure on earth, and let it begin with me."

The Pleasure Principle
with Annie Sprinkle

Annie Sprinkle is mostly known as the porn star/prostitute who became a performance artist/sex guru. She spent many years exploring a multitude of sexual possibilities in Manhattan's kinky sex clubs and through her roles in hundreds of hard-core XXX films, where she achieved legendary status and such earned titles as "the Queen of Kink," "the Mother Teresa of Sex," "the Shirley MacLaine of Smut," and "the Renaissance Woman of Porn." As an exhibitionist who liked to do it all, she posed for every major and minor sex and fetish magazine there is, and she was a "Photo Funny Girl" for National Lampoon *for two years. All along Annie has been a very creative individual, but recently she has emerged as what she describes as a "post-porn modernist," creating her own eclectic brand of feminist, sexually explicit media. Her latest one-woman show is part autobiography, part parody of the porn industry, part sex education, and part sex-magic-ecstasy ritual. It is controversial, powerful, and popular.*

After twenty-two years of devoting her life to learning and experiencing all she could about sex and doing sex work, Annie has become a unique kind of expert. She has authored three hundred articles on the topic, as well as an autobiographical book entitled Annie Sprinkle: Post-Porn Modernist. *She produced and directed several videos, including the lesbian classic* The Sluts and Goddesses Video Workshop, or How To Be a Sex Goddess in 101 Easy Steps. *She has been invited to teach and lecture at many museums, universities, and holistic healing centers, including such prestigious institutions as Columbia University, the Museum of Modern Art, the Wise Woman's Center, New York University, and the New Museum of Contemporary Art. Some of the topics she's presented are the "Pleasures, Profits, and Politics of Women's Sexualities in the '90s," "Sacred Sex Technologies," "Cosmic Orgasm Awareness," and the "Secrets of Sacred Slutism." HBO ran two specials on her work. She's such a "character" that someone has even created a comic-book series about her.*

Midway through Annie's career, her views about sexuality changed radically when the AIDS crisis hit and Annie's lover was infected (although Annie never was). Through having to practice totally safe sex, she learned

*that sex is not just about bodies coming together and the electric embrace
of genitalia, but also about the exchange of energy. Consequently, her work
merged with the long tradition of achieving health, well-being, and spiritual growth through meditative sexual union. Annie metamorphosed into
the more multidimensional incarnation Anya, whose goal is to get a handle
on the source of orgasmic energy, and who is inspired by the archetypes of
the sacred prostitute and the Goddess.*

*At present, Annie is half-finished with a feature documentary about
orgasm, Orgasm Scrapbook. She is also making a deck of "Pleasure Activist Playing Cards" from photographs of women she has taken over the
years, and marketing her own designer dildo, the Sacred Sex Tool. She is
experimenting with monogamy, "Zen sex," gender play, and training her
girlfriend's dog, Hillary, to give her cunnilingus.*

*Annie has a big, warm heart and a very sweet spirit. She seems to
completely lack any inhibition or guilt regarding sexuality, yet she is actually kind of shy. She's optimistic, funny, sensuous, and she appears to be a
genuinely happy person, often hovering, it seems, on the verge of orgasm.
Rebecca and I interviewed Annie on November 1, 1992 at her parent's
house in Granada Hills, the Southern California home in which she grew
up and where she was visiting at the time. The house was quite ordinary,
rather conservative, and nothing gave the slightest hint that this place would
have produced an Annie Sprinkle. We conducted the interview in the back
yard by the pool. When her mom walked by, Annie whispered, "Sh . . . I
don't want her to hear us talking about my sex life. It makes me nervous."
We interviewed her again in Maui, Hawaii, on July 26, 1993. Just as we
began the interview, Annie said that she had to stop because she needed to
orgasm. So I switched off the tape recorder, and she went into the other
room and turned on her vibrator. She returned five minutes later with a
smile on her face. "Okay," she said, "now we can begin."*

DJB

———————

DAVID: Annie, tell us about your sexual development and how it influenced your later career choices.

ANNIE: I grew up mostly in this middle-class Los Angeles suburb, which
at that time was very white bread, sexist, and very sexually conservative. I
wasn't aware of anything to do with sex. The only thing that really turned
me on was swimming in the pool in our backyard. I wasn't a sexual child,
because I didn't so much as even know it was an option. I feel kind of sad
that all that time was wasted. I could really have been enjoying myself, like

the children of New Guinea headhunters. I've read that those kids really get to enjoy sex in a very beautiful way.

DAVID: Can you see what it was that inspired your interest?

ANNIE: It came as a big surprise, actually. Probably what inspired my interest in sex was all the ignorance, fear, and curiosity I had about it. My only sexual memories from when I was a child are of when I used to wake up in the morning having to pee. I was having orgasms from my full bladder pressing against my G-spot or the roots of my clitoris or something, so I've connected peeing with ejaculating and eroticism a lot. They don't call me "Sprinkle" for nothing. But at that time I didn't know those were orgasms. It just felt fantastic. You know, according to the new feminist view, the clitoris is a *huge* structure inside the vagina—it's almost as big as a penis. What most people think of as the clit is the glans, and just the top of the volcano. Anyways, what I was more focused on was menstruation. That was the big, scary thing. All my questions were about that, and I didn't even know about sex. I heard a little bit in the playground at school, but that was it.

REBECCA: So there wasn't any sex education to speak of?

ANNIE: Of course there was the sperm, the ovum, and the fallopian tubes—the biology of sex—but nothing *practical* at all! Finally, I lost my virginity at seventeen, and I thought, "Gee, this is great, everyone should know about this. How come nothing is being done about this?" (*laughter*)

> *Losing my virginity was one of the happiest days of my life.*

Losing my virginity was one of the happiest days of my life. A year later I lucked into prostitution, and that was another really happy transition for me. When I discovered sex, I thought, "I've got to learn more about this, and I want to spend a lot of time doing it." Twenty-three years later, sex is still the main focus of my life in one way or another, so I guess it's not just a passing phase.

REBECCA: Why do you think sex has become so distorted? Do you think it's just the effect of Christianity, or are there other factors?

ANNIE: Everyone knows that Christianity has given sex a very bad rap in many ways. But sex is an enormous subject with millions of aspects. The subject of sex is as big as the subject of life itself. Sex can be extremely dangerous—there's disease, rape, it can break up marriages . . . Sexual knowledge and experience can be a tremendous source of power which some folks do not want others to have. People are imprisoned over it. Then there is the intimacy and the bond that it creates between people in relationships, which can be heartwrenching when you want to break up. It can cause a lot of problems, and it can solve them, too. It's so very dangerous on the one hand, and on the other it's total liberation, transformation, and joy.

REBECCA: What do you think are some of the worst social consequences of a culture that denies the body and sexual freedom?

ANNIE: War, drug and alcohol abuse, suicide, loneliness, skin diseases, cancers, violence, rape, obesity, frustration, dissatisfaction, and perhaps worst of all, numbness.

REBECCA: Zits? (*laughter*) So you regard sex as fundamental to a healthy life?

ANNIE: For many people, not all. With sex there are never any absolutes. Any question about sex can always be answered with "It depends." Having a great sex life doesn't solve everything, but it certainly helps a lot.

It's amazing how deeply wounded, fearful, and confused people are about sex. I know for a fact that even the world's greatest sex experts are wounded, fearful, and confused. But then, that's part of what makes it so fascinating.

REBECCA: It seems that sex was beginning to be viewed with more openness in the sixties. Then AIDS came along, and alarm bells went off again with this whole fundamentalist exclusiveness against homosexuality. Do you think AIDS has polarized the issue of sexual freedom so much that there is little hope for constructive understanding between the two sides?

ANNIE: From what I perceive of history, it seems that there is always a tug-of-war between freedom and repression, which goes on constantly. You win some, and you lose some. But sex does not go away. AIDS has certainly had a big effect on this tug-of-war. The repression people are tugging a whole lot harder lately, but the freedom people are, too. The freedom people have made some tremendous strides. For example, there is more freedom to be openly gay or lesbian than there has been in centuries.

You go to a high school, and there are all those adorable little baby dykes. They're so cute, and they're considered cool, not outcasts.

DAVID: You see that in California quite a bit, but this doesn't necessarily reflect what's going on in the rest of the country.

ANNIE: Well, that I wouldn't know. I'm scared to go there. (*laughter*)

REBECCA: You haven't been affected by the fundamentalist backlash?

ANNIE: For me personally, it's simply made my work more interesting, more important, and more in demand. Nationally there is a whole lot more sexually explicit work being made than ever before. Look at Madonna. She might not have made her *SEX* book if it wasn't for the backlash. As long as the antisex people don't go too far, the backlash seems to be having some quite positive effects. I'm all for it. I generally try to look at the positive sides of things.

DAVID: What are some of the positive aspects of the phenomenon of AIDS? You've talked about more people being openly gay—what are some other things?

ANNIE: You get free condoms. (*laughter*) Plus, there are all those very erotic safe-sex posters plastered all over the subways. There are a lot more family values—more love and caring and deeper bonds created among friends. A lot of great community was created because of the AIDS crisis. People are expanding their ideas of what sex is really all about and what it looks like. People are learning more about health and healing techniques. Many of us appreciate life more and live it more fully because we've been around so much death. Children are getting more sex education, although it's still far from enough. But of course, AIDS is a major nightmare, and we've got to stop it.

REBECCA: What other aspects of sexual awareness do you teach?

ANNIE: A wide variety of different things, from the basics, like getting over guilt and shame, to learning to build, move, and utilize subtle sexual energy. How to use sex as a healing tool, as a meditation, and in ritual. I teach an elaborate series of pussy massage strokes, which I developed with my good friend and teacher Joseph Kramer. These are combined with breathing and Taoist techniques, which then get put into a very carefully structured ritual that we do in groups. That's probably the most powerful thing I've taught. Major transformations, realizations, and transcendental things occur. We just did one called Cosmic Orgasm Awareness Week, which took place at a magnificent retreat center in the woods. It was beautifully produced by the Body Electric School in Oakland. They're really on the cutting edge of the sexual vanguard.

REBECCA: You've said that just *thinking* about sex can strengthen your immune system. Have you had experience of this yourself?

ANNIE: I read about some scientific tests that were done where it was proven that just thinking about sex creates disease-fighting neuropeptides. In my personal experience, it works on everything but hemorrhoids. Although I've heard claims that it *does* cure hemorrhoids. (*laughter*)

> *. . . it was proven that just thinking about sex creates disease-fighting neuropeptides.*

REBECCA: How do you experience the healing powers of sex? There's a great story in your interview in *Research* magazine about how you saved the life of someone who was having an asthma attack by giving him a blow-job.

ANNIE: From the very beginning, sexual healing was something I knew about subconsciously. Now I use it more consciously in all kinds of ways. For example, when I had gum surgery a couple of years ago, the pain killers weren't working and my gums were throbbing. I felt like shit, I looked like shit, and sex was the last thing I cared about in the world. But I had this lover who would go down under the sheets and give me orgasms, and it would totally help. It would take the pain away. It worked better than any painkillers.

DAVID: Right after an orgasm, the production of endorphins is increased in the body. It's like a heroin rush.

ANNIE: Recently I was in Toronto teaching a workshop. A woman came to me complaining that she had a pounding headache, a horrible migraine, and would have to leave the workshop. I got two vibrators, and I prescribed that she put one vibrator on her clit and one on the back of her neck. I told her to relax, to breathe very deeply, take time, and to visualize sexual en-

> *. . . if she used the vibrator regularly she eventually wouldn't . . . get migraines anymore.*

ergy filling head. Then I told her to blast the headache out the top of her head with the orgasm. I put her in a private room, and she followed my advice. It worked like a charm. She was thrilled, because she got a lot of migraines. I gave her the vibrator as a present. (*laughter*) I suggested that if she used the vibrator regularly she eventually wouldn't even get migraines anymore. I really should follow up on her progress.

REBECCA: Do you think this is the same kind of healing that occurs with practices such as t'ai chi and chi kung?

ANNIE: Yeah. Or aspirin, or acupuncture, or enemas. Or possibly even surgery. Use it as a sedative, to cure jet lag, relieve back pain, for cardiovascular health, to clear sinuses, hangovers, menstrual cramps—it really works. It can be great emotional therapy as well. A good, long, deep, ten-minute multiple orgasm can do the same thing as four months of weekly therapy.

REBECCA: Do you discriminate between chi, kundalini, and prana, or do you regard them as simply different aspects of sexual energy?

ANNIE: There are subtle differences, which are reflected in the culture or discipline or technique that uses them. I use all three words and would choose one over another depending on the occasion. But I don't claim to be an expert about those subtle differences. I'm not a traditional yogi. I have a lot of respect for those traditional yogis, but I like to think of myself as a postmodern, avant-garde, radical yogi.

DAVID: What are your feelings and thoughts about why there's such a connection between sex and death in music and art?

ANNIE: I think it has to do with surrendering and letting go, losing control. Sex is great training, or practice, for dying. Orgasm especially is great training for dying. Death could be seen as being like another kind of sexual thrill. In that respect, I'm really looking forward to it. I would like to think I've practiced orgasm enough now to have an orgasmic death. Sex and death are both about body and spirit.

REBECCA: You worked as a prostitute for a long time and claimed to love it. Many would be cynical hearing a prostitute say, "I love what I do." They'd think, "There's no way—she must be covering something up."

ANNIE: I've never denied that it's a hell of a hard fucking job. You need enormous amounts of patience and compassion. Sometimes you have to put up with a lot of shit. You're in a society that is misogynistic and full of sexual guilt, and you can take that on. You have to be really strong, and if

> *You're in a society that is misogynistic and full of sexual guilt, and you can take that on.*

you're not, yes, you are miserable. It can get to you. You can get what I call "prostitution burnout." Whenever that happened to me, I didn't love my work. I compare it to being a nurse. You take care of people. You see a lot of sad, horrible things. You deal with some people who have no respect for you and who try to take out their frustrations on you.

For me, about one in ten clients was a bit of a drag, one in a hundred was bearable, and maybe two in a thousand were a nightmare. But with the hundreds of others there were wonderful, mutually beneficial experiences. I really liked the immediate intimacy of getting naked with a total stranger. It was surreal. There was a lot of love and respect between me and most of my clients. I liked most of the sex. Even the lousy sex I liked a lot—it was intriguing to me. I was lucky. Liking sex a lot made being a prostitute a very satisfying job. Some prostitutes don't like sex. Plus, I was a pretty privileged prostitute and always worked in the best places—except once, when I worked at the Pink Pussy Cat, because I wanted to see what is was like for a month. I learned a lot and grew a lot working in prostitution. It fulfilled a lot of my needs. I know it's hard for people to believe, but I truly was a pretty happy hooker most of the time.

Lately, some prostitutes are reclaiming the term *sacred prostitute*, which is great. A lot of prostitutes do really sacred, spiritual, healing work, and they need all the positive reinforcement they can get. People are so prejudiced and judgmental about sex workers, just the way they are against blacks or whites, or Jews or Moslems. They have a lot of preconceived notions and misconceptions. You can't really imagine what sex work is truly like unless you've done it. And different people have different experiences with it. A lot

> *A lot of prostitutes do really sacred, spiritual, healing work . . .*

depends on the person doing it and that person's level of self-esteem. Plus, lots of people are very jealous of prostitutes, so they put the job down a lot.

DAVID: What relationship do you see between spirituality and sexuality? How would you describe your spiritual belief system?

ANNIE: I just go by my own personal experience. Basically, when I'm in sexual ecstasy is when I feel the most spiritual. I feel the most in touch with my essence. It's the simplest way I've found to open my heart, to feel the most love and experience life-force energy. I've been to a dozen ashrams, done a dozen different types of spiritual disciplines, been on mountain tops and under the ocean, been in churches around the world, tried drugs, sat at the feet of famous gurus, and I have never felt as spiritual as when I'm in a high state of sexual ecstasy.

DAVID: Is it then that you feel a connection to everything else in the universe?

ANNIE: Yeah. On a good day, sex helps me access my deepest, deepest feelings, my unconscious, and take me beyond my body and mind to "supreme consciousness." I get glimpses of what life is about, besides telephone calls and jobs and pieces of paper and everyday reality. When sex is really great, it goes way beyond the physical into the magical—into timelessness. Truthfully, I don't really know what I'm doing. I just know what I'm *experiencing*. I don't have too many guides on this journey. I just experiment, take creative risks, and put a lot of time and effort into it. There aren't many sex shamans or sex yogis that you can go study with. I don't really know exactly what spirituality is, but in my experience it's pretty erotic.

Of course, I don't *always* have sex that feels spiritual. Sometimes it's bland, very grounded, or simply very physical. Sometimes sex can make me feel less spiritual. It's all part of the whole, so to speak.

DAVID: What about ancient systems: shamanism, paganism, tantra, the archetype of the Goddess? How have you incorporated these into your work?

ANNIE: With humor, mostly. Certainly learning some ancient techniques—the fire-breath orgasm, the microcosmic orbit, casting a circle, invocation, ritual, yoga—has helped me make major leaps toward accessing a more profound sexuality. I've learned a lot from the ancient traditions. I like incorporating all those things into sex. But to tell you the truth, my favorite thing for the last few months has been being with this one person I'm madly in love with and doing very minimal things—no sex toys, no techniques, no kink, no ritual, no frills. Just good, old-fashioned romantic lovemaking. It's kind of Zen sex. I'm very embarrassed about it, but at the moment it's the truth. This could be the end of my career! But I'm really turned on by the simplicity of it. The minimalness of it. It's very blissful. Sometimes less is so much more.

DAVID: It sounds like you're always on the verge of orgasm.

ANNIE: In a way, I am. What I'm realizing is that the more I train myself to go into ecstasy, my body becomes more and more in touch with what it is to be in that state, so I can access it at a moment's notice. Not all the time, of course, because there's a certain point where we have no control over the energy. But for me, sex is better than ever before, because I've built up my capacity for pleasure and I'm much more orgasmic. I'm also much better at being intimate with another person. I can jump from a, b, and c right up to q. Now it's in my blood. Practice, practice, practice.

It's very easy to go into an orgasmic state if you just relax, open your mind to it, and let the orgasmic energy of the universe, which is there just for the asking, wash through your body. I know quite a few people who can simply lie down, take a few breaths, and go into an orgasmic state. It's actually very easy.

DAVID: Do people object to your work?

ANNIE: Occasionally. But I don't hear that many objections. I mostly hear all the really positive stuff. When I was teaching a course at the Learning Annex [in Los Angeles], I was demonstrating energy orgasms on the floor. I happened to not have underwear on, and a few of the women could see that. I thought, "Hell, it's a sex workshop, it's all women, what's the problem?" (*laughter*) Then they wanted to know where their G-spot was. So I invited a few women to put on a latex glove and feel mine. It's the best way to teach them how to find theirs. So a few women found my G-spot. No one said anything. At the time I didn't pick up any negative reactions, but a few women called the annex later to complain. It was too much for them. I wasn't trying to shock anyone, but how can you teach sex if you don't get down and show it?

REBECCA: What kinds of positive changes have you seen in women as a result of your work?

> *I'm always amazed when a woman tells me how much she has gotten from a work-shop . . .*

ANNIE: I'm always amazed when a woman tells me how much she has gotten from a workshop, or from a good performance, and how much it's improved her life. But I don't usually feel that I have that much to do with it. I think they're just ready for the change. I just give them the space to explore, and sometimes I midwife their change. Just being in a circle of women for a few days is transformative in itself. Workshops are truly a great way to learn. When else do people devote three, four, seven days straight to exploring their sexuality? Most people don't put time into it. I always learn a whole lot from taking a sex workshop—or for that matter, from teaching one.

REBECCA: Do you think that not only confronting but *celebrating* a woman's sexuality can empower her to realize she cannot only take control of her own life, but also make changes in the world?

ANNIE: Our sexuality is not just something that can be used to enhance an intimate relationship, or for physical pleasure, or for procreation. It can also be used for personal transformation, self-realization, spiritual growth, and emotional healing. Something that versatile and powerful definitely has the potential to contribute to the well-being of all life on earth.

> *. . . a sexually satisfied woman is a happy woman.*

Notice how powerful women started to become just after the birth control pill came around. Besides, the bottom line is that a sexually satisfied woman is a happy woman.

I've seen some beautiful miracles happen when women explore, and even exploit, their sexuality. When I was working at Caesar's Retreat, this "massage" parlor in Manhattan, a new woman named Simone came in to work. She had been married, had four kids, and was a strict Hasidic Jew. She had worked for years in the garment district, making minimum wage. Her husband didn't treat her well, and she was always shat on by all the Hasidic men at her job. So she decided to take her kids and leave her husband. Desperate for money, she ends up getting a job at Caesar's whorehouse. I was asked to train her. After a few days, Simone was making tons of money, largely because she had these humongous, pendulous breasts. She had never before had sex with anyone but her husband, and he was a lousy lover. So she started coming out of the back room in amazement, with a smile on her face. She became more beautiful, more powerful, and happily independent very quickly. She still wore her wig and kept a kosher kitchen. Eventually she sent her kids to private schools, and they really benefited, too. She became very politically active. Now she is a lawyer and helping lots of people. Of course, this doesn't always happen, but I've seen some cases.

REBECCA: Do you think many women feel that in some way they don't *deserve* to be sexually satisfied?

ANNIE: Sure. We don't believe we deserve lots of things. I suppose a lot of people in the world are having fantastic sex. But also I'm constantly amazed by how little people know and how unsatisfied they are. We don't have good role models and masterful lovers. Porn movies are a joke. Some people can learn a little from them occasionally. There are aspects of sex you can learn about through porn, but most people making porn don't have a very broad view of sexuality. There is also so much fear around sex. I woke up in the middle of the night last week trembling. I was full of fear. Then I realized that I had taught four workshops in a row, and a lot of fear had come up among the participants. I had taken on some of it. Plus, the responsibility I feel is scary. The trick is to create a very safe space where women can examine their fears and face them head on.

And then there are all the judgments people have about their bodies and all their insecurities about what they don't know. Sex is highly emotional, but that's part of what makes it interesting.

DAVID: You had a transsexual, hermaphroditic lover for a while. As a result of your experimentation with gender, what are your thoughts about the value of androgyny?

ANNIE: My lover was a surgically made hermaphrodite. Although a female transsexual before receiving male genitals, he was totally butch. That's one of the great things about living in the nineties: all the various gender choices. There's nothing like a good gender fuck. My present lover, Mary, is very androgynous. She's a cross be-

> *My present lover . . . is very androgynous. She's . . . the most sexy, beautiful person in the world.*

tween Rod Stewart and K. D. Lang, and the most sexy, beautiful person in the world. I don't know how I got so lucky.

There's a lot more work to do in the gender thing. In my last workshop, we had a woman who as born with hermaphroditic genitals. At one and a half years old, the surgeons mutilated her. They removed her penis, which was really an enlarged clitoris, and her inner labia. Now she has horrible vaginal and psychological pain, and has never experienced orgasm. She's in her thirties. In my workshop, she masturbated for the first time ever. That was a big breakthrough. She's a wonderful, very sexy person. She's very angry about having been mutilated, so now she's organizing other people like herself through a newsletter. Unfortunately, this is very common, but rarely addressed.

People who are not stereotypically male or female suffer so much. Transsexuals and androgynies have so much to offer. The really sad thing is that often they don't appreciate their own uniqueness and specialness.

REBECCA: Do you see this as a trend that's building: more sexual diversity and fewer boundaries between genders?

ANNIE: Sure. You can even see glimpses of it on MTV. Everything's getting mixed together, and stereotypical gender roles are totally breaking down, or actually multiplying. One very obvious change is the popularity of strap-on dildos. Women are getting these big dicks—it's great. And they really know how to use them. (*laughter*) And they never get soft. You know, recently dildo technology has vastly improved. When I first got into porno movies, twenty-something years ago, we used these flimsy hard-plastic things that had a little piece of elastic to hold them on. They were virtually impossible to use. Now that women are designing sex toys, there are so many gorgeous dildo models to choose from, and the harnesses are strong and sexy.

A lot of my good friends are doing great work in the gender thing. My best friend Veronica Vera's business is booming. She created the Academy For Boys Who Want To Be Girls. Diane Torr is doing Drag King For a Day workshops, where women become men for a day. The list goes on and on. For four years a group of female-to-mail transsexuals and transvestites has met at my house. I'm very close to the group. A lot of them are in a lot of pain and confusion. Gender can be such fun to play with, and it can be the source of so much suffering.

One of my favorite things is to go out on the town wearing a sexy low-cut dress, high heels, and a mustache. People always think I'm a man in drag. In spite of my big boobs. It's fun.

REBECCA: What have your relationships with the various sexes taught you about the differences between women and men?

ANNIE: I've learned that it's virtually impossible to generalize about men and women. The two generalizations I can make are that women are much softer and less hairy, but not always, and that most women have pussies and most men have penises, but not all.

REBECCA: How do you feel about monogamy?

ANNIE: It's great for some people and a prison for others. Generally, I don't like to be monogamous, because each individual person I'm with brings out some totally different aspect of myself, and I learn so much from each person. My goal is to find out everything I can about sex, so how could I just be with one person? Of course, there's a lot to be learned through monogamous sex.

Much to my surprise, for the last eight months I've been virtually completely monogamous. I love it! I'm enjoying being discriminating and focusing the energy. It's quite liberating and very romantic. It's hot. It's sweet. It's kinky!

Then again, in a way, monogamy is impossible. If sex is about the exchange of energy, then I'm having sex with lots of people all the time. Today I was on a jogging machine at the gym, and a very sexy guy got on the machine next to mine. Energy-wise, we were definitely having a sexual experience jogging next to each other. I could barely keep from moaning.

DAVID: How do you see technology influencing sex in the future?

ANNIE: Technology is certainly having an electrifying effect. The Hitachi Magic Wand vibrator is revolutionizing women's sexuality. In my opinion, every woman ought to have a good vibrator, especially women who are pre-orgasmic—it's a basic. They can't replace a human being, but they are very special in their own right. Vibrators are definitely helping women become far more orgasmic—and what I call *megagasmic*. Certainly the telephone has had an enormous impact. For the first time in history, millions of people a day are discussing their sexual fantasies and desires totally honestly and openly because it is anonymous, through those phone sex companies. A lot of truths about where people are at sexually are coming to the surface and being expressed, and that has been scaring the shit out of the right wing and anti-sex people. In my opinion, the antisex right-wing backlash has a lot to do, unconsciously, with phone sex.

It's funny. I've been with a few johns who were really into phone sex, and when you had sex with them, it was like you were talking on the phone.

They were totally dissociated from the physicality of sex. It was all about words and thoughts. In some ways technology will take us away or distract us from some beautiful aspects of sexuality, but it is also adding a whole new dimension.

One of the best sexual experiences I've ever had was on the Vibrasound machine, which is the Rolls Royce of those brain-wave therapy machines. It's not made for sexual purposes, but it's ultra sensuous and erotic anyway. You lie on this water bed, which vibrates and waves to music that you hear on headsets, and you put on these goggles with blinking lights. After an hour, I was overtaken, completely by surprise, by a humongous, full-body energy orgasm that kept going and going and going. Then the afterglow feelings were incredibly deep. It was profound. Yogis practice for years to get into that state, and the Vibrasound puts you there quite quickly, without much effort. Most people don't have the experience I did on it. In fact, I did the Vibrasound a few more times after that and had nonsexual experiences.

DAVID: What role do you think psychedelics play in the evolution of sexuality?

ANNIE: I'm not sure. Most all of the psychedelics I did were when I was a teenager in high school in Panama and still a virgin. I'm gearing up to do some psychedelic drugs again. The ancient sacred prostitutes used drugs. I've never been a big drug-lover, luckily, but I have tried most of them, and they've been fun and educational. But drugs are very hard on my body, and I hesitate to do things that drain my energy. Besides, I've found that if I invest enough time and energy in a sexual night or weekend, I can get from sex the same effects as from many drugs. Drugs are kind of the lazy person's sex.

DAVID: Did you find any similarity between the peak of an LSD trip and the height of a sexual experience, in terms of the consciousness level?

ANNIE: Yeah, now that you mention it. When I'm in a state of sexual ecstasy and I go and gaze at the moon, I have a psychedelic experience of the moon. Oddly, it doesn't always work the other way around, where looking at the moon during the peak of an LSD experience is sexual.

DAVID: That was how Timothy Leary popularized LSD—through the sexual connection, in terms of opening up the senses.

ANNIE: It's true. Sex is about the senses. By my bed I have a long shelf with all kinds of things to titillate all the senses. Things to listen to, smell, see, massage with, taste—they're very effective to use during lovemaking. Occasionally, when I have a friend who is very sick in the hospital, I'll visit him or her with a bag of sensuous goodies. Often they don't have any sexual energy or desire, but stimulating their senses brings them a lot of pleasure, especially if they were very sexual when they were well. So I'll give them oils to sniff, brush and tickle them with feathers, ring bells or tap on drums by their ears, stimulate their skin with cupping, use the vibrator on various parts of their body, massage them with cornstarch. They really love it. It's very sexual without being *overtly* sexual, and often a much better way of communicating than the kind of talking that takes place around sick beds. I'm often amazed how being around illness and dying can be such a turn-on.

DAVID: What future possibilities do you see in the evolution of sexual awareness?

ANNIE: I have noticed lately that there are quite a good handful of what Joseph Kramer calls "erotically gifted people" coming into the world. I've seen these young sexual prodigies pick up at the age of twenty-one where a lot of us in our forties, fifties, and sixties have left off. I'm so jealous! They're incredible sexual healers, and extremely aware. They could pioneer a quantum leap in our society's consciousness. Sex magic is going to be very, very popular. Orgasm is going to be a big fad when my documentary movie about it comes out. My video will create more interest in orgasm, and people will have a better understanding of all the varieties of orgasms and the uses of orgasms. Condom technology will get much better, which is important nowadays. We will hear more people talk about having sex with things like extraterrestrials, angels, spirits, ghosts, and other entities. I think sex with dogs and horses will become popular. It's amazing it's not more popular right now. In the very near future, people will be more interested in deeply intimate, very connected, more loving sex exploration happening in that area, especially in the tantric community. Queer culture and modern primitivism have certainly taken a strong hold, and are inventing a lot more options and varieties of sexual possibilities and lifestyles.

REBECCA: Do you have a definition of pornography? Is this a meaningless term to you, in the sense that most people use it?

ANNIE: To me, pornography simply means sexually explicit. I think it's a useful term. It's certainly provocative, and somewhat descriptive. I like the word.

REBECCA: Do you see any value at all in censorship?

> *. . . I do see value in people* **trying** *to censor things. It adds to the excitement . . .*

ANNIE: I don't see any value in censoring anything. But I do see value in people *trying* to censor things. It adds to the excitement; it adds to the value of what they're trying to censor. When I go to a college to give a lecture and show a video or two and there's no controversy, if there's no one against my work or ideas, then it's not nearly as interesting.

REBECCA: Do you think that censorship can help to protect people?

ANNIE: No. Censorship ultimately hurts people. Look at the countries with the most censorship, and they're the most fucked up. When it comes to censoring porn, it's ridiculous. Sex is not the problem. The problems are sexism and violence, which have been going on for centuries, since before there was porn. That's what we need to address.

REBECCA: Do you feel that there is any connection between the way sex is portrayed in the media and violent sexual acts?

ANNIE: I figured the rape and abuse questions were coming up. I find it odd that you want to ask me about rape. I think that deep down everyone in the world wants to have more fun, more ecstasy, more pleasure, have some laughs, be loved, be touched. Isn't that what everyone wants? So I'm trying to be a living example of what that might look like. That's my job, my goal. But inevitably what happens is, I'm constantly being asked, "What about rape? What about abuse? What about child pornography?" I'm always getting asked about all this shit. Why is that? I'm just fascinated by that. Wherever I go, people want to talk about pain and suffering.

REBECCA: Perhaps people talk about what they know.

ANNIE: Why don't they want to talk more about ecstasy and orgasms? I do think that lots of violence on television results in more violence in the world. And that pornography results in more fucking and sucking. And the way sex is portrayed on television does have an impact on people. Certainly rape is far more acceptable to portray on television than intense pleasure and ecstasy. A violent rape is far more acceptable to watch than a simple little kiss between two women or two men. What's wrong with this picture?

> *Certainly rape is far more acceptable to portray on television than intense pleasure and ecstasy.*

DAVID: Something that's hardly ever talked about is teaching children to enjoy their sexuality.

ANNIE: Yes. Big taboo subject. Perhaps the next generation will be better able to tackle some of those issues, because ours is failing miserably. In the past, in some of the Native American traditions, when a child was interested in sex, they sent that child to learn about it from an adult, and the child could have sex with that person when they were ready. I wish that when I was a kid, I'd had an understanding, sensitive adult to teach me all about sex, and how to masturbate.

REBECCA: Of course, the pivotal phrase in what you just said is "when they were ready." It makes a difference if somebody is being forced to engage in a sexual act, against her or his will.

ANNIE: Sure. That's about violence and control, not really about sex. But some children are ready for sex and could greatly benefit from it at a very young age, and some could not. And there are certainly adults who are caring, sensitive, and knowledgeable enough to handle the incredible responsibility of teaching a child sex. But that's not allowed in our culture. You go to prison for life for that.

> *. . . some children are ready for sex . . . . But that's not allowed in our culture. You go to prison for life for that.*

   You know, having a lousy, fucked-up sexual experience isn't the end of the world. There are no mistakes in sex. It's a great tool for learning. My lousiest, worst nightmarish sexual experiences were in a way some of my most interesting. In my late teens and early twenties, I liked to live dangerously. I found it very erotic. I'd go to a party, and would leave with the guy most likely to murder me. I hitchhiked a lot and put myself in dangerous situations. I wanted to see if I could get out of them. Luckily, I always did, and relatively unscathed. I'm not *that* afraid to die. What I'm really afraid of is getting fat. (*laughter*) That's my worst fear. Fortunately, I'm not interested in any kind of dangerous sex any more. But I'm actually proud of my worst, most stupid sexual adventures, even though sometimes they hurt. Why not make the best of it?

DAVID: I'm having a little bit of a hard time understanding that, because to me the whole thing about eroticism is trust.

ANNIE: There are many kinds of eroticism. Sex with trust is very erotic. Actually, I had to have lots and lots of trust in those dangerous situations. Perhaps it's my trust that saved me.

REBECCA: So you think that the reason people want to talk about the negative stuff is because they get turned on by it, a reversal of the pleasure principle?

ANNIE: Maybe it's the same reason people go to horror movies.

DAVID: Perhaps part of the pleasure comes from being scared out of your wits then knowing that you're safe, which is the thrill of watching a horror movie or being at an amusement park.

ANNIE: That's interesting. Well, as I learn that sex is more about energy than anything else, when you add that violent aspect or fear aspect, it raises a lot of energy. And I think that people don't know how to raise their sexual energy.

REBECCA: Without that.

> *If you're into pleasure, you're labeled . . .* **hedonist. . . .** *If you're into suffering, you're a . . .* **saint.**

ANNIE: Right. If you're into pleasure, you're labeled with words with negative connotations: *pleasure seeker, hedonist, nymphomaniac*. If you're into suffering, you're a martyr, a hero, a saint.

DAVID: It's very difficult to write a book that doesn't have some element of violence. It's hard to stay on the topic of pure pleasure if you want to keep people's attention.

ANNIE: People get bored. Most people can't sustain happiness for very long. Most people's orgasms are extremely short, and they want to stop at once. We're capable of very long orgasms that go on and on. I think we need to stretch our pleasure muscles, like working out at the gym.

DAVID: Have you noticed that there's an inverse relationship in cultures between openness toward sex and frequency of violent behavior?

ANNIE: I don't know the statistics on that. Certainly the United States has quite a bit of openness, and quite a bit of violence. I've heard that the aborigines in Australia had a good idea. They had a system in which everyone was totally taken care of sexually. Everyone had a mate, plus everyone could have a lover on the side if they wanted. They also engaged in various kinds of group sex during rituals. In some rituals, they would act out rapes. Because they acted out rape in a safe way, there was never, ever any actual violent rape in the community.

In the old days, I did several porno movies where I got to act out being raped. It was very interesting. I admit I'd had rape fantasies. Once I had acted them out fully, roughly, they went away quite quickly. Perhaps on some level this kept me from ever actually having been raped. Nowadays, it's not allowed to act out rapes in porno movies.

REBECCA: What are your thoughts about rape?

ANNIE: It sucks—excuse the sex-negative expression. I understand that rape can be devastating. It can take a long time to heal from a rape. You can't believe how many women, and men, I meet who have been raped, especially by family members. It's unbelievable. Personally, I don't know that much about rape. I know about pleasure. What's sad is how some people use their rape experiences, or the fear of rape, to keep themselves in a cage. Because they were raped or abused, they use it as an excuse not to deal with their sexuality. But in some cases you can actually use sex to heal a rape trauma. Sometimes talking about a rape experience in therapy for years won't create a breakthrough. But then you get your hands up into the root of the problem, where some of the trauma took place, and you can bring it right up to the surface, look at it, and heal it. That requires trust.

> *. . . people use their rape experiences, or the fear of rape, to keep themselves in a cage.*

DAVID: I know a woman who was raped, and she enjoyed it very much.

ANNIE: That's probably how I'd try to cope with it, too. My motto is "Eroticise Everything."

> ***My motto is "Eroticise Everything."***

Some women stay in relationships with abusive, violent husbands partly because they enjoy violent sex and they don't know how to enjoy other kinds. Soft, gentle, sensitive lovemaking just doesn't do it for them, and they don't know how to create a sexual intensity in other ways. Violent sex is very popular. But it can be so bad for your health. I was just invited to teach a sexuality seminar at a battered women's shelter. I think that will be very, very interesting and educational.

If we could teach people to have more intense sexual experiences other ways, I think a lot of the violence could stop.

I have talked with men who were in wars and who admitted getting sexually turned on, erect penises while killing people. I can imagine that killing is very penetrating, very visceral, very intimate.

REBECCA: What are the most common problems you come across as a sexual counselor and workshop leader?

ANNIE: There are lots of performance-anxiety-type problems stemming from insecurities, negative mind chatter, and lack of information. Boredom

> ***There are a lot of concerns pertaining to orgasm. Guilt and shame.***

in long-term relationships is a biggie: "bed death." There are lots of concerns pertaining to orgasm. Guilt and shame. The number one most common thing women complain about is that they can have great orgasms alone but never with a partner, and they're really upset about it. Many women don't have vaginal orgasms and feel they're missing something. I've had all those problems myself over the years, so I can relate. There certainly are lots of women who had something horrible that happened to them sexually and they just can't get past it. I just say, "Oh, forget about that. Go to therapy and work on it there. But let's go. Let's have a good time." I show them that they don't have to dwell on it. They can rise above it. I try to give them a new view of sex and encourage them to get back up on that horse they fell off, so to speak, and go for a beautiful ride.

Here we are talking about pain and suffering again. How come no on ever asks me when was the most wonderful sexual experience I've ever had?

DAVID: Hey, I'd like to know.

ANNIE: Two days ago. (*laughter*)

DAVID: What do you think about the importance of keeping a sense of humor in regard to sexuality?

ANNIE: I use humor a lot. For one thing, a good, hard belly-laugh is so orgasmic. Also, sex is really scary to a lot of people, and one way of dealing with fear is through humor. So a lot of my work is kind of funny. It helps the medicine go down. Besides, sex in itself can be so silly and funny. Like, for a year I had a masochistic lover who liked his food stepped on before he ate it—it really turned him on. I loved the humor in it, plus it really was surprisingly erotic.

DAVID: Tell us something about post-porn modernism.

ANNIE: Post-porn modernism is a term that a Dutch artist named Wink Van Kempen came up with and let me borrow. The words imply something *after* porn, something artistic, and something postmodern. It gives a name to a genre of porn that is more intellectual, more creative or experimental. It doesn't have to focus on the erotic, like mainstream porn does. Erotica is just one aspect of sex. Most of my recent work hasn't been about being erotic.

DAVID: What has it been about?

ANNIE: Ideas, feminism, politics, visuals, controversies, education, gender, humor.

DAVID: Why is it that you live in New York City, when California is so much more pleasure-oriented?

ANNIE: I think because it's such a communications center. It's the throat chakra of the world. I like the feeling of hundreds of thousands of people living very close together. I think Manhattan is sexy. I really appreciate the eroticism of nature, but buildings are sexy, too. I look out my window at the Manhattan skyline, and I see the Grand Canyon. There's a lot of energy. But I'm certainly very open to moving soon.

REBECCA: Have you had much experience of censorship?

ANNIE: Almost every day for over half my life.

REBECCA: You don't seem to have much anger in you at all about the resistance to your work.

ANNIE: I'm not totally in another world, although sometimes I try to be.

REBECCA: You're doing a good job. (*laughter*)

ANNIE: It's funny you say that, because I'm actually full of anger, even rage. Anger and orgasm are very connected, you know. If you want to have better orgasms, practice expressing anger. For a long time, I didn't express my anger. I still have a long way to go there. I'm always grateful for a situation where I can get really angry. It's such a relief. But compared with many, I'm generally not a very angry person.

> *If you want to have better orgasms, practice expressing anger.*

I still have so much to learn. I don't claim to be the world's greatest lover. I do claim to be the best lover that I can be. I'm not a prodigy. There's a lot that I lack as a lover—natural born talents that I don't have. I lack some types of sensitivities, some types of energies, an ability to thrust. (*laughter*) I'm not great at thrusting. But I do have my gifts: a sense of adventure, creativity, a nonjudgmental attitude, playfulness, enthusiasm. Everyone has their sexual strengths and weaknesses.

I'm just so grateful for my sexuality. I don't know what I'd do without it. I'm just amazed that everyone doesn't want to make pornography, or be a prostitute, or learn more about sex—but they don't.

REBECCA: How has it felt to conduct this interview in the house where you grew up?

ANNIE: Fine. I feel good about it. It's funny, because years ago I used to keep my family pictures totally separate from my porno pictures, and then eventually they got all mixed up together and kind of finally grew over each other.

Second Interview (*conducted in Hawaii*)

REBECCA: The interview so far has mainly been with Annie Sprinkle, but I'm interested in talking to your alter ego, Anya. Anya, could you tell us how you experience sexuality, and what some of your fantasies are, and how they differ from Annie's?

ANNIE: You know, before we get started, I think I'd like to have a quick orgasm. It will help me think better. Clear my head. Excuse me.

DAVID: [fifteen minutes later] Better?

ANNIE: (*laughter*) Definitely. Now my mind is much more clear. Sex is so handy.

REBECCA: So, I was asking about how Annie's sexuality differs from Anya's.

ANNIE: Well, Annie's fantasies used to be everything from being hooked up to electronic torture machines by the Nazis, to performing a live sex act with a horse on stage in Tijuana, to someone squatting over me and shitting into my mouth. (*laughter*) I went into the depths of my kinkymost self and never censored myself. Eventually all the kinky fantasies melted away. Nowaday, Annie fantasizes exclusively about her girlfriend, Mary. Mary's pussy rubbing against mine—simple stuff: Mary's shoulders, Mary's eyes, Mary's lips on my pussy, my lips on Mary's pussy.

As Anya, I focus mostly on my breath and let my mind completely go. I don't fantasize. I might occasionally visualize, which really is just about the same thing. Same muscles. If I visualize something, it's very cosmic. I become the sun or the moon or the stars or something very expanded. I make love with the Goddess. Or I become nothing; let my ego go. I imagine becoming empty or my heart opening and pouring out love. Sometimes I become a hissing snake or a volcano. Often I pray or give gratitude. I see myself as a devoted disciple of something, but I'm not sure what, and it's my job to midwife as much bliss into the world as possible. As a wise gay man once said, "As I receive pleasure, so the whole universe receives pleasure through me." That's Anya's fantasy at the moment.

REBECCA: Are you becoming Anya full-time, or will she and Annie always share the stage together?

ANNIE: I think I'll jump back and forth and definitely becoming Anya more and more whether I like it or not. She's simply more mature, wiser. Maybe they'll integrate. Sometimes I still enjoy being Annie, the party-girl slut. My neighbor Karen is a call girl, and every so often she'll call me and say, "Come on down and turn a trick with me," and I'll put on my Annie Sprinkle gear and go turn a trick. Occasionally I really enjoy it—it's kind of a hobby. I'm glad I'm not dependent on prostitution. I couldn't do it on a regular basis any more. But I like to keep my finger in the pie, so to speak.

DAVID: As Anya, do you feel that you're plugging into an archetype?

ANNIE: I don't know. Yesterday someone told me I was the "bodhisattva of the first chakra." (*laughter*) That was quite a compliment. Sometimes I'm amazed at my own power. Sometimes at the end of my show, when I finish the ecstasy ritual, I just sit on stage and sort of meditate, and amazing things happen. People in the audience sometimes have spontaneous orgasms, or start sobbing hysterically, or start doing weird yoga poses, or go into trance. They come up and give me their jewelry, their good luck charms, their baby's photos. They throw away their crutches! Just kidding about the crutches.

A couple of days ago, about twenty of us were on a boat on an outing that my friend Kutira organized. Most everyone there was a tantra teacher. Kutira teaches what she calls "Oceanic Tantra." So we were out in the middle of the ocean, and we all jumped in the water to try doing her brand of sex magic, where you breathe, undulate, hold your breath, and dive down while you visualize what you want to create with the sex energy. I had never swum out in the middle of the ocean before, and I was really scared. But it was beautiful. For two hours I don't see a single fish, so finally I relax. Then we start the sex magic. We're in a circle, we dive down, and all of a sudden, there's a big shark right below us—my worst fear! I should never have seen the movie *Jaws*. Anyways, I'm not doing any more sex magic in the ocean for a while.

REBECCA: Camille Paglia claims that the feminist movement sees female sexuality as something that has been exploited by men, and has encouraged women to abandon their sexual power. One of the things I found liberating about your show was that it used that sexuality in a multitude of forms, as a form of self-expression. What reaction have you had from feminists? And what would you say to women who claim that you're simply buying into a male-dominator fantasy and betraying women?

ANNIE: When I first started doing this show, I was much more used to relating to a male audience, and I probably was heavily influenced by male fantasies. My only stage experience was in burlesque. But as I've changed and become more of a feminist, the show has changed. Certainly I got feedback from some feminists that really made me think and re-evaluate myself. Now, whenever I do a run of my show, I always try to have one night that is for women only. The all-woman audience is my best audience. The show I do is really more for women. One of the things I do in my show is insert a speculum and show the audience my cervix. When there are men in the audience, it's a much different piece than if it's all women. A lot of how what I'm doing is perceived is in the mind of the beholder. You can't please everybody when you're doing this kind of work, that's for sure. In fact, you're bound to upset a few.

I haven't had much opportunity to connect with the Women Against Porn. I've been curious. But when I've seen them on the street with their signs, they've been far too violent and scary to approach.

I did have one very interesting encounter with one of the Women Against Porn. I met her at a funeral of a friend. We got to talking, told each other what work we did, and went out for tea together. For four years she had been touring the country with an anti-porn slide show, advocating censorship to protect women, to protect girls like me from being exploited and tortured by the porn industry. It was like a cosmic joke, because as we talked it became obvious that she was totally miserable and I was quite happy. She was living with her mother because she couldn't afford an apartment, she was horribly depressed, she hadn't had sex in four years, she didn't know if she was a lesbian or a heterosexual—she was a wreck. I was having a good day, was quite happy, had my own apartment, had money, had a fabulous sex life, and seemed to have it all together. She dropped out of Women Against Porn shortly afterward. A couple of years later, she even came to one of my sex workshops. She's the one who invited me to come to the battered women's shelter, where she works now.

Don't get me wrong. There's a lot about the porn business that is sleazy and disgusting and yucky and dumb. There are women who are treated less than respectfully and who don't come out of it ahead. But lots of those women wouldn't come out of anything ahead. There are some Women Against Porn types who are doing some good work, I think. It's great that they talk about the violence and abused-women experience. Someone's got to do it.

I'm very happy that I'm not involved with the mainstream porn industry. What a relief. I loved it in the old days, but the biz was different then. Now mostly I find it simply boring and stale. Plus the fact that they hardly use any safe sex really freaks me out. They have such a great opportunity to educate and influence the public and do the right thing. But they won't, because they're in denial and they think they'll lose money. I started a group called Pornographers Promoting Safer Sex, but it quickly fell by the wayside. All my video work now is totally safe sex.

REBECCA: I found your live performance to be a very powerful experience. What kinds of responses have you gotten from your audience, positive or negative?

ANNIE: Mostly, I get positive responses, because the people who have negative responses don't stick around to tell me. (*laughter*) People sometimes say, "Well, I really enjoyed your show, but it wasn't erotic." They expect to be turned on. So they think the show fails. But it's not meant to be erotic.

DAVID: What are you trying to get across in your shows?

ANNIE: Originally I did the show simply to understand myself better and to heal my life. It helped a lot. Now I do it more for others, and because it's a fun way to make a living. I want to show people what it looks like to not have any shame or guilt about your sexuality and your body. So many people suffer unnecessarily. I want to show that a lot of taboos are silly. I'm trying to give people a little real contact with a real sex worker, so that hopefully they'll get over some of their prejudices and preconceived notions about women who are in the sex business or who are promiscuous.

In the first half of the show, I try to show sex as something that can be fun and light, as something that most people take way too seriously. In the second half, I try to make it sacred again and show that most people don't take it seriously enough.

DAVID: You're trying to dissolve some of the superficial mystery so that you can get to a deeper level of mystery?

> *. . . you can never demystify a cervix, because it will always be a great mystery.*

ANNIE: Yeah. Like when I show my cervix to the audience. What's inside? It's a big mystery. So let's shine a flashlight on it and take a casual look. But you can never demystify a cervix, because it will always be a great mystery.

DAVID: In your opinion, what is the key to really good sex?

ANNIE: Hmmmm. There is no master key. Different keys unlock different people's doors. It depends. Love and romance are certainly great aphrodisiacs. Learning about conscious breathing is a very powerful key for one person, and getting down on your hands and knees and worshiping somebody's feet can be a really great key for another person. Getting over guilt and shame opens a lot of doors. To have no expectations is a good key. Acceptance of and compassion toward where you're at in you own personal sexual evolution is another. For some people it's learning to say no, and for some it's learning to say yes. Learning about energy is a major key.

For me, one of the big keys is time. Quickies can be spectacular, but really transcendental, deeply satisfying sex takes hours—hours to prepare, hours to savor, and hours to clean up after when it's over! I can't really go into such depth and intensity and into those altered states without putting in the time.

Group-sex energy can be very powerful for some people. I personally don't care much for casual orgies, but I like structured group-sex rituals very much. I love to raise that cone of power. One key for me is shaving my legs. I can't have good sex until I've shaved my legs. (*laughter*)

DAVID: If you were to sum up the basic message of your life's work, what would it be?

ANNIE: Let there be pleasure on earth, and let it begin with me.

Jerry Garcia

"There is a human drive to celebrate, and we provide ritual celebration in a society that doesn't have much of it."

Tales of the Living Dead
with Jerry Garcia

When you've had a street named after you, then you can congratulate your-self on a certain notoriety. But when you've had an ice cream named after you—well, that is the kind of recognition which dreams are made of. After thirty years of playing with one of the most successful bands in rock and roll history, Jerry Garcia finds himself, at the age of fifty-one, at the zenith of his popularity. The Grateful Dead, the sixties-gone-nineties rock band, has recorded over a hundred albums and plays more live shows than al-most anyone anywhere. And their concerts are always sold out.

With its own magazine, Internet status, and booming merchandising industry, the group is a musical phenomenon of mythical proportions. But Jerry Garcia shrugs his shoulders with genuine innocence in the face of it all. Is it the band that has spawned the semi-nomadic tribe whose members roam the country like medieval minstrels, living on veggie burgers, psychedelics, love, and, of course, the promise of a ticket to the next show? Or is it that the aspirations and values of the sixties just refuse to die, and the Grateful Dead is simply a conduit for their continued expression?

Jerry Garcia began playing with the Warlocks in 1965, and in the same year, the Grateful Dead was formed. He developed his improvisational style at the infamous "acid tests," where the Grateful Dead was often the house band. The Jerry Garcia Band, formed in 1975, is as popular as the Dead. It has a more blues-oriented, gritty sound, but maintains Jerry's distinctive psychedelic edge.

Garcia's almost supernatural status got an extra boost when he jour-neyed into the jaws of Death and back, after falling into a diabetic coma. He has reached a point in his career where, if he were half-asleep and out of tune, the audience would still hang on every note with a reverent sigh. Who is this man who has catalyzed peak experiences in young and old for three decades. He describes himself as a "good 'ol' celebrity," although at shows you're likely to see at least one starry-eyed youth coddling a sign declaring that "Jerry is God." Many fans are convinced he is not from this planet.

56

The interview took place at the Grateful Dead's homey headquarters in San Rafael, California. With his full, white beard and wise-owl eyes, Jerry Garcia looks ready to pass out the clay tablets, yet when he smiles, the Old Testament prophet is transformed into a self-parodying garden gnome, who has walked the yellow-brick road of success simply by doing what he loves.

RMN

———————

JERRY: I'll take off my glasses. They don't convey much humanity.

DAVID: Jerry, how did you start playing music?

JERRY: My father was a professional musician, my mother was an amateur. I grew up in a musical household and took piano lessons as far back as I can remember. There was never a time in my life that music wasn't a part of.

The first time I decided that music was something I wanted to do, apart from just being surrounded by it, was when I was about fifteen. I developed this deep craving to play the electric guitar. I fell in love with rock and roll; I wanted to make that sound so badly. So I got a pawnshop electric guitar and a little amplifier, and I started without the benefit of anybody else around me who played the guitar, or of any books.

My stepfather put it in an open tuning of some kind, and I taught myself how to play by ear. I did that for about a year, until I ran into a kid at school who knew three chords on the guitar and also the correct way to tune it. That's when I started to play around at it; then I picked things up. I never took lessons or anything.

DAVID: Who particularly inspired you?

JERRY: Actually, no particular musician inspired me, apart from maybe Chuck Berry. But all the music from the fifties inspired me. I didn't really start to get serious about music until I was eighteen and I heard my first bluegrass music. I heard Earl Scruggs play five-string banjo, and I thought, "That's something I have to be able to do." I fell in love with the sound, and I started earnestly trying to do exactly what I was hearing. That became the basis for everything else—that was my model.

REBECCA: Jumping ahead a few years, during the sixties you played a lot of acid tests, when you could fit all your equipment into a single truck. How do you compare those early days to now? Do you enjoy it as much?

JERRY: Well, in some ways it's better and in some ways it's not. The thing that was fun about those days was that nothing was expected of us. We didn't have to play. (*laughter*) We weren't *required* to perform. People came to acid tests for the acid test, not for us.

> *The thing that was fun about those days was that nothing was expected of us.*

So there were times when we would play two or three tunes, or even a couple of notes, and just stop. We'd say, "To hell with it, we don't feel like playing!" It was great to have that kind of freedom, because before that we were playing five sets a night, fifty minutes on, ten minutes off, every hour. We were doing that six nights a week, and then usually we'd have another afternoon gig and another nighttime gig on Sunday. So we were playing a lot!

So all of a sudden you're at the acid test and, hey, you didn't even have to play. Also, we weren't required to play anything even acceptable. We could play whatever we wanted. So it was a chance to be completely free-form on every level. As a way to break out from an intensely formal kind of experience, it was just what we needed, because we were looking to break out.

REBECCA: And you're still able to maintain that free-form style to a certain extent, even though you're now more restricted in certain ways?

JERRY: Well, also we're required to be competent. The sense of accomplishment has improved a lot. Now when we play, the worst playing we do isn't too bad. So the lowest level has come way up, and statistically the odds have improved in our favor.

REBECCA: What do you think it is about the Grateful Dead that has allowed you such lasting popularity, which has spanned generations?

JERRY: I wish I knew. (*laughter*)

REBECCA: Do you think you *can* define it?

JERRY: I don't know whether I *want* to, particularly. Part of its magic is that we've always avoided defining any part of it, and the effect seems to be that in not defining it, it becomes everything. I prefer that over anything that I might think of.

DAVID: When you say "everything," do you mean something different for everyone?

> *We're whatever the audience wants us to be; we're whatever they think we are.*

JERRY: Well, that's one way of saying it, yeah. But the other way of looking at it, from a purely musical point of view, is that it becomes a full-range experience. There's nothing that we won't try. It means everything is available to us. It also works from an audience point of view, too. We're whatever the audience wants us to be; we're whatever they think we are.

REBECCA: Do you think there is a timeless quality about your music that appeals to people?

JERRY: I'd like to believe there's something like that, but I have no idea, really. There is a human drive to celebrate, and we provide ritual celebration in a society that doesn't have much of it. It really should be part of religion. It happens to work for us because people have learned to trust the environment that it occurs in.

REBECCA: Do you feel at all disillusioned at the rate of social evolution? In the sixties, many people thought that massive social change was just around the corner?

JERRY: I never was that optimistic. I never thought that things were magically going to get better. I thought that we were experiencing a lucky vacation from consensual reality to try stuff out. We were privileged in a sense. I didn't have anything invested in the idea that the world was going to change. *Our* world certainly changed. *(laughter)* Our part of it did what it was supposed to do, and it's continuing to do it, continuing to evolve. It's a process. I believe that if you open the door to the process it tells you how to do it, and it works. It's a life strategy that I think anyone can employ.

DAVID: How do you feel about the fact that many people have interpreted your music as the inspiration for a whole lifestyle, the Deadhead culture?

JERRY: Well, a little silly! (*laughter*) You always feel about your own work that it's never quite what it should be. There's always a dissonance between what you wish was happening and what is actually happening. That's the nature of creativity—that there's a certain level of disappointment in there. So, on one level it's amusing that people make so much stuff out of this, and on another level I believe it's their *right* to do that, because in a way the music belongs to them. When we're done with it, we don't care what happens to it. If people choose to mythologize it, it certainly doesn't hurt us.

REBECCA: How do you feel about the fact that you enjoy divine status in the eyes of so many of your fans?

JERRY: These things are all illusions. Fame is an illusion. I know what I do, I know about how well I do it, and I know what I wish I could do. Those things don't enter my life; I don't buy into any of that stuff. I can't imagine who would. Look at David Koresh. If you start believing any of that kind of stuff about yourself, where does it leave you?

DAVID: What about the subjective experience a lot of people talk about—that there's a group-mind experience that occurs at your shows?

JERRY: That's been frequently reported to me. And also, even more specifically, a direct telepathic connection of some kind.

REBECCA: Do you experience that yourself?

JERRY: I can't say that I do, because I'm in a position of causality. So, I don't look at the audience and think, "I'm making them do what I want them to do."

REBECCA: I'm thinking of it more as a spontaneous, noncausal experience that is being mediated by something greater than either yourself or the audience.

JERRY: You might think of it as a kind of channeling. At the highest level, I'm letting something happen—I'm not causing it to happen. We all understand that mechanism in the Grateful Dead, and we also know that, fundamentally, we're not responsible.

We're opening a door, but we're not responsible for what comes through it. So, in that sense, I can't take credit for it. We're like a utility, like a

> **We're opening a door, but we're not responsible for what comes through it.**

conduit for life energy, psychic energy—whatever it is. It's not up to us to define it or describe it or enclose it in any way.

REBECCA: It's rumored that the Grateful Dead can control the weather. Can you shed any light on this?

JERRY: (*laughter*) No. We do not control the weather.

REBECCA: You've heard those rumors though?

JERRY: I've heard them, of course. Sometimes it *seems* as though we're controlling the weather.

REBECCA: But that is synchronicity?

JERRY: It's synchronicity, exactly.

REBECCA: So what *is* the dynamic between you and the audience when you're on stage?

JERRY: When things are working right, you gain levels. It's like Tibetan *bardos*. The first level is simply your fundamental relationship to your instrument. When that starts to get comfortable, the next level is your relationship to the other musicians. When you're hearing what you want to and things seem to be working the way you want them to, then it includes the audience. When it gets to that level, it's seamless. It's no longer an effort. It flows and it's wide open.

   Sometimes, however, when I feel that's happening, the music is really boring. It's too perfect. What I like most is to be playing with total access, where anything I try to play or want to happen, I can execute flawlessly. For me, that's the high-water mark. But perfection is always boring.

REBECCA: I've heard that musicians using computer synthesizers are complaining that the sound produced is so perfect it's uninteresting, and that manufacturers are now looking to program in human error.

JERRY: Right. I think the audience enjoys it more when it's a little more of a struggle.

DAVID: What is it that you feel is missing in that case?

JERRY: Tension.

DAVID: Tension between what and what?

JERRY: The tension between *trying* to create something and creating something, between succeeding and failing. Tension is a part of what makes music work—tension and release, or if you prefer, dissonance and resonance, or suspension and completion.

DAVID: Joseph Campbell, the renowned mythologist, attended a number of your shows. What did he experience?

JERRY: He loved it. For him, it was the bliss he'd been looking for. "This is the antidote to the atom bomb," he said at one time.

DAVID: He also described it as a modern-day shamanic ritual, and I'm wondering what your thoughts are about the association between music, consciousness and shamanism.

JERRY: If you can call drumming music, music has always been a part of it. It's one of the things that music can do—it can transport. That's what music should do at its best: it should be a transforming experience. The finest, the highest, the best music has that quality of transporting you to other levels of consciousness.

> *The finest, the highest, the best music has that quality of transporting you to other levels of consciousness.*

DAVID: Do you feel sometimes at your shows that you're guiding people or taking people on a journey through those levels?

JERRY: In a way, but I don't feel that I'm guiding anybody. I feel as though I'm sort of stumbling along and a lot of people are watching me or stumbling with me or allowing me to stumble for them. I don't feel, "Here we are, I'm the guide and come on, you guys, follow me." I do that, but I don't feel that I'm particularly better at it than anybody else.

For example, here's something that used to happen all the time. The band would check into a hotel. We'd get our room key, and then we'd go to the elevator. Well, a lot of times we didn't have a clue where the elevator

> *... if nobody else does it, I'll start something—it's a knack.*

was. So what used to happen was that everybody would follow me, thinking that I would know. I'd be walking around thinking, "Why the fuck is everybody following me?" (*laughter*) So, if nobody else does it, I'll start something—it's a knack.

DAVID: A lot of people are looking for someone to follow.

JERRY: Yeah. I don't mind being that person, but it doesn't mean that I'm good at it, or that I know where I'm going, or anything else. It doesn't require competence; it only requires the gesture.

DAVID: Is there any planning involved about choosing songs in a certain sequence to take people on a journey?

JERRY: Sometimes we plan, but more often than not we find that when we do, we change our plans. Sometimes we talk down a skeleton of the second set, to give ourselves some form, but it depends. The important thing is that it not be dull and that the experience of playing doesn't get boring. Being stale is death. So we do whatever we can to keep it spontaneous and amusing for us.

REBECCA: You play more live shows than any other band I know of. How do you manage to keep that spontaneity? Is this a natural talent you've always had, or is it something you've had to work to achieve?

> *... the idea of doing something exactly the same way is anathema. It will never happen.*

JERRY: Part of it is that we're just constitutionally unable to repeat anything exactly. Everyone in the band is so pathologically antiauthoritarian that the idea of doing something exactly the same way is anathema. It will never happen. So that's our strong suit—the fact that we aren't consistent. It used to be that sometimes we reached wonderful levels, or else we played really horribly. Now we've gotten to be competent at our worst. (*laughter*)

REBECCA: How do you compare a Grateful Dead show to a rave? There seem to be strong similarities between them.

JERRY: Well, if we would let people get up out of the audience and add their two cents worth, then it would be kind of similar. The acid test was like a rave, the same sort of idea.

DAVID: Do you see the acid tests or Grateful Dead shows as being the inspiration for the raves, or do you think it goes back to something more ancient, more tribal?

JERRY: Back in the fifties, there was a place in North Beach called The Place. They used to have "blabbermouth night," and everybody who wanted to could get up and rave for ten minutes. I don't believe it's anything new, but I think the modern version of it is a spill-off from the stand-up comedy explosion. Plus, there's been a resurgence of poetry readings and performance art.

DAVID: I'm curious about how psychedelics influenced not only your music but your whole philosophy of life.

JERRY: Psychedelics were probably the single most significant experience in my life. Otherwise, I think I would be going along believing that this visible reality here is all that there is. Psychedelics didn't give me any answers. What I have are a lot of questions. One thing I'm certain of: the mind is an incredible thing, and there are levels of organization of consciousness that are way beyond what people are fooling with in day-to-day reality.

DAVID: How did psychedelics influence your music? What was your music like before and after?

JERRY: Phew! I can't answer that. There was a me before psychedelics and a me after psychedelics. That's the best I can say. I can't say that it affected the music specifically—it affected the whole *me*. The problem of playing music is essentially one of muscular development, and no matter what, that is something you have to put in the hours to achieve. There isn't something that strikes you and suddenly you can play music.

DAVID: You're talking about learning the technique. But what about the inspiration *behind* the technique?

JERRY: I think that psychedelics were part of music for me insofar as I'm a person who was looking for something, and psychedelics and music are both part of what I was looking for. They fit together, although one didn't cause the other.

REBECCA: If you were made Clinton's drug policy advisor, what would you do?

JERRY: I would advise him to make everything legal immediately.

REBECCA: Now, when you say that, do you mean readily available to everybody, without restrictions?

JERRY: Yes. Because the first thing to do is to take the criminality out of it. Take the profit out of it, and the whole criminal structure will collapse. The next part is the health aspect: make drugs that are clean and make them in knowable, understandable doses. Why not spend research money on making drugs that are good for you, that are healthy? Is the problem that we don't like people changing their consciousness? I don't think that's a good enough reason not to have drugs.

> *. . . humans love to change their consciousness, and so there will always be drugs.*

The point is, humans love to change their consciousness, and so there will always be drugs. You can either deal with this situation by acknowledging it, or you can pretend it's not real and outlaw it. If you're going to make laws about what human beings should and shouldn't do, you need to have a template.

Without moral imperatives, you have to be able to say what humans are and what they're capable of. You have to start with what humans are *really* like, not what we *wish* they were like or what Western civilization or Judeo-Christian doctrine wishes they were like—but what they *are* like.

REBECCA: Do you think that people in government have a knee-jerk reaction to drug use because they are afraid of unleashing the autonomous sensitivities that come when individuals explore their own minds?

JERRY: I don't think they're doing it on purpose; it's just part of the traditional way to act. It's part of that questionable quality called "responsibility," of somebody thinking that somebody else should behave themselves somewhere. The ideas about what that means are very narrow and sadly in need of rethinking.

REBECCA: So even hardened addicts—and now, of course, I'm talking about heroin, cocaine, and crack users—have a right to use these drugs if this is what they feel they need to do, in the same way that society allows people to become alcoholics?

JERRY: Why not? What's the objection?

DAVID: Well, the objection would be that it puts a strain on society. If addicts need medical care, it has to come out of taxpayers' money.

JERRY: I think addicts represent very little strain on society in terms of medical care. If society is worrying about taking care of people, it could start anywhere. Part of the whole rehabilitation of people is taking them out of the criminal spiral of having to get money to score their dope. If addicts have the drugs they need, it may be possible for them to get steady enough to start doing regular stuff, like holding down a job.

REBECCA: Just such a system was put into effect in England, after they gave up on the war-on-drugs approach, and it's proven to be a success. People are overcoming their addictions while maintaining their self-esteem. They're allowed to remain with their families and are able to hold down regular jobs.

JERRY: Right. There's nothing that says you can't be productive if you're an addict. The problem is the illegality. It puts such a stress on the whole system. The war on drugs is a failure, but people won't admit it.

REBECCA: Isn't part of the drug problem also the social environment we've created for those less fortunate, the dog-eat-dog attitude of capitalist philosophy? Psychedelics are so different from a drug like crack. You use psychedelics to expand your experience of life, but many people use drugs to deaden an otherwise painful existence.

JERRY: Perhaps. But if life is miserable, what's wrong with adding a buffer to it so that your experience of it is a little gentler?

> *... if life is miserable, what's wrong with adding a buffer to it so that your experience of it is a little gentler?*

REBECCA: Do you have hope that the legalization of drugs will come about?

JERRY: I have hope that something like that might happen some day. But I don't think it will, not realistically, not as long as there are people in power who believe that they know how other people should behave.

REBECCA: What would you say to someone who described the Grateful Dead as simply a grand nostalgia trip?

JERRY: Well, that's certainly an opinion. I don't think anybody who comes to our shows would see that. First of all, there are kids at our shows. It's not nostalgia for them—it's happening now.

REBECCA: But they might be nostalgic for what they missed out on in the sixties.

JERRY: They might be, but I don't think that's the case. The Grateful Dead has evolved—it does things. It isn't steady state; it's not a remnant. Really, the whole thing has been slowly growing all this time. It didn't level off at some point and then people started re-energizing it. It's been gradually picking up energy.

DAVID: When you project into the future, how do you see your music evolving?

JERRY: I have no idea. I was never able to predict it in the past; I certainly don't feel confident to predict it now.

DAVID: Did you ever imagine it would get this far?

JERRY: Oh, God no! It exceeded my best expectations fifteen, twenty years ago. We're way past the best I could come up with. (*laughter*)

DAVID: How did you come up with the name the Grateful Dead?

JERRY: We called ourselves the *Warlocks* and we found out that some other band already had that name, so we were trying to come up with a new one. I picked up a dictionary and literally the first thing I saw when I looked down at the page was the Grateful Dead. It was a little creepy, but I thought it was a striking combination of words.

Nobody in the band liked it. I didn't like it either, but it got around that that was one of the candidates for our new name, and everybody else said, "Yeah that's great." It turned out to be tremendously lucky. It's just repellent enough to filter curious onlookers and just quirky enough that parents don't like it. (*laughter*)

DAVID: What's your concept of God if you have one?

JERRY: I was raised a Catholic, so it's very hard for me to get out of that way of thinking. Fundamentally, I'm a Christian, in that I believe that to love your enemy is a good idea somehow. Also, I feel that I'm enclosed within a Christian framework so huge that I don't believe it's possible to escape it, it's so much a part of the Western point of view. So I admit it, and I also believe that *real* Christianity is okay. I just don't like the exclusivity clause.

But as far as God goes, I think that there is a higher order of intelligence, something along the lines of whatever it is that makes the DNA work. Whatever it is that keeps our bodies functioning and our cells changing—the organizing principle—whatever it is that created in its incredible detail all these wonderful life-forms that we're surrounded by.

There's definitely a huge, vast wisdom of some kind at work here. Whether it's personal, whether there's a point of view in there, or whether we're the point of view I think is up for discussion. I don't believe in a supernatural being.

REBECCA: What about your personal experience of what you may have described as God?

JERRY: I've been spoken to by a higher order of intelligence—I thought it was God. It was a very personal God, in that it had exactly the same sense of humor that I have. (*laughter*) I interpret that as being the next level of consciousness, but maybe there's a hierar-

> *It was a very personal God, in that it had exactly the same sense of humor that I have.*

chical set of consciousnesses. My experience is that there is one smarter than me, that can talk to me, and there's also the biological one that I spoke about.

DAVID: Do you feel that there's a divine plan at work in nature?

JERRY: I don't know about a plan. I don't know whether it cares to express itself that way or even if matters such as developmental constructs along time have any relevance to this particular God-point-of-view. It may be a steady-state God that exists out beyond space-time, beyond our experience, or around it, or contemporary with it. Or it may function in the moment. I have no idea.

REBECCA: I understand that you became very ill a few years ago and came very close to death. I'm interested in how that experience affected your attitude toward life.

JERRY: It's still working on me. I made a decision somewhere along the line to survive, but I didn't have a near-death experience in the classical sense. I came out of it feeling fragile, but I'm not afraid of death.

REBECCA: Were you afraid of death before?

JERRY: I can't say that I was, actually. But it did make me want to focus more attention on the quality of life. So I feel that now I have to get serious about being healthful. If I'm going to be alive, I want to feel good. I never had to think about it too much before, but finally mortality started to catch up with me.

DAVID: You say that you didn't have a near-death experience, but did anything happen that gave you any unusual insights?

JERRY: Well, I had some very *weird* experiences. My main experience was one of furious activity and tremendous struggle in a sort of futuristic spaceship vehicle with insectoid presences. After I came out of my coma, I had this image of myself as these little hunks of protoplasm that were stuck together kind of like stamps with perforations between them that you could snap off. (*laughter*)
  They were run through with neoprene tubing. And there were these insects that looked like cockroaches, which were like message-units that were kind of like my bloodstream. That was my image of my physical self, and this particular feeling lasted a long time. It was really strange.

DAVID: That sounds really similar to a DMT experience.

JERRY: It was DMT-like as far as the intensity was concerned, but it lasted a couple of days!

DAVID: Did it affect what you think might happen after death?

JERRY: No. It just gave me a greater admiration for the incredible baroque possibilities of mentation. The mind is so incredibly weird. The whole process of going into coma was very interesting, too. It was a slow onset—it took about a week—and during this time I

> *I started feeling like the vegetable kingdom was speaking to me.*

started feeling like the vegetable kingdom was speaking to me.

It was communicating in comic dialect in iambic pentameter. So there were these Italian accents and German accents, and it got to be this vast gabbling. Potatoes and radishes and trees were all speaking to me. It was really strange. It finally just reached hysteria, and that's when I passed out and woke up in the hospital.

DAVID: Do you feel that psychedelics might be a way for the vegetable kingdom to communicate with humans?

JERRY: I like that thought, but I don't know if it's true. The thing is that there's no way to prove this stuff. I would love it if somebody would put the energy into studying the mind and psychedelics to the extent that we could start to talk about these things and somebody could even throw forth a few suggestions as to what might be happening. There's no body of information—we need more research. These are questions that we should be asking. This is the important stuff.

REBECCA: When you came out of your coma, did you come out of it in stages?

JERRY: I was pretty scrambled. It was as though in my whole library of information all the books had fallen off the shelves and all the pages had fallen out of the books. I would speak to people and know what I meant to say, but different words would come out. So I had to learn everything over again. I had to learn how to walk, play the guitar, everything.

> *It was as though in my whole library of information all the books had fallen off the shelves . . .*

REBECCA: Did you always have faith that you would access it again? It didn't scare you, the idea that you might have lost it forever?

JERRY: I didn't care. When your memory's gone, you don't care because you don't remember when you had one. (*laughter*)

DAVID: What do you think happens to consciousness after death?

JERRY: It probably dies with the body. Why would it exist apart from the body?

DAVID: People have had experiences of feeling that they're out of their body.

JERRY: That's true. But unfortunately the only ones who have gone past that are still dead. (*laughter*) I don't know what consciousness is apart from a physical being. I once slipped out of my body accidentally. I was at home watching television and I slid out through the soles of my feet. All of a sudden I was hovering up by the ceiling, looking down at myself. So I know that I can disembody myself somehow from my physical self, but more than that I have no way of knowing.

REBECCA: So I take it you don't believe in reincarnation, in the recycling of consciousness?

JERRY: It may happen in a very large way. It may be that part of all the DNA coding, the specific memory, returns. There's definitely information in my mind that did not come from this lifetime. Not only is there some, but there's tons of it! Enormous, vast reservoirs.

Dreams are kind of a clue. What are these organizing principles that make it so you experience these realities that are as emotionally real as this life is? You can feel grief or be frightened in a dream just as badly as you can in this life. And the psychedelic experience is similar, in that it has the power to convince you of its authenticity. It's hard to ignore that once you have experienced it.

REBECCA: What does the term *consciousness* mean to you?

JERRY: I go along with the notion that the universe wants consciousness in it, that it's part of the evolutionary motion of the universe, and that we represent the universe's consciousness. Why it wants it I don't know, but it seems to want it.

Here's the reason I believe this. If the point of an organism is survival, why go any further than sharks or simple-minded predators that survive perfectly beautifully? Why continue throwing out possibilities? So my sense is that, conceivably, there is some purpose or design. Why monkeys with big heads? Because that's the most convenient consciousness-carrier, perhaps.

REBECCA: Do you think that humans are evolving en masse to be more conscious?

JERRY: I do think there's a drive toward more consciousness. There are huge setbacks all along the way, but all the aberrations that we see—holy wars, et cetera—are metaphors for more consciousness. They are expressed as conflict because we haven't come up with enough good models to express it in other ways. We *are* it. We're the same stuff as stars and galaxies, so we're indivisibly part of it. We're the part that speaks, that plays music, that creates abstractions.

The atomic bomb is a good metaphor for consciousness. If you are able to describe a possible way that things work in this universe—with enough rigor inside some kind of belief system—you're going to be the creator of fundamental change expressed as a huge eruption of energy.

> *The atomic bomb is a good metaphor for consciousness.*

You first have to have the idea about energy and mass. Once that idea is expressed perfectly enough, then it's possible to create something that will do it physically. So the atomic bomb is a physical model of the mind gaining control of the material world. The question is, are we able to do it without blowing ourselves to smithereens?

DAVID: Are you talking about being able to organize reality the way we want to, say, with nanotechnology?

JERRY: Yes, that would be a good example. If the universe's mind—meaning us—is able to say what it wants about itself, to describe itself well enough, it can make decisions about where it's going and what it's doing *consciously*. That's like bringing the big mind and the little mind together.

DAVID: Have you had any experiences where you felt you were in contact with extraterrestrials or multidimensionals—beings not of this world?

JERRY: I can't say not of this world. I believe that anything that I was ever in touch with was fundamentally a part of this world. I would even go further to say that the concept of extraterrestrial is not applicable in this universe. Everything in this universe is part of this universe.

DAVID: Have you ever felt like you've been in communication with beings of a higher intelligence than humans?

JERRY: I've had direct communication with something that is higher than me! I don't know what it is; it may be another part of my mind. There's no way for me to filter it out, because it's in my head. It's the thing that's able to take bits and pieces of things and give me large messages. To me, they are messages as clear as someone speaking in my ear—they're that well-expressed, and they have all the detail that goes along with it.

Sometimes it comes in the form of an actual voice, and sometimes it comes in the form of a hugeness, a huge presence that uses all of the available sensory material to express an idea. And when I get the idea it's like, "Duh! Oh, I get it!" And it's accompanied by that hollow, mocking laughter: "You stupid fuck! You finally got it, uh? Geez, it's about time." (*laughter*) For me, enlightenment works that way, but it's definitely a higher order of self-organization that communicates stuff.

> *... when I get the idea it's like, "Duh! Oh, I get it!" And it's accompanied by that hollow, mocking laughter ...*

My psychedelic experiences were sequential. They started at a place, and they went through a series of progressive learning steps. When they stopped happening, it was like "This is the end of the message—now you're just playing around." That was when psychedelics stopped having the relevance they originally had. It lasted for about a year, I'd say.

DAVID: What do you think a Grateful Dead show in virtual reality would be like?

JERRY: Deadheads would want to be part of the band, I would imagine. I think it would be fun if they could be, because it would make them see the experience differently. But I think they would be disappointed if they saw our version of it.

REBECCA: Why do you think that?

JERRY: I don't know why. Remember, I don't *know* what the Grateful Dead are like. I've never seen the Grateful Dead, so I don't know what it is that the people in the audience experience that they value so highly.

REBECCA: You facilitate the potential for an experience. People have full-on religious experiences at your shows: they pass out, speak in tongues, and are even picked up by flying saucers. Are you aware of the impact you have on people's minds?

JERRY: Not like that. I've made an effort to not be aware of it, because it's perilously close to fascism. If I started to think about controlling that power or somehow trying to fiddle around with it, then it would become fascism.

> *If I started to think about controlling that power ... then it would become fascism.*

REBECCA: Have you ever been tempted to dabble in the power?

JERRY: Oh yeah. For the first eighteen years or so, I had a lot of doubts about the Grateful Dead. I thought that maybe this is a bad thing to be doing, because I was aware of the power. So I did a lot of things to sabotage it. I thought, "Fuck this! I won't be a part of this." I dragged my feet as much as possible, but it still kept happening! So in that way I was able to filter myself out of it and think, "Well, it's not me. Phew! What a relief!"

REBECCA: When you said before that you weren't responsible, you were saying it in a very modest way—you're not responsible for the wonderful experiences people are having—but at the same time, you're also shedding responsibility for the negative experiences.

JERRY: Absolutely. It's a cop-out. I don't want to be responsible. But this is also something I learned from my psychedelic experiences: you don't want to be the king, you don't want to be the president, because then you're responsible for everybody!

REBECCA: Have you heard of the Spinners? They wear long dresses and do this whirling-dervish dance at Dead shows.

JERRY: They're kind of like our Sufis. I think it's really neat that there's a place where they can be comfortable enough to do something with such abandon. It's nice to provide that. That's one of the things I'm really proud of the Grateful Dead for, because it's kind of like free turf.

REBECCA: It doesn't bother you that they use you as their religious focus?

JERRY: Well, I'll put up with it until they come to me with the cross and nails. (*laughter*)

REBECCA: What are your priorities now? Are they very different from what they were twenty years ago?

JERRY: Not very. Basically, I'm trying to stay out of trouble. I'm trying to play well. For me, playing music is a learning experience, and it's satisfying to me to still be learning stuff. Also, my object is to have as much fun as I possibly can. That's a key ingredient.

REBECCA: Some people believe that this is a pivotal time in history. Do you feel there is a New Age or, to use Terence McKenna's term, an archaic revival coming about?

JERRY: Sure, I'll go along with that—I love that stuff. I'm a Terence McKenna fan. I prefer to believe that we are winding up rather than winding down. And this idea of 2012, when everything tops out, well, I would love to be here for it. I'll buy into that belief. I don't want to miss it! It's like the millennium. At this point, it's a matter of personal pride. We have to survive; the band has to be able to play at least the turn of the millennium.

> *I prefer to believe that we are winding up rather than winding down.*

REBECCA: Upon what do you think the future of the human race depends?

JERRY: Getting off this lame fucking trip, this egocentric bullshit. There are entirely too many monkeys on this mudball, and that's going to be a real problem. People have to get smart. I've always thought that the thing to do is something really chaotic and crazy, like head off into space. That's something that would keep everyone real busy and would also distribute more bodies out there.

> *There are entirely too many monkeys on this mudball . . .*

Otherwise, we end up staying here and kill each other and damage the planet. I've gotten into scuba diving, so I've developed a great affection for the ocean. I just don't want to see it get worse than it is. I'd like to think we could get smart enough sometime soon to make things better than they are, instead of worse.

REBECCA: When people say they're optimistic about the future, they usually mean the future of the human race. But you can be optimistic about life and perhaps pessimistic about the future of the human race.

JERRY: I think the earth doesn't have any real problems, in the long run. I think we're just another disturbance. I don't think even we can really fuck up the earth.

REBECCA: Do you think it's arrogant to think that we have the ability to save the earth? And even if it is, do you think it's a healthy attitude to develop anyway?

JERRY: It's arrogant, but I think we should develop it anyway.

DAVID: How did you get involved in helping to save the rainforest?

JERRY: Well, I remember we started hearing about these things twenty-five to thirty years ago. The clock kept ticking by, and nothing was really happening. So we thought maybe we should call attention to this. Then there was the matter of finding out who the true players were, because there are a lot of bullshitters in the environmental movement. There are a lot of frauds.

You have to really go into it to find out who's *really* doing stuff and who has the right perspective. So for us it was about a two-year process of finding the players and then getting them to agree to work together so we could do something that would matter. I think everybody wants to do stuff about these problems. We didn't want to just call attention to how powerless everybody is. Instead, we wanted to do some things that were really hands-on, using direct action, and it's worked out quite well.

REBECCA: Can you tell us about any current projects that you're involved in?

JERRY: I'm involved in an interesting project with a little symphony orchestra down the peninsula called the Redwood Symphony. I'm getting about five or six musicians to write pieces for me and this orchestra. Danny Elfman is one. David Byrne seems to want to do one, and also my friends John Kahn, Bob Bralove, and David Grisman. The interesting part about it for me is that my oldest daughter plays first violin with this orchestra. So it'll be kind of fun to be involved in a project where she and I play together.

REBECCA: That sounds wonderful. What are some of the basic messages in your music?

JERRY: We've always avoided putting any kind of message in there. But, as life goes on, I find myself more comfortable with committing to emotional truths. I'm not an actor, so I can't get on stage and sing a song that doesn't have some emotional reality for me. Sometimes it's only something about the sound of the lyrics—it may not be the sense of it at all—but there has to be something in there that's real for me. Robert Hunter's really good about writing into my beliefs. He understands the way I think, and he knows me well enough to know what I'll do and what I won't do. He knows that I'm always going to be battling with my intelligence about whether I can sing this lyric or whether I'm going to feel like an idiot singing it. It has to resonate in some way.

> *. . . I find myself more comfortable with committing to emotional truths as life goes on.*

REBECCA: I've been impressed throughout this interview by your modesty. How have you managed to remain so unaffected by your fame?

JERRY: If you were me you'd be modest, too. (*laughter*) Deadheads are very kind. When they enter my private life, they almost always say, "I just want to thank you for the music, I don't want to bother you." When I feel that I really don't want to know about it, I just tell them. I treat everybody who speaks to me with respect. I've never been hurt by anybody or threatened in any way, so I have no cause to be afraid of this kind of stuff. It just isn't part of my life most of the time.

> *Deadheads are very kind.*

Besides, I'm kind of like a good ol' celebrity. People think they know me. It's not like "Oh gosh! Look who it is." It's more like, "Hi, how ya doin'?" I'm a comfortable celebrity. It's very hard to take the fame seriously, and I don't think anybody wants me to. What's it good for? The best thing about it is that you get to meet famous people and you get to play with wonderful musicians.

> *It's very hard to take the fame seriously, and I don't think anybody wants me to.*

REBECCA: If you hadn't been a musician, what might you have been?

JERRY: I'd be an artist. I was an art student, and that was where I was going in my life before music sort of seduced me.

DAVID: What inspired you to design a line of ties?

JERRY: I don't really have any control over them; they're just extracted from my artwork. I don't design ties, for God's sake! (*laughter*)

> *I don't design ties, for God's sake!*

REBECCA: You mentioned earlier about how something that you could call "God" had the same sense of humor as you. Some people get extremely fractured as a result of intense psychic happenings, and I was wondering how you feel about the importance of humor when faced with such mind-blowing experiences?

JERRY: I think humor is incredibly important. It's fundamental. You have to be able to laugh at yourself and your place in the universe.

REBECCA: What do you think happens when you lose your sense of humor?

JERRY: Well, at the very least you won't have much fun. (*laughter*) Humor characterizes consciousness. For me, life would be so empty without humor. It would be unbearable. It would be like life without music.

Jaron Lanier

"[Virtual reality] defines our agenda with machines as being primarily cultural and sensual, as opposed to power-oriented."

Reality Check
with Jaron Lanier

When virtual reality became a cultural obsession and took the national spotlight, Jaron Lanier stood center stage. The diverse scope of possibilities created through full sensory immersion into computer-generated worlds caught the collective imagination, and Jaron became the hero of cyberspace. He began his journey into virtual reality after quitting high school, when he engineered his own education in computer science by spending time with mentors such as Marvin Minsky at MIT. After a stint performing as a street musician in Santa Cruz, Jaron began programming electronic sound effects into video games. He quickly became a pioneer in computer programming, and soon he started the first VR company out of his home— VPL Research—which produced most of the world's VR equipment for many years. He is the co-inventor of such fundamental VR components as the interface gloves and VR networking.

Jaron coined the phrase "virtual reality" and founded the VR industry. He appears regularly on national television shows, such as "Nightline" and "60 Minutes." His work with computer languages and VR was twice chosen for the cover of Scientific American, *and it also appeared on the cover of the* Wall Street Journal, *in a piece entitled "Electronic LSD." But music is his first love. Since the late seventies, he has been an active composer and performer in the world of new classical music. He writes chamber and orchestral music, and is a pianist and a specialist in unusual musical instruments. Jaron has the largest collection of exotic instruments from around the world that I've ever encountered, and the most remarkable thing is that he can play them all. He has performed with artists as diverse as Philip Glass, Ornette Coleman, Terry Riley, Barbara Higble, and Stanley Jordan.*

Jaron has a powerful presence. His large eyes, which alternate between dreamy reflectiveness and focused intensity, peer out from behind long, brown dreadlocks. He appears gentle and relaxed, although he gets very animated when he starts talking about something that excites him. His nervous system is unusually balanced with a blend of artistic sensitivity, sharp scientific mindfulness, and great imagination. Referring to the unique neurochemistry that must contribute to Jaron's genius, Timothy Leary once said that he would like a cerebral spinal fluid transfusion from Jaron's brain. Jaron currently divides his time between New York and California. He has an album out on PolyGram, Instruments of Change, *and two books in press, one from Harcourt/Brace and the other from MIT Press. Amid a sea of exotic musical instruments and a tangle of electronic equipment, we interviewed Jaron at his Sausalito home on February 3, 1993.*

DJB

DAVID: Jaron, what was it that originally inspired you to develop virtual reality technology?

JARON: Not that question! Oh no! (*laughter*) There are three different things that got me involved with virtual reality—or really, four. One of them had to do with the philosophy of mathematics. Another had to do with direct-action politics and the frustrations thereof. The third had to do with musical instrument design, especially a really fantastic thing called a theremin. And the fourth had to with the psychology of early childhood, specifically my own. Do you want to hear about all four of them?

DAVID: Well, how about how they all came together?

JARON: Well, that's the most mysterious of all, because, of course, life is experienced mostly in anticipation and retrospect, and only at rare moments in the present. So I anticipated wondrous things without really believing them, and then suddenly I found they'd happened. I can hardly even remember when they did. But somehow this whole virtual reality thing has been taken seriously by the world and has become a field in its own right.

DAVID: I first became acquainted with your computer work many years ago, when it was featured on the cover of an issue of *Scientific American*. What was that about?

JARON: That was probably the first of two different *Scientific American* covers. It relates to one of those four tracks, which is the philosophy of mathematics. I studied math in graduate school. If you've ever been around a math school, you notice a very strange phenomenon, which is that people who have already learned some new math thing refer to that thing as trivial, while the people who are learning it for the first time refer to it as abominably difficult. Same people, same items, just different moments in time.

So the question is, what's going on? Is this just a sort of a hubris, or is there something particularly unusual about the process of learning math and understanding it? I was suspicious that the way that math was communicated and the way it was understood were completely different, that math had to be understood somewhat visually, or perhaps in something of a process way—playing with images and shapes inside one's imagination.

Math was taught and expressed in notation systems, and I thought, "Maybe the notation system is the problem." But then, as soon as you think that, you have to ask yourself, "What of mathematics is left once you take away the notation system?" And that's a very hard question, because the traditional view of most mathematics almost equates it with at least some kind of notation system.

DAVID: But isn't the dynamic pattern left, which the notation system is expressing?

JARON: It depends on the type of math. Some types of math, such as algebra, are largely a byproduct of notation. At least that's my interpretation. There are some kinds of math which are a little ambiguous—if you're talking about the mathematics of dynamic flows and that sort of thing. The flows indeed exist without the math, but a lot of abstract math might not exist effectively without some kind of notation. It's just not clear; it's a hard problem.

So I became interested in the idea of having computer pictures of mathematical structures, pictorial interpretations that would be modified in real time to express the movement of mathematical ideas. I was fortunate to get hired as part of an NSF (National Science Foundation) project—I was just a kid in my teens—and I worked with a group of people doing a college-level curriculum in mathematics using pictures. These days that would not be too radical or exciting, but in those days it was pretty unusual.

That project had mixed results, but I became very interested in the process of programming. I started to think, "Well, maybe you can look at computers and computer programming as a simplified mirror of the problem of mathematics and mathematical notation, but where the situation is much less ambiguous." There are some similarities. In computers, you have a notation, a programming language, that tells the computer what to do, and then there's what the computer actually does. Unlike math, there's no trouble defining the reality of what the computer actually does as a separate matter from the notation.

So you can ask yourself, "Is there some better way to understand what the computer is doing than using the usual programming notation?" And if you *could* come up with something that was an interactive visual representation of what the computer's doing, would that give you any inspiration (getting back to the original question) toward being able to express math ideas in a better way?

DAVID: Was that an original thought? It sounds like a really unique way of looking at it.

JARON: No. Although I didn't know of his work at the time, the first person to think about visual programming languages, as far as I know, was a particularly brilliant guy named Ivan Sutherland, who also invented the head-mounted display and computer graphics in general, and who is a very important, seminal figure in twentieth-century culture and science. The idea of a visual version of math, on the other hand, has fascinated many people, like G. Spencer Brown.

So I became immersed in the world of programming language design, and I was very fortunate to be able to spend a lot of time and be somewhat taken under the wing of some of the people who had invented the standard programming languages in use. I started developing a big "virtual" programming language, and it was an offshoot of that work, which was oriented toward children, that was on the cover of *Scientific American* in 1984.

The early team included some wonderful and brilliant minds, such as Chuck Blanchard, Young Harvill, Tom Zimmerman, and Steve Bryson. The biggest problem we had in that early work was that the screen was too small a window—a frustratingly tiny peephole into the world in which a program was visualized. We originally began developing what I decided to call "virtual reality systems" to have a better way of handling these programming representations. Of course, when we showed those to the world, particularly to people who were funding research or investing in companies, they got excited about the interface and missed the whole point of the programming languages, and thus we started to focus much more on virtual reality than on the original idea of a new type of programming language.

I should stress that the programming language we were doing was really very different from the current generation of visual programming languages—of which there are many, including commercial ones—in that this one did not have any sense of source code at all. It didn't have any fixed representation. Rather, it was composed of spontaneously regenerated representations of the internal state of the computer that simulated the existence of source code.

DAVID: That sounds like such a paradox. You mean not using icons, kind of create as you go?

JARON: Well, the traditional way that computers have been controlled is by making a differentiation between source code and object code, where source code is a human-oriented representation of what the computer's going to do. It usually looks like a series of awkward, broken, written English commands. Object code, on the other hand, is made of the ones and zeros that the computer itself can read. This scheme was set up primarily by a very brilliant woman named Grace Mary Hopper. It dates back to a time when hardware interfaces were very limited and incapable of handling pictures. It made a great deal of sense to make the best of the computer's ability to read in a string of letters and to try to use a natural language, such as English, as a metaphor.

What we were doing, however, is radically different from that, in the sense that rather than having a fixed type of source code—be it visual or text—the computer would instead analyze its own code and present one of a number of visualizations of an infinite variety, so that you could pick and choose different visualizations of the same material and invent new ones. The visualization was always spontaneously created, and the source code, as such, was a passing illusion.

There are some reasons why that turns out to be very useful and avoids a lot of problems. Mostly what it does is, it forces the computer to represent and understand its own code well enough that it can make a more broadly based analysis of decisions than it can with the traditional source code idea, which forces it to have an incredibly narrow point of view on its own code in order to turn in into a linear representation.

REBECCA: So the computer can make variations on a theme. Does this mean that it's actually being creative?

JARON: Well, this is a whole interesting other diversion, because whenever a computer does something, it can only be understood according to your own psychological projections upon it. You can either decide you're going to project autonomy onto it and treat it as doing something or you can treat it as a tool that you're using.

> *. . . whenever a computer does something, it can only be understood according to your own psychological projection . . .*

Both points of view are functionally equivalent and cover exactly the same actions and events. I prefer not to think of the computer as autonomous, because I feel that creates a more finite metaphor for how I define myself, and I find that's a dangerous path to go down and leads to nerdiness and blandness and Silicon Valley. But that's another story. (*laughter*)

REBECCA: Tell us about your childhood influences. You said this was another of the four inspirations for your work.

JARON: Well, I think everyone as a small child has an experience of a drastic contrast between their internal experience of themselves and what they're able to share with other people. You might have the same memory as I do, if you remember back to when you were a little kid, of having this kind of infinite freedom of imagination and optimism. As you get older, though, you discover something that can only be described as God's greatest infliction of indignity on children. The shocking truth is that the only world in which other people reliably exist, particularly your parents, and the only world in which things like food exist is this physical world in which you're a pudgy little pink weakling. (*laughter*) You struggle to accept it. It's very, very hard, and the acceptance of that fact is more or less what adulthood amounts to.

I think it's one of the two great limitations that we adjust to—the other one being mortality. I think that the reason people get excited about virtual reality, the reason it's not just another gadget, is because it does suggest a new way around the dichotomy between the infinite interior imagination and the limited world shared with other people.

DAVID: What is your definition of reality, and how do you think it's created? And in that context, what is virtual reality?

JARON: You'll be shocked to know that I don't have definitive answers to all deep philosophical questions. (*laughter*) I do have some thoughts on it, though. I'll start with one definition, which is a biological one. Reality is the global expectation of the nervous system for the next moment. In other words, the most flexible parts of the psyche and your body mold themselves to a rolling guess of what will probably come next.

The continuous, cinematic-style experience of reality that we have is an illusion created by our nervous systems. Our direct perception of this world is actually highly flawed. For starters, the blind spot is a great example. Near the center of each of your eyes is this big, black hole where you don't see anything, but you're never aware of it. Your mind fills it in perfectly for itself, which it can do because it holds all the cards. Even aside from that, what your eyes actually see is not what you perceive them seeing. Your eyes see edges and boundaries and patterns. They don't really see the picture that you see—that's constructed on a running basis in your brain. Physiologically, they just do not pick up the picture that you're seeing now.

> *The continuous, cinematic-style experience of reality that we have is an illusion created by our nervous systems.*

REBECCA: And there are all those associations you have developed throughout your life that get psychologically attached to what you're seeing.

JARON: Yeah. Have you ever had the experience of looking at something, and for a moment it's just an abstraction, and it's weird and you don't quite get it, then you recognize it, then you can only see it in the proper way, no matter how hard you try to see it "wrong" again? Sometimes the top of a building in the distance will blend with the sky in an impossible way. That sort of thing. That's an example of how every level of your being works together to create your sense of reality. What a computer person would call a high-level idea of recognizing objects such as building tops and understanding their functions and relationships helps the supposedly very low-level function of just interpreting colors and edges and the visual scene.

So what's happening is there's a sort of rolling effect. I hate to use the word "model," and I'm trying to avoid using it, because I don't really think that your brain represents the outside world in any kind of codified and consistent way. You don't need to study the brain to decide that. You can make philosophical arguments to show that that's an unlikely thing to be going on.

But I think, on a more global level, your brain and your body together are adapting themselves to the reality, and that's also the process that lets you perceive it. So there's this moment-to-moment process where your expectations happen to match up with the apparent consistency of the stimulation from your physical world, and those things together are reality for you.

DAVID: Isn't that a model?

> *Another definition of reality has to do with the mysterious or sublime stubbornness of things.*

JARON: Yeah, okay, it's a model. But it's not the usual kind of model that can be represented as an abstraction. I don't want to say the word "model," because if I do then a bunch of academic philosophers will write me nasty letters saying, "How *dare* you say that?" (*laughter*) And yet it's the closest thing you can say easily. Another definition of reality has to do with the mysterious or sublime stubbornness of things. There are a few things that are just intensely, stubbornly there all the time.

DAVID: Philip K. Dick once said that "reality is that which doesn't go away when you stop believing in it."

JARON: That's absolutely excellent. There are only a few things that fall in that category—I think there are three. There's this everyday, mundane, physical world, which seems awfully persistent, and the fact that Marin hasn't made it disappear is good evidence that nobody could. (*laughter*) And then there's the world of moods and essences and artistic feelings and styles, and those things are intensely real to me on a deep level—the sense of experience itself, including the differentiation of experiences. The other stubborn item is that mysterious thing called mathematics—it's just really stubbornly there.

DAVID: And just a brief definition of mathematics in that context?

JARON: Mathematics is an inevitable path you go down when you start thinking about things in some way other than as an undifferentiated whole—which is any kind of thinking, really.

DAVID: So what is virtual reality?

JARON: Virtual reality is the use of technology to generate the sensory experiences of people, under human control. Virtual reality is the first thing since the physical world that fits into the same niche, between people, of being what you call an "objective" reality.

DAVID: Because it's consensual—more than one person experiences it, and it doesn't go away when you stop believing in it?

JARON: Right. And also because the neurophysiological strategies used to perceive, manipulate and learn about it are the same that your body has evolved to use. So your experience of it is with the natural language of your own body, as opposed to your intelligence or culture of perception.

> *... your experience of [virtual reality] is with the natural language of your own body ...*

DAVID: How do you then adjust virtual reality, when you change the physical laws and do things that you're not accustomed to doing?

JARON: If you deviate too far, virtual reality becomes imperceptible because it is too weird for the brain to recognize. But there is a wide gray zone in which you can experience a radically unnatural world. You can slow everything down. You can make your arm two miles long relative to the rest of your body.

DAVID: The brain is still using the same neurophysiological mechanisms.

JARON: Right. When you want to really create a surreal experience in virtual reality you don't play with physics, you play with your sensory motor loop. For instance, one of my favorite ones is to trade eyes with another person, so that one person's head controls the other's point of view, and vice versa. So you have a very intimate and trusting approach to the other person. It's a remarkable experience of a shared body.

All of the great art that will happen in virtual reality, I think, is going to be—I hate words like "all"—playing with the very intimate sensory motor loop in that way, as opposed to the current, early trend of making weird external virtual environments.

Another example of an extremely radical experience would be as follows. It's possible to control a virtual body with more limbs than a physical body. Ann Lasko, who was at VPL for a long time, made a lobster body. Initially, the extra limbs just kind of sat there. Typically, it showed up as a twelve-foot-tall

> *It's possible to control a virtual body with more limbs than a physical body.*

big red lobster, and it scared people. (*laughter*) There are a few approaches to how to control the extra limbs. A very interesting one is to take all the movement data from all over your body and put it through some tricky algorithms, so that you have a function that relies a bit on all that global data to control just one local joint on an extra limb. So maybe even though your body doesn't understand the function, or formula, that's creating that control, you can sort of learn it. And so, with relative freedom for each of your physical body parts, you can learn to control extra virtual body parts; you can squeeze in an extra parameter.

DAVID: Without being totally conscious of how you're learning it? Is that what you're saying?

JARON: The whole question of conscious versus unconscious is a little misleading. The real question is whether your body learns it, which could also be conscious. There's nothing necessarily inhibitive about consciously understanding something that your body knows, but it's a different type of knowledge. So you can learn to control new limbs. This was an enormous surprise to me—that people could learn to control limbs that were differently proportioned, much less new ones. This is very strange. You wouldn't expect this to be something people would adapt to quickly.

> *. . . you can put a buzzer on one hand, and another on another hand, and create a sensation that's from an out-of-body point.*

There's another interesting thing you can do. There's a field of study of tactile illusions that are vital to the development of tactile feedback in virtual reality. One of the illusions has to do with putting buzzers or vibrators against the skin and creating phantom third buzzers between them. It turns out that, apparently, the way the brain understands that type of sensation is very nicely linear or metrical. So you can put a buzzer on one hand, and another on another hand, and create a sensation that's from an out-of-body point.

Now, if you match up the position of such a sensation with one of these phantom, visually existing limbs that you're controlling, all of a sudden you have a new limb to your body that you can control *and* feel. I just cite this example and the example of trading eyes as two of the types of things you can do with playing at a deep level with the way you perceive your own body and the world, and how you interact. That, to me, is the most fascinating area for aesthetic exploration of virtual reality.

REBECCA: What are some of the current applications of VR? Most of us by now have heard of the virtual kitchens in Japan. What else is going on?

JARON: Well, at VPL we put together literally hundreds of sites using virtual reality around the world, so it's really impossible to summarize. Right now, I'm excited about using it in medicine, particularly in surgery.

REBECCA: What about applications in education?

JARON: In education, wonderful things have happened both in K through 12 and in college. But there's not adequate funding, because our society doesn't make this a priority. We did a pilot class for fifth and sixth graders using virtual reality systems at VPL, and they would put their dreams into VR and all sorts of stuff. It was great.

DAVID: Put their dreams in it—what do you mean?

JARON: They would come into class and build their dreams as a virtual world. What *else* would you do? (*laughter*) Sharing their dreams—they're good at that. The generation of kids growing up with computers has an enormous facil-

> *We're really seeing a new type of literacy.*

ity, and their kids will have an even greater facility. We're really seeing a new type of literacy.

REBECCA: You've talked about VR as a tool for communication and empathy; you've described exchanging eyes and growing limbs. But how can VR help someone really to empathize, to understand another person?

JARON: How does anything help you with something like that? I want to stress that I'm not claiming that this is a panacea. All it is is that our particular culture is completely in love with technology and gadgetry, so this seems like it might be a slightly more inspiring sort of pursuit than some others. In another culture, in another time, it might not have any value at all. So I'm not claiming it has any intrinsic, universal value.

REBECCA: But you have said that you feel that perhaps its greatest potential is for communication and empathy?

JARON: Absolutely. But I'm thinking in the very long term. I'm not thinking about tomorrow, but about generations hence. This really hinges on the idea of post-symbolic communication. Some generations from now, if we've survived as a species—which is not clear—there will be many wonderful, cheap VR setups around, and there will be access points everywhere, and a generation of kids will grow up using tools with great user interfaces for inventing stuff in virtual worlds.

So they're going to grow up differently from previous kids, because, aside from using symbols to refer to the things that they can't directly create and do, they'll have this other way of just making up for each other any imagined stuff as objective sensory objects. They'll develop a facility for "reality conversations," or "intentional waking-state shared dreaming," or co-dreaming. And that's what I call post-symbolic communication.

DAVID: I can understand that intuitively, but for some reason I can't seem to quite grasp it rationally. (*laughter*)

JARON: That's only evidence that it is a truly new thing. Post-symbolic communication is genuinely hard to understand, and it's genuinely going to be a generational chasm. I can dream about it, but I'm sure I don't really quite get it myself.

REBECCA: When you say "post-symbolic," you're still talking about the symbol-based language involved in basic visualization, right?

JARON: No. Let's go back to symbols and childhood, okay? Remember our child? That was the pudgy weakling who's very frustrated. When you're a little kid, you find that there's only a very small part of the world that you can control as fast as you think and feel. Your tongue and your mouth move as fast as you think and feel, your hands do to a certain extent as you grow older, and then the rest of your body comes along. So your body is the part of the world that you can move and change about as fast as you think and feel; the rest of the world, you can't.

Now, symbols are simply a trick where you use the part of the world that you can change easily to refer to all the other things that you can't realize. So, for instance, you can compose a sentence out of symbols—like I can say, "We're all antique lamp shades that are sentient, and we're crawling up the back of a giant trilobite."

Now, it's not absolutely inconceivable that such a thing couldn't be physically realized. You could have nanotechnology experts change us into lamp shades, perhaps, and you could have genetic engineers breed giant trilobites, but it would take centuries and billions of dollars. It's an enormous project just to realize that one thing that I put together with a sentence.

So that's the power of symbols. They operate on this vast time-scale without using resources. They're a trip, referring to the things you can't do. Post-symbolic communication amounts to a spontaneous way of creating a sensual world between people without requiring interpretive symbols. It's sort of like cutting out the middleman, and you actually *make* stuff instead of just referring to it.

There are a lot of nonverbal, partially nonsymbolic attempts to bridge this tragic interpersonal gap we've been stuck with, too. Like, you can make paintings, you can do architecture, but none of them quite get there. They all approach it from one direction or another. Architecture's a little like post-sym, but it's way too slow. Paintings can be like that, but they're not really interactive, and from a sensory-motor point of view they're not real, not what your body treats as reality. Fantasies are solitary. Movies are kind of like that, but they're not inclusive of the perceiver. Music improvisation comes close, but it's all form, no content.

Each of the ways we've approached this problem in the past hits some kind of big, monstrous disqualification, but so far as I can tell, virtual reality just goes right on through and does it. So it's really hard to imagine what this communication will be like.

DAVID: Well, if we were conducting this interview right now in some kind of post-symbolic world, how would we be doing it?

JARON: Well, the first thing to say is that the types of things you'd communicate and your whole world view would start to shift, and I think this would be in a very wonderful way. There are some things that you'd only say in a symbolic context, such as puns.

Let me also just clarify that language isn't going to disappear. There's actually a part of our cortex that's specialized to it. That's how committed we've become to it. This is going to become a new, wonderful adventure that grows up *alongside* the adventure of language, increasing our sensitivity to language.

I know that abstraction doesn't need to exist for communication, which is something some linguists don't believe. For instance, in VR, if you need to refer to a quality, you don't need categories to communicate because you can have every single thing that's perceived alike in some way in some giant planet that you can carry around. I

> *Instead of saying something's red, just put everything that's red in a planet and let others look at it . . .*

mean, why not? Instead of saying something's red, just put everything that's red in a planet and let others look at it and perceive for themselves what these things have in common. So that's an example of how the whole idea of communication changes.

DAVID: So, then, it'll get more specific?

JARON: No. In language we have a notion of a quality, such as redness or pudginess or something. In post-symbolic communication, why bother with those things, because there's no limitation? I can bring a jar and inside it I can have everything that I think is pudgy. Then the concept of pudgy becomes unnecessary, because you can look at them all at once and experientially get what's alike about them.

REBECCA: You've mentioned only sensual communication, which is just one aspect of human reality. How would it be possible to express feelings—love, hate, greed, indignation, ecstasy, et cetera—in virtual reality without some kind of symbolic language?

> *. . . the capacity of symbols to smooth over differences has probably been vital as a social lubricant . . .*

JARON: When we use symbols alone to refer to our internal states, we are kidding ourselves. But the capacity of symbols to smooth over differences has probably been vital as a social lubricant, and our survival thus far may have depended on it. Without our blanket of little white lies, we might have killed each other off. The capacity of symbols to communicate a little bit of truth mixed in with a lot of illusion is remarkable.

There is a critical nonsymbolic component to intimate communication, though. This stuff will flower in a post-symbolic context. The stuff I mean is exactly what's absent in an E-mail-only romance.

If you're talking about communicating internal states, then the poetry of gesture spiced with a little experiential metaphor might be the truest expression. A metaphor is different from a symbol, because the choice of a symbol is arbitrary—it is only a pointer. Post-symbolic communication is the ultimate playground for metaphor. You might experientially meld the moment's activities with childhood memories and mythical events. If, on the other hand, what you're talking about is the categorization of human *behavior*, then a planet-jar can hold the truth behind the category.

What's left between these two? The characterization of people in their essence is a dangerous business, and the difficulty of doing this in post-sym is actually, I think, evidence of its value.

REBECCA: How could definitions be agreed upon unless the person already knew me? Someone else might see my planet of beautiful things as ugly. How do I get my concept of beauty across?

JARON: Just like you do in language, through ongoing experience and feedback. You each add things to the planet, and if there is coherence, you have reached each other to a far greater degree than you could with the use of words. The difference, really, is that words let you keep the illusion of commonality longer when it is not present. Anyway, beauty's just a judgment.

> *. . . symbols require a sort of characterization and judgment of things that might turn out to be happily expendable.*

That's less important than finding that you groove on the same jar with someone, or with everyone. Once you're used to post-sym, the judgment that the jar means "beautiful" fades away as a symbolic holdover. What I'm getting at is that symbols require a sort of characterization and judgment of things that might turn out to be happily expendable.

REBECCA: I'm still grappling with this. You talked of expressing pudginess, but what about boredom or surprise? If I listed all the things that surprised me to express that I had been taken by surprise, for example, not only would it take forever, but the person I was communicating with would be dumbfounded as to what I was trying to get across.

JARON: How do you teach a kid the meaning of the word "surprise" in the first place? Symbols are actually not primary, though they do take off on their own and stake out a territory in which they seem to be indispensable. But what is hardest to understand is what *fluency* would be like in post-sym. It might take a long time to express that moment that you'd now simplify into "surprise," but it might be worth it, a kind of gourmet communication. Or the post-symmers might become so fluent that they'll do it fast. I don't know.

REBECCA: Isn't it more likely that there would be some kind of compromise between post-symbolism and language, where some kind of symbolism is used when things fail?

JARON: Ha! It is more likely that you'd have to resort to some VR when words fail, which they often do. But truly, I think that the relationship between symbols and post-sym in the long-term future will be a little like the relationship between language and music now. You have language-free music, you have music-free language, and then you have all the gradations between, such as the various kinds of song, from senseless Irish "mouth music," which uses words without meaning, to rap, which supplants melody with prose. So sure, there'll be marvelous shades of gray, but the pure stuff is the most intriguing to contemplate from this distant moment.

REBECCA: So you're saying that you won't need descriptions of the world because you would be experiencing things spontaneously?

JARON: Let me give you a couple of examples that can help to demonstrate this. The simplest example is when you travel to a foreign country and don't speak a word of the language and still get by. You get by through projecting emotion and miming and all kinds of things. This is the same thing; the only difference is that, in that case, you can't do very much. You can point to a banana, but you can't suddenly create whole worlds. But that's the basic idea, except that you could make the world into anything at any time, with spontaneity, if not spontaneously.

DAVID: When you're in a pre-symbolic stage of development and you experience something—some overwhelming burst of color and pattern—and then someone lays a symbol on it, all of a sudden, it condenses all that down. Are you saying that post-symbolic communication can unravel that?

JARON: I'm not proposing that the purpose of post-symbolic communication is to experience the world as undivided sensation, where everything is completely noncontextual and meaningless. Things would have context, and there would be clarity of reference and clarity of intent, but it would be created through the direct interaction between people rather than through an abstraction held separately from them.

DAVID: It may not be an English language abstraction, but it would still be a mathematical code abstraction.

> *. . . if you want to cause a stampede among linguists, this is the stuff to bring up.*

JARON: No, it's not. Let me give you another example. This is subtle stuff, and if you want to cause a stampede among linguists, this is the stuff to bring up. (*laughter*) I want to stress that I'm not making any judgment against language at all; it's just that mankind needs big, long-term adventures.

It's kind of like, if you have kids locked up in a house, they're going to need something to do. So on this planet we need something to do. That's the justification for it, and it's the only one that makes any sense. So it's an adventure; that's the reason for it. Let me address the issue of whether the perception of things requires symbolizing or not. When you have a lucid dream, you are able to control the dream, and the question is, what is the language that you use to tell your dream how to be?

DAVID: What is the language? Well, it's something to do with will and intention.

JARON: But do you actually have to go through concepts, go through words, to change your dream?

DAVID: I'm not really sure. I'm thinking it through in English, I guess.

JARON: Yeah, but how do you actually change the dream? What's the interface to your dreaming self? Do you put in a request—"I'd like a fantasy with a red balloon"—or do you just sort of feel the world as it would be and it gets that way?

REBECCA: But you have to isolate, from all the possibilities, where you want the dream to go. I think I use language to do that—at least I've thought about things I want to do, and I've found myself doing them. But perhaps that didn't make it happen, because there was something else involved, such as will. Whether the thought preceded the will or not, I'm not sure.

JARON: The process the mind follows in using symbols might not be so linear as to provide an answer. It's very mysterious, and these are deep, difficult problems. I don't claim to have all the answers, but it seems to me that we are able to both apprehend the world and imagine it changed without having to symbolize it. I think dreams are created directly out of the stuff of experience, not out of platonic forms. And I think we will eventually communicate with the same kind of continuity, instead of with a vocabulary.

REBECCA: How would you effect changes in the world of virtual reality in order to post-symbolically communicate?

JARON: This is the most important practical question. I think the way people will change the world in order to accomplish post-symbolic communication is not through some kind of psychic hook-up, but rather through craftsmanship, through using tools with their bodies. The mind without the body isn't smart enough to do it. I imagine the tools being a lot like musical instruments that you can learn to use intuitively—that would, with practice, spin out changes to the VR world very quickly.

DAVID: Didn't you say that one of the most exciting things about virtual reality is that it helps to blur the distinction between imagination and reality?

JARON: No. What it does is it creates a new objective reality between people that is more quickly malleable than the physical world is. In fact, VR will probably have a clarifying effect on the boundaries of imagination. In our everyday physical lives, there's a very confusing division between the internal and external worlds. In virtual reality, however, there is a much sharper division between what is objectively created and what is subjectively perceived, because the external world is exactly defined by computer software.

Now, there are some things about virtual reality that are not perfect. Once again, I don't want to shock you. (*laughter*) Virtual reality will always be of a lower quality than the physical world. After the next few early decades of development, the veracity of virtual reality will not depend on how good the technology becomes, but rather on how good we become at perceiving the difference between it and nature. A good precedent for this is the way stereophiles can compare a $50,000 pair of speakers to a $70,000 pair of speakers and hear a difference. But they also can hear a difference between that and natural sound.

So here you have a whole aesthetic of creating ever-better speakers, but it never ends, because we're also increasing our own sensitivity to sound. Sensitivity is sort of a global or systemic property of perception; it's not a simple, measurable parameter that can be maxed out. I think it goes on forever and that you can achieve entirely new, unforeseen strategies of sensitivity that cannot be predicted. Good media technologies make us more sensitive to nature by providing a basis for comparison. That should be treated as one of their best gifts.

> *Good media technologies make us more sensitive to nature by providing a basis for comparison.*

DAVID: But if you can directly interface with the senses, how would the brain be able to differentiate?

JARON: Your brain is so flexible that it's a moving target. There's no such thing as a final model of the brain and what it does, because brains are changing and moving all the time. You learn your own sense organs better as you grow and age. Throughout their lives, musicians change their hearing, change their hands, change the way they see.

DAVID: If you're in direct control of all the sensory signals entering the body, why are the signals coming from this reality any more specific or precise or defined than something you can generate from a computer?

JARON: One of the properties of the physical world is that it's infinitely mysterious, and I mean that as a sort of precise definition. (*laughter*) In science, there's never absolute truth, only theories that are waiting to be disproven. We can never know that we have come to the end of understanding ourselves or the way we appreciate the world.

DAVID: I completely understand that, but why wouldn't anything we create inside this infinitely mysterious universe have those qualities as well?

JARON: I think inside virtual reality there will be a new type of infinite mysteriousness, but it's different from the infinite mysteriousness of the physical world. In the future, when there are a lot of people using virtual reality at once, the intersection of all those different reality conversations playing on each other and overflowing will become a massive wilderness with something of a Jungian nature.

REBECCA: So you're saying that because this primary world is what we are trying to simulate the situation demands that the virtual world be inferior, in terms of its precise correlation to this world.

JARON: One of the things about virtual reality is that even though our creation of objects can be accomplished through our spontaneous craftsmanship in using these interfaces of the future—which I imagine to be great musical-instrument-like things that spin out all the properties of reality—everything that a virtual reality system does has to be represented on a computer, which limits its mysteriousness.

That's because computer programs have to be made out of our ideas to start with, as opposed to that mysterious nature stuff, which we analyze after the fact with successive approximation. We're "drinking our own whiskey," so to speak, when we interact with artificial things, even if they

> *We're "drinking our own whiskey," so to speak, when we interact with artificial things . . .*

are "out of control," as in the artificial-life ideal, where we've let our whiskey ferment. Our sensitivity to the difference between a possibly very great level of sensual mysteriousness in VR, versus the infinite level that the physical world presents, will never disappear. To say that it will is the same as saying that science can be perfected to absolute completion.

REBECCA: Do you think that virtual reality might help people to lower their inhibitions, as they find they are freed up from the conventional styles of communication?

> *I'm arguing that this is a great adventure; I'm not arguing that it's going to make people better.*

JARON: I'm arguing that this is a great adventure. I'm not arguing that it's going to make people better. I think it has the *potential* to make people better, but not because of anything specific about it—just simply because it is an adventure. Whatever increase in empathy and maturity might happen that might be partially inspired by VR would only rely on the technology as a fetish object. We're talking about the same old internal growth, which is very hard and with which we all struggle.

REBECCA: Technology also enables us to de-sensitize and de-sanctify the world. If you can create virtual environments with virtual trees and bring back extinct animals, you can end up having less reverence for the world outside. Why would you care about the environment and other people when you can just plug them in?

JARON: There are a bunch of reasons. (*laughter*) One thing about virtual reality that I found to be true for almost everyone who uses it is that when you leave it you get this thrill of seeing the physical world again. Actually, one of the patterns of use that I've noticed with people is that they tend to want to build up some time in VR so that they can experience that thrill of the transition back to the physical world.

You have such an increased sensitivity to detail when you come out— it's like your sense organs have been widened. The first time I came out of virtual reality I noticed the rainbows in the individual threads in the weave of the carpet for the first time. So it actually increases sensitivity, rather than decreases it.

REBECCA: Because of its limitations, it would seem.

JARON: That's exactly right. And as I pointed out, that will continue always. It's very easy to confuse virtual reality with television or movies, because that's the media technology we're used to. With those, you sit there and your sense organs are filled with sensation, even though your body isn't doing anything and has no opportunity to affect experience. That's a very unnatural mode of perception. The natural mode of perception is entirely interactive and very physical.

So, by having this sort of artificial source of sensation without action, you turn your body into a zombie, and that's why kids sometimes look like zombies when they're watching TV. Virtual reality is entirely different. The very thing that makes it come alive and what makes it seem real is its interactivity. By the same token, if you're not physically active inside virtual reality, it becomes suddenly unreal and its magic pops away. What that means is that you get tired after using it for a while. It corresponds a lot more to riding a bike than to watching TV.

> *[VR] corresponds a lot more to riding a bike than to watching TV.*

Another thing about it is that any particular form of a virtual object at a given moment can become rather dull and uninteresting, because they're all so easily available and so easy to change. Therefore they become less real and less valued, and the things that become noticeable and real are the personalities of other people, and the spontaneous interaction with them, and the movement and the flow of change and creativity.

A long time ago, one of my catch phrases was "creativity is the money of virtual reality," because it's the only thing that can possibly be in short supply. But it's really not just creativity per se; it's interaction with other people's personalities and their presence. Other people feel very real in virtual reality because they *are*. Since a person can take on any form, a person viewed from the outside looks like a wave of creative change with a distinctive personality.

It's kind of like the telephone, in a sense, where you only hear the voice, but the gesture, the body music, is also preserved, so you have this real sense of physical presence with them. So real people are truly the life of the party in

> *. . . real people are truly the life of the party in virtual reality.*

virtual reality. There might be somewhat amusing fake people at some point in the future, but our sensitivity to the difference between fake people and real people will increase well ahead of the technology. I think that individuality, creativity, sensitivity, the quirks of personality, individual style— these things are going to be really highlighted and very highly valued.

REBECCA: That sounds nice, but I'm wondering who's going to end up controlling this technology. Media entertainment systems, video games, and, to a lesser extent, TV have been co-opted by military or otherwise violent themes. Why would VR be any different?

JARON: In the short term, it's not necessarily going to be different. There's already been stuff like that, and it's very disappointing. But you have to think in a longer term. Marshall McLuhan was right. The structures of media tend to become the effective content, so the content of these things is determined by what they are and also the way they're sold.

The reason you have military games is because if you're paying to have an interactive experience the only way to get it to end—so that you have to pay more—is either to have "The End" flash in front of you or to have something kill you. Of the two, having something kill you has been more accepted by the users, because having "The End" suddenly appear seems to crush their autonomy. I'm aware of only one solution to that problem, which is to have live guides who kind of run the show and herd people forward to get them to end on time. That's the approach that we're using at the virtual reality theater project I'm involved in. Of course, the nicest solution would be to let people interact as long as they want, but that is not economically compatible with site-based entertainment.

So some of these things are just structural. I have no doubt that there'll be a great deal of ugly, schmaltzy, crappy virtual reality along the way. But I do believe that the dream is worth believing in, and it's certainly necessary to replace television with something better, if we are to imagine a world where we survive.

REBECCA: Except for a few fortunate individuals, corporations are going to pretty much monopolize this technology. How much freedom will there be for autonomy in virtual reality programming? Will people have to be content to buy another person's dream?

JARON: That's the single most important question about the future of virtual reality. Obviously, the way I want it is for everybody to be able to make their own world all the time. I'd like that to be so standard that it's spontaneously happening at conversational and improvisatory speeds all the time. That's the future I want to see, but it won't be there right away.

REBECCA: Do we have the technology now for this to be possible?

JARON: That's more of a cultural question than a technological one. On the one hand, there's the evolution of wonderful user-interfaces for creating content of worlds quickly, and on the other hand, there's the social phenomenon of a generation of kids growing up using that with fluidity and expertise. Both those things have to happen, and it'll take a while. The shortest time I can imagine is maybe three or four generations hence.

DAVID: What potential dangers do you see in terms of government regulation of VR?

JARON: That's so complex. Right now, I'm pretty optimistic. Right now, the government is playing an active role in peace conversion and the military is interested in it and all the defense contractors are interested in it. There's kind of an alignment of interests between people who are concerned about trying to disarm the world and people concerned about America being competitive in the world economy. That's a very fortuitous alignment of interests at this particular time, when it's so critical. But of course, as circumstances change that alignment could disappear.

REBECCA: Do you see censorship being a consideration in VR?

JARON: Virtual reality as a solitary experience is not that interesting; it's as a shared group experience that it becomes fun. So its primary mode of use will be over the advanced phonelines of the future. One of the

> *Virtual reality as a solitary experience is not that interesting . . .*

interesting things about the telephone is that it's the most moral of media technologies, in that the companies that make the most money from it do so by simply shipping content around rather than by affecting the content. And the content is so vast that it's completely untrackable. It's like a huge jungle. I'm sure virtual reality will be the same way. It will be effectively unregulatable, and money will be made by connecting people together, because the content will be too easy to create and too voluminous to control.

> *[Virtual reality] will be effectively unregulatable . . .*

REBECCA: Why do you think it is that American industry is so slow in responding to potentially innovative technology, while the Japanese end up marketing so many U.S. inventions, such as VCRs and HDTV (High Resolution TV), semiconductors, and, probably soon, nanotechnology?

JARON: There are a few reasons for that. One of the reasons has to do with it being too easy to make money in the United States through scams. The way an economy works is, it's like an ecology.

Especially during the Reagan years, in a climate of decreased regulation, there were so many ways to make money from scams—the savings and loans or the junk bonds or the acquisitions that were phony . . . it goes on and on. There were endless weird ideas that people came up with for making money that were nonproductive. When you can make better money through doing something that's nonproductive, it's lower risk, because it's just a scheme. You don't have to worry about whether people want to buy a product or something like that, and it sucks all the investment money away from the productive means of making money. During the critical Reagan years, the Japanese started manufacturing everything, and we gave up a bunch of industries because, I believe, our investment capital was seduced away by scams.

Also, our corporations are not really American corporations; they're sort of world corporations. When you're in Japan, what's really striking about the Japanese is that they have a remarkably coherent sense of who they are and what their self-interest is. It fits into this nice little hierarchy. There's the Japanese country made of Japanese people who are in a group of Japanese companies in Japanese cities, and it all sort of lines up. In America none of those things line up, so the sense of what self-interest is is completely confused.

I think that power is more or less the same thing as a clarity of self-interest. When people have an unchallenged sense of what self-interest is, it's pretty easy to go for it. It's when life becomes complicated—through self-searching or through a confusion of circumstances—that people lose power. The diffusion of national powers may be a trend—and may be a good thing, by the way, as long as it isn't replaced by something worse.

Part of it should justifiably be called corruption, because a lot of American officials were working with the Japanese promoting their case during the Reagan years. When the history of the Reagan years is written, they're not going to be seen as patriotic at all. They're going to be seen as scumbags.

REBECCA: Hasn't part of the problem been that the Republican attitude to business is very hands-off and shy of investment, whereas in Japan they're into consortiums between government and business?

JARON: It's not so simple. For instance, in American agriculture the Republican agenda is very hands-on.

REBECCA: That's true, but in agriculture you know what you're getting into. There's not the same risk involved as in investing in a new technology, where possibly you're not going to get the dividends back for many years. Isn't there something about America's habit of demanding instant gratification that keeps it from progressing in this area?

JARON: There's definitely some truth to that. I'm tempted to blame television again, for ruining the attention span of the people who became captains of industry in the United States. (*laughter*)

If you look at what happened with American and Japanese trade in the Reagan years, it's a little bit like a repeat of what we claim we did with the Indians—trading beads for Manhattan. They traded us trinkets in the form of disposables, such as tape recorders and cars, in exchange for strategic valuables, such as real estate and just plain, old money. That's a pretty interesting trade.

We're hopelessly in love with gadgetry, and when you know what your enemy's in love with, you have quite an advantage. That brings us back to why virtual reality is valuable. I have a

> *We're hopelessly in love with gadgetry . . .*

great deal of sympathy for people who advocate a decreased use of technology in the future, but it's not realistic, because we're just in love with it.

REBECCA: That reminds me of when Bill Moyer asked Ronald Reagan what his answer to poverty was, and he waxed poetic about some guy who had invented a magnetic soda-can handle. (*laughter*)

JARON: The whole American dream is based on a social contract to maintain a class system in which, with luck, you can switch roles. That's why we're so cruel to our poor, because everybody wants to make a clear distinction between the rich and the poor so that their own fantasy of becoming rich has that much more meaning. See, you invalidate the motivation and the dreams of everyone if you take care of the poor. That's why we treat them so much worse than other industrialized countries.

REBECCA: We touched briefly on the applications of VR. What are some of the other possibilities that excite you?

JARON: Well, education is one of them. Our species evolved in complicated natural terrains, and our learning was very much keyed to an environmental or social situation. If you look at the types of stimuli that create the most recall, they are probably other people—seeing a friend you haven't seen in a long time and collectively recalling things. Smells are also very important, and then environments. Environment is the only one of those that you can really package, using VR.

It's really striking to me that children are expected to learn a variety of things, but always in the same environment, with the same social group, with the same smells and the same stimuli. You have this incredible drudgery in which you're supposed to retain variety of memory and learning. It's completely absurd. Your memory of school just grinds and collapses into the memory of one room, and that's counter to the natural way of learning new things. So one can imagine creating a virtual world for the express purpose of making a memorable place in which you learn something new.

> *. . . the kids can become the dinosaur— they can become the thing they're studying and achieve identity with it.*

Let's use dinosaurs as an example. You can simulate the old forest and have these big dinosaurs tromping around. But then you can do a wonderful thing—the kids can become the dinosaur. They can become the thing they're studying and achieve identity with it. They can become molecules such as DNA, or mathematical shapes—it goes on and on. And of course, kids are interested in themselves—they're egotistical little buggers—so it's a very effective way of learning something.

Unfortunately, I don't think this society has a commitment to spend any money on education. I've talked to schools a lot about this, and there are very few that can afford this. Many in the country today can't even afford a new basketball hoop. It'll happen eventually, but it might not happen very well at first.

I'll tell you a scary story. In the mid-eighties, I was very involved with trying to get virtual reality, or just quality computer tools, into classrooms. I talked with some of the largest corporations in the United States, and their image of the future of technology in education was truly chilling.

They said, "Okay, let's look at undeniable demographics, which predict that in the future there's going to be a tremendous shortage of teachers and public funds for schools, and there's really going to be a two-tiered school system, inevitably. We can sell all the fancy things we want to the good schools, but they'll be so small in number that the market is limited, so there won't be a whole lot for them. The vast number of schools are going to be this other type, which won't have real teachers but teaching technicians or something. Our customer is not the child or the parent or the teacher, but the state budget." It's going to the governor and saying, "Hey, look, we can sell you this computer that will reduce the cost of your schools." "Great, send them in. It'll help our deficit."

The inevitable trend of demographics, resources, and so forth indicates that this is a permanent situation. They had these school automation systems that I thought were horrendous. They had an image of kids in these cubicles interacting with computers. It was clearly a security-oriented thing, so that the kids couldn't hit each other and they could be monitored easily, and there was minimal human contact, because they couldn't afford it. It was also notable that the kids were all minorities.

DAVID: It's reminiscent of the Industrial Age.

JARON: Yeah, it *is* like a retreat to the nineteenth century. It's a difficult situation. Then there's another player, the companies like Apple and Microsoft who are creating a software infrastructure. This particular historical moment is immensely important, because we're really creating the very fabric of ideas with which our own culture will be represented for a long time into the future.

There's another possibility. If people do get good at improvising reality, they may get good at improvising the insides of computers again and just undo everything that Microsoft has done, when they get skilled enough. I'm not saying that what Microsoft is doing is bad—in fact, I think a lot of it's probably quite good—but the point is that there's this codification of how we represent our culture in order to computerize it, which is extraordinary. This is something fundamentally new, and really scary to me.

DAVID: Tell us something about VR's potential for physically challenged people.

JARON: There are many approaches, because there are so many types of disabilities. It's something I've been very active in—in fact, in the next month I'm going to three different conferences on that topic. Cal State Northridge, near Los Angeles, had a wonderful conference on virtual reality for people with disabilities. We actually brought a VR system there, and during the conference we were building custom worlds for people to try things out.

There was a woman who had very limited hand mobility, and Chuck Blanchard created a virtual hand for her. She had a glove on her physical hand, which amplified her hand movements so that she was able to learn to use it and pick up virtual things in a way she could never pick up physical things.

I did a juggling teaching demo a long time ago. If you juggle virtual balls, you can sort of simulate the experience of juggling. You don't feel the balls hit your hand as much with the current types of gloves, but you can still approximate the experience. Let's suppose you decide to make the balls move slowly, but keep your hands moving at the natural speed. So now you have lots of time to get your hand under the balls. That by itself is just a cheat, but what's really interesting is that you can slowly speed up the balls and have a gradual approach to learning a physical skill that previously required a leap. For people recovering from strokes, this could give them some learning feedback earlier than they would get otherwise. So there's a whole range of learning uses.

There are some special things for blind and deaf people. For the deaf you can use gloves to synthesize sign language, and for the blind there's this three-dimensional sound capability of virtual reality. It potentially gives the blind a portable spatial display, so that they're not left out of this age of spatial interfaces for computers. It goes on and on.

REBECCA: Do you see virtual ritual as being a turning point in humanity's relationship with the machine?

JARON: Well, it is in a number of ways. First of all, it defines our agenda with machines as being primarily cultural and sensual, as opposed to power-oriented. For a long time we've had an agenda for doing science and technology that can be stated very simply—"Make us more powerful," ultimately to conquer death or something like that. But you have to remember that in the context of when the scientific method was born, coming out of the Renaissance, we're dealing with a whole continent of people living in disease and shit and misery.

> *With the exception of diseases and natural disasters, all of our other problems are created by our own behavior.*

So the desire to be able to control the physical world was very reasonable. We've reached a remarkable moment now that, with the exception of diseases and natural disasters, every other area of science and technological development is unnecessary. (*laughter*) With the exception of diseases and natural disasters, all of our other problems are created by our own behavior.

So if you're working in medicine or natural disasters, you're still on that front, fighting nature and trying to get control of something that's important to us. Anything else you cannot objectively justify any more. It has to be justified culturally, as if it were a work of art. Anyone who doesn't see that is not really thinking rationally.

We can't stop making technology, because we're in love with it. So what we have to do is shift to a cultural way of choosing our technologies and justifying them. Virtual reality is an interesting technology; it's something that's being taken very seriously. But everybody recognizes that its justification is fundamentally cultural. To me, that's a marvelous shift. It's very positive.

Another aspect of virtual reality is that it's sensual, it's embodied. In the use of information technology there's this terrible danger of making the world seem more abstract and becoming blind and nerdy, as I mentioned before. Virtual reality really places the body at the center, and I think that's also a wonderful development. Then, of course, there's the dream of post-symbolic communication that we talked about before.

DAVID: Speaking of the sensuality of VR, what about the possibilities for virtual sex, which Howard Rheingold termed "teledildonics"? A lot of people are very hungry for this kind of technology and its potential for sexual experience.

JARON: Howard blames Ted Nelson for the term. The problem I have with people who talk about virtual reality sex is that in the way the question is asked there's an implication about what sex is that I think is really bad. The implication is that sex is a media experience, as opposed to being a mystical communication between people.

DAVID: That's a very blurry distinction.

JARON: No, I don't think so. The very question implies that the reason that you're with a real person when you have sex, as opposed to pornography, is because the media quality of pornography isn't as good yet. That implication for what sex is, I think, is preposterous. That makes sex into this really meaningless thing which I think even horny young guys will eventually not find any pleasure in, because it turns it into nothing but information. (*laughter*)

DAVID: Right. But virtual sex *is* a communication medium, and biological sex is nothing but the exchange of sensory and chemical information.

JARON: Okay. I was giving a talk at UC Santa Cruz, and there were two questions, both about virtual sex, that to me sounded completely different. One question was this guy coming up and saying, "Er, could I experience making love to Marilyn Monroe?" I tortured that person. He will never ask another question at a seminar again. He is permanently stunted for life now. (*laughter*)

Then the other one was a person who asked, "Could me and my lover become octopi?" That, I thought, was a very attractive question. So these are two different attitudes toward it, and they have completely different subtexts underneath the question about what they think sex is. It's not that I'm opposed to the concept of virtual reality sex per se, but the way the question is asked is usually really abhorrent to me, and I feel as though I'm immediately at war with it, because it implies a very limited idea of what sex is.

REBECCA: But it is the prevalent idea, as you say, and the combination of sex and technology is a huge industry.

JARON: Sure. When copiers first spread, what a lot of people did was to copy their privates. That was a big thing for a while. Now nobody thinks about it anymore because it just seems stupid. And you have the same thing going on with 900 numbers now.

DAVID: Right, but telephones have been around a lot longer than xerox machines—which, by the way, aren't interactive—and the 900 phenomenon doesn't appear to be a passing fad. The interesting thing about phone sex is that it's the first time that we have come close to being able to enjoy nonlocalized sex, so that people on different parts of the globe can engage in imaginative erotic exchanges. Don't you think that virtual reality will open up more dimensions as a medium to explore that type of communication?

JARON: If you're talking about using virtual reality for sex, there are a few critical questions here. Are you inventing your own body? Are you making it up? The question about octopi is interesting because there's a playfulness there—it's kind of like flirting or being at a masked ball.

But suppose you have somebody who gets excited about an experience that's not like that, where the co-creative experience with the other person isn't at the center, but that person is interacting with a simulated partner. The person is essentially becoming sexually excited about something that is abstract and also very malleable. What is sex, as opposed to what is not sex? Sex is one of the most interesting concepts because it refers to so much and so little.

The fact that two people can communicate is a fundamentally mysterious thing. It's not understood. You can go out and buy books that try to explain how two people communicate, and you will see very clearly that the authors do not know. It's philosophically mysterious, it's scientifically mysterious, it's an area of totally wild unknown. There's not even the beginning of a possible explanation for it.

I think one of the greatest intellectual sins that we've committed is that we've somehow created this world view that we don't live surrounded by mystery. This is something that is abhorrent to a real scientist and to a real artist. Science is based on mystery and on not really trusting your theories thus far, but having them always be subject to change, right?

DAVID: Supposedly.

JARON: See, technology has been successful enough that we treat it like a comfortable net that will always catch us. So sex is one such communication—it's a mysterious, mystical, unexplained thing. To the degree that you pretend that media technology can capture it or explain it, you've just extinguished your own experience of life.

> *. . . technology has been successful enough that we treat it like a comfortable net that will always catch us.*

REBECCA: Earlier you were talking about how virtual reality gave you an extra appreciation of your senses. In the same way, couldn't VR open people up to the dimensions of sex they haven't yet explored and give them a sense of what they've been missing?

JARON: Anything can happen. But the key is to keep in touch with that fundamental mysteriousness. I think anybody who "understands" sex has just lost it. Virtual reality sex implies a non-mysteriousness to the contact, and that's the fundamental problem.

> *Virtual reality sex implies a non-mysteriousness to the contact, and that's the fundamental problem.*

DAVID: Why does it imply that?

JARON: Because it implies that you can capture it as sensory information and pipe it around. I think you *can* have authentic communication that would include sex over media. I'm not saying that's impossible. All I'm saying is that it's a question of intention.

REBECCA: What kind of relationship, if any, do you see between nanotechnology and VR?

JARON: You might be able to make some pretty good computers with nanotechnology, but you might be able to make some equally good computers using other techniques. The first thing about nanotechnology you have to understand is that it's not going to happen quite as fast as Eric Drexler says. Just because you have the ability to move atoms around doesn't mean you really know how to program them. It takes a while to figure this stuff out. Also, a lot of the vision depends on computers becoming smart enough to program themselves, where suddenly by making a computer big enough and fast enough the machine automatically figures out how to do a lot of stuff.

The idea is that you have this qualitative difference that makes computers "smart," which comes about automatically with a quantitative difference. But there's no way to know that this will happen. So I'm sort of in an in-between camp, compared with those people who think that the nanotech guys are ridiculously over-optimistic and the people who are sure the world's about to pop into a completely different state.

REBECCA: Do you see it as being as big a leap as virtual reality?

JARON: Potentially it's an enormous leap, of course. What's interesting about Eric Drexler's writings is that he's keyed into the same thing that comes out of the frustrations of early childhood. What if the world could be whatever you wanted? And what an extraordinarily different landscape that opens up.

To me, the key to the future of science and technology is not just increasing power, but coming up with large-scale cultural adventures that can last forever. That's why the post-symbolic idea is really more important than anything specific about virtual reality or nanotechnology. That's really where the action is. I mean, one way or another we're going to live in a fluid universe. (*laughter*)

> *... one way or another we're going to live in a fluid universe.*

My only comment would be that there might be an ethics in the future where you would choose the mode of experience that affects other people as little as possible. In that sense, there might be a lot of situations where virtual reality would be considered a more moral way of attaining some types of experiences than actually changing the physical world, which inevitably will have side-effects, since there's only one of those physical worlds, so far as we know.

REBECCA: VR could be a way to experiment with some possibilities without having to commit to them.

JARON: VR's a way to experiment with anything that involves human experience. But if you want to learn about the objective world of nature using VR instead of physical experiments, that's limited by how good your models are.

REBECCA: But you can experiment with what it would be like to have lobster hands!

JARON: That's true. (*laughter*) One of my cohorts over the years is a guy named Joe Rosen. He had a project for a long time called the "nerve chip." This was a prosthetic nerve made of a computer chip with holes burned in it by a laser that a severed nerve bundle would grow through. With it, you could remap the nerve connections during the healing process. As things stand, nerve bundles heal together with the wrong nerve connections.

Joe is a reconstructive plastic surgeon, and he often talked about how you have some extra things in your body. There's a couple of extra muscles and tendons that are used in reconstructive surgery, and there are even extraperipheral nerve bundles that don't go anywhere and are just vestigial pieces. He would say, "Why don't we just take some of that with plastic surgery and just build a tail?" On the

> *I'm imagining the next generation will be building new physical appendages in order to annoy their parents.*

face of it, it would seem possible. Since many of my students have been radically pierced, I'm imagining the next generation will be building new physical appendages in order to annoy their parents. (*laughter*)

I also told my students that their kids will probably put very powerful microscopic video projectors into their zits and project bizarre animations on the wall as they walk by. See, this generation has sixties parents. That's why they're into piercing, because what are they going to do, get drunk and go to rock and roll concerts and have sex? The parents will just say go ahead. So the next generation is really going to have to go all out. (*laughter*)

REBECCA: Do you see VR becoming as commonplace as television?

JARON: Yeah, sure.

REBECCA: What abuses do you foresee when this happens?

JARON: VR is a very powerful communication medium, just like books, so if you want to understand the abuses just look at the abuses of other communication mediums, like books or telephones. It's different from television in that it's not a broadcast medium. But in one-to-one-type communications media especially, such as talking or using telephones, you can find precedents for all the types of abuses that might come up. You have the person who can yell, "Fire!" in a crowded room. You have *Mein Kampf*. When you're involved in creating a new media technology there's a kind of faith you have, that you're empowering mankind in a certain way to better communicate with itself. There's a faith that in the broad picture there's a goodness and a sweetness in people. It's a kind of optimism, and I believe it's justified.

> *... if you want to understand the abuses, just look at the abuses of other communication mediums ...*

I believe that history has shown a gradual improvement in our conduct. But certainly many bad things will happen.

DAVID: In terms of your reaction to the *Wall Street Journal* calling your work "electronic LSD," I've gotten the impression that you don't think the multiple-reality perception that a psychedelic generates is a very good metaphor for understanding VR. Certainly philosophers, such as Timothy Leary and Terence McKenna, have often drawn the analogy. Do you think that long-term exposure to VR could have similar effects to the long-term effects of psychedelic drugs?

JARON: There are very few people who've actually used high-quality VR systems a lot, and I'm not aware of anybody who's very experienced at both the use of psychedelics and VR. I've never taken psychedelic drugs. I'm stubborn, you know. Tim and Terence have had some VR experiences, but not a whole lot. So there's a degree to which we talk about each other's experiences but we don't really know, and in a certain way it becomes nonsense. I can say a little bit, though. One thing is that virtual reality doesn't involve a sudden change in the state of consciousness. It might involve a gradual one or an eventual one, but in terms of the state of consciousness going from being in a normal waking state to going into virtual reality, it's continuous.

There are little things, such as that increase in sensitivity I talked about, but it's not anything like what you'd associate with a psychedelic drug. A drug, because it's operating directly on your brain, is changing your subjective perception. Virtual reality only happens outside your sense organs, so it only directly addresses what you objectively perceive. Your subjective style of experience changes, of course, in response to circumstances, but a lot more slowly and gradually, just as it does if you go on a vacation or something.

DAVID: You could actually create a drug that would come on very slowly though, and the external world can have a psychoactive effect on us. The line between internal and external isn't clearly defined.

JARON: The word I love to use to describe the VR user's mindset is "craftsmanlike." Virtual reality doesn't happen to you. If you space out in a virtual reality situation, the medium lit-

> *... it's the interactivity that makes [VR] real.*

erally disappears, because it's the interactivity that makes it real. The visuals are crummy compared even to TV. It's not a great sensory medium in terms of conveying passive images. VR feels more real than TV, but it looks less realistic. There will always be a passive visual medium that is higher in quality than the interactive ones.

DAVID: A psychedelic experience is a very interactive one, though. What you do, how you respond, what your intention is—all affect the experience.

JARON: You're really going to wrestle me to the ground on this one. (*laughter*) I think that's probably true, but I think it is different. A psychedelic experience does have its own momentum, it lasts a certain amount of time, and to a certain extent it's something you interact with. But a virtual reality experience is not happening to you; it's entirely dependent on your activity with it. There's no persistence to it whatsoever that's not by your intention.

REBECCA: For many people, long-term use of psychedelics gives them this idea that reality is malleable. With long-term use of VR, do you think you would also form this realization that you do, to a large extent, create your reality?

JARON: This is a tricky area. The idea that reality as we know it is just a passing illusion that can be changed at a moment's notice is sort of the state religion of Marin county. (*laughter*) And yet, as apparent as that might be, there is this stubbornness of—I don't like to say "the physical world," because I'm not sure if it's the physicality of it that's the stubborn part—this mundane world out there. I should also say that the stubbornness of reality is the only thing that makes science sensible. So it's a mysterious area. I don't know that anybody has articulated a tremendous way to reconcile the stubbornness and the apparent flexibility, which both exist at once.

REBECCA: But your *experience* of the world is flexible.

JARON: Our experience is absolutely malleable. Furthermore, in a hypothetical future world of virtual reality you have the added experience of the objective world being something that's very fluid and changing and controllable. Of course, on top of that you'd have your internal experience, which has always been fluid and changeable. It's like balancing a unicycle on top of a unicycle; you have this more flexible situation. But I still say that your experience of using virtual reality is probably a lot closer to riding a bicycle—or double-decker unicycles!—or building something than it is to an altered consciousness experience. It's more intentional, and it's more waking-state, and more craftsmanlike.

DAVID: What do you think might be some of the long-term perceptual changes that would result from someone using VR?

> *. . . sensitivity is a learned, ever-growing capacity, just like learning to play a musical instrument.*

JARON: Well, this hasn't happened yet, so I'm purely guessing. As I already mentioned, VR can increase sensitivity to the natural world. I want to stress that sensitivity is a learned, ever-growing capacity, just like learning to play a musical instrument.

I think that virtual reality will create a profoundly increased sense of distinction between natural and manmade parts of the physical world. Most of us have had the experience of building only a few things. Things like houses and streets are just so common that they come at us as if they were from nature. You discover in virtual reality that you can make houses and streets, but you can't make trees. Well, actually you can sort of make some trees that are okay, but they're not magical like real trees. You're able to own all those man-made artifacts because in virtual reality you can essentially make them yourself, from an experiential point of view. So they become something that's clearly distinct from that which you can't make, which is the natural.

I think also there will be a kind of focus on experience. The word "experience" to me is the most provocative, mystical word in the language, because that word, in itself, undermines the whole scientific view. Experience is something that from an experimental point of view can't be shown to exist at all, and yet it's all we have. It's the only thing that we have in common that we can't measure—it's not part of the objective world. In a virtual world, because your experience is more clearly separated from stimulus, because the stimulus is all defined in a computer

> *Experience is something that from an experimental point of view can't be shown to exist at all, and yet it's all we have.*

and can be enumerated, your angel-self of experience is sort of exposed and you become more aware of it. That creates a kind of sensuality and a direct apprehension of oneself.

Virtual reality may have some other effects. It may change the way that people walk or something—in all seriousness—because it may give them a lot more experiences of the ways their bodies work. Who knows? There may be all kinds of crazy things. The changes are really up to whoever's there to use the stuff, and I hope all this will be explored as if life were a work of art.

DAVID: We asked Stephen LaBerge about VR, and he described lucid dreaming as "high-resolution VR." How would you compare VR and lucid dreaming?

JARON: That's true; it's just that lucid dreaming is solipsistic. That's the same old boundary between the infinite solipsistic universe and the more limited shared universe.

REBECCA: Some people think technology is going to take us back to the Stone Age because of humanity's love affair with the science of destruction, while others see it as the answer to all our prayers. How do you see technology's role in evolution? Where, if anywhere, do you think it's ultimately taking us?

JARON: Evolution only proceeds when people die before they reproduce, or when they just fail to reproduce as a result of their adaptation to their environment. Without death you don't have evolution. The way you are now, almost everything about you—the way your fingers work, the way your nostrils point down, the way you think, to a large degree—all this is the result of countless millions of deaths, of incredible suffering. It's an extraordinary thing.

So, in that sense, technology reduces the degree to which evolution takes place, because people live longer in a technological society. We are breeding a population now that's tolerant of cancer-causing agents and radiation in the environment. So in a sense, evolution continues. But our environment changes so quickly. An environment has to stay relatively still for a while to have evolution occur in a coherent way.

There's a little book I like a lot called *Finite and Infinite Games*. The title almost says it. There are two types of games, games that have to end and games that go on forever. If we are playing with technology a "game" that has to end, then we'll end. The quest for more power goes in only one direction, so it doesn't cycle. It must end, if not in nuclear war, then in biological war or something else. This is basic logic. You have to have something that cycles around in an infinite dance of some sort in order to have something that survives. If people find an "infinite game" for technology, it will be based on aesthetics, not power, and it'll involve some sort of massive cultural adventure with technology—virtual reality, nanotechnology, God knows what.

To address the cosmic long-term, I have this ultimate creation myth I made up as a way to think about people and technology. A long, long time ago, our ancestors were very highly technological people. They even built time machines that worked and transporter booths like they use in *Star Trek*. They had all this great technology, and at a certain point, they suddenly *stopped experiencing anything*. They already had the future at hand because of their time machines, so there were no surprises, and everything just kind of stopped. So they had a meeting, as they knew they were about to, (*laughter*) in which they said, "Well, this sucks! Let's create a situation in which we drop all this technology, forget all of it, and we'll become cave men and women and fight saber-toothed tigers, and then we'll just gradually build it up again. They knew that they and their descendants would go through tremendous pain, but it didn't matter to them because they could see the whole future and see that they would just come back to the same place eventually. And we descended from them.

REBECCA: What are your thoughts on the relation of technology to Gaia?

JARON: Well, right now it's somewhat antagonistic. (*laughter*)

REBECCA: Terence McKenna had a thought about technology being the earth's way of becoming sentient, and the fear of machines is just the male ego's fear of relinquishing control to the Gaia matrix.

JARON: I think that's exactly, perfectly wrong. I think technology is the male's *defense* against the wilds of nature. I think men, in general, are kind of scared of nature and overwhelmed by it. Technology always looks as unnatural as possible—that's the aesthetic of technological design. All the rhetoric about technology is always about

> *The ultimate fantasy of most computer scientists is backing themselves up onto a tape . . .*

overcoming nature, one way or another. The ultimate fantasy of most computer scientists is backing themselves up onto a tape, so they no longer have to deal with biology or, of course, with death. So I think that Terence McKenna's idea is just about completely opposite to my point of view on the ultimate meaning of technology to "men."

REBECCA: A lot of people talk about the importance of "value-free" science, having no regulation on the use of a scientific discovery. Do you agree with this, or do you think that scientists should have some say in how their discoveries are used?

JARON: I wish that scientists would apply the standards of scientific method to understanding their own motives, so that they could be honest about them. You have to understand—it's irrational and impossible to do science without an agenda. Science requires resources. The universe is so large and multifaceted that there are enormous choices to be made in what's to be studied. Furthermore, by its very nature, a lot of science is wrong at any given time and waiting to be destroyed by the next generation of results.

So the choice of what to study next is not based on some kind of magical, value-free overview—that's a complete illusion. It's not available. The engine of science is rigor, but the ignition is emotion. On the other hand,

> **The engine of science is rigor, but the ignition is emotion.**

the reason scientists have to pretend there's a rigorous ignition is that they have to protect themselves from counterforces that are even worse, such as these moralists who don't even understand science going in and telling them, for instance, that they can't use fetal tissue for research, which is completely lunatic. [Note: Since this interview was conducted, President Clinton was elected and the fetal-tissue controversy was resolved in the favor of the researchers.]

> **Scientists must develop a cultural agenda to have meaning in the future.**

Scientists must develop a cultural agenda to have meaning in the future. When you do science, that means somebody else is not using resources for some other research, or for survival or pleasure or whatever. So it's really a social decision. It has to have some meaning for the rest of the culture outside science.

In a market environment it seems increasingly necessary to market scientific agendas to the public with clever campaigns, because there may not be products to buy for a long time, if ever. That is, after all, why the concept of "virtual reality" came to be.

REBECCA: Who determines the benefit to the culture? The scientist?

JARON: I think it has to be pretty broadly based. I do believe there's a grand adventure in getting to know the universe better, so science has an adventure value, just as post-sym might someday. But adventure, including science for science's sake, is like sex—increasing the pace doesn't necessarily make it better. It's not like we have this manifest destiny to go into as much science as possible in every direction as fast as possible at all times. I really feel that scientists have to share some responsibility with the rest of the society in setting the agenda, and I think they do. Most of the problems that I notice aren't coming from the scientific community. They're coming from the religious community, from a James Bond-like fantasy life in the defense community, and from politicians and businesses with excessively short-term agendas.

REBECCA: Do you think that science and mysticism can ever be reconciled?

JARON: They've never been separated, and the best scientists are often mystics, as a matter of fact. There's this awe at the fundamental mysteriousness of the universe that drives both science and mysticism. There's a great book of the writings of the founders of modern physics called *Quantum Questions.* All these folks wrote beautiful mystical essays.

This is not as true for computer science, because it's not a study of nature but a creation of a man-made world, and it doesn't usually inspire that kind of awe.

REBECCA: But many scientists, in seeking to keep up a determinable, repeatable objectivity in their experiments, have tried to keep the mind well out of their experiments.

JARON: What do you expect them to do? Mysticism can be part of one's personal understanding of the universe revealed by science, and it can be the "ignition" for science, but it can't be part of the conduct of science. Science is a specific, philosophically narrow discipline. The limitations can be viewed as making it irrelevant to many kinds of understanding, but they are, at the very least, beautiful.

I was around Richard Feynman, the Nobel Prize-winning physicist, one time when he was on acid. Before he started to come on I asked him, "What do you really think about the mind-body problem? Now come on, don't just shove it under the rug. You probably experience yourself existing on the inside. How do you think that reconciles with the matter of the brain? Do you think there's any problem there?" He said, "I've thought about that a lot, and I really just don't understand it." That was just an example of the immense honesty and integrity that he had.

REBECCA: It was proof that he really *had* thought about it. (*laughter*)

JARON: Exactly. I asked him again when he was on acid, and he said, with this most wonderful smile and this effervescent glee, "I don't understand it." That sort of glee at the fundamental mysteriousness of the universe is the motivational core of science, and you always run into that with a great scientist. Just to be clear, though, Feynman didn't state any mystical ideas. He just was rigorous about what he did and didn't know, which I think is one of the hardest mental disciplines.

DAVID: Around seven years ago you asked me a question that I've spent years puzzling over. "If you could, through nanotechnology, replicate every single atom in your nervous system, would that structure be you?" Would you care to venture an answer to your own question?

JARON: That's a trick question. The answer to the question doesn't matter, and the intention does. (*laughter*) It's really a variation of the virtual sex question. Do you treat the glaring mysticism of your experience of every moment as the center of your life, or do you treat some kind of measurable phenomenon as being the important thing?

> *Do you treat the glaring mysticism of your experience of every moment as the center of your life . . .?*

I don't know what would happen if you made a copy of somebody's head. Presumably you'd have two heads that talked, but you wouldn't know if they were both conscious or not, because that's not a measurable, scientific thing. So it would be just sort of a confusing result. But I don't think the result of the question matters nearly as much as the intention with which it's asked. The key is, are you in touch with the mystical sense of experience you have, or do you suppress it by the way you categorize and think about the world?

By the way, I consider my position to not be "dualist," which is the dirty word used by these new "information positivists" to talk about anyone who acknowledges the existence of experience. I'm not claiming some second track of reality for souls or something. I'm just demanding that we show some humility in assessing our understanding of things. You have to walk the razor's edge between reductionism and superstition, and through humility you find your way.

The dominant idea about people in the information world comes from Alan Turing. He saved England during World War II by breaking a Nazi secret code. He was a really brilliant mathematician and a founding computer scientist. He also was imprisoned by the English courts for being gay. He was given female hormones in prison, started to develop breasts, got depressed, and committed suicide.

Shortly before he committed suicide he wrote the Turing Test paper, which is the foundation of computer-science culture today. It's a thought experiment in which you have a computer in one booth and a person in another booth and they're both typing at you. If you can't tell the difference between them, Turing claims, don't you just have to admit that they're the same, at that point? Turing noticed that there might be no objective measurement of consciousness.

DAVID: It's not so much whether I could judge if you were the same person; I'm wondering what you think *your* experience would be if your head were copied. Do you think there would be some kind of continuity of consciousness?

JARON: I have no idea. If you actually did it, you still wouldn't know.

DAVID: The real intention behind the question is whether you think there's something beyond the physical atoms that make you who you are?

JARON: You're still asking the question from an objective point of view. That doesn't matter; that's just a choice among implementations of the universe. Who cares? (*laughter*)

DAVID: What do you think happens to you when you die?

JARON: Well, I don't really know. (*laughter*)

DAVID: I *know* you don't know, Jaron. (*laughter*) But you must have given it some thought. There's no mystery greater than death.

JARON: That's true. It's really impossible to know. I used to worry about it more when I was younger. (*Long pause*) I think the only thing it's possible to talk about is how our ideas and perceptions of our own death affect our lives now. I mean, it's just out of the bounds of the possible for discussion and thought.

As I mentioned before, there are the two big limitations you have to live with. By a certain age, you've dealt with the lack of total godlike power over the universe and the limitations of the body, but your own mortality usually takes longer to come to grips with.

One way to explain mortality is to imagine a universe where we were unlimited and to see that that wouldn't lead to no experience at all, like in the techno-creation myth I told. A person with a time machine is essentially immortal. The people in my story overcame the two basic human limitations, and the penalty they paid was to cease to have experience.

> *A person with a time machine is essentially immortal.*

Now let's suppose my creation myth is true. It's just a techno-version of the old perennial philosophy, so who knows? Then the ultimate truth of our situation would be found in the eternal cyclical story of our ancestor-descendants having their meeting without any sense of surprise or experience, which results in a perpetual grand cycle of induced amnesia that allows our lives to happen. Some sort of stillness that has to forget itself in order to give birth to experience seems like a reasonable metaphysics. What else could be going on?

Now, if this is right, we don't know how many worlds there might be between us and that ultimate reality in which there is no experience. So maybe there is some kind of afterlife or heaven that's between us and that ultimate thing. But that ultimate thing must be there, however many layers there may be between us and it. And in that ultimate place there is no experience. Experience only happens within the context of ignorance of the next moment and ignorance in general. So our deaths allow us to experience.

> *... death represents a necessary ignorance without which you couldn't have experience.*

Having said that, it would be nice if life were longer, but that's another problem. So death represents a necessary ignorance without which you couldn't have experience. It's an inevitable thing, and I think that all beings and all realities in all possible planes of existence have something analogous to it.

DAVID: That's a pretty good answer for someone who claims to have never taken a psychedelic.

JARON: I live in Marin. (*laughter*)

Joey Tranchina

Alexander and Ann Shulgin

"... anything that the human is capable of doing through the
mind is duplicable pharmacologically ... "

Chemophilia
with Alexander and Ann Shulgin

Alexander (Sasha) and Ann Shulgin stand on the frontier of designer neu-rochemistry, developing a plethora of miraculous pharmacological keys that unlock different aspects of the brain's hidden potential. They are known to many as the authors of the underground best-seller PIHKAL: A Chemi-cal Love Story, *the title of which is an acronym for Phenethylamines I Have Known and Loved. Alexander is a long-standing, well-respected re-search chemist and professor of pharmacology at the University of Cali-fornia at Berkeley, where he earned his doctorate in biochemistry in 1954. He is the author of 150 scientific research papers, twenty patents, and three books. Although Alexander has been quite outspoken regarding his opposition to the so-called war on drugs, he has been a scientific consult-ant for such state-run organizations as the National Institute on Drug Abuse, NASA, Lawrence Radiation Laboratory, and the Drug Enforcement Agency (DEA).*

But in private, in his government-licensed research lab, he has spent the last thirty years discretely—yet legally—designing hundreds of new psychoactive compounds, particularly psychedelics. Along with his wife, Ann, and a small, brave, and dedicated research group, they sample each new drug as it is developed. Through the cautious escalation of dosage, they discover and map out the range of each new drug's effects, experi-menting with the various aspects of their psychological and spiritual po-tential. Most of Alexander's psychoactive designer molecules are unknown to the public, but a few, such as 2CB (an MDMA analogue) and DOM (better known as STP), have received widespread distribution. Their re-search continues to this day, and a new book, TIHKAL *(Tryptamines I Have Known and Loved) is on the way. Their previous book,* PIHKAL, *details their truly remarkable adventures and, for those with a solid back-ground in chemistry, provides the esoteric recipes for recreating hundreds of Alexander's finely crafted magic molecules.*

Alexander and Ann make a very compatible research team: they comple-ment on another, and their relationship reflects a deep commitment to in-ner exploration. They are extremely warm, and anxious to share what they've learned through their experimentation. We interviewed them at their home in Lafayette east of Berkeley in northern California on May 19, 1993. Ann is strong, solid, and grounded, very much connected to the earth. Before moving to northern California as a teenager, she lived in four countries. She worked as a medical secretary at the UCSF Medical Center and has three children from a previous marriage, to Jungian analyst John Perry. She is presently a psychotherapist.

A wild electrical current seems to buzz through Alexander's nervous system, as evidenced by the white hair that seems to stand on end on his head and face, and the excited manner in which he explains everything. Alexander's research laboratory, just a short walk from the main house, is filled by a complex of interlocking flasks, glass beakers, plastic tubes, heating coils, and countless bottles; it looks dramatic enough to be used as a Hollywood movie set. The only chemicals that we sample, however, are in the cheese sandwiches that we have for lunch before we begin the interview. Even so, we do feel ourselves to be in an altered state.

DJB

DAVID: What was it that inspired you to write *PIHKAL?*

ALEXANDER: I was inspired partly by the history of Wilhelm Reich. I discovered that in his very last years he got into very unusual and not totally acceptable areas and hypotheses, such as making rains fall by means of electrostatic guns and other such ventures.

The FDA filed a lawsuit against him for promoting radical equipment that had not been approved by them. They put him in jail, and he died there. After his death the FDA took all his lab books and papers and burned them. One of the reasons I wrote *PIHKAL* was because I could see the need to get a lot of information that had not been published into a form that just could not be destroyed.

ANN: And I couldn't imagine him writing all that fun stuff without my help. (*laughter*) I'd co-authored one paper with him before and discovered that it's a great ego boost to do good writing. And I've never had anything published before. It became the most exciting thing in the world to do, especially because it was pushing against the establishment.

My model and my hero was Castenada, but what I wanted to do was bring in the personal, which he failed to do: marriage, kids, love, soup— everyday reality. Our feeling about psychedelics is that if you use them the right way, they enrich your everyday life. You learn to think a different way about the ordinary things you see.

REBECCA: What is a phenethylamine, why is it so special, and what role has it played in your research?

ALEXANDER: There is a collection of neurotransmitters in the brain, and two of the largest families are the phenethylamines and the tryptamines. And it turned out that all the known psychedelics around the time I got curious in this area—back in the fifties and sixties—were either phenethylamines or tryptamines. It's now been shown that this is a very good guide. Nature said, "Here are the two basic building blocks, and if you're going to do something with the brain, it's going to be with one or the other."

DAVID: Why did the two of you use fictional names in the book, when the story was obviously autobiographical?

ANN: Among the drugs we were writing about, some—such as LSD—are illegal. It was risky enough writing the book in the first place. We didn't know what to expect from the establishment, if anything. Some people late at night with baseball bats smashing up the lab was a perfectly reasonable possibility. Using fictional names gave us deniability.

The second reason was so that I could tell my children that the sex in the book wasn't actually us. (*laughter*) Also, we didn't want to jeopardize our next book. At this point, when not only has there been no fire from heaven descending on our heads, but the DEA itself is one of our best customers, it's easy to look back and ask why were we worried.

ALEXANDER: One of the things I did was to send a copy of the book to people within the DEA, with covering phrases like "Here's a book that will provide you with a lot of information that may be useful to you."

> *One of the higher administrators of the DEA in Washington said, "My wife and I read your book, and it's great!"*

DAVID: What was their response to it?

ANN: They loved it. One of the higher administrators of the DEA in Washington said, "My wife and I read your book, and it's great!"

DAVID: Sasha, how did you become a chemist?

ALEXANDER: My doctorate is in biochemistry, but I found that it didn't have the magic and the music of chemistry. In my teaching class at Berkeley I would ask, "How many people are taking organic chemistry?" And you'd hear this groan. Why? Because the typical instruction would be "Go and read pages 83 to 117 in the textbook, and we'll have a quiz on Monday." People hated it. Chemistry, however, is an art, it's music, it's a style of thinking. Orbitals are for mathematicians; chemistry is for people who like to cook!

Some of my colleagues would have a goal, and if something went wrong, they'd try to find out how else they could get it to go right. My argument has always been, if something went wrong, oh wow! Out of this will come something unexpected. That led me into a very great curiosity about the mind process, which was greatly amplified by my first mescaline experience.

Drugs do not do things; they allow *you* to do things. It's not an imposition from the outside. People tend to say, "What did that drug do?" or "How did the drug do what it did?" or "I took a drug, and it did such and such." In each

> *Drugs do not do things; they allow* **you** *to do things.*

instance this is giving up your power to an inert white solid. The drug catalyzes and facilitates, but it doesn't *do* things. That puts it in perspective. You don't have to give credit to a drug.

DAVID: It also encourages the person to take responsibility.

ALEXANDER: Completely. You can't live without that.

REBECCA: Do you ever find yourself making a judgment that what you're experiencing is a quality of the drug rather than something inherent in your own psyche?

ALEXANDER: If I do, then that experience is sure to be a bummer! (*laughter*) Look at yourself in the mirror; it's a good catharsis. It's *me* and the drug. It's a relationship that is available to everyone. Everybody has the possibility of going into some sort of ecstatic experience, at any time, without drugs, perhaps even at the grocery store. Now there's a thought!

ANN: If this were a property of the drug, it would be the equivalent of the atom bomb! It's very useful for us that Sasha's metabolism is just about as different from mine as it could possibly be. I had a crisis week that was brought about by forty milligrams of something that turned out later to be absolutely inactive. That's the placebo effect, which can happen on any drug. But often he's often taken a drug on which he seems to have a perfectly okay time at an active level, and I'll take it and have a terrible time!

REBECCA: But haven't you found that these drugs do have a certain character to them, a tendency to bring out a particular aspect of the psyche?

ANN: The drug has a physical effect if nothing else, and how my own individual chemistry and metabolism use that drug may be quite different from the way somebody else does it.

DAVID: Do you think that the states of consciousness you produce with your molecules could be produced by the endogenous neurotransmitters in the brain, or are you producing states of consciousness that are unique and have never been and could never have been produced without the drug?

ALEXANDER: I think they are deeply embedded in the human animal.

ANN: [*to David*] I have a compulsion. It's a mother thing. Could you put your left foot up please? [*She ties his shoelace*]

ALEXANDER: I was asked almost the same question a few years ago, so I made up a chart about telephones. The finger-dial system can be seen as an analog of the brain. All you're doing, if you dial the number one and release it, is making one very fast break in the integrity of the system. If you dial the six and release it, it makes six breaks in the system. Then the relay gets broken three times when you dial three, two times when you dial two, and then five times, and you have the number 6325. You see, you make the circuit by the number of times you break the relay. In fact, if you are very fast with your two fingers, you can dial 911 by hitting the cradle that gives you the dial tone nine times very fast, and then once, and then once again.

Then you have the push-button system. Every time you hit a button, you're actually activating two frequencies simultaneously. They devised frequencies so that there's no harmonic interference that could give you a false signal. You're not imposing breaks in the system; you're superimposing two nonconflicting frequencies in the system.

I look upon this as the true analog of the human brain. The numbers represent serotonin, dopamine, et cetera. If you want a signal to come through, you get this neurotransmitter combination that combines with this and that, and the next thing you know, you have a thought process and memory.

But when they designed the phone system, they didn't make it three by four, they made it four by four. These extra four stops have the rather unimaginative names of A, B, C, and D, and to operate them there is a very secret frequency of 1633 cycles per second. So if you play around with these, you get into areas you wouldn't believe! The military and deep computer language use these four additional stops. But they're not visible on your telephone.

And of course, these stops represent your psychedelic drug neurotransmitter, which also gets you into weird places. All the wiring is there but you don't have access to it, because two million years ago it got bred out of us because it didn't have survival value, in spite of what Terence McKenna says. So the wiring of the brain can use a psychedelic, but the transmitter that makes it a functional network is not available.

DAVID: How did you first start designing drugs? And from where do the two of you draw this courage to take unknown substances into your body?

ALEXANDER: It doesn't take that much courage. You're not foolish. You don't take a whole teaspoonful to see if you burp. (*laughter*) You start out with a reasonable estimate of what you think might be an effective level, and you divide that by whatever number your wisdom and judgment tell you.

> *You don't take a whole teaspoonful to see if you burp.*

DAVID: Nonetheless, you're venturing off into the unknown.

ALEXANDER: Admittedly, the first time is an unknown, but you start with a level at which it would be hard to believe it would have an effect. Almost never are you surprised, and when you are surprised, you learn from it.

ANN: What takes real courage is being on the street or at a rave and somebody gives you a little packet of something and it doesn't say what it is or how much it is.

DAVID: Well, some people would call that stupidity rather than courage.

ALEXANDER: People call what I do stupid, too. (*laughter*) But I know what I have, and I know its purity, and I know I can take it a second time.

REBECCA: You also have a number system that helps you to measure your reaction to a drug. It certainly beats having to come up with a barrel-load of adjectives to describe what's happening.

ANN: Yes, and it's helpful to the research group also. Everybody knows when it's not just a plus 2. Perhaps it's a plus 2.65. (*laughter*)

ALEXANDER: It does have the value of being applicable not only to psychedelic drugs but to anything, from stimulants to sedatives. At the first level, you're aware of something going on, but you're not aware of how long it goes on. At the next level, you're aware how long it goes on, but you can't give a *name* to what's happening. At the third level, whether or not you know how long it goes on or can give a name to what's happening, you don't choose to go out and do anything else because you're not totally in command of your physical and mental capacities. Each of these levels is a different degree of acceptance of the drug's action.

REBECCA: What therapeutic value have you found for the drug MDMA? Why was it made illegal?

ANN: I worked for two years as a co-therapist with a highly trained hypnotherapist before MDMA was made illegal. But psychotherapy with any kind of psychoactive drug was still not generally accepted in the medical community. The many therapists who were using it did not publish, because it was not widely known and accepted by their peers.

   One of the reasons that MDMA was made Schedule I so quickly was that the DEA found it in a lab that was making something else that was illegal, and decided to sweep it in with the rest of the stuff. They knew nothing about it.

ALEXANDER: One of the rationalizations for it having been scheduled at all was that a group in Chicago was studying the effects of MDA and had found some serotonin neuron changes in experimental animals. A member of this group was on *Donahue* and spoke about this. Immediately they said, "Well, if that happens with MDA . . . MDMA has almost the same name, it's almost the same compound, maybe it would also be a negative." In the report that came out it was stated that there are a lot of similarities between the two drugs, and that was one of the rationales for immediate emergency scheduling.

DAVID: But there actually is some evidence that MDMA causes degeneration of the dendrites.

ALEXANDER: Yes. It's temporary. The consequence of that is not understood. It's also species-specific: monkeys do, rats do, dogs don't, mice don't, and the effects in humans are unknown.

DAVID: So it's questionable how accurate the spinal tap studies were that showed that there was less serotonin.

ALEXANDER: The results are ambiguous. There were two basic studies. One of them found no measurable changes. All these were of people who were alleged to have used the drug recently, but they did not make the very necessary check to see if the drug was in the person. If it's not in the person, you may be looking at long-term residues of something that may not be MDMA. The other study showed no significant difference, but it was "suggestive." (*laughter*)

REBECCA: Describe to us some of the applications of MDMA.

ANN: The most valuable effect of MDMA is that it enables insight. The patient or the client may regard the possibility of having insight into himself as a very threatening thing. One of the problems that most human beings suffer from is the suspicion that the core essence of who they are deep down is a monster. There is this terrible fear that when you get down to it, you'll discover that the essential you is a rotten little slime-bag.

> *The most valuable effect of MDMA is that it enables insight.*

MDMA, in some way we don't yet understand, removes that fear. It not only allows you to take a really deep look at who you are, but also shows you that you're a combination of angels and demons and that they're all valid. Apart from the removal of the fear, there is also a kind of good-humored acceptance that this drug allows you to feel. There is a validation of the self, which is a miraculous and marvelous thing to experience. MDMA does not remove common-sense caution—you don't cross the road at the red light—but this deep-seated fear is gone.

It is also an extraordinary tool for discovering repressed memories. When I was doing therapy, a great many of our patients were women who were professionals in the child-abuse field. An extraordinary number of them had gone into the field not knowing that they themselves had been sexually abused as children. MDMA brought out these memories. It is a tremendous uncoverer, but with the uncovering is a gentle, compassionate validation and acceptance.

We also worked with married couples. MDMA allows two people who are having problems to forget the defensiveness of you-said-that-first-no-I-didn't. They can drop all that and get hold of the feelings of love again.

One of the most moving things that happened was when Sasha and I gave MDMA to a couple who ended up holding hands again and being able to reaffirm the commitment they had. Two weeks later their older son was diagnosed with leukemia. He died four years ago. They said that if they hadn't had that day with MDMA, they didn't know if they could have supported each other through what was an extremely difficult time. One of the things I want to do in our next book, *TIHKAL,* is to write about psycho-therapy with psychedelics.

> *The patient would also have to be able to deal with the fact that they would be committing a felony.*

After MDMA was made illegal, all the therapists who had been offering it told us they would never quit. Of course, the entire method of offering it would change. They would have to know the patient for at least a year in ordinary therapy before they even mentioned it. The patients would also have to be able to deal with the fact that they would be committing a felony. I've used the phrase "MDMA is penicillin for the soul," because that is exactly the way therapists feel about it. It is already used legally in therapeutic settings in Switzerland.

REBECCA: MDMA seems to work very differently from traditional therapeutic drugs. Thorazine is designed to *suppress* what's happening to the patient, whereas MDMA opens it all up.

ANN: It also requires a different kind of training of the therapist. Handling one particular person's psyche for six hours is very different from doing it for fifty minutes.

REBECCA: PCP has a bad reputation because many people have become extremely violent while under its influence. Is there a drug, do you think, that could turn the Dalai Lama into a raving sociopath?

ALEXANDER: In my case, PCP didn't release any aggressive tendencies at all.

REBECCA: Why does it have this reputation, then? Isn't it perhaps more likely to cause aggression than, say, marijuana?

ALEXANDER: PCP, like ketamine, is an anesthetic—people don't get the feedback of pain. They don't know that they're exceeding their normal muscular capacities. So the anesthetic aspects of it could allow violent behavior simply because people may not be able to feel the consequences of their violence.

DAVID: I spent years working in psychiatric hospitals, and when somebody came in with a psychotic episode triggered by LSD—which was very rare—it was far less extreme than one triggered by PCP.

ALEXANDER: It's an entirely different action on the nervous system. Most of the psychedelics, as with most of the stimulants, are usually considered *sympathomimetics*—they imitate the sympathetic side of the nervous system. PCP, ketamine and datura are *parasympatholytics*. Instead of actively participating in encouraging one side of the nervous system, they fail to discourage the other side of the nervous system when these two sides are in balance. Things shift in a direction either because you're pulling a certain way or because you are releasing the restraints that keep you from going that way.

The analogy I give is the dilation of the eye. The pupil of the eye is dilated because of two opposite things. One, you have things that are pulling it open, and two, you have sphincter muscles that try to keep it closed. So if you give a stimulant or a psychedelic, that activates the puller-opener mechanism, and the eye dilates. The sphincter muscles are okay; they're just overpowered. If you force a light in that person's eye, you get a reflexive closing down of the pupil, and then it'll open up again.

Now, if you give something that craps up the sphincter muscles, like ketamine, the eye dilates because the radials are pulling it open and the sphincters don't have any power to keep it from happening. If you flash a light in that person's eye, it doesn't close, because the mechanism that closes it doesn't work.

REBECCA: Why is it that the parasympatholytics—datura, belladonna, PCP, and ketamine—have this reputation for being the somewhat darker and weirder members of the psychedelic family.

ALEXANDER: You have amnesia for what's going on in there. There's a dreamlike quality. You have an idea of what's happening, but the details are elusive.

> *I have never experi-enced what could be called a hallucination.*

ANN: I have never experienced what could be called a hallucination. The word *hallucinogen* is one we really don't like.

ALEXANDER: I've talked to people to whom that has happened. But the same thing can be said of finding Christ at a revival meeting. Suddenly, there it was!

ANN: I have a prejudice against anything that causes amnesia. What's the point? If you can't remember, you can't learn anything!

ALEXANDER: There was a person who was giving his impressions while on ketamine. Just before he stopped talking entirely he said, "I think I see it, I think I finally have it, in fact I know I have it, it's completely clear, it's obvious . . ." This went on for hours, and it turned out that it was the sole of someone's shoe!

ANN: I like your question: Is there a drug that could turn the Dalai Lama into a sociopath? I suspect that the Dalai Lama has developed his own consciousness sufficiently that he is already acquainted with this animal.

> *During psychedelic therapy, you eventu-ally have to go to the monster and get to know it.*

So he's already made his choices. During psychedelic therapy, you eventually have to go to the monster and get to know it. The Jungians go as far as getting a good look at it and accepting that it's there. What we do is we go into it and *look through its eyes*, so that we become it.

I think the worst terror a human being can experience is when he or she is facing doing that, because we're all afraid that we're going to get stuck in the demon. What you have to realize is that you have already made your choices of what side you're going to be on in this life. You have basically chosen whether you're going to be a nurturing person rather than a de-stroyer, and so on.

Once you get inside the demon, the first thing you experience is the absolute lack of fear, and then you begin to recognize that this is also the survivor aspect of yourself. There's a part that takes care of *you*. Then it begins to transform, and you recognize its quality of total selfishness—it's going to take care of you and nobody else, right?—but it *is* your ally. And then you begin to recognize its positive aspects.

DAVID: That's interesting, because part of the therapeutic process for people with multiple personality disorder involves an understanding that each personality has a particular function.

ANN: Absolutely. This is why I believe that all psychedelic use, even if it's at a rave, is part of a spiritual search. My suspicion is that psychedelics are going to be accepted, if they ever are, only when they are seen as tools for spiritual development. But the trouble is that the West basically treats the unconscious as the enemy, as if only an ax murderer will be found in there! "For God's sake, repress it!" (*laughter*)

> *. . . the West basically treats the unconscious as the enemy, as if only an ax murderer will be found in there!*

DAVID: Because drug use can present serious problems, every society needs a well thought-out drug policy. The American government's persecution of drug users through the criminal justice system has, in the face of rational thinking, been a totally unsuccessful attempt at fighting drug abuse and has seriously eroded many of our constitutional rights. What do you see as the cause behind the zealously fought "War on Drugs," and what kind of drug policy do you envision for a tolerant society of the future?

ALEXANDER: Well, there are two changes I see as indispensable. One is that the laws will have to change, and that is going to require the other part, which is honest education and distribution of information about drugs and their actions. The term *abuse* is used nowadays to mean any use of a drug that you don't approve of.

> *The term* **abuse** *is used nowadays to mean any use of a drug that you don't approve of.*

DAVID: For a long time I thought all drugs should be legal and available to everybody. Then I read Mark Klieman's book *Against Excess*. The cost of drug abuse to the taxpayer is a point he brings up.

ALEXANDER: Well, if someone has a drug abuse problem and he requires medical treatment, is that worse than having a drug abuse problem and being in prison, which also puts a strain on the tax system? One of the reasons you can't rationally pinpoint harm reduction is because you cannot measure harm. What is the harm of a person using a drug that is not approved by society? To one person it's trivial, to another person, whose son has just died from an overdose, it's immense.

So you can't put a quantitative value on harm. Also, if you want to reduce harm—and this is the argument for the drug war—you can't measure the reduction. Lastly, the thing you do to reduce harm itself does harm. If you remove drug laws, you have ten thousand unemployed law-enforcement people—and they are going to see that in an entirely different light. On the other hand, they passed a law in Florida that if you're on welfare and you go into prenatal care and test positive for illegal drugs in your urine, you may suffer the confiscation of your child. Instead of facing the possible loss of her child, a woman just won't go in for the prenatal exam. What's the harm? You can't calculate it.

What would be the damage to society from changing the drug laws? If you look at it through one lens, you can see that it's going to be horrendous, and if you look through another lens, you can see that it's going to be a lifesaver.

REBECCA: I was in a hardware store, and there was this big sign up that read, "We ensure that our employees are tested for drugs." A strong *1984* feeling came over me. What do you think about urine tests?

ALEXANDER: It's intolerable! There's no basis for a urine test unless there's a reason to believe that a person is incompetent in some way.

DAVID: Even then, you should measure their performance, not their urine.

ALEXANDER: Exactly. If you run a bus into a group of pedestrians and you stagger off the bus and go into the nearest bar for a drink, there may possibly be reason for a urine test. If a person is going to fly an airplane, and before he boards the plane you take a sample of his urine and send it off to Florida for analysis, it doesn't protect the people on that flight at all!

> *You have no protection, even today, for the presumption of innocence ... the taking of a urine sample is a presumption of guilt.*

You have no protection, even today, for the presumption of innocence—that doesn't exist in the Constitution. The taking of a urine sample is a presumption of guilt.

REBECCA: The drug laws haven't changed anything in the Constitution, so why are we all getting this nasty feeling that our constitutional rights are being eaten away?

ALEXANDER: It's how they are being interpreted. The perversion of the laws that were written with good intent but have been allowed to be eroded is something that the Constitution can't even touch. I can show you the original writings of the social security law, which says that your social security number should remain private.

The original laws of income tax documents say that your submission of an income tax form to the federal government shall be a private correspondence. Needless to say, that has been scrapped. You now have to get fingerprinted to obtain a driver's license, but California state law states that fingerprinting serves one function only: to identify a person in conjunction with a criminal charge. The measures that they can go to is frightening.

REBECCA: You talked in *PIHKAL* about how racism has been one of the root causes of prejudice against various drugs.

ALEXANDER: Right. The connection between racism and drugs started in the public consciousness with the building of the transcontinental railway. To save on labor costs, we hired Chinese immigrants, and they brought with them the practice of opium use. More and more regulations were put into place to limit and control access to opium, which was soon considered a social evil. The marijuana laws were put into effect to control Mexicans coming over the border, and crack cocaine is nowadays very much associated with blacks in the inner cities.

REBECCA: What benefits have you both received from taking psychedelic substances?

ALEXANDER: I think I've learned about myself a little more thoroughly from the inside out, and I've learned to take myself a little less seriously. I've also learned not to take anything I hear as gospel—even if I say it myself! (*laughter*)

> *I've also learned not to take anything I hear as gospel—even if I say it myself!*

ANN: Psychedelics have allowed me not only to explore myself and my own levels of consciousness to an extraordinary extent, but by doing so I feel that I'm beginning to understand what the human consciousness is. I also have a compulsion to understand what the universal consciousness is. Let's aim as high as we can! The exploration is never dull.

There are so many kinds of knowing, and the kinds of knowing that have the most impact are unexplainable. But I like to try to put into words the incomprehensible things that I find. These same experiences are in everybody's psyche, so if I find the right words, I may be able to elicit some sort of response from the unconscious of the reader and perhaps encourage people to be less afraid of understanding themselves.

REBECCA: What would you say to someone who suggested that drug use was simply a form of escapism?

> *It is amazing to me that people use the term "escape" in association with psychedelics.*

ANN: It is amazing to me that people use the term "escape" in association with psychedelics. I've found them to be the most incredibly hard work, and I've never "escaped" with any psychedelic experience.

ALEXANDER: The same thing could be said about going to a symphony orchestra and listening to concerts, or going to church. These could also be looked upon as escape.

ANN: The fact that we use the word "escape" that way implies that everybody in this culture regards what they call reality as a grim and miserable thing.

ALEXANDER: The prefix "eu" means "normal." "Euthyroid" means you have a normal thyroid function. The word "euphoria" means that this is the way you should feel. If you don't feel the way you should feel, that would be *dysphoric*.

> *This culture regards a state of euphoria as something abnormal!*

ANN: This culture regards a state of euphoria as something abnormal!

REBECCA: Have either of you had to face the problem of addiction?

ALEXANDER: I have with nicotine, but not with any of the other substances I've used.

ANN: The whole idea of using psychedelics is to train yourself to a different kind of perception, which you should be able to use without drugs. Most spiritual teachers say that you should develop the altered states in a "natural" way and not use drugs to do it. Sasha says that is the equivalent of saying you should never go to a symphony or listen to a recording but that you should produce the music yourself, and you should not use any tools other than your own body.

Well, heck! Life is made interesting by giving yourself different forms. Yes, it's wonderful to sing and play the flute yourself, but it's also wonderful to go to a symphony.

REBECCA: You do need to be disciplined and motivated to reproduce that state when you're not on the drug.

ANN: Right. You must have an incentive to develop your own abilities. I've found that insight is something that can be learned. You can learn to observe your own thoughts. You begin to get a different relationship to time, and to yourself, and to the mayfly. These things don't need drugs, but drugs can show you where you can go.

REBECCA: Although you both believe strongly in legalization, do you think that some guidelines must be established for drug use?

ALEXANDER: Absolutely. Giving a drug to a person who is not, in the opinion of people who have worked with it, developed enough to use it, giving a drug without consent, giving out false information about a drug—all these need to be controlled.

ANN: I'd like to make the rather obvious comparison of psychedelics with sex. Nobody in their right mind would say that sex is bad for us, but no one would advise someone under a certain age to try it! There is a certain stage of growth you need to go through before you're ready for either.

DAVID: Terence McKenna claims that there is a spirit, or a conscious intelligence, that dwells within certain psychedelic plants. In *PIHKAL*, you discuss how at times you've felt the presence of some entity or force guiding your work. Do you see this as being related to what Terence has claimed? And how do you explain this phenomenon?

ALEXANDER: I think this is like the intuitive going through a dark room and being able to find the door. You don't see in the dark, and yet you know there's a door there. As you get more and more experienced at working with plants, or working in the laboratory and designing new structures, you get more of a feel for why they are and what they are.

> *Is this talking to leprechauns? No. But it has some of the smell of that.*

One of the beauties of organic chemistry is that you cannot make a relationship between a continuing change here and a continuing result there. You cannot extrapolate from one molecule to another with any more confidence than you can extrapolate from one plant to another. So you begin to assign certain characteristics to what you're working with. Is this talking to leprechauns? No. But it has some of the smell of that. (*laughter*)

ANN: I think that there are forms of energy that some people see as elves or fairies. Whether they see these or not seems to depend more on whether the culture they live in allows for seeing such things. The Irish are famous for it. Is this because a certain kind of energy associated with natural things is translating itself telepathically into an acceptable form for the human who is looking at it? It's an open question.

ALEXANDER: How do you discover the action of a molecule? A molecule, when it's hatched, is like a baby. There's no personality there. As the baby develops, your relationship to the baby develops, and eventually the baby forms into something with its own shape and character.

The first time I made MDOH I distilled it, as I like to do before I make the salt. I found that it began a threshold activity at around eighty milligrams, but I didn't know that something was amiss. I ran some tests and discovered that when I did the distillation of MDOH, I had gotten it sufficiently hot to split up the hydroxy group. I had made a mixture of the base without the hydroxy group, which had gone on to the MDOH and become an oxine. The material I was left with was MDA. So I had accidentally rediscovered the property of MDA.

I went back and made MDOH again, keeping the vacuum temperature down, and I came out of it with a brand-new compound that I never would have made before. So from a divorced position, I had to come back and reinstitute a rapport, because the material I had thought I had met, I had not met. You don't discover these things; you interact and develop them together. If you want to incarnate elves into the materials, that's fine, but either way it's a relationship.

REBECCA: That sounds very similar to the way alchemists viewed their work.

ALEXANDER: Very much so. I was listening to Terence McKenna years ago at Esalen. He was talking about how if a drug comes from nature it's okay, but if it comes from a lab it's suspect. Suddenly he realized that I was sitting in the audience. (*laughter*) In essence I said, "Terence, I'm as natural as they come. To me there's no difference between making a chemical in the laboratory that's new and that you can get to learn and interact with, and interacting with a plant."

DAVID: As John Lilly said, "Plants are chemists, too."

ANN: Exactly. And some of them will kill you. Just because it's natural doesn't mean it's benign.

ALEXANDER: I've studied alchemy a bit, and it's very much about feedback. Who cares if you melt and fuse lead ten thousand times? At the end of it, you don't come out with anything but ten-thousand-times melted and fused lead! But the doing of it—that's *meditation.*

DAVID: Do you see a relationship between alchemy and shamanism?

ALEXANDER: Yes. They are both teachers. A shaman is a person who allows you to be healed by the interaction with him, and alchemy is the same way.

REBECCA: The biochemist Rupert Sheldrake proposes the idea that the characteristics of a compound develop through time, creating a morphic field that influences all similar forms. Because of this idea, people such as Terence McKenna suggest that newly developed drugs are soulless compared to something like psilocybin, which has been used by shamans probably for thousands of years. How do you respond to this?

ANN: That's like saying a newborn baby is soulless. There is a soul there; it just has to learn to relate.

ALEXANDER: Initially I had a scientific reluctance about Rupert's theory, but I've seen how he does it and I've grown to like the idea. He has complete candidness and honesty. He's trying to find things that *don't* fit into his theory—and that I like.

REBECCA: Have you experienced parallel discovery?

> *Secrecy is anathema. Everything you do, you share.*

ALEXANDER: Secrecy is anathema. Everything you do, you share. But I remember the first time I got into sulphur. Nothing was going right, just black tars and terrible smells. I was working along the same lines as a person in Indiana, and about the same time we both developed separate psychedelics. It was almost as if the stars had aligned.

I'm reading a marvelous book at the moment, which talks about how, up to the time of Galileo, there was a complete synthesis of religious orthodoxy and science, because it was part and parcel of the church. They broke apart because of Galileo and Copernicus's contributions. In a sense, we've reconverged back to a synthesis of Genesis and the Big Bang, to a dogma that everyone takes on faith. And you don't allow the slightest challenge!

REBECCA: I interviewed the head of the Flat Earth Society, and I found it very liberating to allow myself to question something so ingrained as the roundness of the earth! (*laughter*) In your book you describe many mind-expanding experiences when you developed a sensitivity to the sacred life forces. With this consciousness in mind, how do you feel about the practice of vivisection?

ALEXANDER: I believe there are times when it is necessary. I used to do all my studies on rats and dogs, but I wasn't learning enough to justify it, so I stopped entirely. I think if it's possible to extend a person's life at the expense of an animal, then it's justified. Until recently pigs were essential to maintain the life of people with diabetes. If you were a total vegetarian, would raising pigs to obtain insulin to protect the lives of people who have diabetes be justified ?

REBECCA: No, it wouldn't. I know of a woman who claims to control her diabetes without insulin by eating something called bitter melon, which is native to Sri Lanka. There is much evidence to suggest that there is a vast reservoir of untapped medical lore and resources on the earth.

ANN: One of Lauren Van der Post's books is about a race of pygmies in Africa. Before they kill an animal, they send out deep thanks and gratitude to it, asking to be forgiven for the fact that they are going to kill it. In a sense, they enter into an emotional contract with that animal. My feeling is that animal experimentation is necessary in this culture, but I would pass a law that the only people allowed to work with animals in a laboratory would be those who love animals. If you love an animal, you are not going to be able to stand giving it pain.

In laboratories, people are encouraged not to form any kind of attachment to the animals they're using. I think the opposite should be the case. Using an animal's pain to develop cosmetics is inexcusable, but when it is to save lives, I think that is a different question. I believe that the whole environmental movement was largely influenced with the taking of psychedelics in the sixties, because the first experience that everyone has is the oneness of nature.

REBECCA: Do you believe that there might be a teleological reason for why psychedelics exist?

ANN: Sure. How on earth did anyone ever discover the psychedelic properties of the peyote cactus, or something that's only active as a snuff? Have you ever tasted peyote? Your instinct says, "That's poisonous!" Considering the fact that we create consensual reality, some part of us may have assigned certain plants the ability to open those doors.

ALEXANDER: The evolution of the animal and plant kingdoms seem to be complementary to one another. But whereas you have the origin of the human in the Old World, ninety percent of psychedelic plants have been seen natively only in the New World. It's certainly not from a lack of diligence in searching for them! (*laughter*)

> *. . . ninety percent of psychedelic plants have been seen natively only in the New World.*

REBECCA: That's interesting. What procedures do you use when testing out a new drug? And what do you do if everyone's experience is different?

ALEXANDER: When I test a new drug on myself I use extremely small levels, with much space between each time to eliminate the effects of tolerance. When I get up to a level that I feel comfortable with, Ann and I share it and see if indeed we have the same responses. Then we introduce it to individuals within the research group.

We often find that some of the materials have radically different responses within the group. I had to abandon a whole family of compounds, which I called the Alephs because they were too erratic. Someone would have an overstimulating experience on two milligrams, and on seven milligrams the next person would experience nothing at all! We also have the occasional idiosyncratic difference from day to day of one person to one chemical.

TMA6 was a compound I had worked on and abandoned because it was not that interesting. We were exploring it because it was an opening to a new family of compounds. It was clearly active. You knew you were in an altered place, but you couldn't give it a name or a character. There were no visuals and no time distortion—nothing. So we threw it open to the group, and we were all up against the wall! When I went to take a pee in the bathroom, the wallpaper came out and shook hands! (*laughter*) Everyone had an intense experience.

> **When I went to take a pee in the bathroom, the wallpaper came out and shook hands!**

ANN: Sasha goes through the boring stuff—tiny bits increased very gradually over weeks and weeks. I come in at the exciting point. (*laughter*) If we find certain things, we don't pursue use of the substance. For example, if my emotions are flattened it's an absolute no-no to go on with it. Also, if we're not interested in touching each other, then there's something wrong. Also, of course, you learn to spot signs of impending nervous-system trouble, like the possibility of a convulsion.

ALEXANDER: It's like soldiers marching across the bridge. If you break step, you're not going to have the rest of the bridge getting to some resonance that could lead to a catastrophic event. You search out your thought patterns and abort them before they come to any consequence. Then you start another thought pattern and stop it. If you don't let things consummate, that diffuses things, and pretty soon you realize that it's not necessary any more. The other answer is phenobarb, which is much easier. (*laughter*)

ANN: The group doesn't get any of these things until we've gone up to a plus 3, and usually beyond that to the point where it's too much. So we know for sure that it's not going to attack our nervous systems.

DAVID: What are some of the basic guidelines that you would recommend to an individual who was experimenting with psychedelics?

ALEXANDER: Learn everything you can about the material, and stay away from all information that's clearly geared to encourage or discourage its use.

ANN: Doing your first experience with a very trusted friend who has taken the substance before is very important. That sort of companionship can turn a very bad trip into a very good learning experience. Your psyche is very eager to have you learn things, and if you can develop an acceptance and a calmness, you can overcome a lot.

DAVID: What type of drugs do you see being developed in the future? How do you see pharmacological tools being used to expand potential in the areas of creativity, intelligence, and spiritual understanding?

ALEXANDER: In this direction, I think anything that the human is capable of doing through the mind is duplicable pharmacologically—it's all chemistry upstairs. I think anything from insight to paranoia to joy to fear can be reproduced chemically.

The fact that there are specific receptor sites for specific materials in the body, which duplicate the actions of drugs from outside the body, implies that the receptor sites at which the drugs operate are there because the human produces neurotransmitters for that same purpose.

ANN: I think that depending on the way you interact with any particular psychedelic, creativity and imagination can arise. Basically, you're giving yourself permission to use these powers. I can't see a psychedelic being particularly creative.

DAVID: But they may be developed with more specificity. You developed a drug whose only property was to create auditory distortion.

ALEXANDER: Right, that's a good example. I'm intrigued by that one because most of the spontaneous schizophrenic states have auditory rather than visual components. If there is a physical correlate to schizophrenia, you could deposit this material in a person and see where it accumulates. You could play strange noises and see if it accumulated faster or slower.

REBECCA: How many psychedelics have you synthesized?

ALEXANDER: Around one hundred.

REBECCA: And how many of those are illegal?

ALEXANDER: About fifteen. The analog law will label a drug illegal on the grounds of it being "substantially similar" to an already existing illegal drug. I was once asked in a drug case down south if two drugs were substantially similar. I said that the question had no meaning. The chemist, who came from the Ventura County crime lab, said that two things are substantially similar if they are over fifty percent identical. I just abandoned ship at that point. It's a lot of gibberish!

DAVID: How has your relationship influenced your psychedelic journeys?

ANN: If you're going to do psychedelic exploring the ideal is to have a partner who is on the same wavelength. There is, needless to say, a certain amount of vulnerability when you take these substances, and you have to totally trust the other person. The only disadvantage is that I suspect we pick up each other's responses a little faster than we should.

I had one experience that really startled me. I got up in the morning and went to wash the dishes from the night before, and I realized I was not at baseline. It was nice, but I was wondering, "What caused this?" Sasha came in, and I was wondering if I should say anything to him when he came up with the information that he had taken a sample of a new drug that morning!

DAVID: Do you think you might have been exuding pheromones, which the other person was picking up?

ALEXANDER: That's possible, but you're normally unaware of the extraordinary vocabulary of body language. Just the way people carry themselves or the way they respond to a stimulus can give them away. And if Ann's washing dishes, I know we've got a problem. (*laughter*)

DAVID: What projects are you currently working on?

ALEXANDER: Tryptamines. (*laughter*)

Matthew Fox

"To connect with the great river we all need a path, but when
you get down there there's only one river."

Counting Our Original Blessings
with Matthew Fox

*While for many being a Christian implies generous portions of intoler-
ance, self-righteous proselytizing, and patriarchal zeal, some have dug
deeper into the well of the Western mystical tradition and have drunk from
sweeter waters. Instead of embracing the religions of the East, they are
finding parallel philosophies and equally enlightened gurus amidst the dis-
carded relics of the Christian church.*

*Matthew Fox, a Dominican priest, theologian, writer, and teacher, is
one such person. He has been called "a green prophet" by the archbishop
of Canterbury, and, by the Vatican, a dangerous radical, heretic, and blas-
phemer. The author of over a dozen books, his best-known work,* Original
Blessing, *rejects the idea of humanity's innate sin and inevitable punishment, and instead proposes a creation-centered spirituality—a philosophy
of mystical artistry, universal compassion, and the celebration of the divine within each human soul.*

*In 1960 Fox joined the Dominican order. He was ordained seven years
later, and after acquiring a master's degree in philosophy and theology, he
went to study in Paris, where he earned a doctorate in spirituality. In 1977
he founded the Institute of Culture and Creation Spirituality at Holy Names
College in Oakland, California, and began to formulate educational programs, encouraging participation from all creeds, races, and subcultures.*

*In 1988 the Vatican, fearing Fox's popularity, silenced him for a year.
He used the time to visit and listen to the liberation theologians of Central
and South America, and he returned to the States more dedicated than ever
to sharing his message. After the year had expired, his first words were
"As I was saying . . . " In 1993, after a number of failed attempts by the
papacy at proving him a heretic, which would have led to his excommuni-
cation, Matthew Fox was dismissed from the Dominican order.*

*As church pews gather dust in the twilight, Matthew Fox's lectures are
standing room only. The clergy at the Vatican must be wringing their hands
as he speaks freely about the motherhood of God, the spiritual relevance of
environmental consciousness and love for animals, the interconnectedness
of all religions, and the acceptance of homosexuality as a viable lifestyle.*

That Jesus' message might actually have something to do with progressive social action is an idea that the church has traditionally sidestepped with dexterity, but listening to Matthew Fox, it is easy to entertain the idea that the true spirit of Christ is arising to turn the tables once again. This interview was held on August 8, 1993 at Matthew Fox's home in Oakland.

RMN

DAVID: What were you like as a child, and what childhood experiences shaped your spirituality?

MATTHEW: Well, I grew up in Wisconsin, and I was certainly influenced by the beauty of the land there. I was also influenced by the presence of the Native American spirit, and from the time I was very little I had Indian dreams. It was a university town, and the whole issue of ideas became very important to me. I was Catholic, and my best friends were Jewish or agnostic, and we'd get into these philosophical debates that were a lot of fun. There was a priest I knew, and he got me reading Thomas Aquinas, G. K. Chesterton, and so forth. So the intellectual side of faith became very important to me.

REBECCA: Were you brought up a strict Catholic?

MATTHEW: My father was Irish-Catholic; my mother was half Jewish and half Anglican, and although she became a Catholic, she always kept her freedom. So it was a very ecumenical household. When I was a teenager, we lived in a large house near the university with my six brothers and sisters. As they went on to college, my parents would rent out their rooms to foreign graduate students.

So I spent my high school years next door to a sikh from India who wore a turban and cooked wheat germ at three in the morning, a man from Venezuela who would pull his shirt up to show his bullfighting scars, a communist from Yugoslavia, and an atheist from Norway. It was a very broad education.

When I was in college I brought a friend home for the weekend, and afterward he shook his head and said, "God, it's like being at the United Nations!" (*laughter*) I was never that interested in religion, but I've always been interested in spirituality, and that's how I got interested in theology.

DAVID: How do you define the difference?

MATTHEW: Well, I wish there *weren't* such a big difference between religion and spirituality, but people have to be very clear about the difference and not simply settle for religion. Spirituality is about *experience,* and religion, unfortunately, ends up being about the sociology of the structures, in news reports of popes coming and buildings being bought. Of course, they also influence each other. For example, last week here in the Bay Area, the front-page news of the *Chronicle* was that the Catholic church was trying to sell twelve of its churches. Why? Because they have only thirty-five people coming to church on Sunday.

> *Religion has to sell its buildings. Spirituality is connecting to the source of things ...*

So that's religion. Religion has to sell its buildings. Spirituality is connecting to the source of things, to the source of wonder and awe and pain and suffering and creativity and justice and compassion. Religion ought to be about that, but unfortunately it wanders off the path.

DAVID: Would you say that spirituality is based upon one's own experience, while religion is based upon someone else's experience?

> *Jesus was spiritual—would you call him religious?*

MATTHEW: (*laughter*) That's good, but I wouldn't stress the "own" as distinct from the communal. At your deepest depth, you are in touch with other people's joy and other people's sorrow—so it's not just a private journey, it's a journey into the ocean of experience. Jesus was spiritual—would you call him religious? He was taking on the religious establishment of his day. He was trying to bring out the juices of his tradition, and this got him into a lot of trouble. That happens all along the line. It's happening today, too, with liberation theology.

Bede Griffiths was a monk who died recently. He ran an ashram in India for Hindus and Christians for fifty years. He said that if Christianity can't recover its mystical tradition and teach it, it should just fold up and go out of business, because it has nothing to offer. I agree 100 percent. Spirituality is about mysticism, which is about awe and wonder and the prophetic dimension of standing up to injustice because it interferes with our wonder.

DAVID: How did your interest in theology develop?

MATTHEW: I had a lot of mystical experiences as a child, and as an adolescent, even more. I remember when I was in ninth grade walking into the living room when someone was playing Beethoven's Seventh Symphony, and my soul wanted to dance. When I was a junior, I read Tolstoy's *War and Peace*, and it's because of Tolstoy that I went into the priesthood, because I wanted to examine the spiritual experience I was having with literature and music.

I think that people are born mystics. We are all mystics as children, but it's taken away from us as we grow older. It's taken away subtly by education, which trains the left brain and ignores the right brain. They take away your crayons right when you need them most—at puberty. When you should be getting to your cosmic soul, they give you football and shopping malls. I was fortunate. I had polio when I was thirteen, so I let go of my desire to be a football hero like my brothers. When I was sick in the hospital—they couldn't tell whether I would walk again—I met a very spiritual person who had been a monk before he married and had five kids. He became kind of a mentor for me and showed me that there was another path in life, besides the obvious.

> *They take away your crayons right when you need them most—at puberty.*

So when I got my legs back a year or two later, I was very overwhelmed with gratitude, and I said, "I'm not going to waste my legs. I'm not going to take this for granted." I wasn't going to waste my life. I was going to do something interesting.

REBECCA: Gratitude seems to be very much an aspect of your spirituality. Prayer has traditionally been used to ask favors.

MATTHEW: Yuck! That's Santa Claus in the sky! Meister Eckhart said that if the only prayer you ever say in your life is thank you, that will suffice.

> *Meister Eckhart said that if the only prayer you ever say in your life is thank you, that will suffice.*

DAVID: Don't you think that it takes almost losing something in order to appreciate it?

MATTHEW: (*laughter*) Unfortunately, yes. And that's what religion won't tell you—that we're losing the planet. We have everything to lose. It's basic. And that's why the only resolution is an awakening of gratitude and reverence for the planet, and falling in love in more than an anthropocentric fashion. In that experience there is an excess of gratitudinal energy, and that's what we need to change our destiny.

REBECCA: Could you explain to us some of the core values of creation spirituality, and how they differ from Fall/Redemption philosophy?

> *Animals . . . don't sit around feeling sorry for themselves and counting their sins.*

MATTHEW: Well of course, one is why I called my book *Original Blessing*, as opposed to *Original Sin*. My problem with Original Sin is that, first of all, it's so anthropocentric. Sinning is what humans do; all other creatures do not sin. Thomas Merton says every non-two-legged creature is a saint. That's why my spiritual director was that guy [points to a painting of a white spitz on the wall], who died a year ago—my dog, Tristan. Animals and other beings, they just go about their work; they don't sit around feeling sorry for themselves and counting their sins.

REBECCA: My dog does.

MATTHEW: (*laughter*) Well, they do pick up the ambiance. So original blessing is so much more accurate. We know from the nuclear stories that for 15 billion years the universe has been preparing our way—getting the temperature right, the ozone layer balanced, the oxygen level perfect—and it's taken for granted *not* to acknowledge this. Religion that begins with sin is ignoring 15 billion years of amazing preparation.

Another difference is the emphasis that we put on all the images of God. I love that rabbinic phrase that says every time humans walk down the street, we're preceded by hosts of angels who are singing, "Make way, make way, make way for the image of God." What does it mean to be an image of God? It means that we are creative.

Creativity is very important to this whole tradition. In fact, the basic prayer form is what we call *art as meditation*. This is what we do in our teachings. I hire a lot of artists, and we do painting, sculpture, and dance as meditation.

Art is the yoga of the West. Art has been co-opted by capitalism, and so it's always about product and what it costs. The essence of art is the relationship between one's own creativity and matter, whether it's the muscles in dancing, or paints, or the strings of an instrument. Art as meditation awakens the artist in everybody, and when that happens spiritual energy flows.

REBECCA: And in the Fall/Redemption philosophy, creation is seen as a once-and-for all event.

MATTHEW: Well, creativity is not emphasized. You can read those theologians until you're blue in the face. They'll never talk about art or creativity; they just talk about sin and redemption and Jesus, forgetting that Jesus himself was a storyteller, an artist. Another difference is the way they deal with the *via negativa*, the darkness and suffering. You hear these fundamentalists—and *the* Fall/Redemption institution is fundamentalism—saying such things as "AIDS is God's punishment," and "Earthquakes in California are because there are so many gays there." But of course, all those good people out in the Midwest were badly treated by Mother Nature when they got flooded out, right? (*laughter*)

So the darkness is not about guilt. It's about doing something about it and facing it, not denying it or blaming it. The asceticism of Fall/Redemption Christianity has people wearing hair shirts and beating themselves in front of crosses in the basement. I think that

> *You don't have to make up enemies inside or out*—they're already there!

if you're living a full life, you don't have to do that. You don't have to make up enemies inside or out—*they're already there!*

There's a wonderful Native American dance that has to do with facing the enemy, and the teaching is of the enemy being outside *and* the enemy inside. But the point is to pay attention and deal with them, not to wallow in guilt. Cheap religion builds on fear and guilt, and I don't think that was what Jesus was about. He was about driving out the fears.

REBECCA: I'm intrigued about why you chose to remain a Catholic when your philosophy seems so much more closely aligned with Eastern religions.

MATTHEW: Well, a lot of my work has been on the medieval mystics, who have been ignored and condemned. Meister Eckhart was condemned by the church in the fourteenth century and is still on the condemned list, but so was Galileo, for three hundred years. Then there was Hildegard of Bingen, a Renaissance woman of the twelfth century, a musician, poet, painter, healer, scientist, and mystic. The Middle Ages were amazing times. Thomas Aquinas, who my last book was about, was the last theologian to really care about bringing science and religion together. He was condemned three times before they canonized him a saint.

I am a Westerner. We're not going to change the West by going East. The East has a lot to teach us, but essentially it's like a mirror, saying, "Hey, can't you see what's here in your own religion? What are you, stupid?" Carl Jung said that we Westerners cannot be pirates, thieving wisdom from foreign shores as if our own culture were an arid land.

Our religious ancestors were not all stupid, and they were certainly not as stupid as some of the people running the churches today. People like Aquinas, Eckhart, Francis of Assisi, Julian of Norwich, Nicholas of Cusa were all of the same movement. David Bohm, an English physicist, says he owes more to Cusa than to Einstein.

There was a period of about two hundred years, beginning in the eleventh century, when the Goddess came roaring into Christianity. Have you ever been to Chartres Cathedral? It's an incredible experience to be there. It's a temple to the Goddess. And they built five hundred like that all over Europe—to Mary the Goddess.

> *We have a cultural DNA; we have to stir things up and demand things of it.*

So I try to draw on the Western tradition, first because I'm interested in social transformation—a few can go East, but that's almost elitist. We have a cultural DNA; we have to stir things up and demand things of it.

REBECCA: I can understand remaining a Christian, with the insights you've gained, but why did you remain a Catholic? Catholicism doesn't seem to have much to do with personal spiritual experience.

MATTHEW: Catholicism, going back to its medieval mystical tradition, has a rich heritage of spirituality, which it needs to recapture. But I am interested in deep ecumenism. I think that the deeper you go into your own tradition in terms of spirituality, the closer you come to the living waters of wisdom. In this image, God is a great underground river. There are many wells into this river: there's Buddhism, Taosim, Judaism, Sufism, the Goddess, native traditions, and Christianity.

To connect with the great river, we all need a path. But when you get down there, there's only one river. What I'm doing *is* connected with the East. I have a Hindu from India teaching shakti yoga in my program. We teach t'ai chi and aikido. We have Sufis, Buddhists, Jews, Catholics and Protestants, and witches. So the future of religion is interdenomination.

DAVID: But you have a certain kind of loyalty to Christianity.

MATTHEW: Why should I? They just kicked me out! (*laughter*)

DAVID: But it seems that you're working to build a bridge back to people in the Christian tradition.

MATTHEW: I'm interested in bridges. I'm interested in truth.

REBECCA: Was one of your reasons for working within the tradition, rather than branching off from it, so that you could reach a greater number of people?

MATTHEW: Well, I do speak English better than I speak Japanese. I read Latin better than I read Sanskrit. (*laughter*)

REBECCA: Well, you don't have to speak Japanese to be a Zen Buddhist. Have you actually been excommunicated by the Catholic church?

MATTHEW: No. I've just been expelled from the Dominican order. I'm technically still a priest. They can't take that away from me. But they can forbid me to practice. I'm not allowed to give a public mass, et cetera.

REBECCA: What specifically about your views do they object to?

MATTHEW: I think that the real issue is the same problem they have with Latin American liberation theology, and that is that there's a movement around this, and the Catholic church doesn't like movements. Our creation spirituality includes women and gays

> *. . . the Catholic church doesn't like movements.*

and lesbians and artists and native peoples, so it involves the kinds of people who don't have strong voices in the Vatican. It's fear. If I had their world view, I would be threatened by the things I'm teaching, too.

DAVID: Why?

MATTHEW: Because they have a pretty good thing going. You could start with the fact that they're all male.

REBECCA: Have they informed you of exactly what it is they don't approve of in your teachings?

MATTHEW: They gave me a list, yeah. (*laughter*) Their first thing is that I'm a feminist theologian, although I didn't know that it was heresy to be a feminist. Secondly, I call God "mother"—well, I proved that medieval mystics do, and even the Bible does. Thirdly, I call God "child." Well, mystics do this, too. Number four, I don't condemn homosexuals. Number five, I believe in Original Blessing more than Original Sin. Number six, I'm not as depressed as they are. (*laughter*)

REBECCA: Did you get the opportunity to respond?

MATTHEW: You see, they have hundreds of years of experience of how to get people, so it was subtle how they did it. They got the Dominican order to give me a command to leave California and go back to Chicago, which would have meant ending the program and the magazine and the community here. So I refused to do that, and they kicked me out on grounds of disobedience. The real reason was obviously that they wanted me to end the work.

REBECCA: They did silence you for a year, from 1988 to 1989. What did you do during that time?

MATTHEW: I went along with that. I'd never had a sabbatical before, and I went to Brazil, Nicaragua, and Crete. During this time I made some decisions, one of them being that I wouldn't go along with the second silencing, because it was against human dignity.

DAVID: In addition to the overemphasis on Original Sin in Christianity, when you take an overview of all the world religions today, what do you see as some of the primary problems they have, and what can be done to alleviate them?

> *We see that there's no such thing as a Buddhist ocean or a Roman Catholic rainforest . . .*

MATTHEW: I think the primary problem is anthropocentrism. When we put religion in the context of creation, we learn a little humility. We see that there's no such thing as a Buddhist ocean, or a Roman Catholic rainforest, or an Anglican river, or a Lutheran corn field, or a Baptist moon.

The second problem with religion is that it's about religion and not about spirituality. It's that whole thing of pointing to the moon and confusing the finger with the moon. So they should be pointing to spirituality. We should be teaching every thirteen-year-old meditation, including sexual practices that are ways into mysticism and also ways into safe sex.

> *We should be teaching every thirteen-year-old meditation . . .*

The human species can't deal with its moods and resentments. Look at Bosnia—it's all about resentment. We did a summer program in New York, and a fellow showed up from Croatia who had just received an award from the United Nations for his nonviolent work. He said, "I don't have anything against the Serbs or the Muslims. The problem is our politicians, who are building on the resentments. It's their war, not our war."

I think a lot of the Reagan years were about building on resentment, on a backlash against women and against black people. Religion ought to be assisting the human heart to cleanse itself of resentments and hatreds. Unfortunately, it's so often used to make things worse.

REBECCA: Why has the Christian church historically expressed so much fear of nature religions, and thus of nature herself?

MATTHEW: I think the best answer to that comes from Frederick Turner in his book *Beyond Geography,* where he says that when the European Christians came over here, they had suppressed the wilderness inside—sexuality and sensuality. When they saw it being lived by the native people, it came up as something unconscious and violent toward them.

The issue is wilderness. The church in Europe ordered the destruction of the Irish woods to try to get rid of the Celtic spirits. This whole thing is about domesticating the wilderness, but of course, it's also about the wild animals in us—the rage, the anger, the desire, and the lust. The idea was that you had to wipe these out. Meister Eckhart says, "Put on your passions as a bridle of love." It's so nondualistic. You embrace your passions and embrace the wilderness and steer where you need to go. But it's not about stomping out the wilderness.

REBECCA: Is this fear of the wilderness partly the reason the church hasn't come out against the crimes of biocide and geocide?

MATTHEW: Well, that's the third objection I make to religion as it is usually practiced. And it doesn't address these areas because religion is preoccupied with the human.

DAVID: Why do you think the church condemned sexuality and eroticsm?

MATTHEW: It goes back to the patriarchy overtaking the Western church in about the fourth century, when it inherited the empire. There's a statement by one of these ascetic philosophers, Philo: "We must keep down our passions just as we keep down the lower classes." That gives you some insight into history, doesn't it? Passion and compassion are related. A passionate response to injustice is what gives you energy to do something about it. If you can keep that energy down, then those who are running things are safe.

In our culture, television and consumerism are the opium of the people. They keep people from getting in touch with their deep passions. People keep getting fed more and more TV, and more and more things to shop for, so that they don't ask the deeper questions.

DAVID: And creation spirituality approaches eroticism and sexuality in what way?

MATTHEW: Well, as a gift of the universe. There's a story and a history to sexuality. We've been told that it happened about 1.3 billion years ago. It was an increase in the possibilities of evolution and creativity. I think if you want to understand sexuality, you go back to its source. It's really an invitation to be even more creative than we are.

The Song of Songs, a book in the Bible, celebrates lovemaking as a theophany, as an experience of the divine. This is something that we should be bringing back in ritual, in our churches and synagogues, and we should be honoring it. The first lesson in sexuality is to honor the power within yourself and to respect that. Then find out how many different expressions of it there are besides genital expression, which is pretty obvious.

I think that religion and other elements of our culture have ganged up to repress eros . . .

How does it feed into or out of our relations with the earth? Can we be erotic toward the earth? We can be erotic baking bread, making love, or vacuuming the living room. Eros is the love and a passion for life that we bring to whatever we do. So I talk about taking Eros back from the pornographers. I think that religion and other elements of our culture have ganged up to repress eros, which is really a sacred experience.

REBECCA: Do you think the repression of sexuality is largely about the fear of surrendering control?

MATTHEW: Saint Augustine, in the fourth century, was the one who set it all up. He himself said that he didn't want to "lose control." And again, notice how sexual politics links to imperial politics. His whole world view was seized by the church and the empire that married it. But since that time there have been people objecting.

Augustine said, "Spirit is about whatever is not matter." Now just think about that. That's the most dualistic statement you could imagine. That means there's no spirit in bushes or trees or dogs or the water, so you can do whatever you like with them. Thomas Aquinas' divine spirit is present in everything, in all of matter.

DAVID: Timothy Leary said that anything we can define as spiritual is just something that we haven't developed the technology to measure yet.

MATTHEW: Oooh! (*laughter*) I don't like that. I've explored mystery a lot, and mystery is not something you're ever going to *solve*. It's something you live! The Jewish word for spirit means "to live." There's that line in the Book of Wisdom in the Hebrew Bible that says, "This is wisdom, to love life." That's eros.

> *. . . mystery is not something you're ever going to* solve. *It's something you live!*

DAVID: What about paganism and shamanism? What role do they play in creation spirituality?

MATTHEW: These represent the forgotten, shadow side of our own traditions. When Christianity was healthy, it didn't stomp on paganism, it embraced it. A good example is Chartres Cathedral, which is built right on top of the cathedral to the goddess of grain. At that time the church was not stomp-

> *When Christianity was healthy, it didn't stomp on paganism, it embraced it.*

ing on other religions; it was embracing them and bringing them in like a welcoming mother. *Pagan* comes from the word *paganis* which means "a person who lives in the country." A *heathen* is a person who lives on the heath.

The church has put so much venom into stamping out paganism, and it's all about a hatred of ourselves, of our own earthiness. The word *humility* comes from the Latin *humus*, which means "earth." Real humility means acknowledging our relation to the earth and what we have to learn from the native peoples. Of course, they also have things to learn from us. But their forms of prayer—sweat lodges and sun dances and so forth—are powerful ways to pray. And they're powerful because they're not anthropocentric; they're cosmological.

They do things in circles—it's about microcosm and macrocosm. And it's not about reading books. It's not boring to sit in a sweat lodge—it might take you close to death! It's an adventure, and it wakes you up! So we have a lot to learn about ritual from native people, and we have a lot to learn about forgotten aspects of our own spiritual capacities. In our culture, they lock you up if you go into a trance. In those cultures, every member of the tribe is regarded as mystical. They think something's wrong if you *can't* go into a trance. (*laughter*)

DAVID: Most, if not all, world religions are very sexist. What value do you see in reclaiming the Goddess-oriented traditions?

MATTHEW: I think that the return of the Goddess is one of the most important movements of today's hope. The last time the Goddess returned was in the twelfth century, and something really happened. That's when they invented universities, which were not like they are now. They were venues where you went to find your place in the universe—it wasn't about the job market and bureaucracies. It wasn't expensive, either. The student paid his professor directly, and if you didn't like what you were learning, you didn't pay!

The Goddess represents the divine creativity in everybody, and that's why she's often depicted as a pregnant female. What we know about that 25,000-year period when the Goddess reigned in Europe is that there were no artifacts of war anyplace. I think there's an incredible insight here. If you pay attention to creativity itself, you might be able to do something about the war impulse. If you can keep busy enough giving birth, you're too busy to make war. As Eckhart says, "All the images we have for God come from images of ourselves."

If we have just a male image of God, that legitimizes the other patriarchal privileges and forms of oppression—including men towards men—

that go on in the culture. So obviously, we need gender justice in our divinities.

In the West, we have a couple of names for the Goddess besides the Goddess. One is the *Cosmic Christ*, which I think is a euphemism for the

> *The first name given to Jesus in the New Testament is Sophia, "lady wisdom."*

Goddess, because it is about cosmic wisdom, and wisdom is *sophia*. The first name given to Jesus in the New Testament is Sophia, "lady wisdom." This shook up the male establishment so much that the second generation came along and brought in *Logos* to put the brakes on all this woman stuff.

The other name for the feminine side of God is the *Godhead*. You don't hear much about the *Godhead* in Western theology, but all the mystics write about it. Godhead is not a very adequate word—it really means "God-essence." What it's about is the mystery that is the divinity. You hear a lot about the God who creates and redeems and so on, but the Godhead doesn't do anything. It's about nonaction. It's like a great big cosmic mama, and we're all in the Godhead's lap. So what we should be doing in the West is balancing our God-talk with Godhead imagery, and then you get a dialectic between the feminine and the masculine, and between action and mysticism.

REBECCA: Did the church actually come out and say that God is male?

MATTHEW: (*laughter*) Well, if I'm forbidden to say that God is mother, then you'd have to draw that conclusion.

DAVID: You said in *Original Blessing* that the whole Fall/Redemption concept was created by the ruling class for political reasons.

MATTHEW: Did I say that?

DAVID: You did say that.

MATTHEW: Good.

DAVID: (*laughter*) Can you explain what you mean by this and why you think it's so?

MATTHEW: Well, if you can teach people that the number one religious problem is their sin and that when they came into the world they made a blotch on existence—and you can really convince them of that—they'll never get over it. The human species is very vulnerable. We talk about sexual abuse of children, but this is religious abuse. If you feed this into children's minds, it reinforces all other abuse that they might be receiving from adults, and it gives it divine legitimization.

So people never come into their own power, which includes trusting their own experience of anger and outrage. Whether you're a woman in a sexist society or a gay person in homophobic society, you don't have that power to stand up and say, "Well, this is what I believe." If we get cut off from our passion, where's our compassion going to come from?

> *If we get cut off from our passion, where's our compassion going to come from?*

DAVID: Do you think that the ruling classes were doing this very consciously and deliberately?

MATTHEW: I don't think that the ruling class thought it through that much; they've just inherited all these ways of coercion. You've heard the phrase "divide and conquer," well, that's what it is. It's dividing people against themselves. In the Reagan era, the Santa Fe Report done by the National Security Council did an analysis of liberation theology in South America that said, "We can't destroy this movement, but we can divide the church against itself." It's exactly what's happening, and we have this present pope going around condemning the justice-oriented movements in the church.

> *Of course, the idea behind Original Blessing is that everyone is a blessing and everyone is original.*

It's all sadomasochism. You have to instruct one group in masochism while developing your own sadism. What is masochism? It's the "I can't" syndrome. We're being taught this through television all the time: you can't have friends until you get the right toothpaste and the right car. It's very subtle, but it's very real. I think that sadomasochism is the basic energy of imperial minds and structures. You can liberate masochists by letting them in on their own power. Of course, the idea behind *Original Blessing* is that everyone is a blessing and everyone is original.

REBECCA: How do you define sin?

MATTHEW: I like Rabbi Heschel's definition. He says, "Sin is the refusal of the human to become who we are." I like that because it's evolutionary. I think that we're here to become something—to become who we are. Who are we? We're creative beings who desire beauty and justice. Aquinas has a great line: "The object of the heart is truth and justice." It's not in the head! So we're here to develop our powers as images of God.

REBECCA: And sin is anything that limits our ability to express this?

MATTHEW: Yes. There can be sin all around us, but we still have some choices. People can pay attention to their own being and not yield to the false and illusory promises. They can try to find the friends and the philosophies and the rituals to develop their soul, instead of selling it.

In terms of community, sin is also a social disease. We're surrounded by a lot of blessings and goodness and a lot of lies, so you have to be alert.

DAVID: Does the devil have any place in creation spirituality? Do you think that evil, as a force unto itself, exists in the world?

MATTHEW: I think there's no question that evil as a force exists, but I think that the danger is in objectifying it as the devil outside ourselves. The force of evil flows through me and through everybody if we don't watch out. When he was first elected, Hitler seemed like a pretty ordinary politician to a lot of Germans.

Evil is the shadow of angel. Just as there are angels of light, support, guidance, healing, and defense, so we have experiences of shadow angels. And we have names for them: racism, sexism, homophobia are all demons—but they're not out there.

REBECCA: Do you see evil as an actual independent force rather than an absence of love?

MATTHEW: Both. It's an absence, definitely. But what happens when there's a vacuum? It sucks something in. I like the way Native Americans put it. They say that God does not make evil spirits, but humans and human institutions do, and that the door for an evil spirit entering the human heart is fear. Prayer is a way to strengthen the heart so that we don't yield to fear, which in turn leads to evil.

Matthew Fox

REBECCA: Considering how powerful Jesus' message was to the poor and the outcast, what explains the church's traditional lack of social activism?

MATTHEW: When I look at the history of the church, I see a lot of moments when there were groups of people who were working with the poor. One example is the invention of the monastic system in the fourth century.

You hear these stories about the desert fathers with long, white beards eating locusts. They actually were young men who went AWOL. When the church married the empire, you could be drafted into the army and kill people in the name of Christ. So they went into the desert to avoid conscription, and they became hermits. So it was really a political movement.

Saint Benedict saw the corruption in Rome, and he went off and became a shepherd in the hills. He eventually developed this whole idea of monasticism, which originally was a very small, simple lifestyle. Of course, after a while monasticism became the big landowner in Europe. Then you had Saint Dominic and Saint Francis in the thirteenth century, who quit all that and started new branches, such as the Dominican friars, who worked with the poor.

Today there are hundreds of Christian nuns, laypeople, and priests who have given their lives, literally and figuratively, for the causes of the struggling poor in the United States and in Latin America. The lack of social activism has not been so much with the rank and file as with the hierarchy.

REBECCA: Fundamentalist preachers very rarely quote from the New Testament, maybe because if they did they would have to admit certain things, like the rich having a responsibility to the poor.

MATTHEW: To be honest, I don't think that fundamentalism has anything to do with Jesus Christ. They call themselves Christians, but if that's Christian, count me out. Fundamentalism is built on fear and greed. They're telling you to give them your money, otherwise you're going to hell. Christian fundamentalism is an oxymoron, it's contradictory. Jesus was about giving to the poor, and he was about driving out fear. He wasn't about raising millions of dollars for theme parks and so on, or about giving religious legitimization to fascist clerical movements. I do not believe that fascism and Jesus' message are compatible, unlike the present Vatican, which wants to canonize this fascist priest Josemaría Escrivá who is head of the conservative theological faculty at Navarre University (and the university's founder).

DAVID: What is your concept of the kind of person that Jesus actually was?

MATTHEW: I was in Malibu, and these people put me up in a home with a Buddha statue. And I woke up in the morning with this idea that what makes Buddha different from Jesus is that Jesus never had a midlife crisis—he

> *. . . what makes Buddha different from Jesus is that Jesus never had a midlife crisis . . .*

died a young man. Buddha went through it all. He died in his eighties, and so he had more of a take-it-easy kind of approach. Jesus was this impetuous young man! He wanted to get it all done, overturn the system, and so on.

I think you need both. You need the Jesus energy, the prophetic energy, the anger to change things. On the other hand, Buddha has the realization of cycles and that everything is fine the way it is. I see Jesus essentially as a very inspired, energetic, passionate Jewish prophet. Prudence was not his best virtue. (*laughter*)

REBECCA: Gautama Buddha reformed Hinduism and created Buddhism, which incorporated many Hindu principles. It seems that, similarly, creation spirituality is intending to reform Christianity while retaining much of its framework. But when so many Christians wouldn't even consider a creation spiritualist to be a Christian, I'm wondering if the framework of Christianity is really flexible enough to accommodate this.

MATTHEW: Well, let's check the facts here. There are also many Christians who don't consider what's been called Christianity worth their time. I was just in Europe, and I was lecturing in Sweden, where two percent of Lutherans practice, and it's the state church! In England, three percent of Anglicans practice; in France, four percent of Catholics practice.

I don't quite agree that I want to keep the framework. I think the forms have to die. I think that the forms with which Christianity has been presenting itself are for the most part dead. Is there stuff worth keeping? Of course: the mystics, the prophets, the gospels, Jesus, and some of the theology about worship and sacrament, but not the forms! That's what killing worshippers.

The theology isn't that bad; it's really very cosmological. For example, in the Catholic church there's the idea of eating and drinking the body and blood of the presence of the divinity of everything in the universe. I think that's pretty far out and erotic. I would say, let's get some worship that lives up to this theology!

REBECCA: But you are using some of Christianity's framework. For example, in *Original Blessing* you pick out some very lovely quotes from the Bible. But rape, pillage, sexism, racism, and other forms of violence are also justified in the Bible, and most Christians accept the Bible as *the* definitive spiritual truth.

MATTHEW: Thomas Aquinas says, "Revelation comes in two volumes: the Bible and Nature." For centuries we've ignored nature, which includes our human nature and the nature of the universe as a revelation of Christianity. It's just as important as the Bible.

What I like about Catholicism is that it's never said that religion is only about the Bible; it's always used the word "tradition." The Bible is only three thousand years old; the universe is fifteen billion. Let's not starve ourselves! You're right, the book has its good days and bad days. But this is what theologians have always done, and at certain times in history, certain passages become more relevant than other passages. Why shouldn't we pick and choose?

I like what Rabbi Heschel says: "The Bible is not a book, it's a drama." It's a story! It's life!

REBECCA: Buddhism doesn't have the passion to convert that Christianity has. Why is it, do you think, that the Christian desire to "gather souls" has led them to defy the first commandment throughout history?

MATTHEW: I think that's the shadow side of the prophetic tradition, like the crusades, for example. When Jesus is reported to have said to go preach this to all the world, your zealous empire-builders took this as an opportunity to create dominion over people. It's similar to other crusades, like capitalism, democracy, or communism. A spiritual person could never think that way.

The key is in converting yourself, and that is a lifetime's task. Now, there is another thing. If you love your world view or your faith, you might well want to hand it out as a gift to other people—to your children, for example. But offering a gift means that the other person can say, "No thank you!"

REBECCA: Conversion by example can be very powerful.

MATTHEW: Exactly. I suspect it's when people unconsciously realize that they can't convert by example that they begin trying to convert by force.

REBECCA: You claim that the earliest Christians had a very different view of Christianity. Could you describe this view? What is the evidence for it?

MATTHEW: The first generation of Christians were mostly women, slaves, and generally nonprivileged people. Jesus' message really appealed to such people, who were very badly treated at that time. Then, of course, Paul, who was educated, took it into the Greek-speaking world and into the empire itself, making it middle-class, in a way. Early Christianity wasn't very well organized. You had every city saying, "We're the Church." There was no central headquarters.

REBECCA: Like in the movie *Life of Brian,* with the followers of the Holy Gourd and the followers of the Holy Shoe. (*laughter*)

MATTHEW: In a way, they were right. The base church has to get back to that—that it's not a denomination. It's all different people interpreting the universe through their cultural DNA and experience.

REBECCA: Do you think early Christianity was more connected to the ancient Goddess religions?

MATTHEW: Otto Rank, whom I consider one of the greatest prophets of the twentieth century, says that Christianity was a Mother Goddess religion from the start and that this is the reason for the virgin birth story. In other Goddess religions, the Mother Goddess gives birth to a divine son who had intercourse with her. The Christians changed that. They insisted on Mary being a virgin because their divine son went out into the world. He didn't create incest in a closed circle, like you get with Isis, but went into the prophetic dimension of changing society in a linear direction. I think that this is a very brilliant insight, and it's also interesting that it came from a Jew.

REBECCA: What have you learned about the role of women in the early church?

MATTHEW: I was asked to review a manuscript about the church of the second century. They have frescoes on some of these churches in ancient Rome, and there's one called *Episcopa Theodora,* which means "Bishop Theodora"—a woman. You can see how someone tried to change the name from *Theodora* to *Theodorus,* which is the male ending. (*laughter*) The fact is that there were no priests for two hundred years, so it's difficult to distinguish mythology from fact.

I want to stress that your generation is post-denominational. You're post-Piscean. Pisces was the age of dualism, of two fish swimming in the opposite direction. I don't think that your generation was born with the same dualisms in your psyche. Christianity is a very young religion, and it's only existed within the period of Pisces.

> *What I want to see is some really interesting worship.*

Now it's moving out, so there's all this confusion and bedlam and boredom. Denomination is not that important. What I want to see is some really interesting worship.

A few weeks ago I was doing a program in Seattle, and four punk Londoners from England came in who had started—using my theology—a community of thirty artists to design a worship service in Sheffield that they call "Virtual Worship." About four young people go to an Anglican mass in Sheffield—this group has six hundred people coming to every service. It's dark as a cave, and they have video screens showing DNA and so on, and people dance. It's ritualistic.

It's really the next stage to some of these rock concerts that are also ritualistic, but aren't quite plugging it in to the spiritual tradition. This group has been kicked out of the church, but the bishop, lo and behold, is actually supporting them, so they have autonomy. It sounds like this might be the most important thing happening in white worship in the world.

Otto Rank points out that the pagan soul is in all of us, and you have to pay attention to it to get your energy going. But I also think that tradition is very important, because once you start evoking mystical power, you can go really crazy with it. Just look at some of the Rajneesh people. It's just another power. To give it direction, you need mentors and elders and tradition.

REBECCA: It seems that science and religion were once very much entwined, but there was a divergence somewhere along the line. What do you think were the reasons for this split?

MATTHEW: I think the key was the breakdown of the medieval cosmology in the fifteenth century, and then the religious wars of the sixteenth century, which scared the hell out of scientists. And what happened in 1600? The church burned Giordano Bruno at the stake. He was a scientist and a Dominican, like I was.

In the seventeenth century they arranged a truce. Scientists said, "We'll take the universe, and you Christians can have the soul." So the soul became more and more introspective and punier, unconnected to the universe. And science went out without a conscience to find the power of the universe: atomic energy. They sold themselves to warmongers, politicians, and nation-state ideology, and the church became more and more trivial and silly.

DAVID: Do you think that Descartes played a role in that?

MATTHEW: Absolutely. He said that the soul was the pineal gland! (*laughter*) In contrast, these cosmological medieval mystics all said that the soul is not in the body, the body is in the soul! So that means the soul is vast, not trivial. But now that science and mysticism are coming together—that's really exciting.

DAVID: Science is based on repeatable experiments, and religion is based on subjective experience and faith. How do you see these areas becoming reconciled?

MATTHEW: I'm not really at home with the word "subjective." There are better words, such as "intercommunal," or even "transpersonal." Eckhart says, "What happens to another, whether it be a joy or a sorrow, happens to me." Compassion is all about interdependence. So there is no such thing as a subjective experience.

DAVID: I understand what you're saying, but a scientific experiment is repeatable, and you always get the same result if you follow the exact same steps. I don't know if you can do the same with spirituality.

MATTHEW: I would say that spirituality is much more interesting than science, because it's always new. The fact is, awe happens. It happens all the time, not just to individuals, but to groups of people and, especially, to children.

> *The fact is, awe happens.*

I would think, however, that even today's scientists would say that no event in the universe is repeatable. You try to rule out extraneous factors, but there's always chaos and chance.

DAVID: And science makes this incredibly audacious assumption that the universe is governed by fixed mathematical laws that never change.

MATTHEW: Right. Our generation has been taught to think in terms of the evolution of the universe. But the fact is that physics didn't get into evolution until the 1960s—it was just this biology thing. Then we learned how the universe is evolving. Now we're going a step further and understanding that even the laws that govern the universe are evolving!

DAVID: For many Westerners, myself included, their first mystical experience occurred when they ingested a psychedelic substance. More than a few people think that some world religions were actually founded on an individual's experience with psychedelics. I'm wondering, have you ever had any experience with a psychedelic?

MATTHEW: No, I haven't, because I've never felt it necessary. I've gotten high on all these other things—music and nature and ideas and friends. However, some of my best students are people who got into spirituality initially through some kind of drug. The best student I had, who I taught years ago, got into spirituality through drugs, and she ended up becoming a nun.

In my tradition as a Catholic, we drink wine, which is a drug. And Jesus drank wine. So even in Christianity, in its more classical sense, there has been acknowledgment of the role of drugs.

I think that the idea that religions were founded by people on psychedelics is hard to prove or disprove. It's like any other initiatory spiritual experience: the question then becomes, where do you go from there? I tried marijuana in the sixties, and it didn't do anything for me.

REBECCA: You didn't inhale? (*laughter*)

MATTHEW: I tried. (*laughter*) But I would say that if you had been taken to a sweat lodge when you were sixteen, you probably wouldn't have needed psychedelics. Also, you need to consider that when the ancient people were doing drugs, it was within a ritualistic context.

REBECCA: You talk in *Original Blessing* about the need for a personal relationship with God. Yet when many people think about that idea, it's often anthropomorphic and sometimes trivializes the experience of God. Do you believe in a personal God, and if so, how does this belief act so as to encompass the vastness of spiritual experience?

MATTHEW: I reject the notion of talking about God as a person. But there's a difference between talking about God as a person and talking about God as *personal*. The term I use is *panentheistic*: "Everything is in

God, and God is in everything." That's pretty intimate, but it doesn't mean that we don't have to find our own way and do our own creating. I see the universe as a divine womb, and we're all swimming around in this soup.

I think eyes are very revealing. I was with a student who was dying of AIDS about two years ago. He had beautiful blue eyes, and just before he died, his eyes went totally black and he sucked me into this vortex. This is just one example of the presence of the divine showing itself through people.

Eckhart says, "The eye with which I see God is the same eye with which God sees me." So when I used to look into the eyes of my dog, I saw so much mystery there, so much more than he could tell me or *wanted* to tell me. I see things in eyes that are mysterious and unfathomable.

REBECCA: So it's personal, not personified.

MATTHEW: Not personified and not private.

DAVID: How do you define God?

MATTHEW: Never. (*laughter*) It's sad that we put "In God We Trust" on our bills and our missiles and bring God down to our projections. Aquinas has a great line: "God is the source without a source." When you see God as a vitality and energy, your question about whether God is personal takes on a different dimension. Is energy personal? Well, sometimes it is and sometimes it isn't. John Muir said, "The best name for God is beauty." During the Cartesian era, during the enlightenment, beauty was lost as a theological category. However, the last time we had cosmology in the West, in the Middle Ages, they called God beauty.

DAVID: But doesn't defining God as beauty create a dualism? If you have beauty, then you must also have ugliness, and is the ugliness then not a part of God?

MATTHEW: Another part of beauty is terror. The world isn't pretty, it's beautiful. Awe is a mixture of terror and beauty. You say that the opposite of beauty is ugliness. Right. I would say that all injustice is ugly, sin is ugly, tearing down the rainforest is ugly. To me, beauty is not about perfection; there's beauty in imperfection. If you look closely at a tree, you'll notice its knots and dead branches. The same with our bodies. What we learn is that beauty and imperfection go together wonderfully.

I think this is part of the false consciousness of the culture. We think that beauty is having a perfect body with all the cosmetics in just the right place. You have to go back to nature to realize what beauty is.

REBECCA: Isn't part of the mystical experience seeing the beauty in things that have appeared ugly to you before? Seeing the Godhead in even the lowliest form?

MATTHEW: That's right. I think the only ugly thing is human sin. Nothing nature makes is ugly.

REBECCA: Could you talk about some of the practical applications of creation spirituality?

MATTHEW: Much of our society is run on Fall/Redemption ideology. Health care is run on the idea of bringing in outside intervention in the form of surgery and drugs to heal your body, which is inert and passive. That's the basic teaching of medical schools. It's not about the original blessing that our bodies are. Our bodies want to heal themselves. They have intrinsic power to find balance, but they need some help when they get wounded.

Education runs on the same ideology. The idea of education is to force ideas into people's minds, but our minds already *desire* to learn. We desire sex because it's fun, and it's good for the species, and in the same way we want to learn because it's fun. But education has taken the fun out of it. We've taken the awe and mysticism out of our work.

Psychology is another area. Instead of asking what your problem is, psychologists should be asking, "Where is your divine energy, and why is it being bottled up?" I think there's a very important shift going on in all our work, and this is how we're going to affect history. Creation spirituality has to be brought into all work, into politics, business, art, education, health care.

Again, I think that ritual is the key. It provides the energy and courage for people to take risks at work, to reinvent work in a way that is not pessimistic or patriarchal. Pessimism comes from the repression of creativity. If we're honoring creativity, then all our work rules will become very different.

Most people are frustrated at work, or don't have any, not because there's so little work to do but because we're still thinking in terms of the Industrial Revolution and factories and control—Fall/Redemption ideology.

DAVID: What do you personally feel happens to human consciousness after biological death?

MATTHEW: Well, I don't think that any beauty is lost in the universe. Hildegard of Bingen says that no warmth is lost in the universe. Einstein said that no energy's lost. I think that the beauty hangs around. Rupert Sheldrake would call this the morphic resonance, and the Christian tradition would call it the communion of saints. The East might call it the incarnation.

DAVID: Do you think that there's an aspect of yourself that continues on and still contains some of its individuality?

MATTHEW: I wouldn't put it that way myself. Eckhart says, "When I return to the source—the core, the fountain of the Godhead—no one will ask what I've been doing. No one will have missed me." What he's really saying is that there's no judgment.

REBECCA: Are you afraid of death?

MATTHEW: There was a time when I was afraid.

REBECCA: Was the loss of your fear a sudden transition or a gradual one?

MATTHEW: I think it was kind of gradual. I suppose it had something to do with facing death so many times and experiencing other people's deaths. Part of coming to terms with death is experiencing the pain and sorrow that can occur in life and thinking that it can't be much worse. (*laughter*)

REBECCA: What's your take on reincarnation?

MATTHEW: The way I look at it is this: there's a shadow side and a good side to it. There is a certain complacency to the idea of reincarnation. It's like, "Oh well, we'll work it out next time around." Gandhi was told by his Hindu followers that he didn't have to worry about the untouchables because next time around they'll get a better deal. But this wasn't enough for Gandhi, because of Jesus and the West, and he demanded justice *now*. I think there's a certain cop-out, especially among wealthy, comfortable Westerners who are into reincarnation because it gives them an excuse not to get involved in fighting injustice.

On the other hand, I think reincarnation is really interesting. It's certainly more interesting than heaven. We've made heaven absolutely bor-

> **We've made heaven absolutely boring—who wants to go there?**

ing—who wants to go there? (*laughter*) As a Westerner, I talk about the bridge between the East and the West around reincarnation. One is the communion of saints. I've experienced Eckhart and Hildegard. This morphic field is for real. Secondly, there's this tradition of purgatory. When purgatory is cut out from the Fall/Redemption ideology, the ideology is not about punishment, it's about learning to love.

REBECCA: What difference does it make to your life whether you believe that heaven is here and now on earth, rather than out there in some time in the distant future?

> **Jesus said the kingdom of God is now. Why wait around?**

MATTHEW: It makes a lot of difference. For one thing, it puts you in a nondualistic state of consciousness, which is the key to realizing your connection to the divinity in all things and all time, past, present, and future. It opens you up to ecstasy now! If you don't make love with the divine now, then are you going to do it later? Jesus said the kingdom of God is now. Why wait around?

DAVID: What role do you think consciousness plays in the evolution of the universe?

MATTHEW: I think that God is the mind of the universe. I don't think there's any other explanation for the accomplishments of the universe except for mind-consciousness.

DAVID: Do you equate consciousness with spirit?

MATTHEW: Partly. I think that spirit includes consciousness, but consciousness does not necessarily include all of spirit. The word "consciousness" is a little too psychological for me, a little too anthropocentric.

REBECCA: Do you see a divine plan in nature?

MATTHEW: A divine plan?

REBECCA: Yeah. It's a very popular idea right now, especially with all this millenial energy getting stirred up, that we're all on our way somewhere.

MATTHEW: Well, let's see, there's the American Way . . . (*laughter*) Science has confirmed that there's order in the universe as well as chaos. What's really interesting is that order comes out of the chaos—which is the creative process. You need the *via negativa* and chaos before you can get creative.

DAVID: Can you tell us about your Institute of Culture and Creation Spirituality, and any other projects that you're working on.

MATTHEW: I started eighteen years ago in Chicago, and it was a deliberate and conscious effort to reinvent education. I'd done a study on spirituality and education and found that they weren't treating justice, feminism, art, or science as spiritual. I realized that you can't do these things in a Cartesian model of education and develop the right brain and the body.

So I threw out the model of education that we take for granted in the West and designed one that has right and left brain work. We do a lot of meditation and ritual; we include a lot of native people and their music and sweat lodges. We also study Western and Eastern mystics. And it's a model that works. It's not boring at all. People go through transformation, and it's very powerful.

I would like to give this model away to universities, high schools, specialty schools. We would like to do conferences for journalists, cyberspirituality people, and artists.

DAVID: Cyberspirituality?

MATTHEW: Yeah, computer nerds. You've got all this wonderful technology and power—what are you going to do with it, make more money for the insurance companies? We ought to be using that technology to do things that are worthwhile, such as birth rituals to heal people and empower them. That's what I'd like to do. All I need is money. (*laughter*)

REBECCA: Do you feel that your message is getting out there and that people are listening?

MATTHEW: There are several hundred creation-spirituality-based communities around the world. We just got word from Aborigines in Australia, and they want to start an ICCS program in Kimberley, which is where the Aboriginal culture strongest. They want to take our model and use it, and get white people and take them into the bush for a week and teach them about Aboriginal ways. I'm very honored by that. At least the Aboriginals understand what we're trying to do! So far the Westerners have been slower to catch on.

REBECCA: It seems that there is a real crisis in the church.

> *. . . the Vatican is in a deep crisis of faith, which they should be praying for.*

MATTHEW: I think that the Vatican is in a deep crisis of faith, which they should be praying for. They don't trust theologians, they don't trust women, they don't trust gays, and they don't trust nature. The rest of us who do, and who are looking for answers, should just get on with the work. Frankly, I think that as we get on with the work, it's going to be so delightful and fun that everyone's going to want to come along. Nothing changes people like delight. The way our culture and religion is running is very undelightful, and the most basic things, like health care and education, are ridiculously expensive.

REBECCA: Do you think it's possible that within your lifetime the power elite of the church will undergo a real transformation?

MATTHEW: Repent of their sins? (*laughter*) Well, one can pray, can't one?

John Allen

—————

"... it is in our capacity to be the brain and the conscience of the
biosphere, to be its self-reflective point."

Music of the Biospheres
with John Allen

*John Polk Allen was a driving force behind the development of the Bio-
sphere 2 project in the Oracle, Arizona desert. Biosphere 2 is the largest
self-sustaining ecosystem ever built, a masterpiece of human engineering
that has been praised and condemned by a media that, for the most part,
misinterpreted what it was all about. Both confusing it with a controlled
scientific experiment or an entertainment spectacle missed the point. Inside the sealed 3.15 acre biosphere are miniature replicas of all the earth's
environments, designed to function together as a single system.*

*Biosphere 2 was more than just a reductionistic scientific experiment.
It was also bold visionary adventure, like going to the moon. As when the
Wright brothers were building the first airplane, the biospherians were
basically concerned with getting the thing to fly. Biosphere 2 has been a
tremendous success; it broke and set many records. The relevance of Biosphere 2 lies in the light it sheds on our understanding of the earth's biosphere and its value as a prototype for permanent life-habitats on suitable
locations in space.*

*John thinks in terms of whole systems, and he is an expert on ecologi-
cal interrelatedness. Former vice-president of biospheric development for
Space Biospheres Ventures, John wrote a classic article on closed life-
systems, which was published by NASA in* Biological Life Support Technologies: Commercial Applications. *He participated in the first manned
biosphere test module experiment in September 1988, residing for three
days in the first fully closed ecological system that recycled all its wastes,
setting a world record at the time. John is currently the chairman of
Cyberspheres™, Inc., a private research and development firm that designs and builds advanced biospheric systems and semiclosed biomic systems.*

*In addition, he is cofounder and director of EcoFrontiers, Inc., which
owns and manages several ecological research projects around the world,
and Planetary Coral Reef Foundation, a nonprofit corporation devoted to
studying the health and vitality of coral reefs. He has traveled extensively—
very extensively—and this has contributed to his multicultural, whole-sys-*

tems perspective. John has led expeditions studying ecology (particularly the ecology of early civilizations) to Nigeria, Iraq, Iran, Afghanistan, Uzbekistan, Tibet, India, Belize, and the Altiplano. As part of the research for Biosphere 2, John traveled in the ship Heraclitus *to the Amazon and many other areas around the world to collect biological samples.*

John is also an actor, poet, film producer, and playwright. He has been a major force in the Theater of All Possibilities acting troupe for many years. He is a true global citizen who seems to be at home everywhere on the planet. He is also an accomplished author, with more than two dozen publications to his credit, over half of which are scientific, while the rest comprise poetry, drama, prose, and film. John holds a degree in metallur-gical-mining engineering from the Colorado School of Mines, an MBA from the Harvard Business School, from which he graduated with distinc-tion as a Baker Scholar, and a certificate in engineering physiology from the University of Michigan.

John is a swashbuckling frontiersman, an eccentric mix of scientist, artist, entrepreneur, and adventurer. He is warm and charismatic, filled with vision, and often appears larger than life. When he hugs you, he lifts you up off the ground. We interviewed John on April 16, 1994 in the living room of our mutual friend Oscar Janiger (interviewed in our previous vol-ume) in Santa Monica, California. Several weeks prior, trouble had been brewing at the biosphere, when its major financial investor, Ed Bass, in his attempt to gain control of the biosphere, accused John and his associates of "mismanagement." Subsequently, Bass took over the experiment. The story of the corporate takeover of Biosphere 2 is the subject of a forthcom-ing book by Abigail Alling and myself entitled Storming Eden. *Even with all the uncertainty hovering about him at the time of the interview, John was radiantly cheerful and contagiously optimistic.*

DJB

DAVID: John, how have your travels around the planet influenced your desire to create a self-contained ecosystem?

JOHN: The unity that is around the planet earth—the biosphere—has only very recently been recognized as a self-organizing entity. That was a hy-pothesis put forward in 1926 by Vladimir Vernadsky. Before that there was a "great nature," a hypothesized "great being," a creation of God or a fortuitous collocation of atoms that accidentally produced life.

But as soon as you really begin to travel around the planet earth, looking at things from the point of view of a biosphere, you see that the oceans, the winds, the mountain ranges, the deserts, the tropical forests are not occurring at random at all. You see that they are organized, that they have a tremendous resilience, and that they're evolutionary.

In science, the question becomes an experiment to test a hypothesis. So the idea of Biosphere 2 was to see whether or not a system modeled on Biosphere 1—that is, the earth—self-organized or not. Many people in the press and many scientists predicted that the ocean in Biosphere 2 would die and that it would all turn to slime. In other words, they fundamentally followed the idea of a fortuitous collocation of atoms, which says life just happens on a planet the right distance from the sun. The wording in that kind of science is that something is *merely*.

> *... many scientist predicted that the ocean in Biosphere 2 would die and that it would all turn to slime.*

REBECCA: So they didn't think you could consciously design a system that wouldn't just collapse into entropy.

JOHN: Well, actually it's *modeling* a system more than it's designing it. The thing about Biosphere 2 that very few people got was that what we did was create conditions that emulated the conditions of Biosphere 1. There is something to produce tides, something to produce water flows, pipes taking the place of rivers, things like that. But the *live* systems were very much modeled on Biosphere 1, although naturally on a highly reduced scale.

For example, the Biosphere 2 ocean is actually portions that came out of certain coral reefs, water from the Pacific and water from the Bahamas. The rainforest is designed by people who spent a lot of time there. The basic way I formulated that for them was to say, "Let's create the *quintessence* of the rainforest, so that when you're standing in the middle of it, you feel that you are in the Amazon."

These were not just ordinary people. They spent decades in the Amazon and studied it intimately. So that's how these terrestrial biomes went into making Biosphere 2.

REBECCA: Which of the cultures that you came across in your travels had the greatest influence on you and your ideas?

JOHN: There were a number of them. Ethnology was the first science I studied, so when I traveled around I used the idea of Ruth Benedict and Franz Boaz that there is an arc of human potential and that each culture is a part of that arc. So I didn't go around looking for *the* specific culture, but rather cultures that had a bigger arc of human potential or a more incisive tranche than usual.

The Berber culture, the Sioux Indian culture, Huichols, the Bora of the Amazon, the Polynesian culture were all examples of this. The Hindu culture is exceedingly interesting because of the division of humans into castes in an old linear breeding and function program.

There is also what I call *globaltech*, which is the culture of the technicians of the West. It's not officially recognized by anthropology, but I think it's one of the most powerful cultures in the world today, with probably about five million members. It includes

> *. . . globaltech . . . is the culture of the technicians of the West.*

people who can move from Moscow to Tokyo to Santa Monica to Biosphere 2 and never miss a beat, people who are basically inventing, innovating, maintaining, and envisioning the next steps in the global technosphere.

DAVID: Was there a particular culture that you encountered that forced you to re-evaluate your entire belief system?

JOHN: Yes. Actually it was a coming together of three cultures in Tangiers. There was the avant-garde art culture of William Burroughs and the people around him; the Berber culture, which is maybe six thousand years old and has its roots in the ancient magical traditions; and the imperial culture of the Spanish, French, and British empires.

So the combination of the Western imperial culture, the native Berber culture, and the Western avant-garde forced a personal transformation of all values, not just on a mental and emotional level, but on a physiological and social level as well.

DAVID: Physiological? How do you mean that?

JOHN: Well, because the people from the avant-garde were into all sorts of exercises, and then there were all the disciplines and fronts you have to put up to be part of the empire group, and then the Berbers have a number of rites, ceremonies, and Sufi types of sciences.

DAVID: Is this getting into what you refer to as "transvangardia"?

JOHN: Yes. Well, eventually I and some other people evolved the recognition that there is a transvangardia. There's not only an avant-garde of the West, there's an avant-garde in every culture in the world that has an artistic tradition that is trying to re-evaluate it and put it into a radically individual, contemporary way.

That culminated existentially in our formulating the October Gallery in London in 1978. We called it the October Gallery because October is the time of the gathering of the fruits. We showcased transvangardia artists from places all over: Nigeria, Ghana, Pakistan, Jordan, Venezuela, Jamaica, Morocco, Mongolia.

We presented young artists who were just ready for their first show and also older artists, such as Gerald Wilde, who, for one reason or another, had crossed the establishment and, after an initial period of fame, been consigned to the dustbin by the powers-that-be. At that time, the only place in London that showed artists from a wide swath of the world was the Commonwealth Institute, which was nice but rather bureaucratic and reserved.

DAVID: Tell us about ecotechnics.

JOHN: Ecotechnics was one of the first things that Mark Nelson and I and a few others came up with, and it was largely inspired by Lewis Mumford, who wrote a book called Technics and Civilization. We found that technics is a very powerful way to understand what is happening. Most people divide science and technology, but technics means the world of science and technology. There is no pure physics—physics depends on the technology around it. There is no pure technology—technology depends on science and body and mind.

Mumford saw in history that there was a series of technics: there was a technics based on wind and water, a technics based on coal and steel, a technics in the 1900s based on the alternating currents in alloys, and so on. What he called biotechnics was based on what is today called ergonomics.

We saw that the next step would be an ecotechnics, that is, an ecology of technics and a technics of ecology. Then we would be looking at the broadest possible scale—that is to say, a biospheric scale—because the biggest ecosystem is the biosphere. We formed that as a concept in about 1973, and it was the think tank that allowed us to put together the ideas for Biosphere 2.

DAVID: How did Biosphere 2 get inspired, then?

JOHN: In ecotechnics we did two things. It was a non-salaried, nonprofit organization, and every year we did an ecotour, through central Asia, through Nigeria, through the Amazon—wherever was interesting to us at the time. We also had a three-day conference each year where we got together many outstanding scientists. We'd generally also have one outstanding artist come, such as William Burroughs or Ornette Coleman. Many of the original participants became the cadre of scientists that enabled us to build Biosphere 2.

Each speaker would have an hour to talk, and there would be an hour or two for discussion, so there was a total freedom of speech. There was no press invited, so people weren't held to anything they said. We had Bucky Fuller, Thor Heyerdhal—many outstanding people. Bucky Fuller helped us design our first dome.

DAVID: So you were doing quite a bit more than just theater and poetry before you got involved in Biosphere 2?

JOHN: The first time I heard the word "biosphere" was at the Colorado School of Mines. That was a revelation in historical geology. The teacher said, that there is a lithosphere of rocks, an atmosphere, a hydrosphere, and a *biosphere.* Wow! I heard it all in one sentence—it was a direct transmission.

Then I carried that idea further, because lithosphere, hydrosphere, and atmosphere are basically physical and chemical. They exist on Mars and Venus as well as on Earth. So I figured that the biosphere must be the control level, and later on I found out that Vernadsky had a formal hypothesis to that effect. James Lovelock and Lynn Margulis, who were completely unaware of Vernadsky, had come to approximately the same thing forty years later, but there are substantial differences between the Vernadskian geological approach to the biosphere and Lovelock and Margulis's atmospheric and microbial approach.

REBECCA: Could you describe some of those differences?

JOHN: Lovelock and Margulis found the medium and the feedback system—namely, the atmosphere and microbes—that made the biosphere operate as a unity. On the other hand, Vernadsky understood geologic history, the key importance of the necrosphere, or biogenetically originated matter, and of the expansive power of the biosphere.

REBECCA: Tell us a little bit about the voyages of your ship, the *Heraclitus.*

JOHN: By 1974, Ecotechnics was launched and our theater was going. Theater is very important because it shows you the evolution of the inner life of man, whereas science deals with the evolution of the outer life of man. Adventure is what holds them both together. We supported ourselves by building and designing over two million dollars worth of adobe houses in Santa Fe, and other kinds of craftwork, including agricultural experiments that led to the Biosphere 2 soil system.

So we designed and built a ship in the estuary in Oakland. The idea behind the ship was that the biosphere was essentially planet water and that the reason no one had really understood the biosphere before was that they always went out into the trees. James Lovelock's daisy model was wonderful, but if the daisies disappeared, the biosphere wouldn't be affected very much. The ocean, at about 70 percent of the surface of the planet, is what drives the biosphere. It can be looked at as its blood.

> *The ocean, at about 70 percent of the surface of the planet, is what drives the biosphere. It can be looked at as its blood.*

The ocean also gives you access to the marshes, and if you build the right kind of ship, you can go up rivers and explore the tropical rainforest. So we built a ship that could go up the Amazon, safely explore the coral reefs, and sail around the world. We called it the *Heraclitus* because he was the last philosopher who united the philosophy of the East with the practical approach of the West.

On our first voyage we sailed out of the bay and across the Panama canal, across the Atlantic, the Mediterranean, the Red Sea, and to Australia. We set up projects along the way, such as what eventually became the Vajra Hotel, a joint project with Tibetan people in Nepal.

REBECCA: What kind of projects were these?

JOHN: In France we were involved in a restoration of an old Louis XIV farm, where we did more agricultural experiments. Also, we had most of our conferences in France because it was a really free country during the Cold War, unlike America, and anyone could get a visa to come there—a Russian scientist, for example.

Margaret Augustine, who co-created Biosphere 2, was a key person in all this, and she designed the Vajra Hotel. It's earthquake-proof and very high-tech, and it was a hotel for the merging of the East and West and North and South. We had the Tibetan canon in there, the Indian canon, and the Western medical and scientific canon. So we had rinpoches in there studying Western science, and Western scientists studying the Tibetan and Hindu sciences. It's still operating today.

REBECCA: So you were creating a sort of mandala of cultural experience.

JOHN: Yes. And we thought this was very essential to Biosphere 2. It had to address itself to the planetary. The North-South dyad had to be transcended—and the same with the East-West—without either being denied.

DAVID: What would you say were some of the most important things that came out of the two-year Biosphere 2 project?

JOHN: Well, it lasted over two and a half years, actually, because we had a six-month transition. Basically what we learned is that the biospheric hypothesis is correct: it is a self-organizing system. Under the conditions that we put into the Biosphere, we had an increase of eighty-seven coral colonies. There was someone from the Smithsonian who said something like "It's impossible for the ocean to live, therefore I know it's dead." They didn't even look at it. *Newsweek* printed these statements as if they were facts.

In fact, the ocean self-organized. We not only showed that the total system self-organized, but also that various ecosystems that we put in there did. The marsh worked, the ocean worked, the rainforest worked, and all as a total system, although it's true that it works quite differently from Biosphere 1. Each biosphere will be unique in many ways, just as humans are.

> *We not only showed that the total system self-organized, but also that various ecosystems that we put in there did.*

Another consequence of the hypothesis that there is a class of entities in the universe called biosphere is that there is an organized entity or being that is higher than man and of which man is just a part. For example, the Biosphere 2 carbon monoxide was running at about half of what it does in Biosphere 1, but the nitrous oxide was running higher and the methane was running higher. Things didn't just all go up or all go down. There was a distinct signature in the way that it was organizing its atmosphere. Its metabolism was quicker: the carbon dioxide circulates two thousand times more quickly than out here, and it also runs higher.

REBECCA: And the initial conditions were that of the earth's atmosphere, right? Do you think that after a longer period of time Biosphere 2's atmosphere would have reorganized again?

JOHN: It would have gone through changes in the same way that Biosphere 1 does. At one time Earth had much more carbon dioxide than it has today, although everybody gets alarmed if it goes up or down even a tiny bit.

REBECCA: So Biosphere 2 is a way to study such changes occurring in a more intensified and dramatic way.

> *It's what I call a* **time microscope.**

JOHN: Yes, it's more dramatic. It's what I call a *time microscope.* In a space microscope you see more space objects, whereas in a time microscope you see more events in a shorter amount of time. Amazingly few people have gotten that. It was the first expedition in time, and we even carried an Explorer's Club flag sent in recognition of the expedition.

Each biosphere has a different time, a different metabolic rate, and a different evolutionary history. The biospherians are *within*, in contrast to the usual expedition, where people get into the plane or rocket, which takes off to somewhere else and leaves the crowd behind. A biosphere opens up and the people inside stay where they are—it's the crowd that leaves.

> *. . . the aging tests . . . showed that the rate of aging decreased.*

The biospherians enter a new time machine. Interestingly, the aging tests that Roy Walford used showed that the rate of aging decreased. How meaningful this is over two-and-a-half years is hard to say, but at any rate, it seems that the physiological time began to change for the people inside.

REBECCA: Wasn't there a problem with the oxygen levels, and more oxygen had to be brought in from the outside?

JOHN: People might call it a problem, but in an experiment you expect to find new things. Something came up with the oxygen that we didn't predict, namely, that because the carbon dioxide was at a higher level of pressure, more of it went into the concrete. Out here, at a carbon dioxide level of 350 parts per million, if you have concrete in a bridge, not very much carbon dioxide goes into it. But the more you have of an element, the more it does whatever it does. So as the carbon dioxide went up, more of it began to go into the concrete.

Also, carbon began to be oxidized in the soil, and what that was doing was pulling oxygen out. We had to put a lot of carbon in the soil because we started out with the approach of successional ecology. We began with about fifteen tons of biomass. When we reach a climax, it will be about sixty tons. Right now, it's probably about thirty tons.

REBECCA: Did the oxygen have to be pumped in because it was becoming difficult to breathe inside?

JOHN: We pumped oxygen in at the first sign the doctors caught of difficulty for the humans. We ran an experiment with the consent of the biospherians. The scientific community that I consulted with on this said it would be very interesting and important to see what would happen. What is the lowest amount of oxygen that people can healthily live with? They called that "riding the curve down."

So the biospherians kept us informed on their health, and we also closely observed their behavior and measured changes in their blood, because in the experiments you get what's called the *heroic mode*: everything becomes so important and so useful to humanity that a person might even kill himself from excess enthusiasm. We also had medical tests and doctors checking blood, et cetera. All the submarine and space people were very interested in this because if you can put less oxygen in, say, a Mars base, you will save immense amounts of money.

This was also especially interesting because as you go up a mountain, oxygen drops—but so does everything else, such as nitrogen and carbon dioxide. Here, everything else was staying at equal pressure, and only the oxygen was dropping. What we found was that people can go down to about 14.5 percent of oxygen and still perform, but they began to become sluggish at around 17 percent. So after that we set the mission rules to be between 19 and 21 percent.

Many people said that the biospherians experienced difficulty in breathing, but the oxygen would have gone in much earlier had that been true. Three of the biospherians did use an oxygen sniffer during sleeping hours. It was an experiment. It was also interesting to see what plants would do with an oxygen decrease. We thought it might hurt their growth, but we found that it probably increased it slightly.

REBECCA: What were some of the qualities of a naturally occurring environment that were difficult to reproduce in Biosphere 2?

JOHN: The biggest thing you get with increasing scale is more diversity and more of what we call "levels of trophic change"—how many situations of "who eats who." There's a rough law in ecology that says it takes ten times the biomass of one level to support the next level. For example, in the ocean the biggest fish we could have was about twelve inches long, whereas, of course, there are whales in Biosphere 1's ocean. They basically were like Biosphere 1 systems, but with that exception. During the transition, we added in species in and thus built up a trophic level, but there will always be some lesser total of diversity because of the scale.

REBECCA: Were the ratios of the various species roughly equivalent to the ratios in which they exist outside?

JOHN: Roughly. The coral reef was almost exactly in ratio to start with, but again, the trophic pyramid would be truncated—it would have a limit. We couldn't support an octopus or a shark, for example. Also, in our rainforest the trees could only grow 90 feet tall, whereas in the real rainforest they can grow up to 150 feet. So the species that have evolved to be a 100 feet or above, which is a lot of species, aren't able to go in.

On the other hand, the agriculture in Biosphere 2 is more diverse than anything outside in any one system—there are over 140 cultivars in there. Everything else is modeled on existing systems outside, but the agriculture is a synthesis of many different tropical agricultures that had a track record of hundreds of years of sustained reproducibility, such as the Polynesian sweet potato.

REBECCA: The Biosphere 2 project has had a number of ups and downs since its first inception. Looking back, what, if anything, would you have done differently?

> *Biosphere 2 was one of the most successful experiments that has ever been done.*

JOHN: Well, first, I don't think it did have ups and downs. It had *media* ups and downs, but I don't subscribe to the idea that the media are anywhere near a valid representation of reality. Biosphere 2 was one of the most successful experiments that has ever been done. We set all kinds of world records: it was the first time there had been a 100-percent recycled closed system; it was the most tightly sealed system that ever was—thirty times tighter than the space shuttle; it was the first time for total water recycling.

It came very close to the biospheric hypothesis. Eight people went in, one person damaged the end of a finger, but, all in all, everyone's health improved. In fact, it's a very interesting question as to why the media presented the project as problem-riddled when it was a straight-ahead accomplishment.

> *... it's a very interesting question as to why the media presented the project as problem riddled ...*

DAVID: As a result of what you learned from the first two-year project, what readjustments do you need to make, and what new research questions have developed that you will study for future projects?

JOHN: Biosphere 2 represents an air ethic. We had a land ethic that was developed in the 1930s. We had a water ethic with the Clean Water Act. We've never had an air ethic. Biosphere 2 shows the way to do that with an understanding of the total measurement and effect of all the molecules in the air.

Neither the American people nor any other people have yet received a readout of what is in the air they breathe. That's only the beginning of an air ethic. Again, the media didn't report anything about this. But many questions have been raised, such as the differentiation of carbon monoxide, nitrous oxide, and methane, just to name three. Why did these act differently and in reverse directions to Biosphere 1?

> *Neither the American people nor any other people have yet received a readout of what is in the air they breathe.*

DAVID: How did Margulis and Lovelock's Gaia hypothesis influence the project? Do you see the Biosphere 2 as being something like a baby Gaia?

JOHN: That hypothesis didn't influence Biosphere 2 at all because the Vernadsky hypothesis is not just the forerunner, it's *the* hypothesis. But Lovelock and Margulis's work did influence it. Lovelock studied the atmosphere with a device that could measure parts per trillion and showed these fine molecules there. Margulis's work with microbes showed that they would increase their populations and eat these molecules. In other words, Lovelock and Margulis found a mechanism by which the biosphere could maintain its equilibrium.

The Gaia hypothesis is a cyclic hypothesis; it's not a geological hypothesis. Vernadsky's ideas are on a much larger scale, and he describes biospheres as a cosmic phenomenon. Any materially closed system with enough energy going through will tend to cause a self-organizing system that releases the free energy—that's the thermodynamic definition of the biosphere. Lovelock doesn't work with that at all.

In the Sisyphus myth, Sisyphus moves the stone up the hill until it falls back down, and then he moves it back up, and on and on. The biosphere is a Sisyphus, with an urge to move the stone up the hill—that is, free energy—and the stone doesn't fall down again. As long as the energy is coming through, it keeps moving it up the hill. The biosphere is *increasing* its ability to make the migration of matter. It is free-energy-increasing; it's not cyclic.

DAVID: It's energetically and informationally open and chemically closed, right? Is there a lifespan to Biosphere 2?

JOHN: We know for sure that it can go for as long as 3.8 billion years!

DAVID: But the earth is chemically open—meteorites can fall, for example.

JOHN: That's a hundred thousand tons a year. It's a minimal amount on a sextillion-ton planet.

DAVID: But it could have been one of those meteorites that brought the first life to earth.

JOHN: That is possible. But you're talking about two things here. One is the initial causal stuff, which we don't really know about right now, and the second is how it operates once it starts. The biosphere was here before life. The definition of the Vernadskian point of view, which I've extended, is a thermodynamic definition. As long as you have a closed system with energy going through and increasing free energy, that's a biosphere.

So the biosphere, the total system, cuts deep as a self-organizing system. It cuts just as deep as the idea of the human mind as a self-organizing system versus the idea of the necessity of building the mind—from first grade to second grade, and so on. The biosphere can begin self-organizing even before the carbon molecules reach the state of what we now call life. That's not accepted in the West, but the Russians think that, and I think there is a lot of evidence for it.

DAVID: Do you have a teleological view of the universe? Do you see life as being an accident or part of a conscious order?

JOHN: Basically, when you look at the history of the universe, first there was energy, then there was matter, then there was life, then there was mind and technics. As soon as you have life, you have purpose or a goal, and when you have purpose, you have a distinction that one thing is better than something else—it's called *tropism* in biology. So as soon as you react in a way of something being better than something else, you have a value or a teleology.

DAVID: You're saying that this could occur at the point when life begins. But could there be a teleology *before* life?

JOHN: When you look at it, you could even say that it must have been before, because there's certainly more potentiality now than in the past. There are cosmic directions, and directions also imply a teleology. That direction is toward negentropy, more free energy, and using self-organizing techniques in an ever-increasing amount, as simplified in chaotic mathematics. I also think that the values of beauty—that is, wholeness—harmony, and radiance are becoming ever-increasing components of the value system at evolution's edge.

REBECCA: Did you consciously develop an aesthetic for Biosphere 2, or was the selection of organisms based solely on their function and usefulness?

JOHN: When we go to Mars, plants and animals will be selected on the basis of whether they're beautiful or not, as well as whether they're useful. We did the same in Biosphere 2. Biosphere 2 was what I call the beginning of *artistic selection* as an adjunct to Darwinian selection. There are many plants or animals that could have served the same function, but when given a choice, you pick the one that is more beautiful.

DAVID: What have been some of the technological spin-offs of Biosphere 2?

JOHN: One is the Airtron™, which is an air purifier, and another is the Wastron™, which purifies human or animal waste.

DAVID: What do you think the Biosphere 2 project has done to help improve environmental awareness on the planet?

JOHN: The main thing it's done is to create the technics of closed systems. Take biotechnology and the question of whether a new genetic mutation is useful or dangerous? Under normal circumstances it could take billions of dollars and a number of generations to find out the answer. But the material circulation of Biosphere 2 goes two thousand times faster than it does outside, so you can get answers back a lot quicker and a lot more accurately than from other kinds of tests.

> *The president of Toyota came by and said, "Why don't you put a Toyota car in there?"*

You could also create a polluted biosphere, which is an idea that we're working on right now with the Russians. You could take the water and air of Los Angeles on a smoggy day and see how much time and biomass it takes to clean it up. The president of Toyota came by and said, "Why don't you put a Toyota car in there?" And I thought, "Well, that would be interesting—how much biomass would it take to support a Toyota car?"

REBECCA: So the potential of using biospheres for increasing environmental understanding is vast. Has the FDA shown any interest in this work?

JOHN: There's been practically a total blockade by the entire American establishment, but it has created interest in Russia, Europe, and Japan. Bill Riley and thirty-five administrators of the Environmental Protection Agency came by, said how great it all was, and we never heard from them again. Tom Lovejoy of the Smithsonian, Gerald Soffen with NASA, and the bankers now in charge, Bannon and Bowen, have tried to limit the use of Biosphere 2 to reductionist science. These people would like to have a Disneyfied project there, which naturally we oppose.

Lovejoy and Soffen, for example, demanded that we use a reductionist approach to it and conducted a ruthless media war against us for using a total-systems approach. Biosphere 2 is useful, they say, if we study some

> *. . . its big teaching is . . . that it's all a total system.*

specific mechanism in the ocean in there, or what happens, let's say, to the passion vine species in the savannah. By doing this they will generate hundreds of doctoral degrees and violate what its big teaching is—that it's all a total system.

I was just in Japan, and the Japanese are terrified because there's going to be a cloud of brown smoke coming from industrialized China, which is using highly leaded coal. Japan has already agreed to give 200 million dollars to China to help try to put the lid on it. It doesn't matter what Japan's policy is—the smoke from China is going to blow across anyway. After Japan is Alaska; it doesn't stop.

The EPA doesn't recognize that. Tom Lovejoy, who is the ecosystem advisor to Bruce Babbitt, represents the present American policy, an improvement over Bush, which was to save the spotted owl. The Lovejoy approach, which is not flying with the environmental community, was "Let's save the Oregon woods." It's not the Oregon woods that need saving; it's the whole fucking thing!

The biggest thrust of the Lovejoy bankers' approach is that we should make Biosphere 2 into a reductionist science apparatus and study small detail. But total systems are more data-oriented than reductionist science. For example, a reductionist scientist will make a study related to methane in a rice field. But you have to look at the methane together with the nitrous oxide—all of it, and their relations.

Reductionist science is very powerful if you want to send a projectile somewhere or if you want to knock out a specific arms system. However, the side effects, the law of unintended consequences, is taken into consideration only in total systems. But total systems, or holism, got a bad name in science, partially because it's not in the interests of the ruling class . . .

REBECCA: To say that we're all connected. (*laughter*)

JOHN: Because they've disconnected themselves from that. Also, some people who call themselves "holistic" aren't scientists and are peddling cheap psychological cures. Total-systems science, which has created cybernetics and biospheres and certain physiological approaches, is much more difficult than linear cause-and-effect science, which *is* hard enough, and is necessary. But it wasn't Biosphere 2's mission.

DAVID: I'd like to know if psychedelics have influenced your work?

JOHN: [*Pause*] The Biosphere 2 couldn't have been built without the help of a number of shamans, who are probably the primary ethnobotanists in the world. It's impossible to fully appreciate the Amazon, or anything as complex as a tropical rainforest, without special states of consciousness.

What's used in the Amazon by the shaman are plants such as *Banisteriopsis caapi* and substances such as beta harmaline. These substances put people in a state where they can see *eidetically*, instead of just sensationally. The forests and this eidetic ability is what makes the shaman an essential partner of all ethnobotanists. The people who painted the Lasceaux caves were eidetic—that is, they must have seen the animal so clearly that they could copy the eidetic image. Nobody could paint like that until the Renaissance.

Without this eidetics of sensation and memory, which are succession-ally linked, you can't, in my opinion, comprehend a complex totality. Eidetics are so unknown to people in the modern world, and without that kind of vision, I doubt that the total systems view will spread very far because people just won't see it.

Our senses are reductionist. If we go by memory, then we're remem-bering only our successive sensations, or we're combining them by an ac-tive imagination, which produces an element of fantasy. But if we've had an eidetic image, then we can have a memory which, when we train it, can then reproduce that image. But it's possible to have an eidetic experience without being able to remember it.

Also, coca chewing is quite legal in South America and is used for endurance. If you're doing major studies in the mountains or in the forest with the Indians, then you need to use it to keep up with them. I've also participated in shamanic ceremonies because I think that it's important to see the total system in a very literal sense.

DAVID: How do you see biospheres leading to or helping us with extraplanetary migration?

> *Biospheres are* **essen-tial** *to planetary mi-gration. If you take up a picnic lunch, when [it's] eaten, that's it.*

JOHN: Well, of course, it won't just be helping. Biospheres are *essential* to planetary migration. If you take up a picnic lunch, when the picnic lunch is eaten, that's it. Anything short of a bio-sphere, by definition, would be an en-tropy increaser and therefore, at best, a picnic. Only a biosphere increases the free energy, and it's the only way for a long-term colonizing settlement to exist. That's why we called our corporation "Space Biospheres." The bank-ers changed it to "Decisions Investment."

REBECCA: What interest has NASA shown in the project?

JOHN: NASA people who are looking to go to the moon and Mars have shown intense interest and have flocked there, except when they've been forbidden by those in NASA's upper management who are committed to a

Landsat approach, which entails a satellite supervision of the planet Earth and is a relic of the Cold War, part of the military-industrial-academic complex.

There is no program to go to the moon and Mars today, so the attitude on the part of NASA, carrying out the official mandate, has always been anti-Biosphere 2. On the other hand, people from the Russian and Japanese space programs are highly enthusiastic. The Russians actually sent up a closed ecological system in 1989. They want to go to Mars, and Japan wants to go to the moon.

REBECCA: What do you think are the benefits of space colonization?

JOHN: I think it's one of the greatest adventures of all time. I think adventure is where human beings can find the best route to the answer of the question "Who am I?" You don't have to justify climbing Mount Everest, you don't have to justify diving deeper into the oceans than anyone before, and you don't have to justify going into space. It's an end in itself because it leads to contemplation. It might also be a practical art, but first and foremost it opens up whole new territories of perspectives.

REBECCA: What about the practical applications?

JOHN: The practical applications are quasi-infinite, if not infinite. Number one is efficiency. We don't learn how to use the space "out there," but the space of the vehicles we go in. With the population at its present level and without a drastic reduction in the standard of living, efficiency cannot continue the way it is.

Also, it inspires an attitude of intellectual rigor and honesty. You cannot go into space and lie, because you die. So I think that space is the one hope of continuing the scientific world view of humanity, because the fundamentalist reaction around the planet Earth is

> *You cannot go into space and lie, because you die.*

so great, the forces are so big, and science itself has fallen under the sway of a reductionist approach that everybody can see is ultimately meaningless.

Outdated world views, thousands of years old, are calling into action masses of human beings committed to violent methods to take over bigger slices of this earth. But space appeals to everybody. Every human being can see the planet Earth, the moon, the sun. It takes you out of superstition and fanaticism. That may be its greatest benefit.

DAVID: Why do you think that children are so eager to go into space?

> *The Sufis have a saying: "Traveling polishes the rust off the mirror of the mind."*

JOHN: As William Burroughs said, "We're here to go." Kids know that. They haven't been told yet that we're here to stay until we die and get buried next to the trees. The Sufis have a saying: "Traveling polishes the rust off the mirror of the mind."

REBECCA: When do you think that fully manned space stations will become a reality?

JOHN: If there were the political and cultural will to do it, then very quickly, maybe in ten years. In fact, we had it at one time with Skylab, but it was deliberately destroyed.

DAVID: I thought the problem with Skylab was that it descended from orbit and eventually fell down to earth.

JOHN: Because they didn't give it a boost to keep it up. By the way, it costs nearly 200 million dollars for the external fuel tank of our shuttles to drop back into the ocean. If you took the Wright brothers' airplane, its first flight could fit inside one of those external tanks. The nose cone alone, with Biosphere 2 techniques, could support two people with the agriculture you could grow there. Anyway, the Russians already have a permanent space station up there: MIR.

REBECCA: So you think that one of the main reasons that space stations haven't become reality in America is that we're still recovering from the Cold War hangover?

> *. . . there's this huge, lumbering momentum from the Cold War where thinking is not appreciated.*

JOHN: Right. In the Cold War they wanted something that went around the earth and stayed there, looking back. The famous phrase they used was that they wanted to see Kruschev pissing off the back porch. They actually got it down so that they could see two soldiers marching in lockstep.

It's also extremely expensive and therefore profitable. You have a tremendous military-industrial-academic investment, with millions of people earning a good living, and there's this huge, lumbering momentum from the Cold War of thinking not being appreciated. Witness the attitude to Biosphere 2 during this management takeover. The American system at the top is now *sot* in its ways—not just set.

REBECCA: So if a space station went up tomorrow, would you go and live on it?

JOHN: Sure. I don't think I'm as qualified as a lot of people, but if I got a chance I would.

REBECCA: Why do you think that humans have this seemingly insatiable urge to create environments that go far beyond basic survival needs? Do you think it has something to do with us trying to prove our independence from "mother" earth?

JOHN: Our ancestors lived in caves for survival reasons, but they also decorated them—they created an environment. There's an old story in Indian theater in which Barata puts on a play and everyone's ecstatic because it's the first play they've ever seen. Then Shiva comes down and says, "That was pretty good, but you could have doubled the effect"—you could have made it *inside a theater,* and the walls of the theater would have reflected the energy, and you could have created a much higher state.

So you have an environment to create space and time, and to redo the boundary conditions of existence. Most people don't realize—even after Einstein—that there is no space out there. Space is generated by the relative movements of things. Time is different in every biosphere and in every human relative to the location in space. So if I can create an environment that basically makes a location in time and space, then I become master of my existence, rather than a slave.

> *. . . if I can create an environment that . . . makes a location in time and space, then I become master of my existence . . .*

It goes very deep in human beings, this artistic and creative urge to make environments. You can say that a spaceship is a moveable cave and that instead of sitting there with cobras and leopards outside, you have freezing cold and solar radiation to combat. We're always vulnerable, but creating these environments is the challenge, the adventure, and you make them artistic—that is, valuable—and you get together with people you like.

REBECCA: I can't imagine a man-made environment that would turn me on more than one created by the superhuman forces of nature. Diving in the ocean or walking in the woods—part of the beauty of that experience is that it's *not* man-made.

JOHN: But, you see, you *don't* dive in the ocean. You have a very manicured beach, you have lifeboats for the undertow—it's a created environment. Even if you found a beach where no human being had ever been before, you're in a certain perceptual-philosophical scheme. Wherever it is, it's a created environment.

REBECCA: I can see that the *perception* of the environment is created by the human mind, but the environment is *affected* by humanity, not wholly created by it.

> *Nobody walks in an unaltered tropical rainforest . . . Natural and artificial are now interpenetrative.*

JOHN: Highly affected. You don't have an unaltered environment left on planet Earth. You don't walk in a natural rainforest anymore, either. I've walked in parts of several rainforests, and the atmosphere has changed: pharmaceutical collectors have been by, and so have surveyors. Nobody walks in an unaltered tropical rainforest. You may *imagine* you're doing that but, with your size and stature, you can't do it. Natural and artificial are now interpenetrative.

REBECCA: But, in purely artistic terms, it's still far more beautiful than anything that has been created by humans. There's a paltry amount of art that's inspirational in the world today, and inspirational environments are even fewer. Why would space biospheres be any different?

JOHN: We need to deepen our perceptions. Stanislavsky said that we should become fighters for truth and beauty. You're right, humans have historically been able to create messes out of anything. Heraclitus called the process "turning into the opposite."

REBECCA: During a recent trip to Las Vegas I was amazed to what extent they're attempting to create artificial environments. Consider that Las Vegas is the fastest growing city in America, is perhaps the future of artificial environment not this visionary exploration of ecosystem interaction, but rather a commercial orgy of materialistic fantasy?

JOHN: Well, let's get rid of this Aristotelian either/or business. When you say artificial environment, it's a long way from Biosphere 1 to Biosphere 2 to Las Vegas. Las Vegas is already itself an artificial environment—if you put a roof on it, it just becomes a little bit more so. But that's an artificial environment dedicated to wasting energy.

REBECCA: Actually, I was using Las Vegas as representational of a *mentality;* I wasn't suggesting that Las Vegas itself was a biosphere. As you've mentioned, the technosphere is by and large unoriginal, with commercial interests overwhelmingly given priority. Isn't it more likely, then, that space station biospheres—in keeping with the definition you've used—would reflect *those* values more than those of artistic, visionary adventurers, at least to begin with?

JOHN: Yeah, but it's necessary to keep these issues alive so that we don't just surrender to the "battleship gray" syndrome. The word *biosphere* has become very popular. I've had people invite me into their living room, which they've decorated with some rocks and rugs, and they say, "Welcome to my biosphere." A biosphere, as I said earlier, is a materially closed system and has energy and information flowing through it that produces free energy. Las Vegas is not an example of this. *(laughter)*

> *I've had people invite me into their living room . . . and they say, "Welcome to my biosphere."*

Like Las Vegas, the technosphere of the planet Earth, which is the major driving force for these artificial environments, is lowering the free energy of the planet, it's lowering the complexity and diversity. It's bad for thinking and feeling. The technosphere needs to be renovated. The word for that is "noosphere," and it describes a biosphere and a technosphere working together. Biosphere 2 is really Noosphere 1.

DAVID: Wasn't noosphere a term coined by Teilhard de Chardin?

JOHN: It's debatable whether Vernadsky or Teilhard de Chardin coined that term. They were both in Paris at the same time and Chardin was a student of Vernadsky. Chardin gave an idealistic tilt to the word and Vernadsky gave it a scientific interpretation.

REBECCA: Was Biosphere 2, as many have claimed, partly inspired by an apocalyptic vision of the world's future?

JOHN: No, no, a thousand times no. This is the media for you. I said the Biosphere was a *refugia*. This word has a technical meaning in biology—it means a place that has a concentration of life diversity. The Amazon, for example, is a place where the genetic diversity of the rainforest concentrates. Well, this term became, in certain sensationalist hands, interpreted as me being the head of an apocalyptic cult of survivalist savages protecting billionaires and the Pentagon in the middle of Arizona! You couldn't live in Biosphere 2 if Biosphere 1 were destroyed, at least not on earth. It was a dumb smear job.

DAVID: What were some of the biggest challenges that you and your colleagues had to face during the project?

JOHN: The media. (*laughter*) I know it seems that the media were all negative, but there was actually a period when some were saying this was the greatest scientific project that had ever happened on the planet Earth, and it was going to save the world, and so on. So then we had people going around totally conceited, and some never recovered. They actually believed that!

Then there were those who said that it was the worst thing that had ever happened, and some of our people went around thinking that and were feeling all guilt-ridden. It's a pattern in the American media: they build you up, then they take you down. The big challenge was how to keep it out of the public eye, and we succeeded in doing that for a long time.

REBECCA: But then there was controversy about that, about the fact that you weren't available—the media took it as your having had something to hide.

JOHN: Right. This added to the media fuel and they said, "Why didn't anybody know about you from 1969 until 1988? What great secret did you have to conceal?" (*laughter*) But some critics were really beneficial to the project. Hundreds of people came up with excellent critiques.

REBECCA: What do you think it was about this project that inspired so much controversy?

JOHN: It was a challenge—to reductionist science, to the idea that space stations should just survey planet Earth, and to the school system. Kids love it. Biosphere 2 has the same impact on a kid as seeing the earth from space. Kids from the fourth and fifth grades would insist that their teachers teach them about biospheres.

> *Biosphere 2 has the same impact on a kid as seeing the earth from space.*

REBECCA: Many people also seemed to have a problem with the fact that you've taken out patents on some of the technology developed for Biosphere 2.

JOHN: Yes, then there's the nihilist left. (*laughter*) They said we were contaminated because we dealt at all with business, but they didn't offer to finance it! We could have gone to the government, but they were too conservative. So we got one adventurous capitalist, and now he's taken it over. But at least he got the idea out, at least humanity now knows that this is possible. And now that the idea is out, it can't be stopped.

DAVID: I was reading in *Science* magazine that there's an attempt being made by the Biosphere 2 team to accommodate more scientific research by outside scientists.

JOHN: The first two years were like a maiden voyage. On a maiden voyage you need to have people who are highly skilled, who can react quickly to emergencies—not your usual scientific type. Now we have it down to where it's operating more regularly. Like NASA at a certain point needed the "right stuff," and now they put scientists up into space because they no longer need somebody with a jet pilot reflex—the same with Biosphere 2.

DAVID: How did the biospherians deal with the psychosocial pressures of living together in such tight quarters for so long?

JOHN: A little better than a nuclear family in a suburban house.

DAVID: A little better? How did you measure that?

JOHN: Oh, by the divorce rate, the murder rate . . . (*laughter*)

REBECCA: Did they live together before they went into the Biosphere 2?

> *The main thing I looked for every morning was if anyone had a black eye.*

JOHN: We did expeditionary training. We'd had ship voyages and we'd worked in remote stations. We had sophisticated medical measurements and psychoanalysts monitoring things. The main thing I looked for every morning was if anyone had a black eye. (*laughter*)

Most importantly—and NASA did a lot of work on this—we saw if anybody refused to eat with anybody the night before. Nobody ever did, even though they sometimes refused to speak with one another. It's a long-held tradition in nomadic tribes that if you eat together, you don't kill the other person.

REBECCA: What do you think are some of the characteristics necessary for somebody to survive well under biosphere conditions?

JOHN: The first condition in a complex experimental situation is that you have to be knowledgeable in many different areas. Also, you have to relate to other people whether you like them or not. If somebody says, "Jump," you have to jump if that person is in charge of that particular area.

Most of all you must see some value in the task. The biggest secret anybody's ever found to high morale is if people think they are doing something interesting and important. As soon as it starts to bore people or they think it's insignificant, then you have to go to a whole morale-building stimulus deal. The present mode in the United States is "I'm okay, you're okay," "Let's all feel good," and so on. But the older school, which I believe is more correct, is that an army outfit that doesn't gripe is going to be wiped out during their first engagement with enemy forces.

DAVID: Can you tell us about the present situation at Biosphere 2, particularly the allegations of mismanagement and what this will mean for its future?

JOHN: Well, they're totally false. We had developed a whole series of products with budgets and five-year plans, so basically the financial partner just took it all away. I don't know what the consequences will be—that's under negotiation—but I hope that a reasonable solution will be found. I'm often accused of being a sanguine type who perhaps tends to take a cheerier view toward life than the facts would justify.

DAVID: I hope it's contagious, I could use a little bit of that. (*laughter*) Can you tell us about the plans for an underwater biosphere and other future biosphere projects?

JOHN: There's a whole series of biospheres that have an extreme importance to human beings. One is underwater, one will be a desert biosphere, there's a low atmospheric pressure biosphere at twenty thousand feet, a polluted biosphere, et cetera. At what point will the planet Earth be wiped out because the large system can no longer adapt to the rate of change? There's a lot of argument about that, and some people say, *[in a dumb voice]* "Well, we can keep on doing it because there's going to be a technofix somewhere along the line."

Let's suppose you take the smoggiest day in Mexico City, or a real disaster such as Love Canal, and build a biosphere around it to find out if it can recover. You see, it's masked out here because you have the total biosphere working to repair it. It's like, if you had a hole in your head you would recover because the total body would go into a healing trip. But at some point, with, say, twenty-three holes, the whole system would break down.

> *Let's suppose you take ... a real disaster such as Love Canal, and build a biosphere around it to find out if it can recover.*

One hole at a time can be repaired. But in a closed biosphere we could figure out—to a degree, allowing for scale factors—what would be the point of no return for the total system. Of course, long before that there should be intelligent mass action against it, and we're probably very close to that. But who can say? The biosphere has lots of resilience. Do we have what it takes to support ten billion people? This is one of the biggest areas where the Biosphere 2 can help us to find answers.

REBECCA: You've been described variously as an entrepreneur, a charlatan, a genius, and a megalomaniac. How would you describe yourself?

JOHN: (*laughter*) A human being behind those four faces and probably a billion others. That's why I'm so interested in theater—because there you get to be all those things. As a playwright or a drama teacher you can accelerate it even more, because if you have fifteen people in an acting class or fifteen characters in a play, you can multiply yourself by fifteen.

I entitled my book about Biosphere 2 *The Human Experiment*. Human beings can come and go, but the biosphere will outlive us all. The real experiment is, can human beings become not parasites but symbiotes? Can human beings learn to do their duty to the biosphere and take it into space? The biosphere is doomed when the sun explodes. To be a human being is the highest state that we know in the universe, except to be a biosphere, which is beyond our capacity. But it is in our capacity to be the brain and the conscience of the biosphere, to be its self-reflective point.

DAVID: Do poetry and theater still play a part in your life?

JOHN: Oh, of course. I have my third book of poems coming out; it's called *Mysteries*. In a way I think that mystery is the highest of all values. Beauty attracts, but mystery . . . lures.

Neil Sundermayer

John Robbins

"... how can we live so that our participation is for the greatest good and the greatest healing for all beings?"

Food for the Soul
with John Robbins

As a vegetarian, I thought I had a pretty good knowledge of the inside dirt on animal husbandry. But it is one thing to know, it is quite another to feel. The fact that I don't eat meat didn't protect me from the onslaught of shame and sadness that crashed through my head when I read Diet for a New America. *I found it hard to believe that we had gone so far. I cried harder than I had in years.*

As John Robbins points out, you don't have to be an animal activist, or even particularly love animals, to be appalled, horrified, and outraged at what is being done in factory farms all over the country, all day, every day. It is so extreme. The book reads like sci-fi horror, a prophetic warning of the ripening of humanity's faceless brutality. But the fact is, it's been going on for years.

John Robbins surfaced from the Baskin Robbins ice cream family gene pool like some strange new mutation—the thirty-second flavor who was destined to leave a bitter taste in the mouth of the National Dairy Council. In his two books, the international best-seller Diet for a New America *and* May All Be Fed, *he explains with straightforward clarity the link between our food habits and the health of our planet, our bodies, and our souls.*

His manner is filled with the contagious buoyancy of a person who is being true to his conscience. He speaks with an impassioned sincerity—never patronizing, never self-righteous. We interviewed John at his home in Felton, California on June 9, 1994. In his mid-forties he still looks like a schoolboy; his wide blue eyes, elfin face, and Disney smile radiate with a childlike innocence. This is the man at the top of the Meat and Dairy Board's most-wanted list, you wonder? The man they consider so dangerous that they have meetings on ways to discredit him?

He is the founder of the nonprofit organization EarthSave, which concentrates on educating the public about health, nutrition, and sustainable energy consumption. He has spoken to a variety of audiences, including Physicians for Social Responsibility, the Sierra Club, the Humane Society of the United States, UNICEF, and the United Nations Environmental Program, where he received a standing ovation.

Do you know that colon cancer is directly linked to meat consumption? Do you know that you save more water by not eating one pound of beef than you would from not showering for a whole year? Do you know the extent of the suffering involved in factory farming? Once you know, you can never act without that knowledge again. Here is the information, says John Robbins. Now it's up to you. Bon appetite!

RMN

———

DAVID: How did growing up in the "heart of the American food machine" influence your motivation to research and write *Diet for a New America?*

JOHN: There was a tremendous investment in my family to deny any link between diet and health, particularly between ice cream and health. I understood it, given the livelihood involved, but I could feel the pressure of that denial like a lid on top of me. As I was growing up and reaching out beyond the assumptions, values, and world view of my parents, I encountered a lot of information that was taboo to them.

REBECCA: How old were you when you began questioning those taboos?

JOHN: Very young. I don't know how to account for it, but the fact of the matter is that I seemed to be destined to do this. From my earliest childhood I was living two lives. I was being groomed by my father to succeed him—being trained in the factory, in merchandising and franchising, and in all the other aspects of the business. But then my inner life was involved in questioning and challenging everything I was being taught.

I couldn't talk to my father about this, or to my mother, my sisters, or my aunts and uncles. It was two separate worlds. In one world life was about material success, and in another world life was about the heart. In one world ice cream made people happy, and in another world ice cream was high in saturated fat and cholesterol and contributed to diabetes and heart disease.

REBECCA: But that's not something that you could have known as a very small child.

JOHN: No, not the details of it. It was more of a feeling.

REBECCA: You never enjoyed ice cream?

> *When people find out that I don't eat ice cream anymore, they get this pained look on their face, as if I'm deprived . . .*

JOHN: I loved ice cream! Are you kidding me? (*laughter*) When people find out that I don't eat ice cream anymore, they get this pained look on their face, as if I'm deprived, and I say, "*Please* don't feel sorry for me. I've eaten enough ice cream for ten lifetimes!"

REBECCA: So the style of your inspiration was more of an unraveling process rather than a revelatory flash?

JOHN: Yes. There were moments that catalyzed me, or where I became aware that I had progressed to a certain point, but I can't pin the development of my consciousness entirely on those moments. For example, in the sixties I was living and going to school in Berkeley. I had been working with Martin Luther King, and the civil rights movement had become very important to me. I was this privileged, upper-class white kid, and sometimes I wondered what business I had being involved in this. But then I felt that I had a lot of business because it was such a profound thing that was happening to everyone.

To put this in context, I have to back up a little. When I was in high school and working closely with my dad, I knew only the world of wealthy people and the country club scene. That's all I knew. I felt restricted and limited by the fact that I only felt comfortable with what I was familiar with. I would look around at everybody else, and I felt completely disconnected.

And I noticed that at Baskin Robbins most of the store owners were white, most of the customers were white, and that it was basically an upper-class trip—it was a luxury ice cream. And then when I was a senior in high school I was offered scholarships to Harvard, Stanford, and Yale because I had been very successful on the debate team. But I chose not to go to those schools because it would have been more of the same: the privileged few.

So I chose to go to the University of California at Berkeley, which is a public school and was then fairly inexpensive. I thought here would be an opportunity to meet people outside the very narrow socio-economic group that I had been in. I had a very powerful desire to understand more kinds of people.

So in 1965 I left Los Angeles and went to Berkeley. I immediately became involved in the free speech movement, the civil rights movement, and the antiwar movement. It was an incredible time to be alive. Openings of all kinds were happening. I took the civil rights movement very personally, and when Doctor King was killed in 1968 I felt as if a bullet had gone through my heart, too. Any thoughts of business as usual felt just ludicrous and empty.

> *when Doctor King was killed . . . I felt as if a bullet had gone through my heart, too.*

I had seen in my own family a high level of material success, and I had seen its limitations. Within the circle of my family's friends were some of the richest people in the world, and some of the most neurotic people in the world.

DAVID: What about your sisters? Were you the only rebel in the bunch?

JOHN: Yeah. My two sisters share a great deal of assumptions and perspectives with my parents.

REBECCA: How do they feel about what you're doing now?

JOHN: I don't think I've been an easy relative for any of them to deal with. When I left the business, my dad was very hurt, and that caused a lot of distance between us. He knew that I was sincere, but he felt that I was crazy. Here I was with long hair, walking away from an opportunity to be extremely wealthy in order to do—what? He couldn't understand, and I couldn't explain it either, in terms that made sense to him.

My uncle Burt Baskin died of a heart attack in the late sixties. I said to my dad, "Do you think there could be any connection between the amount of ice cream that Uncle Burt would eat and his heart attack?" He said, "Absolutely not. His ticker just got tired."

Then five years ago my dad's health was very precarious. His cholesterol was high. He had very high blood pressure, for which he had to take ten of what he called "horse pills" every day, which had serious side effects, which he hated. His diabetes was getting worse. But my dad made changes in his diet, and he's gotten tremendous results in his own health. Today his cholesterol is 150. His blood pressure has come down so much that he only takes one blood pressure pill every other day. His diabetes is in complete remission, so he doesn't need insulin. His circulation has improved tremendously, and he's lost a lot of weight. His golf game has also improved.

We used to argue all the time, and I remember him saying to me, "Look, you're an idealist, and that's very nice when you're young, but you have to get over it in order to be successful. It's too bad, but that's the way it is." And I would reply that if you don't have your integrity, you don't have anything. Recently he said to me, "Thank God some of us have lived long enough to learn a few new things."

REBECCA: So it's been harder for your mother to accept these things?

JOHN: She's doing the best she can. My mother always felt that she was in charge of the food department, and she seems to feel that I'm saying she fed us wrong.

REBECCA: But you *are* saying that.

JOHN: No. She did the best she could given what she knew at the time and given the resources that were available then. She didn't know, for example, about the terrible abuse of animals in modern meat production.

REBECCA: Could you describe, for those who aren't aware, some of the conditions that you have witnessed in factory farms all over America.

JOHN: I could point to the worst places, where the conditions are most stressful on the animals, the diet is the most unnatural, and the people are the most callous. But I'd rather just describe the industry norms.

Veal calves are male calves born to dairy cows. The females are shunted in one direction on their way to becoming four-legged milk pumps, and the males are taken away at birth or the next day. They are baby mammals, and they desperately want to suckle, but they're not allowed to. When you look at their faces, you see that this is an infant here, you see the innocence and the vulnerability and the preciousness, and then you see the exploitation.

They stand knee deep in their own excrement wailing and crying for their mothers.

Standard operating procedure for veal calves is to chain them at the neck in stalls or cages so tiny that they can't even take a single step for their entire lives. They stand knee-deep in their own excrement, wailing and crying for their mothers. The diet the calf is fed is designed to be deficient in iron.

The factory-farm workers play the edge so that the anemia won't kill the creature before it's four months old, which is when it is slaughtered. But a lot of calves die anyway or go blind because the factories play the edge and then go past it. The reason they want to do this is because the flesh becomes a lighter color, and we've been trained to believe that lighter meats are healthier. But it's really just the flesh of a tortured baby animal.

Standard operating procedure for layer hens, from which our eggs come, is to cram them into cages so tightly that the birds can't even lift a wing. The floor of the cage is mesh, and their claws constantly get stuck in it. It's totally unnatural.

Broilers—birds from which chicken meat comes—are kept in warehouses and never see the light of day. These are animals that are extremely sensitive to light rhythms. The industry manipulates their hormonal responses with fluorescent lights, which are sometimes on twenty-four hours a day, but at other times not at all. This is all contrived to get the maximum possible weight gain in the shortest possible time. Part of that process is to mix antibiotics into every dose of feed and to spray them into the air the chickens breathe.

The same mentality is generating the conditions that hogs and dairy and beef cattle are in. Beef cattle are on cement for the second half of their life in the feedlot, penned in so tightly that they can hardly move around. They're implanted with artificial hormones in their ears. We're the only industrialized country in the world that still does that, and we do it to 99 percent of our beef cattle.

REBECCA: What about the conditions that pigs are made to live under?

JOHN: Hogs are in individual stalls as adults, and they're often in tiered cages, three stalls high. Again, the cages are so small that they can't move. The excrement from the upper stalls drops down continuously through the slots onto the heads of the ones below. Contrary to popular belief, hogs don't like to be dirty, and they will never soil their own bedding under normal conditions.

They also have extremely sensitive noses which enable them, under natural conditions, to root around and actually smell edible roots through the earth. Here, piles of their own excrement build up so that the ammonia, hydrogen sulphide, and other gasses give off an unbelievable smell. It's standard for nobody to clean it up for months on end.

DAVID: What do you think is the best strategy for helping animals gain the right to live lives without this kind of cruelty?

> *If you expect people who don't treat themselves well to treat the world well, you'll be sorely disappointed.*

JOHN: There are many things that we have to do. We have to learn to respect ourselves and our needs as animals, and we must respect the entire web of life on this planet. If you expect people who don't treat themselves well to treat the world well, you'll be sorely disappointed. People who smoke and pollute their own lungs cannot be expected to be as sensitive to air pollution from smokestacks.

A society that looks at a forest and immediately starts measuring board-feet objectifies the forest and sees its value only in terms of how it can be converted into revenue. That same mentality looks at another human being and says, "How can I put that person to work for the glorification of my own ego, or for the expansion of my own wealth?" There's no cherishing involved.

REBECCA: So you're saying that if we can develop greater respect for one another, then somehow that will spill over into a greater respect for other forms of life?

JOHN: Yes, and vice versa. I know many people who are not able to love other human beings—they've been too traumatized—but they are able to love an animal, and through that love they are able to learn to relate more caringly to other people. Maybe they can't be intimate, but they can have a more benevolent relationship with other people than they would have been able to have without the animal.

REBECCA: But some people have extremely intimate relationships with their cats or their dogs, and have a whole different category of thinking for a cow or a pig that's lying on their dinner plate.

> *Why do we call some animals pets and other animals dinner?*

JOHN: This is one of the myths that is being perpetrated—that some animals are part of the circle of compassion and others are not. Why do we call some animals pets and other animals dinner? Historically it used to be—and it still is to some extent—that an animal that is destined for human consumption is exempted from the laws restricting cruelty to animals. In other words, you can do anything you want to an animal as long as you're going to eat it. Hence the treatment of veal calves.

DAVID: What if you were going to eat your dog or cat?

JOHN: There are Filipino communities in the United States where they carry on the cultural tradition of eating dogs. Most people who wouldn't think twice about the treatment of veal calves would find it very objectionable to see a dog treated that way.

REBECCA: I've come across a few people who read your book who were genuinely horrified and deeply moved by it, to the point where they became vegetarian or even vegan. And then, somehow, the effect wore off, and one or two years later they were eating meat again. What do you think are the keys to a lasting relationship with vegetarianism?

JOHN: Being honest with yourself about what your values are. Making your life a statement of what you love, believe in, and respect.

DAVID: A basic truth about animals is that in order for them to exist they have to feed on other living things. A lot of people have had experiences that have led them to believe that plants are conscious beings. In your opinion, why is eating the corpses of plants more compassionate than eating the corpses of animals?

JOHN: Look at it this way. It takes sixteen pounds of grain to make one pound of feedlot beef. It takes one pound of grain to make one pound of bread. So how many more plants are you eating if you eat a pound of beef? Secondly, I've harvested cabbages and pulled carrots out of the ground, and I've been in slaughterhouses and seen the animals have their brains bashed out with sledgehammers and their throats cut. The experiences are not comparable.

DAVID: But don't you think that could be a species bias you have because animals are life-forms that are more similar to us?

JOHN: The animals do everything they can to resist: they fight, they scream, they secrete adrenaline. They have nervous systems with pain receptors. In the Middle Ages the church had a conference to decide whether animals and women had souls. Women squeaked by, but animals lost.

But animals do have souls, and they do want to live. I think that plants have group souls, and I don't think that taking an individual plant ruptures the fabric in the same way that the violence of killing an animal does. It is a matter of degree, of course. But I really feel that this question could only be asked by someone who has never been in a slaughterhouse.

REBECCA: Also, plants literally live on their own death. The compost of their material allows other plants to grow.

JOHN: Right. But the deeper issue here is that we are part of and we partake of the biocommunity. The question that I ask is, how can we live so that our participation is for the greatest good and the greatest healing for all beings?

> *I think there's been a great deal of vegetarian evangelism . . .*

Your question points to the fact that we all do take life to live. It's a spectrum, and we are all involved in killing. As soon as you separate people into the violent and the nonviolent, into carnivores and noncarnivores, and you stand in one camp and point a finger at the other in a judgmental way, you're creating more violence. I think there's been a great deal of vegetarian evangelism, with a lot of holier-than-thou or more-vegan-than-thou kind of stuff. And it's created a backlash, because no one wants to be made to feel guilty or ashamed.

> *The ecological impact of meat production is horrendous.*

I feel that it is less violent to eat plants, and of course it's healthier. It's interesting that because you're consuming fewer plants by eating plants than you would be if you were eating animals, you're allowing more of the biomass of the planet to survive. The ecological impact of meat production is horrendous. Of course, the impact of large-scale, agribusiness-dominated, petrochemical-based, pesticide-saturated vegetable and fruit growing is not pretty either, but it's not as bad.

REBECCA: Say that I'm someone who is reasonably aware of the way factory farm animals are treated. I'm a good person in general, and I maybe even do a little charity work here and there, but I still eat meat. When I'm presented with this information I say, "That all makes sense, but there are so many inequities in the world. I have to worry about whether my furniture is made from rainforest wood and whether my phone company is funding political extremists. This is just another thing to think about, and it's just too much.

JOHN: There are a lot of people like that. I think that they would like the limited amount of leverage they have to be used effectively for the greater good. And I think we have found an acupuncture point where, with a minimum amount of effort, you get a maximum amount of benefit to the whole system.

I think that such people would find their own purpose strengthened and validated if they understood that the ramifications of their food choices are incredible—to the animals, to the biosphere, to our own health and ability to function gracefully. The good that can come from conscious food choices is profound, and, by the same token, the evil—even unconscious evil—that can ensue from food choices is also dramatic.

You mentioned the rainforest. Every fast-food hamburger that's made from rainforest beef represents the destruction of fifty-five square feet of tropical rainforest. The person you're describing would never go out and clear a rainforest, but he or she would eat a hamburger. In effect, by the laws of economics, the person's hands are on the chainsaws at that moment.

So I think that alerting people to the consequences of their choices enables them to make wiser choices, ones that are congruent with their desires and heart's purpose.

REBECCA: But some people's biological desires tend to overwhelm their moral desires. I've heard people say, "I love animals, but I also really love meat."

JOHN: Sometimes in life we must choose between a path that leads to greater joy, health, and peace and another path that is maybe more superficially and sensually appealing, but which leads in a different direction. By making these choices we create our destinies.

REBECCA: I find it easy to understand why otherwise conscious people would rather remain in the dark about this stuff.

JOHN: We want to push it away because it is so painful. But we *can* do something about it. I've seen that when people do face the pain and experience the woundedness of our culture in this regard, they experience a deeply human,

> *The pain itself can be the trigger for the clarity about who we are . . .*

clear, thoughtful response to it all that takes them to a greater experience of self. The pain itself can be the trigger for the clarity about who we are, what we will support, and what we will not support.

DAVID: John Allen talked about how the consequences of their actions in Biosphere 2 were very profound and very fast. If they put a toxin down their sink, they would find it the next day in their drinking water. We apparently don't see the consequences until way on down the line.

JOHN: We are a nearsighted species, which was fine as long as our numbers were within a certain range. But now there are so many more of us, and the impact of what we do is multiplied and then multiplied again by our technological advancement. We are definitely called by the urgency of the situation to make some key changes. It is now a survival imperative.

REBECCA: I noticed all the cruelty-free products you have in your bathroom. In your book you don't mention vivisection, but I'd like to know your opinion on testing products on animals.

JOHN: In general, I do not condone research on animals. We don't condone research on people who aren't conscious of the implications, and show me the animal that has signed a release form. (*laughter*) It's part of that mentality that exploits.

DAVID: Let's say that the sacrifice of several animals could save the lives of many humans.

JOHN: I'm not a purist. I think that 99 percent of the animal research is unnecessary, and in many cases cruel. Whether that one percent would be valid and would be something I could support remains to be seen.

REBECCA: Can you think of an instance where you would condone it?

> *The way that most animal experiments are conducted makes for very poor science.*

JOHN: I can theoretically, but practically speaking, since 99 percent of it is appalling to me, I say let's clean that up first, and then we'll talk about the other one percent and see how that can be done in a way that minimizes the suffering to animals and maximizes the value and knowledge to other beings. The way that most animal experiments are conducted makes for very poor science. The cardinal case is thalidomide. Had we not been so reliant on, and therefore so trusting of, animal experimentation, we would have gone through far more careful human testing and realized the dangers sooner.

REBECCA: What are some of the general major health differences evidenced by scientific research between meat-eaters and vegetarians?

JOHN: The differences are staggering. The average vegetarian lives seven-and-a-half years longer than the average meat-eater. But it's not only the length of life, it's the quality. The average meat-eater has a cardiovascular system that is slowly clogging up; the arteries are hardening and tightening, the blood pressure is rising, and the circulation is impaired. The flow of oxygen and nutrition to all the organs is being compromised, so there is a reduction in the quality of life, of consciousness, of flexibility.

> *The average vegetarian lives seven-and-a-half years longer than the average meat-eater.*

The leading cause of death in the United States is heart disease, the second is cancer. People who eat the standard American diet stand over a 50 percent chance of heart and cardiovascular disease, whereas vegetarians have a 15 percent chance of dying from such a condition, and vegans have less than a five percent chance.

When they do autopsies on people who've had heart attacks, they take out what had been stuck in the artery blocking the flow of blood to the heart. It's usually shaped like a sausage and it's gummy and thick. When it's studied they invariably find the same thing: saturated fat and cholesterol. No one has yet come back from the lab and said, "Broccoli and brown rice!" One hundred percent of the cholesterol we take into our bodies and 70 percent of the saturated fat comes from animal fats.

There was an interesting study conducted at Cornell. They started out analyzing the lifespan of smokers, and they calculated the amount of time that smokers smoked a day. They compared that to the decrease in lifespan attributable to smoking and concluded that every minute a person smokes, it costs that person, on average, seven or eight minutes of life.

Then they expanded the study to meat-eating and its mortality statistics, and they worked out how much time a meat-eater spends eating meat. Their analysis was that every time people eat meat they lose eleven minutes off their lifespan.

REBECCA: What mistakes do vegetarians sometimes make in their food choices?

JOHN: One mistake is to think that if you change your diet, you're now exempt from the other laws of living, as if vegetarianism alone cured everything. It's such a powerful, maverick thing to do that people sometimes think that that takes care of things. It's a holier-than-thou mentality that means that people just stop there.

At the diet and health level, I see some vegetarians eating a lot of dairy products: yogurt, cheese, and ice cream. They substitute dairy products for meat to try to keep their protein levels high. This culture has protein paranoia.

REBECCA: If the health benefits of high protein consumption aren't backed up by medical research, as you state in your books, where did this philosophy come from?

JOHN: The original protein experiments were done on rats and mice. And here's another example of faulty conclusions being drawn from animal research. Rats need a lot of protein. Rat mothers milk is 47 percent protein. Human mothers milk is five percent protein. A baby rat gains weight rapidly on a pattern of amino-acid balance that is very close to the pattern found in eggs, and is approximated in meats and dairy products.

When Francis Moore Lappe wrote *Diet for a Small Planet,* she was accepting those studies and held the egg pattern as the ideal. She pointed out that if you combine grains and beans and other vegetarian proteins, there's a certain synergistic complementarity that develops, and you get an overall package that approaches the egg. It was a landmark book because it showed that even if you accept the egg as the ideal pattern, you do quite well if you combine your proteins.

Since that time she has changed her viewpoint dramatically. In the subsequent editions of her book, she says that her emphasis on protein complementarity was mistaken. It isn't needed because our protein needs are much lower than we thought. The epidemiological studies are very clear, and the biochemistry of the body is much better understood than it was in 1971.

REBECCA: Do you think that the success of the idea that a lot of protein is good for you stems from the belief that bigger is better?

Maybe we're not all supposed to be the same size!

JOHN: Yes. The pediatrician comes in and says, "How's the child doing? Is he gaining weight?" Who cares? Maybe we're not all supposed to be the same size! Some of us are supposed to be much bigger than the norm, and some of us are supposed to be much smaller.

REBECCA: In *Diet for a New America* you quote numerous studies, conducted by leading medical authorities and health institutions from all over the world, that time and again point to meat consumption as a major health hazard. How is it that this information remains relatively underground. Why don't more people know?

JOHN: You have to understand how the medical establishment works. It's as if there were a problem with people falling off cliffs. At the bottom we have stationed the most expensive and sophisticated system of ambulances in the world, but we do not erect fences on top of the cliff. As a matter of fact, the companies that manufacture the ambulances and the people who drive the ambulances would like to see laws passed that forbid the erection of fences.

There is a built-in investment for illness in the medical establishment. Of course, it's not an individual conscious desire on the part of the doctor for his patient to get sick. But the pharmaceutical orientation has made disease profitable. Sick people are a market. The pharmaceutical companies support and endow the medical schools. In four years of medical school, the average M.D. gets two-and-a-half hours of coursework in nutrition. They don't know much of anything about nutrition building health.

> *There is a built-in investment for illness in the medical establishment.*

REBECCA: There are so many people who are on medications that cause horrible side effects. How come the medical establishment isn't investing more in education and prevention of illness?

JOHN: There are more prescriptions written for hypertension than for any other condition. They're very often prescribed for older men, and the interesting thing is that most of them are blood thinners. One of the consequences of blood thinners in older men is impotence. Then you have a whole spin-off from the other drugs that are called into play as a result of this.

If you can invent a pill that will lower blood pressure, even if it has all these side effects, you can make a great deal of money. But if you teach people how to eat so that their blood pressure will not be high in the first place, it's an uphill battle to make a living from doing that.

So it's not that people aren't good, it's just that everyone has to support themselves and their families. How many people are going to be able to live in the genuine service of others, given the economics of the situation? In a healthy society medical people are paid when their patients are well, not when they're ill.

REBECCA: What are the meat and dairy industries doing to counter the information that *is* getting through to the public?

JOHN: Oh, a great deal! (*laughter*) We get transcripts from their internal meetings, and one of the major topics at one of their conferences was "What are we going to do about John Robbins?"

DAVID: Have you received any threats from the meat and dairy industry?

> *. . . it doesn't matter what happens to me, because I'm just one voice who happens to have the microphone at the moment.*

JOHN: Oh yes, but it doesn't matter what happens to me, because I'm just one voice who happens to have the microphone at the moment. The truth is the truth.

REBECCA: Are they stepping up their PR campaign?

JOHN: Are they ever! It's a parallel situation to what happened with the tobacco industry ten to fifteen years ago. As the medical information was finally making its way to the public, the first thing they did was step up their PR and advertising campaigns.

They're trying to confuse the issue. Also, there are people in the FDA who would like to have the power of approving everything that you do and position themselves as arbiters. They say they do it for benevolent purposes, to protect the public, but God save us from such benevolence. It's a power trip, and it's just another way of dominating people.

REBECCA: I love the story told by Tolstoy's daughter in which her aunt came to dinner and demanded to eat meat, so Tolstoy tied a chicken to her plate, gave her a knife, and said, "Go ahead." The idea of slaughtering an animal is horrifying to most people, and yet they have no problem having others do the killing for them. How is it, do you think, that so many people are able to eat meat without even thinking about what they are doing, without making peace with the process?

JOHN: How it is that people can be so unconscious? As a culture we don't value consciousness or awareness; we value performance. In schools there is no attempt to educate and show where the meat comes from. Then the industry has an agenda to keep the veil in place and to keep the denial fixed.

McDonalds will tell children during Saturday morning commercials that hamburgers grow in hamburger patches. When I first saw that I thought it was an innocent fantasy, but there's no innocence to it. It's a deliberate and sophisticated marketing ploy, the purpose of which is to obscure the reality that hamburgers are ground up cows. It is done because children are uniquely sensitive to the animal experience. Hamburgers, if they grew on hamburger plants, would be vegetables. (*laughter*)

> *McDonalds will tell children during Saturday morning commercials that hamburgers grow in hamburger patches.*

The experience of being in a slaughterhouse is so dramatic that it gets us out of our heads, and I'm sure that many people's rationalizations would fall away if they were exposed to that reality. You don't have to be an animal rights activist or a vegetarian to be outraged, grieved, and disappointed, because it's so extreme. It's really gone beyond what most of us could imagine in our worst fantasies.

> *It's really gone beyond what most of us could imagine in our worst fantasies.*

REBECCA: When Native Americans killed a buffalo, they conducted a ritual dance in which they acknowledged and atoned for that act. Today, in many parts of the world where people hunt for food, there is still that respect for the animal as a sacred and conscious being that is part of the universe's living framework. How do you think we lost that connection?

JOHN: Western civilization. (*laughter*) Television is an extreme example of removal from feeling experience. All you're doing is looking and hearing; you're not smelling or tasting or feeling. We've isolated ourselves from nature and our own natures. Until we have communities and families that cherish one another, we will continue to play out this hostility.

Ronald Reagan ran on this platform of traditional family values, and then Nancy Reagan encouraged children to turn their parents in for drug use! There was a young girl whose mother was selling marijuana who took

Nancy up on it. Nancy Reagan flew from Washington to California to have a press conference with this little girl and tell her that this showed that she really loved her mother. The girl's mother was sent to jail, and it turns out that she wasn't even a smoker. They were poor, and she was trying to make some money to buy her daughter a tricycle for her birthday.

What kind of traditional family values are these, where you encourage little children, who are completely out of their realm in issues like this, to do something like that? That's the replacement of family values with government values. It's very patriarchal, and it's very paternalistic.

To me, the value of the family is something that, as a culture, we have yet to discover. What would a people be like who grew up with parents who truly cherished them, and who worked at every juncture to support their fulfillment and understanding and growth? We don't know; we have yet to undertake that experiment. I believe that what the human being is capable of is far beyond what any of us have yet glimpsed.

REBECCA: As you've already mentioned, children are particularly sensitive to the animal. What are the meat and dairy industries doing to hide from children the moral and biological consequences of consuming their products?

JOHN: They undertake what they call "educational programs" in schools, in which materials are provided free of charge. The literature paints an entirely camouflaged picture of the actual situation. In it, all the animals have names like Bessie and are treated with care.

The dairy council produces films that are distributed to schools. They have titles like *A Visit to Uncle Jim and Aunt Helen's Dairy Farm,* and they make it look so idyllic. The animals are just part of the family. The contrast between that depiction and the reality of dairy cows—penned in, not allowed to graze, and pumped up with drugs—is outrageous. It's propaganda for the industry, and the sad thing is that it's not questioned.

REBECCA: When was the last time dairy cows were treated like that in America?

JOHN: There are still a few family farms left, but they simply cannot compete economically with the agribusinesses' highly mechanized mass production. It's not because the factory farms are more efficient— in most cases they aren't. It's because the factory farms have the clout in Congress to get subsidies for what they are doing, to get tax write-offs, to get free water, to get agricultural colleges working for them.

In California, the kindergarten children all receive a coloring book from the California Milk Producer's Association. Inside there is an outline drawing of a man's face, and underneath there is a question: "What did Daddy eat today?" Then it says: "If Dad has had his butter, Dad is happy. Draw a smile on his face. If Dad has not had his butter, Dad is sad. Draw a frown on his face."

Then it asks: "Has Dad has his cheese today? If so, color his eyes blue. If he hasn't, color his eyes red." Then you are asked, "Has Dad had his ice cream today?" "Has Dad had his sour cream today?" "Has Dad had his cream cheese today?" And you end up with two dads. One has blond hair, blue eyes, pink skin, white teeth, and a big smile—there is a racial stereotype operating here also, if you hadn't noticed. The other dad, who has not drenched his body in fat, has red eyes, black teeth, green skin, blue hair, and a big frown.

The National Dairy Council is the single largest supplier of the nutritional education materials used in the public schools of the United States. When I first learned about the Dairy Council, I thought it was a gathering of elders of some kind. (*laughter*) It's a trade lobby, and its purpose is to promote the sale of dairy products, specifically the higher-fat dairy products from which the most profit is to be made.

Now, which five-year-old children are going to raise their hands and say, "Excuse me, teacher, what is being taught here? Who provided us with these coloring books? Aren't all those dairy products the least healthy of the dairy products?"

> *Now, which five-year-old children are going to raise their hands and say, "Excuse me, teacher, what is being taught here?"*

DAVID: So you're saying that what was traditionally seen as a public service is simply free advertising to a particularly vulnerable and captive audience. What do you think can be done to counter the nutritional misinformation that children are receiving in schools?

JOHN: I think people have to be willing to educate themselves and then speak to our children. It's our duty as adults to see to it that our kids aren't lied to. It's particularly abhorrent when we come across this in schools, because we put our trust in the educational system as a means of liberating us from merely commercial agendas.

EarthSave, which is a group I founded, has a program called the Healthy School Lunch Program, and we go into schools and talk to kids and teachers and the food-service people. The idea is to educate kids and make other options available in the cafeteria, such as vegetarian, cholesterol-free, low-fat foods. After we were at Santa Cruz High School, over five hundred students signed a petition demanding that the cafeteria serve our meals and saying that they would buy the food.

The other part of it that is very difficult to overcome is that the USDA supplies six billion dollars worth of free food to schools—mainly ground pork and ground beef. If you want to serve high-fat, high-salt cheese in schools you can get it free from the USDA, but if you want to serve low-fat, low-salt cheese you have to pay for it. It's the same with milk.

So the more impoverished school districts, which tend to be in minority communities, are most vulnerable to this. It's positioned as this generous activity of government, but what it really is, is a guaranteed market for the worst products of the industries that control the USDA program. They get a very fine price from the USDA for the foods that they can't sell anywhere else. The result is that American black communities have the highest rates of high blood pressure, obesity, and heart disease in the world.

REBECCA: In general, do you find that the children you are talking with are more aware or less aware than their parents about nutrition and ecology?

JOHN: Some of them are more aware, others are less. The ones who are prisoners of the television are not, but the ones who are waking up—and there is a certain percentage of every generation who will wake up no matter what you do to them—are extremely committed.

At EarthSave we work with local support groups in many communities, and gather ongoing updates in environmental and health concerns. We focus on a transition to not simply a sustainable society, but a restorative society. Another EarthSave program is called YES, Youth for Environmental Sanity. This is a group of youngsters who travel the country speaking to high school assemblies. They speak in about thirty states a year, and they do about ten summer camps around the country. My son is doing one in Singapore right now. They reach hundreds of thousands of young people.

The feeling I get is that there are colossal powers at work in the world that mean us well. Perhaps they're sending in some new troops. Why would someone like me be born into the family that I was born into? I see it as something of a practical joke, but there is also a power in working from within. To accomplish change, some people try to become as pure as they possibly can: they won't drive a car, they won't eat anything that has a face, they recycle everything, and they push their personal lifestyle to the max.

REBECCA: People who have become so pure that when they are exposed to any pollution whatsoever, they immediately get sick.

JOHN: Right. They do have a role to play, but they are disconnected to a certain extent from the process. Others of us feel that we will create more change if everybody moves six inches than if a small group of people move to the extreme edge. So how can we accomplish that? You're not going to do it from the edge. If you challenge too high a percentage of people's assumptions, you lose credibility and are seen as a fringe phenomenon.

Some of us, born within the culture, stay within it—even when part of our hearts and psyches sees through it completely—in order to play a role in the turning.

DAVID: How do you—or do you?—think it is possible to solve the world hunger crisis?

JOHN: The first thing is to recognize that it exists and to stop shutting it out. As a culture we have to move away from valuing a meat-based diet as a reflection of prosperity, because there is not enough to go around. It takes too great a toll on the agricultural base.

The problem is that when some people do become aware of the scarcity, their reaction is "There's not enough to go around. Therefore I'm going to get mine." They say, "I'm sorry if the animal has to be killed or tortured or people have to go hungry, but my primary imperative is to survive." That state of consciousness is a reflection of the level of fear in the world.

REBECCA: I imagine that it would be extremely hard for you to continue your work without hope. But you must also have dark moments when you are reminded of what you are up against. Are you optimistic about the future of humanity?

JOHN: No. Optimism for me tends to wane very quickly, and it fluctuates with pessimism in a cyclical manner. If I depended on optimism for my work, I would burn out very rapidly or feel like a hypocrite.

> *If I depended on optimism for my work, I would burn out very rapidly . . .*

DAVID: What do you depend on then?

JOHN: *[Long pause]* Love. Look at the human being. We can produce a Hitler, but we can also produce a Mother Theresa. The moral spectrum of humanity is vast. You begin to feel, "Well, if I don't take responsibility, who will? My parents? Bill Clinton?" (*laughter*) We'll all die waiting.

REBECCA: What are some of the less obvious environmental consequences of the meat and dairy industries?

JOHN: It takes thirty-nine times more energy to produce a pound of protein from beef today than it does to produce a pound of protein from soybeans. It takes twenty-two times more energy to produce protein from beef than from corn or wheat. So people who are deriving their protein from plant sources are in effect consuming far less energy than those who derive their protein from animal sources.

The average pound of beef in the United States takes 2,500 gallons of water for its production. That isn't to say that the animal drinks that much, but it's involved in the watering of the crops that the animals eat, and the animals eat a lot more crops than we would if we were simply eating plants ourselves.

In California, which is a relatively dry state by national standards, the situation is worse. The average pound of beef there requires 5,214 gallons of water, according to the agricultural extension of UC Davis. In the same study they also analyzed how much water it takes in California to produce other agricultural crops. Apples take 49 gallons per pound, lettuce takes 23 gallons. Over half the water in California goes to beef and dairy production, and they *still* have to import most of their beef from other parts of the country.

And we're told to turn off the water when we brush our teeth or when we're shaving! (*laughter*) But if these aren't just little gestures to make ourselves feel better—like wearing a "Save the Whales" button—we have to ask, "Where is our real leverage here? Where can we save the most water?"

In California it takes 5,214 gallons of water to produce a pound of beef. Now, if you were to shower seven days a week and your average shower used two gallons a minute and you took seven minutes per shower, you would use roughly a hundred gallons of water a week. This comes out to 5,200 gallons of water a year. This means that in the state of California, you would save more water by not eating one pound of beef than you would by not showering for an entire year.

REBECCA: And roughly how much beef does the average meat-eater eat a year?

JOHN: In the United States, the present per capita consumption is sixty-three pounds of beef a year.

REBECCA: You've written about how some of the chemicals and hormones presently used in dairy and meat production take a generation for their effects to be fully realized, and you cited incidences of premature sexual development in children. What do you think we have to look forward to as a species if we don't change our eating habits?

JOHN: We'll end up in the direction we're headed. (*laughter*) You're referring to the earlier and earlier menarche of females. In traditional cultures, girls get their first periods at around 16 or 17 years of age; in the United States, on average, girls begin menstruating at the age of 11.

Early menarche has been shown to be related to animal-fat consumption, which throws off the estrogen cycles in the body, and it's also been related to the hormones in the animals products. The statistics show that the earlier a girl begins to menstruate, the more likely she is to have breast cancer, ovarian cancer, or uterine cancer. The earlier a young man enters puberty, the more likely he is to get prostate cancer. These are all hormone-related cancers.

The reliance of agriculture on pesticides is the equivalent of crack addiction. There's an immediate rush. For the short term it feels better, but in the long term it's reinforcing a destructive cycle. The first time that the farmers sprayed the infested plants with DDT, it seemed like a miracle. The first time someone shoots heroin—oh my God, the relief! It seems like a panacea. But the wisdom is to learn what the longer-term consequences are.

We found that the bugs develop resistances very rapidly. Meanwhile, you're scorching the soil and destroying the microbial population, which leads to soil erosion and to poisoning everyone who partakes. The average breast milk in the United States is so contaminated with pesticide residues that it would be confiscated by the FDA if you tried to ship it across state lines.

> *The average breast milk in the United States . . . would be confiscated by the FDA if you tried to ship it across state lines.*

REBECCA: There seem to be a lot of people who abuse their bodies and eat junk food, and nothing seems to happen to them; they still function reasonably well. Do you think there could be some adaptation going on to the environmental pollutants?

JOHN: No, I don't. I think a lot is happening to those people. People who are breathing very polluted air are very challenged and stressed by that. Their immune systems, kidneys, and livers are doing everything they can to detoxify, but there are limits to what the human being can handle. They may not have cancer yet, but their whole appreciation of the human experience is a fraction of what it could be.

DAVID: Have you ever had an experience with psychedelic plants that influenced your perspective?

JOHN: I was a child of the sixties, and I definitely participated. They say that if you can remember the sixties, you weren't there. Well, I have wonderful memories of the sixties. I took LSD for the first time in 1965. I had never had any psychoactive substance before, and it changed my life. It showed me that I was an ant, and it made me humble.

It also showed me that what we take into our bodies—even if it's just a few micrograms of a chemical—can change our consciousness dramatically. It also made me an environmentalist. I saw that everything is connected.

I didn't take LSD very much, because it was so overwhelming. Shortly thereafter, I took mescaline a few times and had wonderful experiences in nature.

In the early eighties a friend of mine talked to me about MDMA. I had had concerns about LSD. I had seen some people get very scattered, and I felt that it sometimes forced a premature opening on a psyche that wasn't ready for it. MDMA seemed to be kinder. I was a practicing psychotherapist at the time, and I began to use it in my practice. I administered it to hundreds of people—while it was legal. After it was made a Schedule I drug, I couldn't justify the risk of continuing its use.

DAVID: What kind of results did you achieve with MDMA?

JOHN: Oh, it was incredible! I saw extraordinary transformations. What a terrible shame that a tool so valuable to people was taken away! When a couple were fighting and stuck in a pattern that both were in despair about but neither could change, suddenly they had the ability to see and go beyond that pattern. They'd have to work it all through, of course—the drug alone didn't do anything. But it gave them the *will* to change.

It made me feel that our policy toward drugs is criminal. I see the drug war as a serious erosion of our civil liberties. We don't have freedom of religion, because some of these substances genuinely do activate religious experiences and are true sacraments.

REBECCA: Your experience as a therapist must be useful in dealing with the resistance to your present work.

JOHN: Yes. Self-inquiry is indispensable to social action. If you want to have an impact on the outside world, you have to go that far inside, too.

> *Self-inquiry is indispensable to social action.*

DAVID: What do you think happens to human consciousness after biological death?

JOHN: I think it celebrates.

DAVID: What is your perspective on God?

JOHN: Well, I'm not into the old man with the white beard. The sense of spirit that enables us to be more present and more honoring of our interconnectedness—to me that's the action of the divine. The surrendering of the individual self, the ego self, into the greater universe *is* my spiritual practice.

Some people find this type of discipline restrictive, just as some people find being a vegetarian a limitation. I find it an honor. And when we learn to honor ourselves fully, we end up honoring each other. It just turns out that way.

Martha Swope

Jean Houston

"There is a revolution going on! We're moving towards
planetization within one century."

Forging the Possible Human
with Jean Houston

When the search was on to find the girl to play Joan of Arc in the Holly-wood movie, she was second in line for the role. It was eventually given to Jean Seberg, but Jean Houston is a mover and shaker with an epicenter of equal mission and purpose. It's easy to believe that she has well over a million ex-students scattered around the globe, and that her plans and strat-egies are listened to by heads of state and other government officials in over forty countries.

A past president of the Association for Humanistic Psychology, Hous-ton is the co-director—with her husband, Robert Masters—of the Founda-tion for Mind Research in Ponoma, California. The foundation has been running for thirty years, and her work has inspired over 1,000 teaching-learning communities. She received the Distinguished Leadership Award from the Association of Teacher Educators in 1985, and in 1993 she re-ceived the Humanitarian of the Year award from the New Thought Alli-ance. She is the author of twelve books, including The Possible Human *and* The Search for the Beloved. *Holder of two Ph.D.'s, a psychologist, scholar, philosopher, and teacher, she specializes in a multi-level approach to education that blends various learning techniques to elicit the potential within each individual.*

Houston works both at the grassroots and government levels, offering her skills to local and international development agencies as they attempt to bring about cultural growth and social change. Most recently she has been collaborating with UNICEF and other NGOs in Bangladesh. Of all the people in this collection, Houston is the most intimately involved with the organizations and institutions engaged in the day-to-day running of planetary affairs. She is also, perhaps surprisingly, one of the most opti-mistic.

For someone who moves around the globe at a rate of a quarter of a million miles a year, Houston is remarkably present—a mountain with wings, a dynamic combination of philosophy and action. She carries her six-foot height with the grace of a person at ease with being larger than life. She is an ancient Greek philosopher ruminating on the hidden mysteries of the universe, yet in the same glance she is a ruddy peasant girl, gazing with delight at the wings of her first butterfly.

She has an uncanny ability to unearth potential. We interviewed Houston on May 27, 1994, but I had seen her speak at a conference a few weeks before. At the conference's end, she conducted the entire audience in singing Pachabel's Canon in rounds—and in tune! When someone congratulated her on the remarkable feat, she just shrugged. Like the protagonist of a Wagnerian opera, her voice resonates with ancient Teutonic tones. Her eyes beam a millennial come-on: "Won't you come on board?" And, as she speaks about the hidden potentials of the mind, you feel a bit like a jury, listening to the defense lawyer's impassioned plea for clemency for her client, the human race.

RMN

DAVID: What was it that originally inspired your interest in awakening human potential?

JEAN: Well, when you ask questions of origins, you necessarily have to go way, way back. In a sense, I was born for it. I am a person of a very great deal of hybridization. My father comes from an old American family. Sam Houston was my great-great-great-grandfather; Robert E. Lee was my great-great-grandfather. And there's also a Jewish-Indian great-great-great-grandfather, whose name, so help me, was the equivalent of "Scarecrow Rose and Blood." My father, Jack Houston, married Maria Anunciada Seraphina Graciella, a Sicillian. So I came into an enormous mix-and-match of cultures.

My father was a comedy writer who wrote for people such as Bob Hope and Edgar Bergen. I went to twenty-nine schools before I was twelve. Often I would go back to the same school after a year-and-half absence, and I would notice that in the first grade everybody was full of potential and capacity. If you could have plotted from the first grade what those children would be, you would have said that you had an extraordinary band of geniuses. Then I would come back in the third grade, and about half would have fallen off, and then in the fourth grade, another half.

So this began to trouble me even as a child. I was being educated on the road by my parents. Geography was something that went by at eighty miles an hour. (*laughter*) My mother decided that the way to put muscles on the brain was to learn huge sections of Shakespeare and poetry and sing Italian opera. So I was allowed to stay quickened and not to fall into habitual learning patterns. I asked myself, "Why is it that we have a million keys within ourselves and we learn to play only

> *. . . Why is it that we have a million keys within ourselves and we learn to play only twenty?*

twenty? Why is it that the child plays about 400,000, and gradually there is that cutting back and down?"

My father had to become a Catholic to marry my mother. He and the young priest traded jokes instead of theology, and finally the priest said, "Jack, you're just a natural born pagan. I'll give you a learner's permit so you can get married, but any kid that comes along, you make sure you bring them up Catholic."

When I was five, I entered the first grade of Catholic school. My father gave me questions to ask the poor little nun every morning. "Sister Theresa, I counted my ribs and I counted Joey Mangabella's ribs, and if God made Eve out of Adam's ribs . . . " I had thirty little girls and boys lifting up their undershirts all at once. (*laughter*)

Or "Sister Theresa, when Jesus rose, was that because God filled him with helium?" She got angrier and angrier. Finally I asked a question I had thought of myself: "Sister Theresa, did Jesus ever have to go to the bathroom?" She blew up. She had this bad lisp, and she started screaming, "Blasphemy,

> *She had this bad lisp, and she started screaming, "Blasphemy, blasphemy!"*

blasphemy!" She showed me a piece of paper, and at the top it read, "Jean Houston's years in purgatory." Every time I had asked a question there was a big X, and each X represented 100,000 years.

At the end of the first grade, on my birthday, we had the great addition. It came to 300 million years in purgatory. I went home crying, and my father found it hilarious. He picked me up and put me on his shoulders and ran down the street saying, "You think you've got problems? Hah! Wait and see what they did to a *real* saint!" He took me to see *The Song of Bernadette*, which was about a little girl who had a vision of the Virgin Mary.

The whole theater was packed with rapturous Sicilian Catholics—old ladies sitting next to me going, "Aaah, Santa Regina!" every time Jennifer

Jones would show up on the screen. Then came the great moment, one of the most religiously luminous moments in motion picture history, when the Virgin Mary appears in the grotto.

Suddenly this horrible whinnying mulelike laugh fills the theater. It's coming from my father. I say, "Daddy, shush. This is the holy part!" He says, "But do you know who that is playing Mary? That's the movie starlet we met at that party in Beverly Hills who was coming on to me. That's Linda Darnell—hot damn!" And the Sicilians are turning around saying, "*Diavolo! diavolo!*" (*laughter*)

As I was going home after the movie, I was heady for purpose. I *knew* that I could see the Virgin Mary—the real one, not Linda Darnell. I went home and up to the second floor, where we had a closet. Chicky, my dog, had just had her pups, so it was a dog nursery. I pulled the dog and the pups away, and I got down on my knees and prayed, "Please Virgin Mary, please show up. I want so much to see you."

Then I remembered that Catholics tend to bribe the saints: "If you show up, I'll give up candy for a week—two weeks, okay?" I opened my eyes, and Chicky had brought one of her pups back. So I tried again. I said, "I'll give up candy and canneloni and ricotta pie." (*laughter*) I kept counting to higher numbers each time. I counted to 167 and opened my eyes, sure she was going to be there—but she wasn't. Chicky had brought all eight pups back into the closet.

So I gave up. I walked to the window seat and looked down at the fig tree in the garden, which was blooming. Suddenly it happened. I cannot say that reality outside changed, but suddenly I was part of a seamless web of kinship with all reality, and I knew absolutely that I and that fig tree and the pups in the closet and my idea of the Virgin Mary and my chewed up pencil and fish off Sheep's Head Bay and old ladies dying in Shore Road Hospital and new wheat in Kansas were all dynamically related to everything else in a symphonic resonance that made for an extraordinary unified cosmos. It was *very* good.

This went on forever. Lifetimes went by, but technically it was probably only two seconds. Then my father entered the house laughing—he was always laughing—and immediately the whole universe began to laugh—great, huge joy. Years later, when I was able to read Dante in Italian, I recognized the truth in the phrase *deriso de l'universo*, "the joy that spins the universe." I was regrown out of the field of that experience. It became the template for everything in my life.

> . . . *immediately the whole universe began to laugh—great, huge joy.*

REBECCA: So the studies you developed after that were to allow people to reclaim this kind of experience?

JEAN: Yes, to reclaim the experience *and* all its implications: that we have the sensory systems to be part of a much larger sensory universe, and that we have the psychological systems to be not schizophrenic or uniphrenic, but polyphrenic.

I've talked to many people who've had experiences similar to this as children, but unlike many of them I was encouraged to reflect my experience in language. My father came home and asked me what had happened, so I told him and he said, "Hot damn! That's really good!" He didn't knock it. That was not my *only* experience, but key experiences tend to recur as fractal waves throughout one's life.

When I was eight years old, I had another huge opening. My dad was writing *The Edgar Bergen and Charlie MaCarthy Show*. We went to deliver the script, and Edgar Bergen was sitting with his back toward us and talking to Charlie, his dummy. There was nothing unusual about that—I was used to seeing ventriloquists rehearsing with their dummies.

But as we listened, my father said, "I didn't write this." Edgar was asking Charlie ultimate questions: What is the nature of life? What does it mean to truly love? Where is the mind? Where is the soul? And this little block of wood, with clacking jaws and a head full of sawdust, was answering with the wisdom of the finest thinkers of all the millennia. Edgar himself was listening, and you could see part of his mouth moving, but his eyes were in complete astonishment.

Finally my father, the agnostic Baptist, couldn't stand any more, and he coughed loudly. Edgar turned around, and his face went beet red. He said, "Hello Jack, Hi Jean. You caught us." My dad said, "What in the world are you doing?" Edgar replied, "I sometimes talk to Charlie. He's the wisest person I know." My father said, "Hey Ed, that's you, that's *your* voice. You've just read a lot." Edgar replied, "Yes, I suppose ultimately it is. But you know, when I ask him these questions and he answers, I have no idea what he's going to say, and what he says is so much more than I know."

Again, it was like someone walked across my future. I knew that I was being reintroduced to the cosmos within. It was as if we lived in the attic of ourselves, with all the floors relatively

> *. . . it was like someone walked across my future.*

uninhabited and the basement locked, except when the plumbing explodes. I knew that part of my job was to help reinhabit those floors.

REBECCA: What were some of the early influences that helped to formulate your understanding of consciousness?

JEAN: Around my eighth or ninth year I became interested in the world's religions. I was mathematically retarded but theologically precocious. I began to correspond with sikhs in India. After about the third letter, they would ask about job opportunities in America. After the fourth letter, I would get a proposal of marriage, and I would angrily write back saying that I was only ten years old, and they would say that's the perfect age for marriage! (*laughter*)

Then I read a book that just spoke to my soul—it was Joseph Campbell's *The Hero with a Thousand Faces*. It set me off on all kinds of metaphysical quests. When I was fourteen I was sent down to Texas in the summertime, and I got a band of boys to follow me. I set myself up as a teenage messiah, and we went on the road with motorcycles. At first we had "saving booths," but people got bored with our preaching, so we then branched off into healing.

So I had a double life. In the summer I was a teenage messiah with an old Harley Davidson and cowboy hat and cowboy boots, and during the rest of the year I was taking walks with an old man I had literally run into. I knocked the wind out of him, and he said, with a thick French accent, "Are you planning to run like that for the rest of your life?" I said, "Yes sir, it looks that way," and he said, "Well, *bon voyage*." The following week, I met him again. He had a long name, but he asked me to call him by the first part, which to my ears was something like Mr. *Tayer*.

He had no self-consciousness whatsoever. He had leaky margins, and he was falling into lovingness with things all the time. He would fall to the ground in the park in ecstasy to look at a caterpillar, with his long Gaelic nose raking the ground. "Oh, Jean, look! A caterpillar! What does a caterpillar become, uh? Moving, changing, transforming—metamorphosis. Can you feel yourself to be a caterpillar? What is it to be a *papillon*, a butterfly? The butterfly is within *you*! What is the butterfly of Jean in ten, twenty, thirty years, uh?" I replied tentatively, "I think I'll be flying around the world, meeting different peoples and helping them to be what they can be." This question was my adolescent initiation.

He was something. He had all kinds of strange ways of relating to reality. He'd talk to trees and rocks, addressing them *tu*, *toi*, thou. We would lean into the wind and say, "This same wind was once sniffed by Jesus Christ. Alexander the Great—very interesting. Genghis Khan—not so good. (*laughter*) Here it comes, Jean d'Arc—be filled with Jean d'Arc! Be filled with the tides of history—same molecules." People followed us around, not laughing at us but with us. He created a kind of conversational gestalt. He would look at you as if you were God in hiding, and I would leave my littleness behind when I was with him.

> *He would look at you as if you were God in hiding . . .*

We walked together twice a week for a year and a half. The last time I saw him was on April 7, 1955. He was very pale. He went off on this extraordinary riff about spirals. It began with a talk about the floor of Chartres Cathedral and brains and intestines and galaxies and evolution. He said, "Jean, the people of your time at the end of the twentieth century will be taking the tiller of the world, but they cannot go directly. They must touch upon every people, every culture. You must do that, Jean. It will be a great field of mind. We will be turning the corner on the human race."

He said, "*Au revoir*, Jean," and I said, "Good-bye, Mr. Tayer. I'll see you on Tuesday." My dog Chicky didn't want to go and was whining. The next Tuesday, he didn't come. For eight weeks I went to meet him, but he still didn't come. He had died that Easter Sunday, but I didn't know it. Years later, in graduate school, somebody handed me a book without a cover called *The Phenomenon of Man*. I read it and the words were very familiar. I asked where the cover was, and my friend showed it to me with the photo of the author. "Mr. Tayer" had been Pierre Teilhard de Chardin.

REBECCA: That's great! What have you discovered about the different ways that children learn, and about how a child who is having difficulty with the traditional system can be helped?

JEAN: Every child has difficulty with the traditional system, it's just that some have certain mind-sets that are appropriate to the limited, dominant system of the time—linear, analytic, verbal, or whatever.

I've been engaged in educational experiments for thirty years, setting up alternative programs in schools—and now programs in whole countries—where art is central to the curriculum, not off at the periphery. There is no such thing as a stupid child, just incredibly stupid systems of education. Often I feel that I was educated for around the year 1926, not for the immense complexities of today.

Some people think in images, some in words. Some think kin-aesthetically like athletes. People like Proust have a sort of interior imagery activated by the senses. People from different cultures think differently.

I was in Brooklyn in a largely black and Hispanic neighborhood, where I was brought in to observe very fine teachers trying to reach these kids, and they weren't. The kids couldn't care less. They were dull and apathetic. I followed the kids out into the playground, and they were brilliant. They were coming up with complex ideas and developing a whole Byzantine intrigue. Then they would go back into the classroom and *bam!* Dead again.

I couldn't stand it. I pulled a boy over, and I said, "Tommy, what's five plus three plus two?" He said, "Oh man, get lost." I said, "Tommy, what's this?" and I tapped out the problem with my hands on the table. He said, "That's ten." "Why didn't you say that before?" "You didn't ask me." You see, I was asking in terms of northern European notions of intelligence and abstract information.

I went home with him. His father had been a jazz musician, and he had grown up with rhythmic patterns related to everything. So I went back to the school and began with the basics—spelling out *cat*. I said, "Let's make a C with our bodies, then an A, then a T, and close your eyes and see a cat." I played it out on many levels and of course they got it. Well, you might say, "What about rhododendrons?" (*laughter*) But once you heal the wounded learner by finding the particular frame of mind, then kids *will* learn.

As you go along, you realize that we are really state-dependent in our learning. If you begin to change the whole frequency domain of brain and mind, and you play the orchestral symphonic form of different states of consciousness, you will find talents just lying there in wait.

> *He invented upside-down lighthouses for submarines, revolving goldfish bowls for tired goldfish . . .*

I was brought to the home of a child who was an inventor. He invented upside-down lighthouses for submarines, revolving goldfish bowls for tired goldfish, easy-off whisker remover—the man puts the paste on his cheek, it causes his whiskers to grow inward, and he bites them off the next morning. But this child was flunking at school. When we tested him, we found out that he just couldn't do the ordinary mathematics. But when I asked him to work out the problem his own way, he began to sing and dance and make movements, and he gave us the right answer. I said, "What are you doing, kid? Are you thinking in images?" and he said, "Yes."

We took this boy to the University of Michigan and gave him an IQ test. He did terribly—85. I said, "Never mind, Billy, do it your own way." He said, "That's not possible, because this test was made for people with your kind of mind. Can you make the question sing and dance?" I tried.

Next question. "Jean, can you make it look like a building by Frank Lloyd Wright?" I tried. We got through this exhausting process, and his IQ was scored at 135. It would have been higher if I had been smart enough to know how to ask the questions the right way.

Then, working with the teachers, we began to create new forms so that these kinds of children could be educated in many ways. And they stopped failing. Not only that, they became very creative. Billy never got beyond a B-minus until he got to graduate school. I asked him why, and he said, "There were too many questions A, B, C, D. I couldn't help it—I always saw E, an alternate version."

What we have done in our Western reduction of intelligence, in marshalling industrial and economic progress, is we have greatly shrunken the mind's domain. We have placed an enormous overemphasis on certain styles of thinking, which has resulted in the ecological holocaust, for example. It's what Francis Bacon referred to as "extending the empire of man over things."

What I try to do in my work is to give people access to the richer levels and frames of consciousness, and also the autonomous personas who are there. If a child is learning math through dance, if a child is learning culture through drama, or fractions through weaving, and has many modes of tie-ins of mind and body into the educational framework, that child is not going to fail.

REBECCA: What was the nature of the foundation that you and your husband, Robert Masters, set up? What understanding did your work there lead to?

JEAN: After the LSD research ended in 1965, my husband and I went on to create the Foundation for Mind Research, in New York, to explore—in nondrug ways—the breadth, the range, and the depth of human possibilities. Over the years we had something like 3,000 research subjects. We explored thinking in images, thinking in words, thinking with the whole body, and we began to apply our work to schools, hospitals, and prisons.

Margaret Mead became the president of our foundation, and she sent me out into the world to explore other cultures. Our associates and I have found it necessary to work both intraculturally as well as transculturally. In our transcultural work, we try to speak to the potential in every human being, regardless of local and cultural conditioning—the perennial human, whether a rickshaw peddler in Delhi or an oil company owner in Dallas.

If possible, we always try to use techniques embedded in a story. We've found that people go much farther, faster, and deeper if they have a story

> *... a great story, like a great piece of music, will take you over the difficult passages.*

upon which to unfold their developing selves. And a story, like a great piece of music, will take you over the difficult passages.

We show people that they have a natural access to such capacities as being able to think with many different frames of mind: visual, verbal, kinaesthetic, interpersonal, subjective, intuitive, logical, mathematical. These capacities improve the physical use of the body and enhance memory, creative expression, and problem-solving.

DAVID: What about the people you come across who are really poor and haven't received any education? How are you able to influence their lives?

JEAN: Given the education and given the opportunity, we find that most people are able to make remarkable improvements in their functioning and learn new ways of being in a relatively short period of time.

REBECCA: Do people in third world countries really have the incentive for all of this? Aren't many just busy surviving and trying to emulate the Western trip?

JEAN: It's even *more* true in so-called third world countries. We find that people there are closer to their potentials because they have not yet been shattered by education and social objectives that inhibit and coerce their natural capacities into approved tracts and templates. Wherever we have worked, we have found the possible human just beneath the surface crust of local culture, and the consciousness of a possible society is not far behind.

REBECCA: Could you tell us about the influence of Aldous Huxley on your work, particularly his book, *Island?*

JEAN: In 1963, when I was just barely out of my teens, a friend called me to tell me that Aldous Huxley wanted to meet me. I couldn't figure out why, except that I had the only legal supply of LSD in New York City. (*laughter*)

His books *The Doors of Perception* and *Island* had become virtually scripture for me, but I was quite unprepared when I opened the door to discover a man who looked like one of William Blake's archangels, or perhaps the average man from a distant but optimal future. He was very tall and very beautiful. His eyes were misted over with near-blindness, but he seemed to be gazing into other worlds.

He had the gift of being interested in everything—and of being able to talk about it. But you never dreaded the extraordinary range of his knowledge, because he also brought you into the conversation and made you partner to it. I can't help comparing the conversation we had together that day to one of the conversations in his novels.

We began by discussing the phenomenon of looking at flowers in the psychedelic state, and he asked me to read out loud the relevant passage in *The Doors of Perception.* We talked about the mythology of flowers, the garden of Eden, and the meaning of paradise. As we continued to talk, we were no longer a young girl and an elderly man. We were comrades in speculation, co-adepts in the mysteries of visionary vegetables.

I plucked up the courage to question him about *Island.* In this book he had carefully created a society based on optimum education and enlightened interrelationships. It was the utopia that stood in absolute contrast to the dystopia he had created in *Brave New World.* It inspired much of my own work in the education of the possible human, and was his consummate vision of what human beings and their societies could be. At the book's conclusion, this ideal society is utterly destroyed as the fascist military forces take over. Try as I might, I could not contain my resentment over this ending, and I asked why he had permitted the book to end that way. He said that he had thought of having a longer book with a different ending, but there had recently been a fire that had destroyed all his manuscripts. He said that as he hadn't been feeling well, he had wanted to get the book out.

I persisted, saying that the ending discouraged people from even making the attempt at creating the experiments that could lead to a better society. "Well, then," he said, "you must do something about it, mustn't you?" And once again, I could feel my whole future rising. I never saw him again. He died later that year, the same day JFK was shot.

DAVID: Tell us about you work in Bangladesh.

JEAN: Huxleys' *Island* population came from Scotland and Bengal, which now of course is Bangladesh. In the world's eyes this is the most tragic of countries, a nation relentlessly afflicted by flooding, poverty, illness, and futility. But Bangladesh is also a world of metaphor, of high and low theater, of great poetry and music. You talk to a rice farmer and you find a poet. You get to know a sweeper of the streets and you find a remarkable singer.

> *You talk to a rice farmer and you find a poet.*

I went and worked with thousands of leaders there. In the various meetings and seminars we gave, we found that the participants were very responsive to our methods of learning, and they spoke to us about how, for the first time, they were being affirmed in what they had long sensed and already knew.

REBECCA: You don't mean reworking their original educational style, but the one imposed during colonial times?

JEAN: Yes. It was as if the imported culture from the West—mainly England—had dropped a curtain over their more natural, artistic thought processes and modes of expression. One fellow told us that he'd always felt that in his studies he'd been made to operate as if he'd had his hands tied and his lips taped up, and that now he felt free for the first time.

> *I go into a culture and look for the genius within it.*

I go into a culture and look for the genius within it. How Africans think and move, how Chinese paint, how American Indians speak to the land—this is all coming together and making for a new cultural context.

Some years ago I was in West Africa investigating a tribe that had had no warfare for a very long time and that had very little neurosis as we understand it. They also had some of the best problem-solving capacities that I have ever seen in my life. They sang and danced and dreamed around the problem! They were cooking on more burners. (*laughter*) Now, you may say that this would never work at the University of California, but you would be wrong.

DAVID: How did your experiences with Margaret Mead influence your perspective?

JEAN: Margaret once said, "You're just like me." I said, "No, Margaret, I'm much nicer than you, just not as smart." (*laughter*) I was her adopted daughter—it's no great secret. She lived with us off and on for six years. I watched her work and saw that she was doing what I had been studying for years. She was thinking in images; she was thinking with her whole body. She had these tremendous explosions, and then she would go and hug you hugely. She had one of the richest, deepest, and widest personalities that I had ever seen. She was the smartest human being I had ever met—not the nicest, but the smartest.

We were eating together at a women's conference one time, and I said, "Margaret, you have the most interesting mind. I would like to study it." She put her fork down and paused. Then she said, "That's wonderful. All my life people have been interested in what I think. You're the first to be interested in how I think." She called me up a month later and asked why I hadn't been in touch with her. I said, "Well, you're so busy, Margaret, I didn't want to intrude." She said, "Oh, Jean, don't you realize that people have to pursue me. Please call me."

She calls me up a month later: "Jean, remember that mind of mine you wanted to study? Well, it's going. You'd better get over here fast. Today I called a typewriter a bicycle." So I went over, and indeed she was making verbal ellipses. I had seen this before, and I said, "Margaret, you know what? I don't think it's your mind. I think it's your body. When was the last time you did any exercise? I bet you don't remember?" "Yes, I do. It was August 24, 1964." (*laughter*)

I thought that if we could get her body image restructured, these problems would disappear. She was seventy-one years old, and she had a body image of an eleven-year-old girl. So she came to my house, and my husband worked on her using mainly Feldenkreis techniques. After two months of her yelling like mad, she had her body back and the mind ellipses went away. And then I began to study with her.

She was a genius for process. Most of our ancestors knew process all the time. They planted the seed, they chased away the birds, they nourished the plant, they harvested the plant, they baked the bread. We just stand in the supermarket line. Maybe much of our social pathology is a lack of process—we have no sense of the moral flow of things. She would give me incredible

> *Maybe much of our social pathology is a lack of process—we have no sense of the moral flow of things.*

tasks, such as writing a complete forty-page report on stress in two days. She would call up President Carter and say, "Now, Jimmy, this is what you have to do . . ." I was in my early thirties, and I thought I was running the world!

REBECCA: I'm interested in how you've been able to take your ideas, which are considered quite radical in circles even outside the mainstream, to the levels of governments, bureaucracies, and industries. I find it hard to imagine the managers of Chevron visualizing universal oneness. (*laughter*)

JEAN: You know, I've never really thought about that. Maybe that's it: I've never become self-conscious about it. I also have two Ph.D.'s—that helps. But when you work at the highest levels with chief executive officers or heads of countries or institutions, you will find in many cases— though not always, of course—that they are very innovative people who have played upon the panoply of mind and body.

> *My way of being in the world is to call people forth; it's not to put forth an idea.*

You find this at the top and the bottom. The problem is with middle management. (*laughter*) Margaret always told me never to go in as the expert within the structure of expertise. You come in like a crab, from the side, within another form of expertise. My way of being in the world is to call people forth; it's not to put forth an idea.

REBECCA: Your preaching days are over. (*laughter*)

JEAN: Yes. The ideas are secondary to the primary premise of people's potential. I'm always in wonder and astonishment.

REBECCA: Is there an example you can give us of real positive change at governmental levels that you feel represents some sort of a turning point?

JEAN: There are so many, but one of the most interesting was in 1979. It was during the Carter administration, which was wide open to these things, by the way. It was a kind of golden age for new ideas, and it attracted remarkable people. I was then president of the Association for Humanistic Psychology. I'd probably taught a million and a half students, and they were scattered throughout high levels of government. They asked me to come in and do something, so I set up a conference on policy alternatives.

There was a very large number of all the assistant secretaries of commerce, of health, education, and welfare—all the heads of various agencies. First there were good, fine speeches by solid, substantial people, and then very intensive small-group work using some of the most advanced procedures of how to envision and dream. Then we had aikido with George Leonard, including living without hurting the other. It went on and on until I had all of these people, more or less in trance on the floor, going to the possible society and coming back with real ideas about how it could happen. During the Reagan administration, all those people left, but they went into corporations, into companies, into setting up new designs, and they began to make differences all over the world.

On her deathbed Margaret Mead said to me, "Forget everything I've told you about working with governments and bureaucracies." I said, "Now you tell me?" "Yes. I'm lying here being an anthropologist on my own dying—fascinating experience, there's no hierarchy to it. If we are going to grow and green our time, it's a question of citizens and volunteer groups. Growing in body and mind and spirit and ideas, and testing each other, and challenging the growth, and then going out and making it. You take care of it, Chief." I said, "Yes, ma'am."

REBECCA: So the other aspect to teaching is the continuation of learning.

JEAN: I write a small book every month. I have to read a book practically every day. I'm on this constant learning curve. If you are repeating the same thoughts and feelings that are 90 percent the same as the day before, you are in trouble.

REBECCA: What are some of the frustrations you experience in your work?

JEAN: You know, my frustrations are not around the world. If I were to be desperately honest about it, I would say that my frustrations are more centered around my own family. My mother is very old now, and I wish I could spend the time doing for her as I'm able to do for other people. She's very fey and happy, and she's being well taken care off, but I know that if I could work with her every day, we could reverse the aging process. That's a frustration. There are everyday frustrations that you run into with your health, your life, your family, and with old ways of being always trying to rise up and reassert themselves.

REBECCA: So you're not finding as many frustrations at the institutional level?

JEAN: No. I travel about 250,000 miles a year, and I can tell you that the world I see out there is very different from the one that's being described in the media. There is a revolution going on! We're moving toward planetization within one century. Not a planetary culture, but more cultures becoming more of what they are. The term *planetization* is not as simple as it sounds. It isn't one happy, homogeneous brave-new-world society. On the contrary, it involves a high individuation of culture.

When you walk through a jungle in Orinoco and you see a naked Indian coming out with a transistor radio clapped to his ear, you realize just how linked we are becoming. People are going to be able to tune in with almost anybody. By the year 2000 we will have information banks, small enough to be held in the hand, that can download anything. This is a different mind.

DAVID: Do you work a lot with the Internet?

JEAN: Oh, yes. I'm one of these computer nerds. I'm very glad that I wasn't born fifteen years ago, because I would weigh four hundred pounds, have bottled glasses, and be eating twinkies in front of the screen. (*laughter*) Every night when I'm home, I'm talking to the world! I'm playing Dungeons and Dragons with fifteen-year-old boys who think I'm a fifteen-year-old boy with a weird vocabulary. I also work with Green parties around the world. It's an extraordinary confluence of consciousness. Teilhard's noosphere is alive and well.

REBECCA: What are you discovering in your visits outside the Western hemisphere about the changing social role of women?

> *In parts of Africa, the women are just moving in and saying, "Enough of this!" . . .*

JEAN: I've witnessed the rise of women to full partnership with men. But it's not always *even* partnership. In parts of Africa, the women are just moving in and saying, "Enough of this!" and are taking over the welfare and education of whole villages. There are so many things happening at such profound levels that the media barely cover at all. It's not considered "news" because it's new. News is old stuff—it's habituated response.

We're in this town a hundred miles from Nairobi, and I'm working with the Institute of Cultural Affairs. The women have spent 80 to 90 percent of their time going down to the river and getting water. They have a rich tradition of doing this, talking and sharing stories and information. Somebody builds them a water tank, and suddenly they have access to all this time. "But, sister, what about our side-by-side, our exchange, where we told our stories, our ways of healing our kids? What shall we do?"

They asked us to help them build a tea house. That change of perspective brought in a whole new energy. They sat around facing one another. "Our men are drunk on palm wine in Nairobi, and they're not sending money home." They're drumming, and they have a big feast, and they start talking about what's on their minds, and they say, "This is what we can do about sanitation. Let's bring in a new school . . ."

This place is becoming a model town—it's the rise of a whole new way of thinking about the world. The rise of women is the most important event in the last five thousand years, because of women's emphasis on process, on making things cohere, work, and grow, and not simply on product. I think that the tragedy in Rwanda represents the absolute end of the patriarchy and the old isolated warring tribes.

DAVID: Could you tell us about the work you did with the Apollo astronauts?

JEAN: I was one of those who was fortunate enough to work with NASA at the time of the moon landing. I was doing work that had to do with helping astronauts remember what they saw when they were on the moon, because they didn't remember a great deal. I tried everything: I hypnotized them, I did various kinds of active imagination exercises, I taught them to meditate, I yelled at them—that's what worked. (*laughter*)

Finally, one of them said, "You know, Jean, you're asking the wrong question. It's not what we saw on the moon, it's what we saw coming back to earth. Seeing that beautiful blue and silver planet gave us a feeling of such nostalgia for what the world can be. My hand hit the stereo button, and the music of *Camelot* came on."

Imagine that!

I have seen that picture of the earth from outer space in a leper's hut in India. I was present in China when a Chinese peasant took a photo of Mao off the wall and replaced it with a photo of the earth.

> *I have seen that picture of the earth from outer space in a leper's hut in India.*

DAVID: How did your experience with psychedelics influence your work?

JEAN: Psychedelics gave me a perspective on the human psyche that would normally have taken me a hundred years to gain. There I was, this young kid, and suddenly I have access to the whole psychodynamic dimension— the sensory levels, the mythic levels, the psychological levels, the spiritual levels, and all the frequencies within.

DAVID: Another play on the fractal wave. What do you think happens to consciousness after biological death?

JEAN: I've nearly died four times. Once was when I was nineteen. I used to jump out of planes, and I had an experience of my chute not opening. My whole life went by. Not every pork chop, but all the major events at their own time. The adrenaline rush turned on life again. Another time, I nearly died of typhoid fever in Crete. It was very pleasant. I found myself leaving the fifth-class hotel and the room of this reality, and going into the next. A light went out here, a light went up there—and there was my car waiting. But I was a young kid, and I said, "I'm not ready, no!" and there was this tremendous psychic effort to pull myself back. I'm convinced of continuity—I can't say reincarnation, because the universe is so complex. We have many different agendas and opportunities, but consciousness, at some level, deeply continues.

When I was in one of Professor Paul Tillich's courses, he kept referring to a word that was central to his theology, and that word was *wacwum*. We theological students met afterward, and we would spin out epistemologies, the phenomenology and the existential roots of the *wacwum*. And we had a whole book by the end of the term. Finally, they asked me to ask the great man a question, so I put my hand up. When he said, "Yes?" I forgot my question, so I asked him one of blithering naivete. I asked, "How do you spell *wacwum*?" "Yes, Miss Houston," and he spelled on the board "v-a-c-u-u-m." (*laughter*)

That's what we are! If you take a body and scrunch it together and get rid of all the empty space, what have you got what for every human being? A grain of rice!

DAVID: What is your perspective on God?

JEAN: Nicholas of Cusa said that "God is a perfect sphere whose center is everywhere and whose circumference is nowhere." I believe that we are always available to the omnipresent grace, and that part of our life is about discovering that we contain the God-stuff in embryo. I like to use a little bit of metaphysical science fiction and say that where we are on this planet is the skunkworks at the corner of the universe. We're in God school, learning to become co-creators.

DAVID: How do you see consciousness evolving in the future?

JEAN: I think it's going to evolve on many levels. I think civilization is going to get to a point where we suddenly become responsible, stewards of the whole evolutionary process. This requires domains of consciousness, not just levels and frequencies. We have psychic structures that are going to be emerging and becoming conscious. Freud said, "All the repressed is unconscious, but not all the unconscious is repressed," and I think that a great deal of latencies of body/mind/psyche are about to emerge.

People are mythologizing this experience as ET's or channelings. I don't think they're necessarily beings from outer space, or because they're dead that it necessarily means they're smart, but a lot of this is part of the psychic continuum that we don't quite understand. We're using the medium of older civilizations and older cultures to explain it.

REBECCA: The resistance to this process is really formidable. There's a lot of fear and a desire to jump back into the old ways, even though they don't work. In view of the evidence that many people are becoming more entrenched than ever in their belief systems, how do you justify your optimism?

JEAN: Because I see more of the world than what is being promoted through the media. It's true that on the surface fundamentalisms are arising, and they're arising because we're on the edge of this immense breakthrough—in fact, we're already there. The dreadful and the wonderful has already happened, and we're in this age of parentheses.

We're at the end of one totally different time, and we're almost at the beginning of the next one. This is the juicy time when the future is coded. People are terrified. "No thanks, I'd rather go back to ideological fortresses of truth." It's the old reptilian brain. "Warning! Warning!" But 10 percent of the creative minority will always make a difference.

> *This is the juicy time when the future is coded. People are terrified . . .*

REBECCA: It seems that you see this potential as something like an attracter, pulling us toward it.

JEAN: Yes, the "omega point" that Teilhard de Chardin was talking about.

DAVID: What projects are you working on right now?

JEAN: So many, I don't remember! I have a book on Isis and Osiris coming out next year. I'm doing a series on American archetypes, and I'm doing projects with UNICEF and other international development agencies.

REBECCA: There must be times when your spirits get low. When that happens, how do you turn it around?

JEAN: I don't, necessarily. Margaret Mead would have a ten-minute depression every day and yell and scream and carry on, and then she'd have freedom from load. I had a lot of projects that fell apart recently and a lot of friends dying. Recently, I've just had too many negatives to support the ecology of a happy spirit.

I think you have to keep your sacred and spiritual life open, to keep your strength during times of adversity. I try to do that, but I don't always succeed. You need to keep your connection going, to the larger self that is always there, even though the public display may belie that there *is* a larger self. (*laughter*)

Years ago, I was the guilty culprit who first talked about "the inner child." I'm very sorry about that. I'm getting a little tired of it. But we have so many different selves within us, and by educating all of them, we begin to bring together the trans-historical crew that can make such a difference in our present life.

DAVID: Why do you think that gaining a mythic perspective is important?

JEAN: We are mythic beings. We contain these great stories of death and resurrection and rites of passage—it's the totemic structure of history. Suppose that all of the meanderings and wanderings of your life were not due necessarily to cause and effect—what your mother did to you, what your father didn't do—but suppose it was a tale told by a master to orchestrate a larger life, unfolding from the mind of the maker, the daimon?

Look at Winston Churchill—dyslexic and stuttering until he was fourteen or fifteen years old, and then writing those great, luminous books of history and speaking the words that charged a nation. Was that compensation? Maybe not. Maybe the daimon knew he was going to be Winston Churchill and was shoring up his tongue.

What about Manolete? The greatest bullfighter that ever lived, who was scared to death of everything and hid behind his mother's skirts until he was fourteen years old. Compensation? Maybe not. Maybe the daimon was shoring up his courage.

Instead of looking at developmental psychology, which says you're born, you have these problems, you get all kinds of wounds, you make some kind of adjustment, and then you die—it's very melancholy isn't it?—maybe there are these great passions and purposes that are encoded in us, and then unfold in and through time.

A myth is something that never was but that is always happening. It is the DNA code of the human psyche. It is available for one generation, and again, in a different twist, for another. It has multiple, myriad facets. It drops into a culture like a crystal seed in a supersaturated solution, and then it blooms and blossoms. Einstein said, "If you want to make your children brilliant, tell them fairy tales. If you want to make them more brilliant, tell them more fairy tales."

> *A myth is something that never was but that is always happening.*

John Varian

Elizabeth Gips

" . . . you get the cosmic badge of honor pinned on you . . . when
you can dance on totally nothing."

Pilgrimage of Change
with Elizabeth Gips

*Born half-paralyzed in 1922, and dictating poetry four years later, Eliza-
beth Gips had interviewed most of the people in the two volumes of* Mavericks of the Mind *long before we even got started. Her infamous radio show*
Changes, *which has now aired in northern California for over twenty years,
has inspired countless individuals to explore new realms of heightened
awareness. She is well known for her lively interviews with virtually everyone who is anyone in the alternative cultural matrix. Her recently published book* Scrapbook of a Haight-Ashbury Pilgrim *is an important historical document, a timeless epic adventure that overflows with contagious
enthusiasm inspired during the peak of San Francisco's citywide halluci-
nogenic experience during the late sixties.*

*Needless to say, Elizabeth has been through a lot of changes herself.
She discovered her power to arouse the emotions in others in 1939, when
she got out of high school a year early because her English teacher threw
an ink bottle at her in frustration. She then attended Mills College, discovered beat poetry, and marijuana, and had a number of experiences "falling in love with the wrong boys." In 1964 her son turned her on to the
peyote cactus, and she metamorphosed into an "errant hippie," wandering around the U.S. trailing after charismatic commune-founder Stephen
Gaskin. She landed on "the Farm" in Tennessee (the well-known com-
mune at which, according to Gaskin, a young Al Gore spent some time). In
1971 Elizabeth left the Farm and started doing radio at her son's station,
KDNA in St. Louis. She began her Santa Cruz radio show,* Changes, *in
1975 and soon started writing articles and reviews for many alternative
magazines.*

*At the age of seventy-one, Elizabeth, now a grandmother, is still very
much at the forefront of cultural evolution. She still loves doing radio, is
working on several new books, has apparently fallen in love with the "right
man," and says that she no longer seeks "enlightenment." We interviewed
her in her cozy home in Santa Cruz on June 10, 1994. Her house is decorated with compelling psychedelic art and exotic religious artifacts from
around the world. Youthful optimism and vibrant enthusiasm stream from*

Elizabeth's spirit. She is filled with curiosity, and her eyes and heart both seem wide open. A passion-filled fireball of energy, Elizabeth gets very excited when she's talking, and laughs a lot. Sometimes like a fountain, other times like a volcano, she is just bursting with life, spewing forth a stream of amazing adventures stories and rainbow revelations, reminding us of those feel-good times in our lives when laughing, loving, and learning all danced hand in hand.

DJB

DAVID: You've been on the air with your radio program for more than twenty years. What is your essential message?

ELIZABETH: I've observed over the last seventy-two years that energy follows consciousness. I don't hold to any one truth; rather, I dance more or less comfortably on nothing. If you press me for a name for my path, I'd say it is the *no path/all path.*

However, for all the infinite possibilities we may have, there are some scenarios for human possibilities that I prefer to others. My essential message—done often with the voice of the Haoka, the fool, "She Who Remembers to Laugh"—is that evolution is real and that it propels us toward kindness, compassion, love. It follows that the more people who agree with this, the sooner it will manifest for everyone, maybe for all species and every thing. The entire universe seems to be evolving.

As more and more of us learn to drop fear, we automatically turn toward a new reality, rooted in kindness. It's an inevitable empathy based on the knowledge of our common unity. And it is changing the world. I don't know any other vision for our race—or for that matter, for all races and things—that's worth hanging on to. If it is a co-creation, why wallow in miserable futures? That's selfish.

So one of my names is Tara. She holds up her hand saying, "Drop fear." Do you want to know some of my other names.

DAVID AND REBECCA: Okay.

ELIZABETH: Isis, Krishna, Sisyphus . . . (*laughter*)

REBECCA: Who's Sisyphus?

ELIZABETH: Every day he had to push a big stone up a hill, and every night it would tumble down. I did a picture a few years back that shows Sisyphus sitting up on the top of the hill like Rodin's *Thinker*. A large crowd of people are milling around down at the bottom. He's saying something like, "I finally got wise. There are hundreds of people who want to push this stone up the hill. I don't have to do it any more!" That's intelligence. At some point we wise up and let go.

DAVID: How did your experience in Haight-Ashbury during the sixties influence who you are today?

ELIZABETH: I'm sure that it freed me to a great extent from the American need of identification through stuff: money, business, power, etc. As I say in *The Scrapbook of a Haight-Ashbury Pilgrim,* I started out with a mansion and a mink coat and ended up a wandering *sadhu.* I went through a long period of poverty—although I didn't experience it as poverty, I just didn't have money. Now I think I've settled comfortably into Buddha's middle road. You know, Buddha tried to starve his way into enlightenment.

> *I started out with a mansion and a mink coat and ended up a wandering* sadhu.

When that didn't work at all, he decided that attachment to not having is as much a detriment to spiritual progress as attachment to having.

I have never been sorry that I opted for spirit. I've appreciated the upper-middle-class heritage I had that turned me on to music, art, and beauty in its many forms, but I've never missed the elegant houses or expensive clothes. Living in a vehicle was a marvelous experience. I joined a magical psychedelicized carnival that went bankrupt. My dog and cat and I went all over the West Coast. Now I live simply with my partner, Paddy. We can hardly keep up with the adventures every day brings us.

REBECCA: What were you doing before?

ELIZABETH: I was a business woman. I had fifty-two employees. My jewelry business did just under half a million in the year before I left. Then I opened a store on Haight Street. [*Knowing laughter all around*]

ELIZABETH: Well, I bought a mansion on Ashbury, and that was the significant thing because I took acid shortly after that. Eventually I walked out on everything—my marriage and my business and my whole way of life. I took all my clothes and jewelry and threw them into the middle of the floor and said, "Everybody take what you want—I'm gone."

REBECCA: Could you describe the quality of that time? And what were your hopes and dreams of what would come out of the sixties?

> *If you wanted to merchandise the American standard experience, experiencing Godhead was not it.*

ELIZABETH: A word that I use a lot in my book is "spirit." It's as though for the first time a whole bunch of people took part in the mystical experience, and there was that camaraderie of shared experience beyond the realm of the American standard. If you wanted to merchandise the American standard experience, experiencing Godhead was not it. (*laughter*)

REBECCA: So the fact that the experience was shared and not just personal made a big difference?

ELIZABETH: I think so. You are here doing an interview to share more of what I am and more of what you are, and that sharing of experience is how evolution happens. We all grow together.

REBECCA: Many people feel that during the eighties the last vestiges of sixties idealism got swept away. Do you think that's true, or did some lasting influence come out of that time?

ELIZABETH: I think that there are more young people aware today than there ever have been in the history of the world, and the best part of the rave generation is proof of it. Hundreds of thousands of people all over the world between eighteen and twenty-five are sharing a spiritual experience with tribal overload and huge sensory input. There was a continuity of spirit in the sixties that has reached into all corners of human work. Even though many people re-entered society, they haven't forgotten their mystical experiences. They've become scientists, teachers, carpenters, farmers, TV producers, poets, house cleaners, CEOs. They not only haven't forgotten, they're actively reshaping the world.

In the Haight-Ashbury time, we really thought that in five years everything would be changed. We thought we would find better ways of communicating, which we have, and that marijuana would be legal, which it is not. We visualized a world at peace. We would cross the omega point that Teilhard de Cardin describes in his books. People would be nicer to each other—that's simplistic, but it's the bottom line.

Obviously our timetable was sophomorically idealistic. Still, there is evidence that those things are slowly, slowly happening.

REBECCA: Do you think people are nicer to each other?

ELIZABETH: [*Pause*] I think there are more people working on how to be nicer to each other, learning to forgive and feel good about themselves. Without that, advance is impossible. If you don't see yourself as God, how can you see anyone else as God. The change involves opening new neurological pathways, dropping the synapses that have left us in fear and distrust and led us in to violence. A new consciousness

> *The change involves opening up new neurological pathways . . .*

is evident as the planet grows smaller and our species becomes more obviously an interdependent colony.

DAVID: What relevance do you think this period will have to the future?

ELIZABETH: It was the first time that a significant number of people knew that evolution could be consciously directed. I think that's what the future holds as we travel around in the Mystery—the idea that we can mold a world that's better for everyone. Because our media chooses to bombard us with evidence of the more difficult parts of our nature, that may sound Pollyanna-ish. But a new awareness is even evident in TV news reporting. I think that conscious evolution is one of the important ideas that came out of the Haight-Ashbury period. The ingestion of psychedelics gave us a hint of the infinitely unfolding dramas of the universe, and beyond that of realms of pure spirit that exist without the duality constrictions of form, which is where most of our consciousness tends to dwell. We opted to try to integrate those experiences in our daily lives, and then, hopefully, to ascend even beyond that. It was the greatest game we could find to play.

DAVID: How would you say psychedelics influenced your perspective on life?

ELIZABETH: Holy mackerel, Andy! Mine? It was almost universal. There was what I call a democratization of God consciousness, never known on such a scale before. Well, I was an atheist, and now I'm a spiritual nothing in great awe. Boy, that's a big change! (*laughter*) The experience of Whatever-It-Is is indescribable magnificence. The narrowness of most science and religion and philosophies is that they try to put a grid on—or make a graph of—the unlimited. I think once humans have enough to eat and drink, they become hooked by a need to know, a serious but grand addiction.

> *There was what I call a democratization of God consciousness, never known on such a scale before.*

REBECCA: Well, if we met you before the experience and then met you afterward, what differences might we notice?

ELIZABETH: Well, let's talk about the similarities. You'd see the same bounciness and intelligence and creativity and insecurities. But right after I began taking psychedelics, I was kind of messianic. I wanted everyone to get on board, because otherwise maybe it was all just a dream and it never really happened. That's the dangerous feeling, the internal doubt, that leads to "Thou shalt nots." Don't do this and don't do that. Don't take psychedelics. Don't really experience. Keep your mind clean, and maybe God will learn to love you. Political organization rather than spirit in religions. My hair was long and I painted my face and I wore elkskin dresses. It was kind of romantic, but too outrageous for society. It became too much trouble to stay in that place. I wandered too far from acceptability, and it was uncomfortable.

I'm not so different, Beck, except that I have known Love and strive to manifest that in my life. Not always so successfully, but the synapses are changing. I'm still learning.

REBECCA: Do you think that if you hadn't taken psychedelics you would have still arrived where you are now, through a gradual process of natural selection?

ELIZABETH: Psychedelics helped me jump to a whole other quantum level. I'm a human chauvinist, in a way, because I think there's something very special about the human brain. If I can take a tiny pill, and forty-five minutes later I've died to my personality and am in contact with realities that are seemingly infinitely unfolding, then it seems that the human brain has some special place in the whole drama of the universe.

DAVID: Was there any link between your taking psychedelics and getting involved in broadcast media?

> *. . . it seems that the human brain has some special place in the whole drama of the universe.*

ELIZABETH: I followed Stephen Gaskin, and I only lasted about seven months down on the Farm in Tennessee. Partly because of the growing hierarchy, but I think the poverty got to me, too. I found myself walking around San Francisco crying hysterically. There was nobody to help me, and finally I got on the train to go back to Tennessee because I didn't know what else to do with myself. I didn't think that I could fit into any kind of society.

I prayed for guidance. I'd never done that before. I said, "Listen, Jesus, if there's an energy or a force that you represent, I need help." I ended up visiting my son in St. Louis, where he had a station called KDNA that was remarkable, creative beyond anything on the air today. It was run by fifteen people who lived together in a great big mansion. They saw how troubled I was and said, "Why don't you just stay here and learn how to do radio." I never went back to the Farm.

DAVID: Have your views on the use of technology changed over the years?

ELIZABETH: I always wanted to use technology for its highest good, and that has not changed. I thought that in learning to communicate with one another in new ways we could somehow help each other more to stay "a-love" and that that's how technology should be used. Being human, we tend to use it on all levels, from the hideous hell realms of nuclear bombs to the heaven realms that draw us closer into the cosmic web. There's always been technology, since the first human struck flint to make fire. We've got autos and airplanes as extensions of our feet. We have telephones as extensions of our ears. We have computers as extensions of our brains. It's only the beginning, but we must learn to use these great tools to further evolution, to make us and all creation happier.

REBECCA: It seems that many people confuse the tool with the experience.

ELIZABETH: There's a Zen proverb that says you should not confuse the finger pointing at the moon with the moon, and that's true whether it's psychedelics or anything else. But I think technology is a miracle. I sat in my room last night listening to music written two hundred years ago, played by a conductor who is dead and heard by my amazing ears because of weird machines such as transmitters and radios, which translate human voices and sounds into waves and back again. Isn't that amazing? Now, because of cyberspace, I'm exchanging ideas and love with people all over the world!

DAVID: It seems that we're developing more and more ways to access the whole universe from a single point.

ELIZABETH: That's nice. It seems that we've invented time/space to play some game I don't understand, but I suspect that's what evolution is about.

REBECCA: Has the game become less serious for you over time?

ELIZABETH: Laughter leads to less seriousness. Observing ants, I've been able to understand how limited any—I mean *any*—human understanding is. The ants don't even realize there is another ant hill twenty feet away. Our horizons are a little larger, but not all that much.

REBECCA: You've interviewed such an extraordinary variety of philosophers, scientists, and thinkers. How have your interactions with people who have such differing belief systems influenced your view of reality?

ELIZABETH: I couldn't have done the interviewing if I didn't already have a multifaceted view of reality. I have had a really charmed life. I was exposed to all different kinds of music and arts from a very early age, from jazz to opera to pop. I know a little bit of this and a little bit of that. I got the idea that universes might be self-defining, and therefore not really universal, when I studied Euclid in High School. Then I married very young, and my first husband was a physicist who boggled my mind with ideas of relativity and quantum mechanics.

On the flipside, my getting so much material from interviews has made it difficult to read. I want my information to come at me fast and precise and verbally. I don't want to read a hundred words when two would be enough. There are other important things I want to do, such as work in my garden. This is more understandable if you know that my third Cosmic Law—now listen seriously—is "There's nothing *more* important than petting the cat." You have to emphasize the "more." It's a koan that gives human logical arrogance some relativity.

> *"There's nothing **more** important than petting the cat."*

REBECCA: When we started out compiling the first volume of *Mavericks of the Mind,* I think we were a little too deferential. We would think, "Oh, he's got the answer," or "No, she's got the answer." Now it's more like a dance, where the mind waltzes with an idea for a while, which then moves back and becomes part of the flow.

ELIZABETH: Congratulations! I think that the secret of success, when you get the cosmic badge of honor pinned on you, is when you can dance on totally nothing. No concepts, no grids, no graphs, no formula—you just dance, and you're happy.

DAVID: What can you do without a context?

ELIZABETH: What's a context, Dave? They're always shifting—contexts within contexts within contexts. Watch out for sacred cows—eventually they all moo at you. No crutches, no crafts, just a little kindness! After we learn that one, perhaps we can go on to other realms.

> *Watch out for sacred cows—eventually they all moo at you.*

DAVID: What are some of the most memorable experiences you've had during your years of interviewing?

ELIZABETH: I've met so many beautiful people, it's hard to recall them all. When I met Ganesh Baba, he was in his eighties and using LSD and marijuana. He was an amazing energy. A Shivite who believed that mystical experiences should be welcomed no matter what the tool used to obtain them.

   There was an Ananda Marga nun, a beautiful young women, inside and out. She was only allowed to stay three days in one place. She said, "You Americans all feel guilty because you have more material plane than the rest of the world. I don't think you're better off, because you also suffer more anxiety than the rest of the world."

I've interviewed the famous, the unknown, and the infamous. Sometimes a person homeless on the street turns out to be a true wandering sadhu.

DAVID: You mentioned how one of the results you've seen from the sixties is that spiritual awareness has increased. But what does spirituality mean to you?

ELIZABETH: [*Long pause*] It's awareness of more and more of the infinite levels of "reality," reaching to an experience where there is absolute identification with all the atoms of the universe. In that place we know ourselves as unique and yet one.

Psychedelics are medicines to teach us who we really are. Spirituality is when we know that there is neither form nor no form, that any realm we can imagine exists somewhere, perhaps all here. Spirituality is recognizing the awesome miracle of all realms, including our own, and seeing the rainbow energy of the unity beyond love in every smallest atom of this and all universes.

DAVID: What, then, is your perspective on God?

ELIZABETH: Well, what's God's perspective on me? That's what I'd like to know! (*laughter*) Unfortunately, the word has terrible connotations because of the Judeo-Christian web into which most of us have been born in this part of the world. Humans, unfortunately, are so anthropomorphic that they assume that somehow God or Goddess has human attributes. God forbid! Sort of an archetypal soap opera up there on Mt. Olympus. So many gods and goddesses have been invented since humans began to think about this that it's very crowded up there!

I think there is a matrix of an energy that's beyond our capacity to touch until we can develop our brains more. A field of infinite rainbow atoms. And we are that. And maybe this matrix—perfect intelligence, or whatever you want to call it—really wanted to feel more, so it invented humans in order to enjoy all this beautiful stuff. Perhaps humans are the nervous system for God. If a tree falls in the forest, there's no sound if no one is there to hear it.

REBECCA: Except for the birds and rabbits.

ELIZABETH: But I think we're better transmitters than animals. They don't have this damnable and sometimes heavenly capacity for self-reflection. They don't *know* that they know.

DAVID: How do you know that?

ELIZABETH: Good question. I don't know how I know. I just know. I think humans have a greater capacity to enjoy and suffer, and to think about it.

DAVID: Do you think self-reflection causes suffering because when you reflect on the past or imagine the future you're not experiencing the moment?

ELIZABETH: No, that's a spiritual cliché, and I'm a New Age heretic. If you reflect on the past and imagine the future, you're doing it right now. There is no other time.

> *... I'm a New Age heretic.*

REBECCA: In what ways do you think that you experience suffering differently from that bird singing outside your window right now?

ELIZABETH: I think about my suffering, and I know that I'm suffering. The bird knows in a whole different way.

To get back to the Haight-Ashbury, I think what we hoped for and what I do see evidence of in the ecological movement and the feminist movement and the touchy-feely workshops is this desire of many people on many different levels to feel better, feel more aware, and to understand more. As I opened by saying, if there *are* infinite possibilities the one I like is that we get our heads together and choose to consciously shape our destiny.

DAVID: What relationship do you see between sexuality and the creative process?

ELIZABETH: The tangible universe in which we exist is the result of a giant orgasm—they call it the Big Bang, don't they? (*laughter*) And it's always happening. On a smaller scale, sex *is* creativity—that's how we make the next generation of stuff. I think the reason that we are so, excuse the expression, "fucked up" about sex is that it's an absolutely guaranteed way to get high, and people are so afraid to get high.

DAVID: Why do you think that people are scared of getting high? Is it because they are so attached to their egos?

ELIZABETH: Well, contrary to Hindu descriptions, I find our ego is our glue; it's what we are this time around. Given half a chance, the ego will opt for transformation and transcendence. But mostly the brain isn't ready for it. We're used to what we are, the old identifications. We need more experiences. We need to feel comfortable being "high" more and more of the time. That's one of the reasons I call marijuana a sacrament. It is a great teacher for learning to operate more optimally on many different levels.

REBECCA: You've been describing the process of growing into something more through mystical experience, and yet at the same time you are also describing a process of individuation. What is coming out of your self when you dissolve your self?

ELIZABETH: A crystal pulls to itself out of the elements what it needs to complete its form, and what accrues to it are separate entities, and yet it is all one thing. The crystal cells don't lose their individuation any more than the cell in your hand does—it's just part of something bigger. And I don't see any need for us to die in order to have this wonderful experience of unity. There is no ongoing self but Self. This time, or some time around, we return HOM with consciousness of both self and Self. Then we are true immortals.

REBECCA: How have your relationships with men influenced your life?

ELIZABETH: My relationships have been my anchor throughout my life. Trying to get validation as a woman through my relationship with a man and setting myself up so it couldn't happen led to some incredibly bad relationships. I spent ten years alone until I met Paddy, my present partner. Old age has been a continuing boon for me, a gift! My life has never been more contented and magical.

We've been together for eight years, and we still have our moments of working things out, but how I ever lucked out as a crone to have a man who is so helpful, I don't know. I couldn't do half of what I do without him. He's so wonderful and supportive, and so kind. Another of my cosmic laws is "The higher up, the fewer," which I got from my mother.

I think we deserve, as a birthright, to be really healthy and happy. I had to get over a lot of stuff in my relationships. I was battered twice, and that helped me. I realized that if I had been battered only once by a man, it would have been *his* fault. But after I got battered by two different men, I had to say, "What the hell am I doing to bring this on?" And I found out.

REBECCA: Do you think that men and women are very different in the way they think?

ELIZABETH: I've always lived in a world where both the men and the women are conditioned into roles that seem to me less than optimal. When women stop wearing high heels and men stop wearing ties, I believe we have taken another step.

REBECCA: Do you consider yourself a feminist?

ELIZABETH: I don't like to call myself anything with an "ist" or an "ian" on the end of it. (*laughter*) I'm glad that women are gradually freeing themselves, learning new roles, and I hope that men will do likewise.

> *I don't like to call myself anything with an "ist" or an "ian" on the end of it.*

DAVID: What did you learn from raising your children?

ELIZABETH: Well, one of my children is brain-damaged. It leads to a different relationship with yourself when you have a handicapped child—it's a love-hate thing. There's a lot of self-blame, a lot of self-pity, a lot of anger. I think I'm over most of that. That's been a huge learning. And my other child is a genius and has been super-wonderful to me in many ways. I turned him on to marijuana, but he was the first person to turn me on to a psychedelic, in about '64. He helped me when I had absolutely no money, and he turned me on to radio. What more could I ask?

REBECCA: What would you like to tell young people today?

ELIZABETH: You're asking a grandma! I asked my mother that when she was ninety-something. She said, "Tell them don't worry about it." That's my advice to young people. Be nice to each other, and when you're feeling really bad is the best time to reach out your hand to somebody else. It makes

> *. . . when you're feeling really bad is the best time to reach out your hand to somebody else.*

you feel a lot better, and you'll help someone in the process. Enjoy the world, work to create change that will help us all, have a good time doing it, and listen to good rock!

REBECCA: That's good advice—there's some really bad rock around. It seems, though, that in spite of all the positive movement going on in the world, there's a seemingly equally powerful resistance to the changes.

ELIZABETH: Well, that's what we want to change by focusing our attention. There are almost no emperors or kings left in the world. The ideals of democracy—freedom of thought—and the ideals of communism—sharing the bounty with our fellow humans—are incredible new ideals in the world. Maybe the two will come together one day. I think that the aberrations are fewer and that the ideals, no matter how they are diminished by our fear and lack of experience, are more numerous.

Imagine a continuum. It's balanced out with what we call "good" on one side and what we call "evil" on the other. Maybe there isn't any good or evil, but we damn well know that suffering doesn't feel as good as happiness. So suppose we take the familiar continuum and shift it in time/space so that the evil is now what good is today, and the good is something that we're not yet equipped to even experience, except in short bursts of ecstasy?

REBECCA: So we're raising the baseline, you think?

ELIZABETH: Exactly. I don't think it can't happen. Terence McKenna says 2012, but I'm dubious. Evolution has never been that fast. I hope he's right. (*laughter*) And I hope I live long enough to see it!

DAVID: Elizabeth, what is the secret to your seemingly boundless enthusiasm, optimism, and curiosity about life?

ELIZABETH: Marijuana! [*Laughter*] From my father I inherited sentimentality and an idea of being gentle with people, and from my mother I inherited enormous energy and creative ability. My body's amazing. You know, I'm really chronically sick with emphysema, and I still have so much energy. I swam half a mile today, and then I was digging my yard before it got too hot. I can't breathe very well, but I'm doing it! (*laughter*) I think that with a mission that's been a part of my life so long, the rewards of love directed at me are so much beautiful energy and I've absorbed some of that.

REBECCA: I'm interested in how your illness has affected your understanding of yourself?

ELIZABETH: Well, on a really stupid level, I sure as hell wish I hadn't smoked tobacco. I wrote an article in *Encore* called "Disease as a Spiritual Practice." When I'm really not feeling well, I find it affects all levels inside me. I admire the people who seem to be above that. However, I'm seventy-two, and even if I lived to be a really old person, it would only be another twenty years or so, and I don't want to live to be that old. My disease has helped me to more and more be grateful for the miracles of my everyday life. And I'm grateful that I'm dying slowly, because it gives me an opportunity to work on myself and to die in a state of grace.

> *. . . I'm grateful that I'm dying slowly, because it gives me an opportunity to work on myself . . .*

DAVID: What do you think happens after biological death?

ELIZABETH: Oh, joy! How wonderful! Wow! Look at this, I'm back home again! (*laughter*) What do I think happens when we die? Man, I don't know. If anyone tells you they know what happens after you die, don't believe them! I get scared of *not* dying; that's really frightening to me. I really love my life, but I feel sure we are born and die every moment of time. It's a continuous process, like a movie, which seems a continuity even though it's a series of stills.

REBECCA: What's going on in the future of your dreams?

ELIZABETH: I don't think we know what we are becoming. Maybe there will be a place where we actually drop form and become a different energy altogether. The worst-case scenario is that we'll blow ourselves up, in which case we'll have to start another experiment. I believe that that what we truly are is absolutely immortal.

The middle-case scenario is that whatever happens to humans, the world is shifting. Australia is moving two feet a year. It's going to hit the Indo-European continent and create mountains twice as high as the Himalayas. So you've got to get some perspective on this! (*laughter*) I hope that not too long in the distant future we'll be able to access now-hidden realms of consciousness—before something catastrophic happens, like a meteor hitting the earth.

> *... I won't be ashamed of the fact that you know some of the horrible images in my mind.*

In the shorter term, I really feel that we are going to create new ways of governance that will make the present forms look medieval, new ways of healing the body, new ways of opening ourselves so that telepathic communication can be easier between us and I won't be ashamed of the fact that you know some of the horrible images in my mind.

REBECCA: Your radio show is called *Changes*, and it seems that your whole life has been a series of transformations. What do you think is the secret of learning to roll with those changes?

ELIZABETH: I think Buddha's message of nonattachment is very helpful, but I'm not sure that I don't want to be attached to some things. I really enjoy people and beautiful objects, and I'm not ready to let go. On my first big acid trip I wrote a note to myself. In wiggly letters it said, "Hold on by letting go." I believe that's valid, and it's at least a lifetime in the learning.

REBECCA: Where do you get the courage to let go?

ELIZABETH: Well, I don't always have it. But sometimes just the invitation of the possibilities in life is so enormous. As I've gotten older, I've gotten around to thinking that I don't like changing so much—the overt form, anyway. In many ways, old age is a process of letting go—of stuff on the 3D plane, of emotional contacts with your friends and relatives who are dying, and of lifestyles. Also, the memory dropping away may be a blessing, because it narrows your focus to what's happening in front of you right now.

DAVID: If you could condense your life into a message, what would that be?

ELIZABETH: I think the human birthright is joy and that the only thing that keeps us from that is fear. I urge everyone to break the habits that they know have chained them in circular patterns of fear and to open themselves up to the fact that once that fear is gone, it's gone for ever, it will never return! Be content in the passing magic, but work for change, knowing that there really isn't any other work to do. This may be an illusion, a dream, but it's a real illusion, worth working with toward the perfection we knew was possible when we ingested so much LSD. The rest of human activity, even beauty and art and ritual and religion, are frosting on the cake of conscious growing. Let the challenges come. Reach out to help and to be helped. Listen respectfully to all teachers and teaching, including this, and find your own truth, knowing that it too will change. When our work has succeeded, the human race will know the joy of an open heart, and that is our entry into a kindergarten beyond which are infinite and infinitely exciting universes to explore forever.

Finally, to use the old analogy, we can learn to focus on the half-full part of the cosmic cup. When enough of us recognize that our joint thoughts can be directed to change this reflexive universe in a direction we choose, we will recreate the cup, and it will brim over for everybody.

William Irwin Thompson

"The history of the soul is always the history of the voiceless, the
oppressed, the repressed . . . "

The Science of Myth
with William Irwin Thompson

He spends his time contemplating such nuances of thought as the relationship of birdsong to light changes in a sunset, the mythic levels of meaning in the fairy tale of Rapunzel, the relationship of oral sex to the development of consciousness, and the rain dances of chimpanzees. He is a cultural historian, poet, and mystic, weaving his imagination deep into the fabric of scientific theory.

William Irwin Thompson received his doctorate from Cornell and has taught at Cornell, MIT, York University, and the University of Toronto. In 1972, feeling the need for a more improvisational forum, he established the Lindisfarne Association, an intellectual community where artists, humanists, and scientists can share their ideas and insights, beyond the confines and agendas of academia. A meeting of minds and friends, Lindisfarne is a model for the realization of a planetary culture. Over the years, it has attracted some of the most envelope-pushing thinkers of our day, such as Bucky Fuller, Marshall McLuhan, Gregory Bateson, and, more recently, Ralph Abraham, James Lovelock, and Lynn Margulis.

Thompson is known for his staggering trapeze acts of thought. Performing without the safety net of empiricism, he spans the subjects of sexuality, cultural origins, science, and mythology in giant sweeps, grasping them in metatheories of poetic grandeur. He is completely at home at the hearth of his intuition, where his rational intellect can sit and warm its hands. He received the Oslo International Poetry Festival Award in 1986 and is the author of fifteen books, including the classic At the Edge of History, *which was nominated for the National Book Award. He brings a mythic perspective to just about everything, from homosexuality to Darwinian theory. His beef with sociobiologists centers on what he perceives as the arrogant assumption that their theories, with terms such as* evolutionary momentum, *are free from the flights of imagination that characterize the language of the mystic. Thompson prefers "to take my mysticism neat."*

Every fall and spring he serves as the Lindisfarne Scholar in Residence at the Cathedral of St. John the Divine in New York. In the winter he is the Rockefeller Scholar at the California Institute of Integral Studies in San Francisco, where this interview took place on June 11, 1994. He declined to be photographed, so Victoria Sulski, an artist and friend of mine, came along to sketch him. I think that the drawing captures the spirit of this interview better than any photo could.

A strong upholder of European standards of excellence, William Irwin Thompson seems a trifle out of place only two blocks from the corner of Haight and Ashbury. It's hard to imagine him with flowers in his hair—but then, his Celtic soul is already decked with the garlands of his private spring.

RMN

DAVID: What was the source of your inspiration in becoming a cultural historian? How did you gain your mythopoetic perspective?

BILL: It was from Stravinsky. Before I knew how to read, my mother took me to my first experience of a public theater. I was a four-year-old child seeing the creation of the solar system set to Stravinsky's "Rite of Spring" in Disney's *Fantasia*. While I was watching the camera's point of view approach the planet from the outside, I had a shockingly familiar experience. It triggered a *déjà vu* in my mind of "Yeah, that's exactly how I got here. Finally, here is a human experience that makes sense!" The rest of the time when you're a child, you're surrounded by stuff that doesn't make any sense, whether it's cribs, punishment, or whatever, and you wonder, "What is all this? How did I get here?"

When I was in the theater, Stravinsky's music was so overwhelming and uninterrupted that it had something of the effect of an Eleusinian mystery rite. It imprinted my imagination with visual mythopoeics, and I became fascinated with cosmology and the story of the universe.

I went home and discovered that I could turn the dial on the radio. I would turn on the classical music station and lie down on the couch and go into *samadhi*.

DAVID: I'm curious about your formal educational process.

BILL: Well, grammar school and the nuns were a little after the fact. They were trying to teach me Roman Catholicism when I had already discovered yoga! (*laughter*) But I was a good boy, and I won lots of medals, and I got A's. But I didn't find Catholicism spiritual enough.

> *They were trying to teach me Roman Catholicism when I had already discovered yoga!*

The movie theater seemed to be a really sacred space, but the church seemed just to be filled with images of mutilation and torture, with a mangled Jesus on the cross. When I went to church mass on Sunday, Father Quinn would just scream at us that we weren't giving enough money to the church. So religion was very unappealing.

At age seven and eight I was sent to a Catholic military school. There, if you were bad, you were punished by having to stand to attention for five hours, and some children would faint in the sun. Today they would be sued and charged with child abuse!

I remember one time I went into a library and opened up a children's encyclopedia called *The Book of Knowledge*. There was a picture of a spiral nebula, and it told the story of the creation of the universe. It connected me back to my original Mind. I realized once more that there was this larger universe out there that wasn't controlled by nuns.

The Catholic military school was a double whammy because the headmaster was a shell-shocked major from World War II. He had a paddle that had holes put in it so that it would scream through the air as it came down. The patron saint of the school was St. Catherine, who, as Ralph Abraham points out, is actually Hypatia. She was tortured and killed by the Catholic mob. Even the namesake of the school was a figure of torture! So as soon as I had the opportunity to get out of all that stuff, I did.

DAVID: So your primary orientation was spiritual rather than intellectual.

BILL: Oh, totally. And also artistic. From the very beginning I was writing poetry. The Europeans have the understanding that a writer doesn't have to be a specialist. In America, if you're a poet you're Robert Bly, if you're a philosopher you're Dan Dennet, and if you're a scientist you're Gerald Edelman. In America they're always trying to figure out what it is you're trying to sell and how you can put it in a soundbite. This explains why I've spent a lot of time out of the country. I've lived in Canada, Ireland, and, for twelve years, in Switzerland.

REBECCA: You got disillusioned with academia after a while, and in your books you describe how you went on to explore other modes of learning in community.

BILL: But I liked academia in some senses because, since I came from the working class, it gave me a chance to move up and get out of that kind of life. So I had a good career, in terms of going from instructor to full professor in seven years and being promoted every year at MIT. I didn't leave academia because I failed, but I went through it so fast that suddenly I was a full professor at thirty-four. I thought, "Am I supposed to keep doing this for the next thirty years? I'm bored so I'm leaving." In the seventies, a lot of people were doing the same and trying to create new institutions.

REBECCA: Tell us about the community of Lindisfarne. How did it begin and what goes on there?

BILL: Lindisfarne has been going for twenty-three years, and every year it's different. It's more of a distributive fellowship, a concert rather than an institution, although at various times we've had functions and courses and things.

I had been really impressed with Michael Murphy's work at Esalen, but it was too wild, sloppy, Dionysian, psychedelic, American, and consumer-oriented. It wasn't really disciplined enough for my sensibility. I didn't want to do it in California because I felt that California would encourage those qualities, so I decided to set it up in New York.

Lindisfarne started out as an alternative to academia and as another way of doing the humanities in a technological society. Originally I tried to cross religion and science at MIT and create an honor college within MIT, but the president didn't want to do it. It was during the Vietnam War, and they had another political agenda. So that's when I quit and went to Canada.

REBECCA: How did it all come together?

BILL: From my travels and wandering. I tend to approach things through the back door rather than coming in with trumpets blazing. I spent a week at Esalen, during which Michael Murphy and I became friends for life. I would travel around the world and meet various people. Marshall McLuhan had read one of my books. I forget how I met James Lovelock. I think I just invited him to a Lindisfarne gathering and he came.

So it's kind of like a musical ensemble where you get together with people. You begin to jibe, and like can recognize like, creating friendships that have lasted twenty years. There was a charisma to the period of 1967.

There was a sense that there was a new evolution of consciousness, a new possibility, a new *zeitgeist*—or angel of time in the ether—and that doing the same old thing was just intolerable.

I went out to the Hopi reservation and started checking out all these different communities and cultures to see what I could learn from each of them for setting up Lindisfarne, which I did in 1972. I set it up thinking that it would be a place for students to drop into, once they'd dropped out of college, and study the new planetary culture. Communes and ashrams were anti-intellectual and universities were antispiritual, so I wanted to create a place that was intellectual and spiritual

> *Communes and ashrams were anti-intellectual and universities were anti-spiritual...*

at the same time, a place where I could be comfortable and find other people like me.

REBECCA: It's a great concept—an intellectual neutral-ground, free from the pressure of fulfilling a predetermined curriculum.

BILL: It's also a place to share experiences with people from different fields—like when Gary Snyder went for a hike with Jim Lovelock to the top of the Sangre and shared his vision of nature. When I had the first Gaia meeting, in 1981 in California, I brought the Santiago school of epistemology together, with Humberto Maturana and Fransisco Varella from Chile, Henri Atlan from Paris, Lovelock from England, Lynn Margulis, Heinz Pagels, and Elaine Pagels. These people had never met before.

The composer Paul Winter was there, and he got so inspired by Lynn Margulis's presentation, which was just intoxicating, that he wrote the *Missa Gaia*. So it was a fugue of art and science.

REBECCA: You have said that "intellectual respectability must come from its unavailability and resistance to communication." But information is the currency of thought, and what is the good of a good message if it isn't communicated?

BILL: If you're going to have a great restaurant, you want a cook who loves cooking, and some quality control. America tends to want to mass-produce everything and just have fast-food. If everybody knocks on the door and says, "I'm your wife," then it's pretty hard to relate in any serious way.

> *Part of protecting the integrity of a tradition or an art form is to learn how to say no . . .*

Part of protecting the integrity of a tradition or an art form is to learn how to say no, and to love to say no, to be in charge of the process from beginning to end. Most people on a certain level lose control and get involved in overpresentation in the media.

DAVID: You mean that their message gets diluted?

BILL: Yes, and they also get too many projections from celebrity psychosis in the culture. You get crank mail from fundamentalists and love letters from psychotics, and your life just gets torn apart. But beyond that, it's simply just a question of protecting the integrity of what it is you want to do.

If you're using your work *in order* to gain fame or money or power or political leverage, then that's a whole different strategy, and you can do that with almost anything—being a sports figure, a movie star, or simply being famous for being famous. But because the intellectual in America is such an endangered species, we don't really have a strong intellectual tradition. For the most part, the things that really work in America are diluted forms of European ideas. Joseph Campbell isn't as strong as Carl Jung or Erich Neumann. Ken Wilber isn't as strong as Jean Gebser.

> *. . . if you're a chef you're not going to want to work for Mc-Donald's!*

REBECCA: But even weak tea can perk some people up.

BILL: But if you're a chef you're not going to want to work for McDonald's!

REBECCA: So you're in no hurry to see the *Bill Thompson's Reclaim Your Mythic Imagination in 60 Minutes* workout. (*laughter*)

BILL: When I had my fifteen minutes of fame in the seventies, I had a chance for that, and it was so appallingly inappropriate that I just slammed the door on it. It made my publishers angry, though. But I think it's just a question of aesthetics. From the very beginning the formation of my psyche was aesthetic, and there are just certain things that to me are vulgar, distasteful, and ugly, such as American pop culture, or being a celebrity and going on *Good Morning, America*.

REBECCA: Are you accused of being elitist?

BILL: Oh, all the time. And I don't mind because I think that you *have* to be elitist. If you were going to study the guitar, would you pick the worst guitar teacher? I think that elitism is precisely what America needs if we're going to have fine wines, good cooking, and good philosophy.

> *I think that elitism is precisely what America needs . . .*

But remember, I'm working-class. I did this all on my own. My parents didn't have an education beyond the eighth grade. At the economic level, I'm anything *but* elitist. But at the levels of commitment to excellence, I'm totally elitist, and anything else I find reprehensible.

One of the reasons that I've changed over the past twenty years is because the technologies have changed. When the media technologies came out in the sixties, they were all very intrusive. You were small and the media were large. The business manager at Lindisfarne wanted to videotape an entire fellows conference. There were these incredibly bright floodlights, and they had wired the room so you could barely get around. I simply told them to get out. The same thing happened with my publisher when *At the Edge of History* was nominated for the National Book Award. They wanted me to go on Dick Cavett and David Frost, and I said, "I'm sorry, I don't want any part of that world."

If I hadn't done that, then the Lindisfarne fellowship wouldn't exist, because the fellowship is a collection of lifelong commitments to people. If people just end up getting used for some other agenda, they're not going to make that level of commitment. But now you have these hand-held devices as big as a Kodak. I'm not a Luddite—I love my Apple Powerbook—and all my mystical experiences as a child were with LP's and radio and even Disney, so I'm not at all opposed to media. But there has to be an appropriate scale of relationship. Anything out of scale gets evil.

I love the idea that this course of mine that's being taped in San Francisco could be taken by someone working on an oil-rig in the North Sea during a tough winter. At the same time, I love that I can walk down the street and nobody is going to recognize me. I feel sorry for Jane Fonda and those people who don't own their own face.

DAVID: I'd like to hear about what myth means to you, and the four different levels of mythic interpretation.

BILL: Oh no, I don't want to do that. It's all written up on page five in *The Time Falling Bodies Take to Light.* The metalevel of this question is more interesting than the content, if we actually attend to what's really going on here rather than to your agenda. This is precisely the difficulty of the media.

If a writer is to stay alive, you don't want to just continually repeat yourself. What America demands in the media is sound-bites and having a certain trip. Joseph Campbell says, "Follow your bliss," and then everybody memorizes it, and it goes out into the culture and becomes an icon. That is the kind of fossilization that I resist.

DAVID: I completely understand and I admire your integrity, but I would just like to learn more about what your perspective is on the subject of myth. You define mythology as being the "history of the soul." I'm curious about whether you see mythology as being history from the genetic code's point of view?

BILL: No, that's too concretized. Myth is much larger than just crystallized DNA.

DAVID: No, not crystallized DNA, but could myth be the story of evolution from the point of view of DNA—that physical part of us that is passed on from generation to generation?

BILL: The whole metaphor is wrong. In *The Ontogeny of Information,* Susan Oyama says that DNA doesn't carry a message or a unit. DNA is a topological crystal, and the shape of it has a lot to do with the sequencing. It's also influenced by thousands of enzymes in the cytoplasm, so it isn't even just in the nucleus. The whole cell is such an incredibly complex ecology of consciousness that it's inaccurate to say that information is just being carried in DNA, like it's a Chevy pickup.

What I said in those lectures back in 1976 is that history is written by elites that are the ego of a civilization. If it's written by men in England, it's not about women and slaves in Athens, or Semites with hooked noses who created the alphabet and the Mediterranean trading culture. The kind of history you learned in classics was a white, male, patriarchal narrative. That's the history of the ego. The history of the *soul* is always the history of the voiceless, the oppressed, the repressed—the marginal people, the artists, the women, the African.

To reconstruct the larger evolution involves the study of fairy tales. Grimm called his stories "house tales." It's the story that the maid with the wrong accent would tell the upper-middle-class children. It's information being smuggled in by marginal people who connect with the oral peasant culture. It's not what the reverend would be teaching the children in schools.

Myth also records the events that happened before we were even around. The Christian metaphor of the Eucharist—"Take and eat for this is my body and my blood"—is a way of describing the supernova that exploded and scattered information throughout the solar system, inseminated our earth with heavy metals, and made life here possible.

The myth of St. Michael, the arch-angel, forcing the demons down into the underworld is a description of the anaerobic catastrophe, where the new cyanobacteria, which were breathing oxygen and creating the new atmosphere, forced the anaerobic bacteria down into the slime at the bottom of lakes. I'm a Celtic animist, so I think

> *I'm a Celtic animist, so I think that we* **were** *the anaerobic bacteria and the dinosaurs.*

that we *were* the anaerobic bacteria and the dinosaurs. I believe that Gaia and the whole biosphere are really our collective body politic.

REBECCA: What does that suggest about the nature of mind?

BILL: That it's more immanent and diffused throughout the system than is commonly thought, and that the mind isn't just epiphenomenal and located in the brain. Varella and Maturana have this biology that says that when you really study the whole dynamics of life, you find that the mind is "the realization of the living."

That's the opposite of the American cognitive model, which says consciousness is just in the brain and information is just encoded in your DNA. In 1972 Varella and Maturana talked about mind as the realization of the living and took it down to the level of the cell. That was really far out then, but now people are beginning to wonder if that doesn't actually make a lot of sense. But there are other people who are really hard reductionists and would just find it too European and fancy.

REBECCA: So let me just clarify. You think that myth is the memory of the whole history of the universe?

BILL: Yes. For example, when you begin to unpack the cosmology in the Rapunzel fairy tale, you can show just how much information is in that.

DAVID: You say that this universal memory is not stored in the DNA. So where is it stored?

BILL: It's nonlocality. Everything in quantum physics now is rejecting the notion of storage and locality.

DAVID: But wouldn't it be stored in the nucleus of the atom? Without localization points, how can information be distributed?

BILL: Well, wave functions aren't localized. Bell's theorem is all about nonlocality, and when you're dealing with ten dimensions, then where's the location? Brian Swimme, who is a colleague of mine, talks about how if you draw a circle and you move to the third dimension, of a sphere, it's possible to move out of that circle without crossing a boundary. If you have a sphere and you go from the three-dimensional to the four-dimensional, you can also do that without crossing a boundary. So at three dimensions you can say I'm Euclideanly located here, but in the multidimensionality of my subtle bodies, I'm involved with Andromeda.

Part of the yogic thing is to shift from what's called the *fu chi*. There's the *anamayacosa* and then there's the *pranamayacosa,* which is the energy body that you use in *t'ai chi*. The *anamayacosa* is sometimes called the "astral body," but it keeps shifting to the *pranamayacosa* and back again, and at each one of those you're adding dimensionality. It's getting vaster and vaster, and at the same time it's recursive and enfolded so that each point pretends a larger point.

The whole notion of what is location and what is the body gets really dicey. What I break with in American culture is the notion that things are located in elementary particles, or in genes or brains, and that by manipulating them through elite minds at Harvard or MIT, you can control everything.

I'm much more involved in a diversity and an ecology of consciousness, where an individual flame can't exist if there's not an atmosphere. We couldn't exist if there weren't bacteria in our guts taking care of the poisons. The new theory about bacteria is that they're actually a planetary bioplasm and that we're inside them, they're not inside us. It's like a sheath around the earth. So the whole notion of location is becoming much more complicated—and much more interesting.

DAVID: So the problem you have with location is similar to the problem you have with the idea of representation?

BILL: Yes, that's a good connection. That's why Varella has rejected the whole representational theory of the nervous system and wants to deal instead with concepts like participation.

REBECCA: Can you describe the connections that you see between science and myth?

BILL: If you ask three questions—Who are we? Where do we come from? Where are we going?—my answer to those will give you a myth. You can give a Marxist answer, you can give a sociobiological answer, you can give a Christian fundamentalist or Moslem answer. So myth is basically macro thinking. Technical thinking is micro. It's saying, "I'm a neuroscientist, I'm a geneticist, and I'm not interested in answering the big questions." That was originally why I left MIT—if kids asked questions the professors would say, "Forget it and do your problem sets."

If you step back and ask the big questions, then you're beginning to think mythopoeically. If you look at the narratives of Darwin or even Leakey—all these are constructed narratives that are inescapably mythic. The whole notion of explanation falls into mythic structures. There's a wonderful book on narratives of human evolution by Misia Landau. She says to go back and study the structure of the folk tale, about how the hero leaves a safe environment and is put through a sequence of challenges. He is then confronted by someone who gives him the gift to be able to go for-

> *Science is inherently mythic.*

ward and resolve the challenge and then settle into a new steady state. You can take the structure of that folkloric motif and apply it to all these different theories of human evolution. Science is inherently mythic.

When I was saying this stuff in lectures in New York in the seventies, it was kind of against the grain. But that way of thinking began to come up much more in the eighties, because Michel Serres in Paris was giving a similar sequence to the whole nature of mythic thought. So now it's not quite so radical.

REBECCA: I could see how some scientists might have a problem with their work being described as mythic, not only because the popular understanding of the word "myth"—that it is something that's false—but also because mythic ideas evolve, whereas scientific truth is seen as permanent and unchanging.

BILL: Before he died, I interviewed Heisenberg at the Max Planck Institute in Munich. He said that scientists today are just stonemasons, putting one block next to another without having a view of the whole cathedral. There's always been a difference between scientists who have just been trained and read textbooks and pass on received opinion, and someone who is a creative scientist, like Heisenberg.

If you're talking to serious philosophers in science, they don't have any problem with that mythopoeic quality. It's just that if people are ignorant and think that "myth" means something is false—like there isn't a Santa Claus—then, yes, they would have problems with that. But I wouldn't necessarily regard them as heavies in the philosophy of science.

There was a wonderful book in the thirties called *The Genesis and Development of a Scientific Fact* by Ludwick Fleck, which is actually the source of T.S. Kuhn's *The Structure of Scientific Revolutions*. Everybody's read Kuhn's book, but Fleck's book is more brilliant and deeper and more inspiring. There's always this kind of Marx-Lenin relationship in the popularization of ideas. Anyway, when Fleck first came out with the book, people said, "Wait a minute. A fact is a fact." But he said no. He was one of the first constructionists to say a fact requires a theory the way a flame requires an atmosphere.

> *. . . a fact requires a theory the way a flame requires an atmosphere.*

REBECCA: So you experience scientific truths in a different way than a scientist.

BILL: I've found that more scientists are actually into poetry and culture than poets are into science. Often they're superb pianists or jazz musicians—Heisenberg was a pianist and Einstein was a violinist. Most all the scientists I've met are full, fleshed-out, complicated, interesting, and sensitive people.

REBECCA: You are in the minority in that, as a poet and writer, you have a strong intuitive grasp of scientific concepts. But given your lack of scientific background, do you feel frustrated because intuitive knowledge is largely seen as less valuable than linear knowledge?

BILL: No. I just feel frustrated with my own stupidity. (*laughter*) I'm really not as good at mathematics and science as I'd like to be, and I can *only* come at these ideas from the intuitive level.

REBECCA: Aren't you looked upon with some suspicion, though, as someone untrained in the sciences presuming to write about scientific theories that even many scientists are having difficulty in grasping.

BILL: The surprising thing is how often scientists' eyes have lit up and they have become affirmative. Because I would expect an attack. But it's kind of self-selecting. At MIT it was a very aggressive, competitive, violent kind of environment, and I certainly have had experiences of being attacked by Noam

> *. . . we are all weirdos getting together for our own mutual support.*

Chomsky or Morton Smith. But in general I've had positive experiences with people like Margulis or Lovelock. Most of those people are intuitive types themselves, so we are all weirdos getting together for our own mutual support.

REBECCA: In a gathering of your scientific friends, you're not viewed terribly differently? You're not seen as something of an odd fish?

BILL: It's funny, but I think they like it, even if only as Irish bullshit. (*laughter*) But I'm always a bit afraid. Last summer at the Lindisfarne meeting I didn't want to embarrass my son, who is in the academic world. He had invited some people from the University of Chicago and Stuart Kauffman, who is a heavy from the Santa Fe Institute. I was trying not to be too far out and mystical, and Stuart was saying, "Relax, Bill, it's okay."

It tends to be a self-selecting and self-organizing process, where like attracts like and you get into this chamber music ensemble. I've experienced both ridicule and humiliation, and also flashes that have actually inspired people to go out and do scientific work from suggestions that I've given them.

DAVID: Could you give an example?

BILL: Ralph Abraham and I are working on trying to do a canon on the proportional system for the Paleolithic statues of the Great Goddess, because my intuition was that the ratio of the head to the breasts to the hip, et cetera, is a mathematical sequencing. If that were worked out with musical analogues, that could be interesting. So at the gathering of Lindisfarne fellows in Colorado this summer, I expect that he will share with us what he's done on the computer.

DAVID: I'm curious about your ideas on the evolutionary process, and I'm wondering why do you think that sexual frequency and genital size have increased over time?

BILL: That's an interesting question. Part of it is in the shift from the estrus cycle to menses. The process of hominization involves the eroticization of time as the very foundation of consciousness. A lot of myths deal with the point where language and sexuality come together and make us human, where there is this crossing between the two.

I think there is a recognition that sexuality is an acceleration of time. If you take half your genetic endowment and throw it away to receive a new half from another partner, then what you're getting is a process of innovation in which the children are not like the parents. So, inherently, sexuality is an acceleration of time, a speeding up of evolution, and a consciousness of intensity, of orgasm and ecstatic time. Time and sex are inherently part of the architecture of consciousness and incarnation.

What's interesting is to realize that the most erotic organ is the mind. I think there's also a relationship between the bottom and the top of the spinal column. If you look at the spinal cord, you see that the brain and the genitals are really one organ. It's also what we share with whales and dolphins, because they too have elaborate courtship rituals. Dolphins particularly are open to sex at all times and also have a huge brain. So dolphins and humans seem to be sharing this evolutionary experiment.

Mystics such as Rudolph Steiner have predicted that in the future sexuality is going to shift from the genital chakra to the throat chakra and there will be a kind of *logos spermaticos*, a pure vibrational quality by which the erotic is connected through speech and sound. It may be something that young people are inherently recognizing through the eroticization of pop music.

DAVID: The cultural link between sex and death was foreshadowed by their simultaneous biological arrival. But I'm wondering if you see, on some level, an even deeper link between sex and death, something in the universe's history prior to that which connects them.

BILL: Sex and death are basic to the structure of myth, long before Freud. Death is really a definition of individuation. If you don't have a discrete cell with a nucleus that dies, if you just repeat cell division *ad infinitum*, then the process is plasmic and universal and extended—but, like bacteria that don't have a nucleus, it's not highly individuated. It's so collective that it's not a discretely located, genetically defined individual.

One of the things that I'm fascinated with in myth is how every structural transition within cultural transformation is characterized by loss and a dark age. After that, there is an opening to the unimaginable. Something else happens, like cretaceous extinction and the occurrence of mammals after the dinosaurs. This is one reason I don't buy into cryogenics and the ego's cry of "I don't want to die!" Death is part of what enables individuation to be possible. In a Greek tragedy, death gives it poignancy. What is opera about? The guy is about to die and the woman sings an aria, "*Addio vita!*"—"good-bye life!" So the whole nature of romantic art, poetry, opera, Greek tragedy is all about the intensity of death and its linked opposite, sex and orgasmic ecstasy.

I think that on some level this is an evolutionary commitment to energizing the universal by energizing the unique. It's a kind of Mobius strip where the unique and the universal cross in more interesting ways than with bacteria, where it's the unit and the uniform. So fascist states that try to compress with a single center, like the old Soviet Union, tend not to carry much evolutionary energy.

The reason that America was able to win the race was that we somehow tripped into this experiment—maybe partly inspired by jazz and art—of self-organization from noise. Notice that we have a high tolerance for crime. I can tell you from living in Canada and Switzerland that Americans will put up with more crime, more noise, and more disorder than these more stable nations. Nobody else can understand it. The Chinese can't figure out what the hell we're doing. The Russians, who are imitating us now and are having their own Chicago-in-the-'30s in Moscow, are flirting with us, but I think they're going to say, "We can't take it! Let's go back to Stalin."

DAVID: Do you think that's related to the extraordinary cultural diversity in America?

BILL: Yeah, I do. I think it has a lot to do with black jazz, with Jewish intellectuality, Irish poetry, this whole gene pool of ecological diversity. The greatness of America is that there's no center that carries the whole thing. You have Paris in France and Moscow in Russia, but New York doesn't call the shots for the whole of America. You've got all these different places with different styles and bioregional cultures that really add something to the mix.

So I think that there's a universal quality that's energizing the unique. How far can it go before the collective breaks down? We're right at the edge, and I really don't know how America is going to handle the next step.

REBECCA: In avoiding institutionalized thought, tribes and subcultures are popping up all over the place. Sometimes they seem even more dogmatic than the institutions they are supposedly freeing themselves from; other times they are free-form experiments in community. Do you think that the increase in tribalism, especially in a country like America, where public unity hides such underlying diversity, is an evolutionary advance, or is it a regression?

BILL: I don't think it's either one—I think it's experimentation. I don't think that evolution is so planned and managed. It deals with mistakes and mutations and accidents, and things get enfolded in sloppy ways. So it isn't the linear program of Teilhard de Chardin or Darwin. It isn't moving from chaos to the omega point. It's something more complicated. Definitely surprise and chaotic processes are all part of it.

REBECCA: Do you see the increase in tribalism as a positive development?

> *If you're mystical, you don't necessarily identify just with a momentary piece of meat called hominoids.*

BILL: Well, we might blow it and it might just move into a catastrophe. But even catastrophes tend to be, over the long haul, spurs to evolution. We might even end it for human beings and not be able to keep this experiment going, but the biosphere will not cease to evolve. If you're mystical, you don't necessarily identify just with a momentary piece of meat called hominoids.

REBECCA: There's been much debate about the robustness of complex ecological systems, such as the rainforest. Is greater evolutionary momentum, driven by diversity, always going to create instability in the long run?

BILL: It's equal and opposite energies going on at the same time. At the one level, you get homogenization of the suburban culture. So other people start marking themselves out and retribalize. They start tattooing themselves and diversifying their sexuality. That reaches a point where it energizes the fundamentalists to say, "Now we've got to go back to family values and kill them all."

So it's a question of how those two extremes are going to balance out. America is arming to the teeth because people basically distrust government and are preparing different scenarios of Armageddon. There are all kinds of scenarios out there that could be pretty frightening, where America could just lose it and implode.

China probably believes that that's what's going to happen. One of the reasons they keep selling us these cheap AK47's is that they think, "Why should we bother to invade and have a war to see who is going to be the master of the Pacific Rim in the twentieth century? Why don't we just sell them the guns, make the money, and let them kill themselves?" I don't think I'm being paranoid—it just might work!

When humanity reaches this evolutionary catastrophe, bifurcation, or cusp, some people can't handle the recycling of the noise into new information and just check out. It's like when industrial cultures hit third-world or tribal cultures, their suicide rates go up, their fertility rates go way down, and they pull the plug on themselves.

I think in places like Los Angeles you're really getting a kind of end-of-the-world psychosis. You're getting drive-by shootings on the freeway, and people are worrying about whether the San Andreas fault is going to crack or whether the air will become too polluted—it's just end time.

> *I think in places like Los Angeles you're really getting a kind of end-of-the-world psychosis.*

REBECCA: I've been hearing a lot about the new planetary culture, which is a term being thrown around quite loosely these days. But isn't the diversity of lifestyle, language and mythos part of the artistry of what humanity is, and what keeps it interesting and surprising?

BILL: Well, the term "planetary culture" is a phrase of mine from almost thirty years ago and was meant to contrast with the internationalism of the MIT multicorporate elite that I was trying to counter. I was saying that there's this new form of globalization, with a crossing of Indian yoga and science and electronics, that is creating a new planetary culture. But it didn't work because the planetization seems to just be apologetics for the American empire in a new form.

REBECCA: Could it be that instead of leading to more and more cultural homogenization, planetary culture could be achieved by individuals within each culture beginning to gain a planetary perspective, which would then lead to environmental sensitivity and a decrease in violence?

Planetary culture isn't a monoculture.

BILL: Planetary culture isn't a monoculture. In internationalism the governing science is economics, but a planetary culture suggests a shift to ecology as the governing science. It energizes diversity, it requires a larger gene pool, and it deals with the new sciences of complexity rather than linear reductionism. We're not all becoming one. We might be going in hyperspace to a level of integration in which we all participate in this multi-dimensionality, but it's high in individuation.

Going back to your question about sexuality, sexuality for somebody who isn't mystical is the most intense way of experiencing the vividness of your own body and your own ecstatic existence. It's about being both intensely alive and webbed to another, participating with the encounter in a romantic dynamic. It's a Zen koan, in the sense that it's in you *and* not in you.

In terms of parenting, there's a whole discovery of love. I participated in the birth of my son and experienced the consciousness of the subtle bodies of my children entering the room at their conception. If you're psychic, then the whole process of being a parent is much more multidimensional than people talk about.

REBECCA: What do you think about the idea that we're actually evolving beyond sex altogether?

BILL: We are tending to deconstruct sex. For example, the women's movement is taking apart seduction and romance. Flirtation is now against the law in some colleges. So there's a massive assault on the whole quality of courtship and seduction and, by feminists, on the beauty myth and advertising. Medi-business is taking apart reproduction the way the family farm got usurped by agribusiness. Sex has become a mystery school, and in certain groups it's become a whole way of life, way beyond the goals of reproduction.

REBECCA: Some archetypes seem to have an eternal quality to them, especially the male and female archetypes. But do you think that these archetypes are evolving in keeping with the changing self-image of men and women? If so, then in what ways?

BILL: I don't want to say that they're eternal. I'll just say that their melting temperature is higher, so it takes longer for them to disappear. They tend to last for a couple of hundred thousand years.

Balzac wrote this alchemical novel called *Seraphita*, in which a man
and woman fall in love with the same figure. The woman falls in love
thinking Seraphita is a man, and the man falls in love thinking it's a woman,
and this love is just beyond any sexual definition. So even back in 1830,
Balzac was playing with these themes, which got played out in the culture
of rock music in the sixties.

I saw a picture of an Indian guru in Hawaii, and you could not identify
the sex. It looked totally androgynous. I think there is a quality of fascina-
tion with the androgyny, and sexuality is on its way out. But in some parts
of the culture, people are getting into natural childbirth and natural death,
and recovering biology as the sacred. But it seems to be romantic, like
writing poems to trees before the industrial revolution, or William Morris
talking about handicrafts when factories were taking over. What its real
future is and how it's going to stand up to this double assault will be interesting.

DAVID: You've said that when a way of life is vanishing, people tend to
try to hold onto it even tighter. Do you see the rise in fundamentalism as
being indicative of that kind of phenomenon?

BILL: Oh, that happens all the time. You get the Renaissance, and then
you get the Inquisition.

REBECCA: Do you think we are in a period of initiation?

BILL: I think we've definitely been in a period of initiation since 1967.
Something really weird happened on December 31, 1967. I'm a firm be-
liever in the *zeitgeist,* that this is a myth that has an ontological reality to it.

REBECCA: Did you believe that we would use the opportunity in better
ways than we have?

BILL: Yeah. I suppose I was more optimistic, and I think we could have
done better. But I don't know. If one has the big picture—which is one
good thing about myth—then you don't have to be optimistic or pessimistic in a quarterly report. You can look at something like the cretaceous
extinction and say, "Well, that wiped out 86 percent of life on the planet.
But a forest fire can actually trigger seeds that otherwise wouldn't spread."

On one level, I think we're up against a really big "catastrophe bifurcation" for humanity. But as death is part of the architecture of individuation,
then it's just part of a larger story. I think we're moving toward a collective,

> *I think we're moving toward a collective, shared death.*

shared death, which is maybe one reason we are invoking a catastrophe. Otherwise, evolution might continue in this slow way, and we'd be locked into hell for a longer period.

Actually, by raising the heat we're really destabilizing the planet. Look at what we've done in the past fifty years to the biosphere. We're raising the ante. We don't quite know what the risks are, but we're totally committed to it. We're not going to put it

> *We're raising the ante. We don't quite know what the risks are, but we're totally committed to it.*

into reverse. Everybody's committed to whatever their trip is, whether it's gay or lesbian or fundamentalist or skinhead. They're all turning up the heat, and no one is moving toward comfort and steady state. We're calling down some evolutionary transformation, but we don't quite know what it is.

DAVID: What do you think happens to human consciousness after death?

BILL: I think that when you're alive, you weave a subtle body and that it's composed out of all of your thoughts—the collective ecology of your consciousness. When you die, you've actually woven your next form of incarnation, and you move into that subtle body that you've constructed throughout your life.

> *It isn't punishment, like going to hell, but it is remorseless.*

It isn't punishment, like going to hell, but it is remorseless. When you live in your subtle body in the bardo realm, you begin to meditate on weaving the flesh that will be the carnal form for your next incarnation. You're not alone, because you're actually inside—this may seem flaky, but indulge me—an angelic body that is a collective neighborhood interacting with you.

I talked to Nechung Rinpoche, who was the abbot of the largest monastery in Tibet before the communist invasion. He said that when people come together in practice, they actually constellate a form of consciousness that is larger than them. The bodhisattva sends a beneficent being that takes an energy from a higher dimension, steps it down, and makes it available to the people in the meditation practice. It's like when you go to a great concert and you suddenly feel that something has happened, that everybody has suddenly thrown a switch and turned on another reality.

So our subtle bodies are woven into this larger angelic formation. I'm happy with the concept *angel*, but there are different words for this in different traditions. It's a transcultural phenomenon. These angelic bodies are like midwives to your own rebirth, and so when you interact with them when you die, you actually go into that bardo. The paranoid way of thinking of this is abduction and flying saucers—that you're taken up into a tin can, which is going to carry you to the stars. Well, all of that is misplaced concreteness for what is really angelic multidimensionality.

DAVID: What do you think happens at the moment of death?

BILL: It all depends on what you've been doing in your meditation practice. If you're a yogi, you die consciously every night—you can stop your heart and go into bardo at any time during meditation. At the moment of death, if you're really advanced, you could just stop your heart and go out through the top of your head and not have the process inflicted upon you.

DAVID: And when you say "go out," you mean going out in the vehicle of thought that you wove together throughout your entire lifetime?

BILL: Yes. And you're not alone. When I quit MIT, I gained a whole new fellowship of friends—and in the subtle dimension you have your colleagues, too. Plato discusses this in the myth of Er at the end of the *Republic*, which is one of the first descriptions of the death experience. If you examine your dreams, you'll often find yourself at airports or at college campuses or at places with a lot of other people, and if you start doing dream practice, you notice that this stuff is already coming up.

REBECCA: You spoke about planetary culture not being a monoculture, but isn't the culture largely controlled by who controls the media? America is the media tzar of the world.

BILL: But multinationals control the media. This is not really about nations; this is about multinational or transnational corporations. If you look at the crusades, we Europeans thought that we would invade and get the Holy Land, but what happened was that we uncovered the Platonic manuscripts, Indian algebra, and created the Renaissance. In the culture of Europe, the father is Islam and the mother is Dark Age Europe. The child is the Renaissance, which then moves to America and the New World. So these things aren't really under anybody's conscious control.

DAVID: Do you see any teleology in the evolutionary process?

BILL: No. I think that innovation is nonlinear, that it's a complex, dynamic system. It has certain parameters—you can't play tennis without a net—but it's definitely not a system moving toward a linear goal. The human imagination tends to envisage that evolution is going to hit higher and higher stages, and that the next evolutionary step is going to be an animal like us but just a little better, with a bigger brain and maybe with technology embedded in it. I think that is a total failure of imagination.

If we have this "catastrophe bifurcation" where a billion people die at once, then they all share an imagination and they all share a definition of an event. The holocaust helped to form the identify of the Jews, and their whole experience of history and time. So if human beings experience a collective catastrophe, they will share an imagination in the collective subtle body.

REBECCA: What is your intuition of how this catastrophe might manifest?

BILL: I think it's actually a change in the position of the solar system relative to the galaxy that happens periodically. Mystical elites have kept records of these changes over long periods of time. When the Earth comes into a new position, it is exposed to more comets, like the one hitting Jupiter on my birthday, July 16.

So I think that we'll get swept into some kind of asteroid belt and that there'll be a subsequent variation in the geological stress on the planet. That will effect the reversal of the Earth's magnetic field and its orientation and rotation, creating stress on the tectonic plates. We might get a lot of volcanoes going off, which will begin to affect the albedo. With our high population, if we get one dark summer then there will be massive shortages in the food supply.

Also, socially, when pension funds go bankrupt with hurricanes and earthquakes and floods every single year, then pretty soon the economy of capitalism won't be able to sustain all the demands being made on it. It implosively forces a redefinition of health care much larger than the one that Clinton has in mind.

That's going to force capitalism to change, because you can't deal with such a collectively shared catastrophe with the concept of private property. Even if you have an AK47, you're not going to be able to defend yourself. It forces people to share a historical space. If they go into this catastrophe space of bardo and the angels are kneading their consciousness—like making bread and throwing it back into the oven in the next incarnation to bake again—then I think it can accelerate evolution. I think it might be quite possible to come up with something where the biosphere generates a new evolutionary form as different from us as, say, the mammals were from the dinosaurs.

> *Even if you have an AK47, you're not going to be able to defend yourself.*

REBECCA: So you think that humans are the end of the line on this particular evolutionary track?

BILL: That's what Sri Aurobindo and the Mother said—that man is a transitional animal and we've reached the end of the road. But ultimately, as the story and the cosmos is so vast, it's not really the end, it's just the closing of a chapter. And it's really far out, as far as any sci-fi imagination can take you. I wonder what the next step is going to be? But I'm not a prophet.

REBECCA: You're not a prophet?

BILL: No, I'm not.

REBECCA: Damn! (*laughter*)

BILL: By definition, an open-ended system is not predictable, and to think that it is, is an ego trip.

DAVID: But from your study of cultural history, do you see certain patterns of transition in the past from which you could extrapolate to where we might be going now?

BILL: All the metaphors of different changes are relevant in a sense, because you can say it's a paradigm shift, but it's larger than that because you're dealing with evolution. It seems to be larger than something like the Neolithic revolution, because it's not just a change in technology, it's a speciation.

So it seems that when we look at the myths of hominization and the emergence of humanity, there are some biological lessons about what happens when a species enters a new ecological niche, such as when our ancestors went from forest to savannah. Generally, when there's one of these

> *The church was not going to imagine a Renaissance—they couldn't imagine that it would be the end of their trip.*

evolutionary changes, the dominant institutions don't carry the explanation. The church was not going to imagine a Renaissance—they couldn't imagine that it would be the end of their trip. So what you get are small groups arising and re-imagining the world and coming up with a more effective explanation. That's why Lindisfarne was more attractive to me than staying at MIT.

But with these small groups I think it's possible to expand imagination and release one's control so that you don't concretize into a premature interpretation, like fundamentalists do, and try to clamp down violently. You learn to have more faith in the transformational quality. So I tend to be more attracted to people who have the biggest possible picture imaginable, such as Rudolph Steiner, rather than technological predictors.

In the eighties, *Science* magazine dragged out all the predictions of the seventies, and they were all wrong. All the smart guys had said that we would be taking helicopters to work in 1984. I think that futurism tends to be just a description of the present; it's never prophetic. Artists tend to be much more sensitive to the possible future.

DAVID: Have psychedelics had any influence on your philosophical outlook?

> *Psychedelics are too much like American consumerism—it's fast food.*

BILL: No, none whatsoever. It's totally yogic. Again, I have an aesthetic orientation. Psychedelics are too much like American consumerism—it's fast food. Also, a couple of my friends went psychotic, so I've seen some casualties. In my particular case, I had a mystical vision that said I shouldn't go that way, that I should become a yogi.

Since childhood, I've always been naturally psychedelic. Gregory Bateson's grandfather, who created the science of genetics, had a theory that the reason the Celts were more psychic was that the witch trials that selectively killed all the people with second sight never penetrated to the Celtic hinterland of Ireland and Scotland. It's certainly true that second sight and visions of elementals is still alive in the Celtic tradition. If you combine that with drugs, you run a really good risk of becoming psychotic. You just get overloaded.

I've been with many who have been influenced by psychedelics, such as John Lilly, Timothy Leary, Ram Dass, Terence McKenna, Ralph Abraham, and Joan Halifax. I think it tends to create a hole in your aura like the ozone hole that, yeah, you can open you up to stuff, but the intermediate realms are full of noise and things that are traditionally called demons. In the *Ramayana* there's this wonderful story about how the demons would go out to yogis who were meditating on their own and eat them alive. People who go out into the astral not really prepared for dealing with it open themselves up to psychic inflation—or worse.

There's a certain kind of autism among my psychedelic friends. They've gotten into their own private Idaho and their eyeballs gleam with a personal ecstasy and they lose the compassionate sensitivity to the Other. I've never really found anyone in the psychedelic movement who is as translucent or radiant or as charming as the Dalai Lama or the yogis I've met. A good friend of mine who's a neuroscientist here at UCSF said, "Man, if it wasn't for acid, I just wouldn't be open to any of this stuff." But that wasn't my case.

I've also noticed that sometimes there's a seductive self-delusion where people get stoned and write crappy poetry. There's a certain level of psychedelic kitsch that I'm aesthetically repelled by.

DAVID: It seems that you really are naturally psychedelic. In reading your books my first thought was, "These are all LSD insights!"

BILL: But they're all literal descriptions of experiences I've had. I've noticed that there's a certain loss of discrimination among the psychedelic crowd. Can we point to psychedelic art that's really as great as Bach or Goethe or Yeats? When I come to San Fransisco, I find this strong commitment to the psychedelic subculture, and I feel that if I stayed here all the time there would be a real loss of complexity and excellence.

DAVID: Isn't that the case if you stay anywhere too long?

BILL: Yes, absolutely. The Parisians can get enfolded into themselves and become anaerobic intellectuals. I don't belong anywhere. I'm here on the edge of the Haight-Ashbury, but I'm about the most un-Haight-Ashbury person you'll ever find or probably ever interview. I'm the *real* freak in your collection.

REBECCA: Tell us about your work with the solar village.

> *Everybody had a bazooka in their pick-up truck. These guys were serious!*

BILL: In Colorado there is a hands-on attempt to create a solar village. We brought people together to develop appropriate technology that would lead to the rediscovery of planetary villages and decentralization. It was an attempt to do something political at the ecological level. Maybe in the long run it's beginning to work, but we've run across a lot of setbacks. I wonder if perhaps we were too purist in our strategies. In going to Crestone, we encountered fundamentalists who tried to burn us out. Everybody had a bazooka in their pick-up truck. These guys were serious! It made New York look like a loving and caring place.

REBECCA: And what was their problem?

BILL: Oh, they thought we were creating a one-world, planetary culture that was apologetics for the Rockefellers, who together with the Council of Foreign Relations and the Trilateral Commission were going to create a nuclear war and create their world headquarters in Crestone, Colorado, and we were there as the shock troops. Real Robert Anton Wilson conspiracy stuff.

I tend to be more of a contemplative than a political activist. I'm not a new-left radical. I'm obviously not a Republican, but I'm not a hands-on protest marcher.

REBECCA: Tell us about your electronic stained-glass project.

BILL: It hasn't happened yet because of the funding, but it was an attempt to put an embankment of liquid crystal displays on the wall of the Cathedral of St. John the Divine, in New York, and render the subvisible and invisible realms—like the bacteria in the atmosphere—visible to people. At the same time, there would be a mimetic level where programs would be stored in the computer as films. There would be interactive arts, where composers would compose music and the interaction of your own breath would go through various software transforms. Using the technology developed by James Lovelock, the electron capture device, you could see the trace of you walking through the forest, of the trees, and your perfume interacting with it, for example, and it would play it back as music.

So it's attempting to tell the story of the biosphere from the subvisible level the way that stained glass told the story of the Bible to people who couldn't read. It's a nice collaborative process—Santiago Calatraca, whose architecture is the design of the physical structure, Lovelock with his electron capture device and atmospheric chemistry, the bacteriology of Lynn Margulis, the botany of Paul and Julie Hankiewicz, the bioshelter concept of John Todd, and the visual mathematics of Ralph Abraham.

DAVID: What are you working on now?

BILL: I'm doing a series of talks in New York tentatively called "Mind Jazz on Ancient Texts." I'm taking the *Rig veda* or the *Tao te ching* or the *Baghavad gita* and giving a rap on it, just taking off the way Miles Davis does on the song "My Funny Valentine." My relationship to the text is like that of Miles to the song. You can hear the melodies coming back, and you can sense that it's still about the *Rig veda*, but it's about a lot of other stuff, too. It's going from the homination of the primates to the planetization of humanity, so it's taking about six or seven years. So I'm doing a lot of reading!

REBECCA: I'm interested about what you think of virtual reality.

BILL: I think the main problem with virtual reality is that it's a toxic technology, a rape of your frontal lobes. I think it's going to give people health effects like early Alzheimers. When I was a kid, I used to go into shoe stores and stick my toes in X-ray machines. What seemed to be progress and groovy was actually giving people cancer.

I think that there's going to be a lot of these extremely low-frequency, vibrational fields that are bad for your immune system. When you have the glove on, what's enabling the computer to read you is that you're in a densely saturated magnetic field. Part of the meltdown of sexuality and the body is that we're all pieces of meat in a Mulligan's stew of planetary noise. The qualities of the interactions that this is having with the immune system and physiology are just toxic to how the human body works.

The latest theory is that AIDS is a DNA disease and not an HIV viral infection. Every time we come into a new ecological niche in evolution, like the New World, there's also new information that comes in the form of a disease. Now we're into this post-biological, electronic new world, and the fear is that the autonomy of the immune system is being eroded from the noise. If you add up quartz watches, microwave ovens, power lines, the wiring in the house, and then you add in virtual reality, we're playing Russian roulette with evolution. This is my intuitive feeling, which I always trust. It's just this wild Irish Druid radar.

David Spangler and I went with totally good faith to the Human Technology Interface Lab in the University of Seattle and experimented with virtual reality. First of all, I was put off by the hype and the politics. Everybody was saying that this is going to cure cancer, and they were trying to get megabucks from the Department of Defense, saying that this is the new cutting edge for the defense industries and medi-business.

Why? Time after time we've seen in the history of science the positive predictions of technology fall short. Thalidomide does this and DDT does that. Why can't they say, "Everything we are going to do will have side effects and a shadow side?" They can't because they're fundraising. If they even mention one-tenth of one percent of the problem, everybody's going to be terrified of litigation and say this is the new John Mansville, and the industry will collapse before it's even begun.

So I took the trip, and I thought the visual quality was pretty tacky. It was like being inside a pac-man game. Anyone who does t'ai chi or any kind of yoga is a little more sensitive to the etheric sheath of the body, and I could feel a sort of violation, and I didn't like it.

DAVID: You've said that every society that creates a class of people to protect them ends up having to protect themselves from the protectors. How do you see that happening in America today?

BILL: That's the first criticism of Plato's *Republic*. How do you guard yourselves from the guardians? Who polices the multinational corporation if its scale is beyond direct responsibility to the nation-state? We don't really have laws to deal with that. Part of what we have to figure out is the relationship between the global economy and the global ecology, and the membrane between the two. China is just racing ahead to industrialize, but it's really doubtful that they'll have the water and the air to do it. There's nobody to enforce controls over that.

REBECCA: So is it just down to individual responsibility now?

BILL: But it's at a scale where individuals can only make a small difference. There's no way of leveraging China to change. They've bought into the myth of progress, and they want to have atom bombs and freeways and be just like us—or buy it from us and then compete with us, which is the Chinese way. They get cement factories from the Soviet Union and five years later ask them, "Would you like to buy any cement?"

REBECCA: What do you predict for humanity one hundred years from now?

BILL: I think the "catastrophe bifurcation" we've been talking about is closer than that. I think it will happen in your generation. The UN has a list of problems that need immediate solution—it's about twenty-two thousand items long. Just stop for a moment. Think of Rwanda, Bosnia, the biosphere, Chiapas, gangs and kids with uzis, the ozone hole and the greenhouse effect, low-frequency electromagnetic fields that may cause cancer, airborne viruses from deforestation that come to large cities, antibiotics no longer being effective. Just add it all up, and then imagine how much the human social unit is capable of responding to and dealing with it. It's just too much. I think that's why some people get so frightened, especially if you don't have a mystical base in your consciousness, where you have this resource inside.

REBECCA: If you see humanity as the center of the show, then it's a lot more frightening too.

BILL: Yes. It's also frightening if you've grown up with a growth economy and suddenly you're not going to have it. I remember the first shock I had, when I first came onto the New York streets as a writer in 1971. I was being interviewed by a black reporter for CBS radio. He got really angry and said, "You're basically telling us that now that you whities have made it, it's all over, and we're not going to have a chance to get our piece. We don't want this talk of a new paradigm, new consciousness, mysticism, ecology, living lightly on the earth—fuck it! We want Park Avenue. We want stretch limos." That's basically the whole third-world scene. I think we're really committed, and hurtling toward some major event. Maybe somebody sticking out their arm can make a slight detour of the planet, but either way, we're in for the ride.

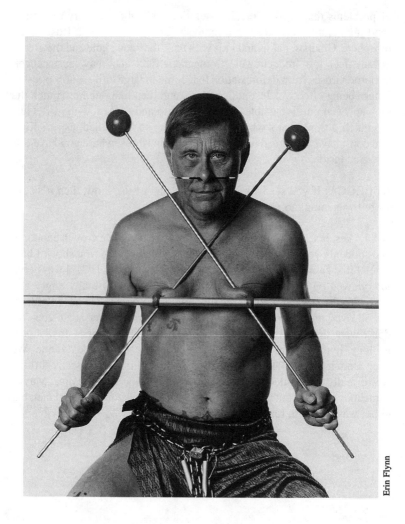

Erin Flynn

Fakir Musafar

———

"Your body belongs to you. Play with it."

Skin Deep
with Fakir Musafar

By the age of four, Roland Loomis was regularly dreaming about his past lives; by six he was experiencing psychedelic visions while riding his bicycle; by twelve he was poking his mother's sewing needles through his skin. By the age of thirteen he had pierced his foreskin in the coal cellar; by fourteen he was experimenting with his newly found psychokinetic powers; and by seventeen he had a full-blown mystical shake-up of the kind recounted by saints, sages, and madmen.

Gradually, the puzzling elements of Roland's childhood began to slip into place, like the ribs beneath a whalebone corset. This odd and awkward boy from a strict Lutheran family in whitest South Dakota had been born again in the regal personage of Fakir Musafar. Fakir Musafar was a misunderstood shaman in thirteenth-century Persia who entered mystical states through manipulating his body and died of a broken heart after a lifetime of ridicule.

This could also have been the fate of Roland had he remained within the walls of his family's cellar, where his experiments began. Instead, Fakir came out, and now, at sixty-three, he has not only been accepted by the tribe but has been granted something of the status of an elder statesman. He is undoubtedly America's master guru of body ritual, offering wisdom and experience in a movement with more than its share of neophytes searching for identity.

Fakir's role models are Hindu sadhus who sleep on beds of nails, African women with necks elongated by metal rings, and New Guinea tribesmen with belts that reduce their waists to a whisper. It was he who coined the terms "modern primitive," and "body play," terms that now, thanks to the information revolution, have become almost as familiar as "cyberpunk" or "generation X." The modern primitive movement is a tribal concoction of neopagans, lesbians, gays, artists, punks—creative misfits who have taken the term "queer" from the exclusive domain of homosexuality and applied it to all who find themselves trying to squeeze their round pegs into the square nipples of society.

His twenty-seven years as an advertising executive allowed Fakir pierc-ing insight into the power of symbolism, a knowledge he exploits beauti-fully in his quarterly magazine, BodyPlay. *He is also the founder and di-rector of the School for Professional Body Piercing, the first in America.*

I interviewed Fakir on October 17, 1992. Sitting in the garden of his suburban bungalow in Menlo Park, California, bespectacled with a but-ton-down haircut, in sports shirt and slacks, Fakir could still be that ex-ecutive. There is little to suggest what lies beneath, except that poking through his nose is a five-inch porcupine quill. Fakir is a misfit who, un-able to find a mold to fit into, simply fashioned one for himself.

RMN

REBECCA:. What first influenced you to start changing your body state?

FAKIR: I suppose it was my feeling that something was missing in what I saw around me. I always seemed to know there was more. When I was growing up, all the people around me lived under Judeo-Christian prin-ciples and rules. It was a very hard and limited patriarchal society. My biggest problem as a child was spacing out, and I would literally go into trance states at the drop of a hat. It was very difficult for me because I thought I was going nuts. I would try to stay "here," but I couldn't help it— I'd fade away. Bells would ring. I'd have hallucinations. I remember riding a tricycle and having wonderful hallucinations, like on LSD.

I had a particular problem with this in social situations, which still bothers me today. I guess it's an escape, a coping mechanism. My family was so repressive and dysfunctional that it was natural for me to use this ability to space out to cope with boredom and loneliness.

REBECCA: What were you like as a child, apart from spacy? (*laughter*)

FAKIR: I was very thin. I was "queer." I was a misfit. I didn't do too well with other kids. I didn't do too well in sports. I couldn't catch a baseball because I was blind as a bat. But I was also very bright. I devoured books because that was my only escape from this very limited society.

In seventh grade I started on volume A of the best looking encyclope-dia. I read the whole thing from cover to cover, and then I started on vol-ume B, and so on. When I got through that set of encyclopedias, I went to another set and read that one. And I found out that I was really interested in how other cultures lived.

REBECCA: And when you first saw pictures of people with body modifications, such as scarification, tattoos, and piercings, did you suddenly go, "Aha! This is it!"?

FAKIR: Oh yeah. Instantly the light went on, and very often I could recognize that whatever was said about these people in the photo caption was *not* what was going on. I could look at them and sense how they felt at the moment the photograph was taken. It was often a curious mixture of fear, pain, intense sensation, awe, and transformation. I thought, "My God! they've got some-

> *... I would secretly try to do these things, such as reducing my waist with a tight belt, like the Ibitoes of New Guinea.*

thing I don't have!" And I would secretly try to do these things, such as reducing my waist with a tight belt, like the Ibitoes of New Guinea.

One of the abilities I had when I was young was psychometry. We lived in an area that was heartland for Indian culture. The farmers would just plough over Indian graves, but I would go out on my bicycle and find old campgrounds, burial mounds, places that were blessed and had a charge in them. At a very early age, I could touch a tree and get a vision of what had happened there. I could take a stone from an Indian burial mound and it would speak to me. I still do this.

REBECCA: And you used to have Indian friends and hang out with them?

FAKIR: Yes. They were misfits, too, and they were treated very badly, worse than dogs. I found a kinship with them because I was a loner.

REBECCA: What kind of reactions do you get from Native American people to the things you do?

FAKIR: I have many friends who are Native Americans. When I did some Lakota rituals at a place called Rancho Cicada, one of them was quite taken with it. We exchanged presents and energies, and he participated in some of the ceremony. In general, I've had nothing but respect from my Native American friends.

REBECCA: You don't ever come across Native Americans who think it's just another example of the white man encroaching on Indian terrain?

FAKIR: Yes, once. In Boston I was on a television program, and they had Native Americans on who were very un-native compared with the ones I grew up with from the Lakota reservations. They had always lived in cities and were very Catholic or Lutheran. They didn't seem to have much connection with Indian culture. Several of them objected to my rituals and said that I was ripping off Indian culture and exploiting it. How do they know?

REBECCA: Going back to your childhood . . .

FAKIR: Rewind, yes. I was the head of the class in the Lutheran confirmation. I knew all the dogma and all the theories and the doctrine of transubstantiation, but it didn't feel right. We had a very aristocratic pastor who came from New York. He was quite a maverick because he didn't preach hell and brimstone as much as he did love. He used to think the world of me.

One of my favorite meditation spots was church. I was in the choir, and we sat in this separate space in front of the organ, which had all of these beautiful vibrations coming out of it. And I had some of the most beautiful fantasies, including erotic fantasies, in that choir loft.

REBECCA: Was there anyone you could share your true urges and visions with?

FAKIR: No. I couldn't share what I was doing with anybody at all. It was so way out and bizarre compared to how everything else was. In school I was an avid lucid daydreamer. So I'd look out the window at a tree, and I'd become sunlight falling on a leaf—I learned how to have intense visions. Some of them were alarming.

REBECCA: If your environment had been more interesting, perhaps you wouldn't have been encouraged to develop your inner world so much.

FAKIR: Yes, that's true. I did learn to accept and love my inner world a lot. For example, at home on Sunday afternoons you had to wear your Sunday best, which was always very uncomfortable, and you had to sit in an upright chair for hours while the family droned on and on about the crops and equally dull stuff. I would sit in this room and stare at my Uncle Milton, and all of a sudden I would start going into a trance state. All the voices would go *vzzzzzzzz*, like turning down the volume control, and everything would start to get dark except for Uncle Milton, who's head would get brighter and brighter. Then it would start to recede until it was a pinhead, and then it would come back. But instead of Uncle Milton it would be an old Chinese man, and he would be speaking Chinese! I was totally fascinated by this.

Up until I reached puberty I had some psychokinetic abilities, too. I could make things move just by looking at them and concentrating—little things like matchsticks or tiny pieces of paper. If I had been discovered doing some of the things I did, I would probably have been committed to an insane asylum.

> *. . . instead of Uncle Milton it would be an old Chinese man, and he would be speaking Chinese!*

> *If I had been discovered doing some of the things I did, I would probably have been committed to an insane asylum.*

REBECCA: Did you ever wonder whether you *were* going insane?

FAKIR: There were times I did. When I started to trance out involuntarily it scared the hell out of me, and I used to fight it. I think by the time I reached puberty I had started to accept this as being a part of me, and I began to realize that perhaps I had a gift that the people around me didn't have.

REBECCA: Did you ever try to explain to your parents what you were doing?

FAKIR: No, it was too risky. I didn't think they'd understand.

REBECCA: The tools you used to change your body state—did you make them yourself?

FAKIR: Sometimes. The first tools were very simple. I discovered a bag of clothespins and clipped them onto my skin and made fans, for example.

REBECCA: What motivated you to pierce your foreskin at age twelve?

FAKIR: A picture in a 1936 *National Geographic* of a Polynesian man getting his nostril pierced. I had discovered that I could disconnect or step aside. My body could feel something, but I didn't necessarily have to feel it. I could watch my body feel it. I could take a sewing needle and slowly push it through my skin. I desperately wanted to pierce my nose like the Polynesian, but that would have been too visible in the choir loft. (*laughter*)

But I had another spot, which nobody ever looked at, and which did not exist as far as these people were concerned, and that was my cock! I liked my cock, and I like the idea of having a hole in it. So I put a pointed clothespin clamp inside my foreskin and let it go. Instantly uncomfortable—painful, you would say. But soon it wasn't pain—it was intense sensation. It was intriguing, and it made me feel alive to feel something and to know I was doing something that I had a right to do, no matter what other people thought.

> *. . . it made me feel alive to feel something and to know I was doing something that I had a right to do, no matter what other people thought.*

REBECCA: What is pain, in your view?

FAKIR: "Pain" is a prejudicial word. Pain to me is intense sensation that you neither expect nor want. Like for instance, if you get up in the middle of the night and you stub your toe on the bed—that's pain, and I feel it just like anybody else. If, on the other hand, it's full daylight and I am deliberately tapping my foot against a bed and it starts to give me intense sensation, that is not pain.

REBECCA: Unless you did it really hard. (*laughter*)

FAKIR: Well, true. It depends on how carried away you get. I run into a lot of people who are out to feel things, they're out for sensation, they're out for kicks. But it isn't coping with the sensation and dealing with the physical that is so important. It's what happens in the process and the transformation.

The same thing goes for any kind of ritual. People are always looking for *the* authentic way, say, to do a sun dance. There isn't any. The Indians laugh. If they talk to anthropologists, they'll invent all sorts of wild stories about the proper way to do something, all of which they know is bullshit.

The people who ask the question don't comprehend the nature of magic and ritual, so why tell them a straight story? They wouldn't understand it anyway.

REBECCA: How did you get away with doing these experiments without your family finding out?

FAKIR: I did all these experiments in secret, in my mother's fruit cellar, under the cover of having a new hobby—photography. It turned out to be a really good cover, because I seriously was learning to do photography. I gradually picked up one body practice after another, and I'd take photographs of it. Something told me it was important to document what I was doing.

REBECCA: You mention a particular experience that you had when you were seventeen as a turning point in your life.

FAKIR: It certainly was. On Memorial Day weekend my parents went away for three days, and I had the run of the house. By then, I had tried many things. I had pierced my foreskin, I had done some tattooing on myself, I had discovered the Ibitoe; and I was doing constriction on my waist. I had made a bed of nails and lain on it. Now I was determined to do one experiment that carried everything to an extreme. I planned to make myself totally immobile in a way I had heard people do in order to have altered states.

[*Reading from the first issue of* BodyPlay *magazine*] "I had fasted for two days and reduced myself to an emaciated robot by dancing for hours with fifty pounds of logging chain. I was seeking an experience, a happening that no other human being I knew had had, even if it meant death. It was two a.m.

> *I was seeking an experience, a happening that no other human being I knew had had, even if it meant death.*

I stood with my back against the cold, wooden wall and laced ropes between the pin staples driven at three-inch intervals up the outline of my body.

"I pulled the ropes deep into my legs from my ankles up to my numb, belted waist. Tied in tight, I felt helpless, glued against the wall. My chest, arms, and head were also quite helpless. I just waited in the darkness, not knowing what to expect. I was resolved to stay that way until something happened. My body ached for relief or sleep, but it could not slip away because of the tight discomfort of the ropes.

"I learned later in life that if I do something like a Samadhi Tank, interesting things won't happen to me. I'll just drift off into a pleasant state. I have to have something that keeps me from drifting into that state, something that's physically uncomfortable. Then more interesting things can happen to me.

"Soon, a pleasant, warm kind of numbness crept up my legs and arms. They dissolved into nothingness. But when the numbness also began to work up my spine into my breathing center, I panicked. I fought for breath. It was like drowning. I was trapped, unable to loose myself, self-sentenced to whatever came next. At this point I began to wonder if I hadn't bit off more than I could handle. Something deep inside shifted to a feeling of indifference.

"I gave up fighting. I was just a watcher now, not aware of breathing or any other direct physical sensation. Only my head still seemed to exist. Next, a vibration, an oscillation, developed. It got stronger and stronger, not unpleasant in the beginning, but soon it felt like my robot body was suspended on the end of a long cable hanging deep inside some huge chasm. A giant, over whom I had no control, was swinging the cable from wall to wall, smashing me to pieces. The smashing went faster and faster and got more violent with each swing—it was later I learned that was my heart-beat.

"In the crescendo of this uncontrolled smashing there was a faint click! sound deep inside my head, in absolute stillness with a slight humming in the background, and I was floating in a pool of warm, sticky glue, uncaring. I didn't know where I was, but I was alive. Disembodied with no fear, no pain, no discomfort. I was hyperalert and feeling good, satisfied like at the moment of sexual climax. I became aware that I could see, dimly in a different sort of way than before. I concentrated my fuzzy vision. I was still looking at me, or rather, at my still lashed-against-the-wall body. What was I looking at? Was it me, or was I the looker? The other reality of this paradox struck me with explosive force, but in this state I couldn't be serious.

"I explored my new reality for some time. One of the peculiarities was the feeling that in this state there was no time. I knew I could go forward and backward in time as easily as I normally walk from one room to another. I studied the lifeless form on the wall. It was beautiful. I had feelings of great love for it. It was always obedient to my wishes, moving when and where I wanted it to, even when it was tired and in pain.

> *I studied the lifeless form on the wall. It was beautiful. I had feelings of great love for it.*

"Then my attention moved away from that body. I stayed in the present. The things to explore were endless, right there. I found I could move right through a concrete wall under the earth outside, or I could think light, and I'd float up through the beams, floors, and roof, above the house, above the trees. This was real! It was magnificent. I watched a cat scamper across the vacant lot beside the house. I could see people moving inside a house a block away. The first rays of dawn pierced the cellar window. I slowly drifted back to the coal-bin wall.

"Without remembering how, I somehow found my way back to the shell-body still lashed there. It freed itself. This beautiful experience colored my whole existence. From that day on, I was liberated. I felt free to express life through my body. I had an insight, an understanding: my body is mine to use. It's my medium, my personal living canvas and living clay to mold and shape and mark as an artful expression of the life energy that flows through it. Your body belongs to you. Play with it."

REBECCA: That's beautiful. You say that it was from this experience that you began to develop an awareness of the distinction between spirit and body. The word "spirit" is so subjective, how do you define it?

FAKIR: I guess the answer would be that the borderline between spirit and body is always fuzzy until one has a subjective experience like I had on the coal-bin wall. I think everybody is confused about where one starts or stops until they've experienced that kind of total separation, where consciousness is definitely not in the body. After that experience, to me, spirit is simply consciousness, awareness, the center point of my attention.

REBECCA: You said that interesting things didn't happen to you in flotation tanks. Yet the inventor, Dr. John Lilly, claims to have had remarkable experiences of quite cosmic proportions in them.

FAKIR: Well, maybe he tried the tank longer than I did. Or maybe he's wired differently than I am. Anyway, all I get in placid sensory deprivation is a slide show on a small screen. And I get bored and ache for some intense body sensation to focus on, some kind of "door" to send my attention through. Most of my shamanic journeys have taken place when I was in a sensory neutral mode with a single body sensation in sensory overload.

REBECCA: You went on to become a successful advertising executive. Advertising is so much about images, and what you've been describing seems to be so much about getting beyond the image to the essence. How did you reconcile these two perspectives?

FAKIR: To get beyond images you have to get totally hooked by them. You have to get satiated. You have to learn how to manipulate and deal with images. If you never get to the point where you realize what is an image and what isn't, and if you don't know much about image construction, then it's very hard to get beyond images.

REBECCA: It seems, in America especially, there is a tendency to get stuck with the image. Do you find the same thing with people who get involved in changing their bodies through what you have termed "body play"? Do a lot of people get into it simply for the look, for a fashion statement?

> *When you start putting large hooks through someone's body, they very soon get beyond the look and the image.*

FAKIR: Yes, many of them do, but not the ones I deal with, because I put them to the test. If they get involved with me, right off the bat they're going to drop out real soon if image is the only reason. When you start putting large hooks through someone's body, they very soon get beyond the look and the image. (*laughter*) You have to get down to very basic stuff—you just can't avoid it. People either dig it and do it, or they don't.

REBECCA: How do people who get into body modification view their bodies, as opposed to people who abhor this kind of practice?

FAKIR: I think that people who get into body modification view their bodies as belonging to themselves, not another. And those who abhor the practice view the body as something not belonging to the one who lives in it. They are laboring under cultural and/or religious programming that strips ownership of the body from the one inside.

Many of the people I know who are practicing body modification are reclaiming their bodies, rightfully theirs from the start, from vested interests who unrightfully try to own it—say, from a possessive father, mother, lover, or other intimate; say, from an abusive spouse or religious leader; say, from an oppressive government, educational, or business interest; say, from a distant, impersonal god like the Judeo-Christian Jehovah.

REBECCA: How much has body modification got to do with sexuality?

FAKIR: A lot! Joseph Bean, former editor of *Drummer* magazine, came up with the idea that there's the *body-first* way, the *heart-first* way, and the *mind-first* way to explore spirituality. We've practiced the mind-first and heart-first way a lot in the West—say, in philosophy or pure science or religious devotion or Zen Buddhism, which I got into for a while.

I did some *zazen*, and I discovered one thing. You're sitting for two hours, you're really getting with what's floating around in your head, and all of a sudden your leg hurts or you've got to pee or you get an erotic fantasy and you get an erection. How do you deal with this? There are forces that are more powerful than the ones you're dealing with in philosophy or devotion or Zen meditation.

REBECCA: Isn't the point of meditation to transcend the physical and learn how not to get distracted by it?

FAKIR: Yes, but most of these disciplines mostly try to exclude—that is, blot out—body sensation and erotic impulses. For that reason, I feel they never really succeed in transcending them. It's like sweeping dirt under the carpet.

> *. . . physical calls and impulses of the lower centers are dealt with first; then the higher centers can function in peace . . .*

In the body-first approaches, such as in tantra, physical calls and impulses of the lower centers are dealt with first; then the higher centers can function in peace, without distraction. Basically, all shamanic tradition is based on the body-first approach. It's basic stuff.

REBECCA: How is sexual energy used within a spiritual context?

FAKIR: There are ways of developing the ability to maintain a certain kind of powerful erotic energy and keep it at a very high level. In American Indian tradition, when a man loses his semen, they say he lost his "moves-moves," his power. You want to learn to have orgasms without losing your "moves-moves," because otherwise you're giving your energy away. It's the same thing that goes on with the Indian sadhus who lie on beds of nails and who do all kinds of austere things.

In the most extreme cases, there are sadhus who take their penis and tie a rock on it and sit around like that all day. They stretch their penis to a point where it's dysfunctional—they can't get an erection anymore. Then they get into an ongoing shamanic state of consciousness. They keep their "moves-moves," they keep their energy. It builds and builds, and they can easily go into altered states of consciousness. It's like always being on the edge of orgasm.

This is what happens when I do a lot of physical body rituals. The trick is to be able to go past the point where I would orgasm and ejaculate, and then continue to have repeated orgasms or, if I carry it far enough, go beyond that. As the arousal level goes up, your feeling or response toward physical sensation goes down. So when you're all hot in a sexual scene, you don't experience pain in the same way. As you get sexually aroused your body naturally starts dumping endorphins, your natural opiates, into your system. This is something that many shamanic cultures have known for eons. I've been able to cultivate it to a large degree.

REBECCA: Yet celibacy is used in almost all the world's religions as a way of release from social responsibility—the distractions of relationships and family—in order to get in touch with the spiritual side.

FAKIR: That's very true. But, as with some of the sadhus and other people who disconnect a lot, I've have found out that it can also have a negative effect. It can withdraw you, it can remove your humanity. I've had this same struggle, and I found after many years of being alone, and being able to space out and do all of this stuff, that in a way I was getting farther and farther away from my humanity.

Celibacy—that is, saving "moves-moves"—is a double-edged sword. It can easily get out of control and overpower you. You can become self-possessed, antisocial, a burden instead of a blessing to those around you. I feel it's important to temper and balance such a practice. That's why I personally swing back and forth between containment and excess.

REBECCA: You mentioned that the body is the last frontier of Western taboos. But we're also obsessed with the body. There are many accepted forms of body modification—plastic surgery . . .

FAKIR: Well, it has to be painless and instant.

REBECCA: . . . liposuction, collagen injections, hair extensions. But then you get a ring through your nose, and it's "Uh-uh, not that." What defines the limits of this taboo?

FAKIR: The people who are getting collagen injections and the people who want the plastic surgery want a nose like Marilyn Monroe or something like that. So basically what their body modification is all about is to conform to an ideal *other*, whereas the kids who are getting tattooed and pierced today are going in totally the opposite direction. The purpose of their body modification is to *nonconform,* to test by ordeal, to reclaim. To do this you have to be a maverick, and this is the way you display your difference, your individuality.

REBECCA: Part of the nervousness of the establishment, then, is due to the fear of the larger nonconformity that is going on inside that person's mind.

FAKIR: Yes. Body modification is definitely a threat to established order. If people are allowed to do what they want with their bodies, how can you control, manipulate, or exploit them? What else might they do? What established authority or power structure are

> *Body modification is definitely a threat to established order.*

they going to bypass next? In a society based on nonprimitive ideas of property rights and ownership, such free expression could be, and is, viewed as a "bomb in the basement."

REBECCA: Are you finding a greater openness toward this kind of thing?

FAKIR: Yes, in younger people. I think there's a radical cultural change happening, but I think it's coming about because the people with these old attitudes are just going to last so long and die, and their place will be taken by people with new attitudes. It's the way society has always changed.

So the kids that have a different view about the body—personal ownership and expression through the body—are going to replace people who will never understand this. People over thirty mostly don't understand this and could never buy it, so you don't even try to explain it. They come to my workshops occasionally, a few broad-minded older people, but for most older people in our culture it's a hopeless cause.

REBECCA: Do you see the rise in fundamentalism as a balancing-act reaction to the new liberalism?

FAKIR: I think it is, because fundamentalism is based on narrowing life options, not expanding them. These things go in cycles anyway, so there are bound to be swings this way or that. But for the most part, I think it's a survival reaction. The world is actually improving—I'm very optimistic. I came from years, in the thirties and forties, that were so limited and exclusive. It's not like that anymore. I've visited my hometown three or four times since I grew up there, and it's changed.

When the television came, it changed things radically. It brought in tons of new ideas and desires, some of which weren't too desirable either, even worse than the ones they replaced. But it did change things that otherwise were fixed in time—there was a time warp there. When I grew up, nothing had changed in twenty years, because there was no communication with the outside world. If you went to Minneapolis, wow! It was like going to Singapore!

I feel that the rise of exclusiveness is having its final death struggles—in apartheid in South Africa, for example. It's going to go down. It's inevitable. I don't see any difference between fundamentalist Moslems, fundamentalist Baptists, or fundamentalist anythings. These are all people who are living by the view "We're the only ones. We're the chosen few. We've got the word, and everything else is wrong! And we have to change it or destroy it!"

I see the vigor and the energy and the viciousness that's in some of the fundamentalists as a last death-kick. And probably, in their heart of hearts, they know they're going to go, because one cannot survive in a global village with that kind of exclusiveness.

REBECCA: I think they're going to be kicking for a little while longer.

FAKIR: Probably, but we can wait. I was very afraid, for instance, to go to Texas. I had visions of fundamentalists finding out a little about what Fakir does, seeing some of our images, and picketing us!

REBECCA: But you didn't have a problem there. I hear the Texans were very receptive. In those kinds of places, where there is a hard core of conservatism, people are hungry.

FAKIR: Desperately. There are queer people there who don't know it's okay to be queer. We've got this fusion going on in the West, in which we've got a lot of people defining themselves now not as this, that, or the other persuasion or practice, but just as *queer*. The feeling is that if you don't fit in with the rest of the crowd in the suits and ties, in churches or halls of power—you're queer. And we'd better stick together, because those people are going to try to destroy us, and we can't afford to let our differences get in the way.

In Dallas we found out there was a lot of division. There were a lot of closeted people there. There were closeted SM players; there were closeted kinky people; there were closeted gay people.

> **We've gone to the next phase of revolution.**

There were gay leather people who wouldn't speak to nongay leather people; the lesbians would have nothing to do with the gay men; and so on. Here in San Francisco we're having great get-togethers, fusions, where lesbians and gay men, for example, are having all kinds of interesting explorations together. We've gone to the next phase of revolution.

REBECCA: Is the modern primitive movement that's happening in the West a desire for a closer-knit tribalism, a sense of community beyond and apart from the cultural homogeny?

FAKIR: Yes. There's this desperate hunger, this desperate, crying need to belong, to find a place and some kind of personal meaning. It's very hard to have meaning unless you have family and tribe. Human beings are basically

> **It's very hard to have meaning unless you have family and tribe.**

social, and we have alienated the things that make us more human. Sitting playing Nintendo or watching sitcoms on television does not necessarily make us more social or connected.

REBECCA: Do you see a future in which this tribalism will spread to the point where people with similar cultural attitudes will live in communities that provide for their lifestyle?

FAKIR: San Francisco is a good example. It's been going on for about twenty years, as far as I know. It's a cultural fusion. I was searching for a tribe for fifty-five years, and I found it in San Francisco.

REBECCA: When did you first meet people you could relate to, apart from the Indians?

FAKIR: When I moved to California in the fifties I began to meet people who were different, queer in one way or another. They didn't necessarily show up and say, "I'm queer, let's get together." But I had needs, and I managed to hunt them out. First, I realized there were things I couldn't do without help. I desperately wanted to do the *O-Kee-Pa*—that is, to be hung up by flesh-hooks—or the *Kavandi-bearing*. It's very hard to do these to yourself. I did little tattoos on myself, but only where I could reach, and I wanted a meaningful, large tattoo.

I had a vision for years and years that I would only be me if I had a certain tattoo on my back. It's a Native American design that depicts flame coming out of the earth. I made a large photograph of my back, and I took what I saw in my vision and sketched it on tissue paper. I started going around to various tattoo artists, and they'd look at it and laugh. They'd say, "You want *that* on your back? How about a nice panther? How about a rose? How about a dagger with 'Mom' in it?" (*laughter*)

Finally, after a lot of searching, I found a tattoo artist in Oakland, Davy Jones, who was receptive. He was the official tattoo artist for the Hell's Angels. He had been a merchant seaman and had been heavily tattooed by natives of Western Samoa. He saw my tattoo and instantly connected with it. He did my tattoo over a three-month period in 1963. As far as I know, that was the first *blackwork* ever done in this country.

REBECCA: *Kavandi-bearing* entails wearing a frame that's filled with sixty or so spears, which are inserted into the torso. Could you describe your first experience of this?

> *Davy had said, "I'll only do this if you'll sign a release that says in the case of injury or death you won't hold us responsible."*

FAKIR: Well, after my tattoo was completed, Davy and a gay friend came over and I prepared myself. I fasted and meditated and did all the things I felt I had to do to get myself psyched up. We did a Kavandi that lasted all day. I totally spaced out, projected out of my body, floated up out through the roof and looked down on all of this with great interest. Davy had said, "I'll only do this if you'll sign a release that says in the case of injury or death you won't hold us responsible." And we did a very formal document, so if my body was found lying there they wouldn't be in trouble.

I had a marvelous experience. The only problem I had was that I wanted more space to move in, but I couldn't communicate because I was projected out of my physical body. I was like an automaton, a puppet, and I felt I couldn't speak through the mouth. I wanted them to open this door of the building we were in so I could run down the driveway and out into the street. The only way I could communicate this was to run up against the door and go, *smash!*, with all these rods in. That scared the hell out of them. All I was trying to tell them was, "Open the damn door!" (*laughter*)

I had experimented and hung myself up *O-Kee-Pa*-style a few times before I met Davy Jones, but I could only go so far. I knew that if I spaced out and hung that way for twenty minutes, I'd strangulate and die. So I appealed to Davy and his friend to come over again and hang me up. That's when I first met the white light. When I got to the point of getting 98 percent of my weight on the piercings I had made in my chest, to go the other two percent I either had to come out of my body or quit. There was no way I could endure this, it was so intense. I was hoping that in this condition I would just *click!* And then it happened and I was free, floating again in warm, sticky glue.

I saw a ball of white light and it was singing. The music was wonderful, and it was talking to me. It said, "Hi, I'm you. Greetings." And the love! I've never felt love on a human level like this. The communication was telepathic and instant. It was a wonderful, wonderful experience. To me, that was the Great Spirit, my higher self, my Godself. My guru had told me years before, "One day you're going to meet your Godself, and you're going to be really surprised because it isn't going to be at all what you think." Well, I did, hanging by flesh-hooks.

REBECCA: Was that the original purpose of the sun dance—to meet with the Great Spirit?

FAKIR: Yes, sometimes it happened that way. It was also a way of getting into a shamanic state of consciousness, where all things are possible, where you escape the boundaries and limitations of a physical life in a physical body.

REBECCA: Is part of the purpose of body ritual to teach people how to deal with pain?

FAKIR: Yes, learning to transcend pain, to separate spirit and body. It's one of the lessons that's missing in our culture. A few people discover it because of what they do. I had an interesting conversation about this with Fran Tarkenton, the football player, on a television talk show. He talked about deliberately getting involved in a situation where he *knew* there was going to be pain and disconnecting from his body the moment it happened. I had a standby position on this talk show and only went on because the main the guest was unable to make it. I didn't find out until a year later who that guest was. Everybody on the show was surprised because they were expecting someone else to be there.

REBECCA: Who were they expecting?

FAKIR: George Bush. (*laughter*)

REBECCA: That's great. But isn't the desire to make things as comfortable and as painless as possible a natural and healthy one?

> *. . . a society that functions by trying to make things as painless and as comfortable as possible might be missing the boat . . .*

FAKIR: Not necessarily. Through ritual you can learn to transform pain into something else. And a society that functions by trying to make things as painless and as comfortable as possible might be missing the boat, because a lot of what we're here to learn in life may be inaccessible. There are people who realize the value of hardship, such as people who climb up cliffs. Physical challenges are where you discover spirit. There's a validity in climbing cliffs other than getting up the wall.

REBECCA: What do you think happens to a society that doesn't offer ritual and rites of passage?

FAKIR: It turns into a bunch of zombies and robots. How are they going to explore their spiritual dimensions without some challenges? You either create them yourself, or someone else creates them and guides you through it. You need challenges—emotional, physical, mental.

REBECCA: Many societies offer a very specific rite of passage for the journey from puberty to adulthood. Like many people, I found puberty a very confusing time and was looking for something to relate to, to help explain what was happening to me. It felt like a transition but . . .

FAKIR: But you had nothing to tell you it was a transition, right? A transition from what to what? Of course you were totally lost. Remember that traditions and rituals didn't happen because someone sat down and invented them. They came out of one person's needs, experiences, and experimentation. Such people were guided to do certain things, and it seemed to work. They became the elders, and they passed on what they had learned to those who came after them, and so on. When the whole system of traditions, families, and tribes vanished, there was nobody to pass on anything to. And now we're all wandering around in limbo, not knowing how to proceed from one phase of life to the next.

REBECCA: You seem to be saying that when the social structure was smaller and simpler, ritual was able to flourish. Do you think that the spread of civilization and the survival of ritual are mutually exclusive?

> *... we're all wandering around in limbo, not knowing how to proceed from one phase of life to the next.*

FAKIR: No, I do not. It depends on the values of the dominant, spreading civilization, I suppose. If the dominant culture has no place for eccentricity, novelty, or individuality, it probably has no place for ritual either, at least "live" ritual. I feel that many cultures that did value ritual just didn't end up dominating the world, that's all.

REBECCA: Much ritual in the major religions of today is purely symbolic, a hangover from an experience that was probably initially quite powerful—baptism, for example.

FAKIR: Ritual, if it has valid intent and real magic in it, is truly transformative. You are not the same person you were before the ritual. So many people want transformation, they want to be freed and cleared of old stuff. When I did piercings commercially in

> *Ritual, if it has valid intent and real magic in it, is truly transformative.*

San Francisco, I would ask people, "Why are you getting pierced?" and to my surprise, instead of getting replies like "Because my buddies are" or "I just always wanted a gold ring in my tit," I often got real answers. They were creating their own initiations, their own rituals. Almost everybody had a good reason for doing what they were doing. It wasn't a hollow thing.

REBECCA: I heard about a girl who got her labia pierced partly because she has a very straight job and was feeling she was losing her identity. So she's got this secret rebellion going on under her clothes.

FAKIR: Right. "I may look like everybody else, but really I'm different from you!" I've had that secret rebellion going for years, ever since I pierced my dick. "They may think I'm fitting in, but I have the secret pleasure of knowing I'm not."

REBECCA: Is body modification largely about reclaiming the body, taking it back from social pressure and control?

FAKIR: Very often, in my experience, it is. I've run into a lot of women who have been raped who, by the act of getting pierced or by doing a body ritual, feel they are reclaiming. Somebody has abused and usurped and used them, and they want to say to themselves and to others, "I'm taking my body back from someone who took it from me, and by this act I bring my body back to me."

REBECCA: Judeo-Christian attitudes that the body is sinful have seeped into the culture so much. Is redemption also a part of this, absolving the body of this idea of Original Sin?

FAKIR: Not at all. The ones I know who are "reclaiming" their body feel no sin to redeem! If anyone has sinned, it's those who took their bodies from them in the first place. And they aren't generally seeking redemption for that act. As I see it, body modification is often a flip-flop reaction to an ongoing, ingrained habit of cultural abuse of unrightful possession.

REBECCA: Why did the body become such a taboo?

FAKIR: Well, to take the ownership of one's body away can give power to another. It was strictly a power game. When Jehovah was invented, the power game started in Western culture, and it's never stopped since. The priests said, "I am the only one who can speak to God, and you can't get any blessings or absolutions unless you go through me." There was a hierarchy, and it was all set up—property rights, including property rights over fellow humans, and the oppression of women—just so the few could have control over the many. No compassion. The "evil body" became a commodity.

REBECCA: Much of Reichian therapy is about drawing emotions out of the body and releasing memories. Is this similar to what goes on in the practices of body play?

FAKIR: Very much. People think you're only doing mechanical things with the body when you pierce it, tattoo it, sculpt it, but you're doing more than that. It's the *process* of creating the change of body state that's transformative, more so than the physical stuff that you see. It also helps you define the boundaries between body and spirit.

REBECCA: How do you define those boundaries?

FAKIR: Well, you push the body as far as you can. By pushing and doing something deliberately to the body, you finally reach a point where you realize there are two things coexisting here at the same time. To find out where the body starts and stops and where the spirit that lives in the body starts and stops is a really important discovery.

REBECCA: So you believe that there is a definite point at which body and spirit are divided?

FAKIR: I've found that there's a very distinct point when you want to go into a shamanic state of consciousness. There is a strong physical and emotional experience, and you do finally reach a disconnection point where you go into the underworld, you go into the cosmos, you go someplace. You have to reach the end of body and get into spirit totally in order to have these shamanic states.

The experience of being aware of the distinction is what I call the *ecstasy state*. You know your body, you can feel everything there is in the body, but you also know you're not the body. You can be totally spirit and just be an observer. You *know* you're outside your body, because you can travel in time and space.

I had the beginnings of ecstasy states and altered states when I was four or five years old. First I had nightmares once or twice a week about being crushed to death. It took about forty years before I really found out what that was all about. It was my death in a previous life, from which I had gone into this life. It was unfinished business, so to speak.

REBECCA: When you dream, you can also travel in time and space.

FAKIR: Yes, but it all happens in the unseen, with only an indirect and tenuous link to the seen. Both feet in one world. A trance state is very different. You have a foot in both worlds, so to speak. Time/space experiences in the unseen world usually have a direct link to the seen world. There is verifiable proof. That's what gives the Shaman real power. What I saw of the seen world during my out-of-body experience on the coal bin wall was exactly what I saw outside the house the next day. I've had intense lucid daydreams, which I consider trance states, and then seen the reality of the daydream's "projected future" manifested exactly, to the smallest detail. At first it's scary. For example, in the famous Seabrook experiment, a bound and deprived and suspended Justine jumped the time wall and lived a day four years in the future. This was perfectly verified in all details when seen-world time got there.

REBECCA: What is the advantage of a body-first approach to greater consciousness, as opposed to one that's mind-first or heart-first?

> *In body-first exploration, one is deliberately walking on the edge, exploring and flirting with the dark side.*

FAKIR: It's faster, less complicated, and is not as prone to "side-tracking." The body-first approach first deals with the most primal, most basic part of being, then it involves the higher centers. But there's another side. There's more risk. In body-first exploration, one is deliberately walking on the edge, exploring and flirting with the dark side. You have to be careful not to fall over that edge!

REBECCA: So it's using the body and extreme physical sensation in order to transcend altogether the experience of physicality.

FAKIR: Yes. The best way to step aside from the body is *through* the body. You're always going to be saddled and trapped with body needs and body problems with the other approaches. You have to be in tune with the body to do the body-first approach. You have to have a great love for it. I've got a good rapport with my body.

REBECCA: Have you experienced healings through the kinds of rituals you're describing?

FAKIR: From the experiences I've had working with people, I would say tremendous healings, and this isn't necessarily physical. There can be emotional and psychic healings. Grief, guilt, sorrow—all kinds of things can be dealt with better in the shamanic state than they can in the nonshamanic state.

REBECCA: The practices of body modification have come from places where they're used within a very traditional setting, and if individuals don't comply with the ritual, they're in danger of being ostracized by the tribe. What is considered alternative here has already been dogmatized in many social situations.

FAKIR: True. But I think that's the nature of all novel practices. They all start out somewhere full of life, get copied, and then lose that life.

REBECCA: But in those places body modification is about belonging, merging the individual with the culture. It's not about rebelling or being a maverick.

FAKIR: True. Body modification in those "other cultures" is a way of merging the individual with the tribe. But that's true in the body modifications of youths in today's Club Fuck, in motorcycle and street gangs, in tattoo or punk circles, or other modern subculture tribes. Body modifications are only seen as a rebellion or maverick behavior to people on the *outside* of the subculture. And remember, the body modification practices among traditional, primitive cultures also started with a few individuals, who at the time were mavericks rebelling against a status quo.

> *Body modifications are only seen as a rebellion or maverick behavior to people on the* outside *of the subculture.*

REBECCA: Isn't the neotribalist movement in danger of succumbing to conformity and dogmatism within its own ranks as it becomes more popular?

FAKIR: In the short term, yes. In the long term, I think not. The spirit and individualism behind neotribalism is so basic and different from the values of the mainstream it is replacing I have a feeling it will never get chiseled in stone. There's too much freedom, and too many options for dogmas to jell.

REBECCA: The repercussions of doing body-modification rituals without a guide can probably be pretty nasty.

FAKIR: Yes indeed. We have kids who want to go out of their body. They see a picture of me in *Modern Primitives*, and they try to do the same things. They don't come and talk to me about it, and things go wrong. They try to hang by flesh-hooks, for example, and they tear loose and get bloody. They need a *ka-see-ka*. That's a Mandan word used to describe an elder, an initiate—a medicine man in some cases—who has been on the trip before, who has mastered the technique to get from ordinary states of consciousness to a shamanic state of consciousness. When young men were initiated in traditional cultures, usually each one had a *ka-see-ka*.

I liken that to SM. We have a sadist and a masochist, we have a top and a bottom. Under the best conditions, this gets to be a shamanic trip where the top is a *ka-see-ka* and the bottom, or the masochist, is the one who takes the trip. But unlike the way some people practice SM, to really be a *ka-see-ka*, you're not just an operator, you're not just the manipulator, you have to go on the trip too. So the kids who pick up some of these things and try to do them have no guidance.

REBECCA: Isn't that tendency to mistrust authority indicative of the whole mentality of underground Western culture?

FAKIR: Yes and no. That's why we need the new tribes. To have a tribe, you have to understand there are people who have more experience, who have been there before, and you have to always acknowledge the elders. We have elders who have no credibility. Our politicians try to be elders, and people are seeing this as a fraud. These people know nothing but dogma. They cannot guide us.

REBECCA: How do you see your role?

FAKIR: Strange as it may seem, Fakir has become a role model for an awful lot of young people. He's accepted as a tribal father, as an elder. I have many sons and daughters, all over the place.

REBECCA: How does that feel?

FAKIR: It feels natural. I'm willing to accept the role.

REBECCA: Does the responsibility ever worry you?

FAKIR: I have a therapist who keeps pointing out that there's a dark side to the Fakir, as well as to everyone else. You have to know who *you* are and that Fakir is primarily an archetype, an image. The father they have found is not me, it's something *behind* me. I have to keep remembering that. If I don't, I could get into serious trouble.

> **REBECCA:** What kind of trouble?

> *The father they have found is not me, it's something behind me.*

FAKIR: I could become a cult figure and go down in flames. (*laughter*)

REBECCA: You recently took psychedelics for the first time. How did this experience compare with the body rituals you've done?

FAKIR: Well, I found out it was the same thing. I went to the same kinds of places.

REBECCA: So it was a reinforcement, or simply a parallel, to what you had already discovered.

FAKIR: Yeah. Except that I had an advantage. Because I already had great respect for people who had gone before. I'd had some guidance.

REBECCA: It's estimated that far more people are taking psychedelics now than in the sixties. What do you think about the validity of psychedelics as a way to expand consciousness?

FAKIR: With the right kind of guidance, I think it's just as valid as hanging in a cottonwood tree with flesh-hooks. But I wish people would get involved in some other disciplines and learn things another way first. And I wish they would have trips with *ka-see-kas* of worth. Otherwise, what kinds of experiences are they getting? How valid are these revelations? Are they revelations at all?

REBECCA: But it's not a body-first approach.

FAKIR: It *is* a body-first approach. You're changing something in the body first, and from that you're influencing everything else. But all the other ways of getting into shamanic states are totally voluntary, and you're in control. In other words, if I start hanging from flesh-hooks I can always stop anywhere along the line.

When you drop a psychedelic, once it's in your system, that's it. You're stuck for twelve hours or whatever. And that's unfortunate, because some-

> *One of the basic things in body play is learning how to manage and direct your own trip.*

thing can be missed. One of the basic things in body play is learning how to manage and direct your own trip. You learn to make natural chemical alterations in your own body and control them, so things don't take off like a wildfire.

REBECCA: Why do you speak about yourself in the third person?

FAKIR: Getting too stuck in identities is a dangerous trap. You can lose your way. When I did a sun dance with Jim Ward in Wyoming, the sun didn't shine and there was a three-day forecast for rain. I said, "We came out here to do the sun dance. If the Great Spirit wants us to do the sun dance, it's the job of the Great Spirit to make the sun shine." I put my arms up and asked for whatever was right to happen, and Jim did the same. And I totally lost my identity. I didn't know who I was. I was not an advertising man. I was not Fakir. I was not a white person. I wasn't even a human being. I was the wind, I was the earth, I was all kinds of things. All of a sudden, after thirty minutes, the clouds parted and the sun came out. All afternoon it shone down on this spot, and we went down and did our sun dance. And the only ill-effect we suffered was a sunburn! (*laughter*)

REBECCA: How did your guru influence your ideas on life?

FAKIR: The work of my guru was long-term. It got more and more clear as time went by, and every time I have an experience and work with others who've had similar experiences, it get's clearer in conscious understanding. At first I hardly understood anything he taught me over a very compressed period of time. He said, "Don't worry about it. It's stuck in your consciousness, and little by little the answers will be revealed, and you will say, 'Oh, that's what Arthur meant.'" And that's what's happened to me for years and years, and it's still happening now.

First he sat in the Mojave desert for seven years in a shack, every day asking, "Who am I?" Then he was a merchant seaman, and would occasionally jump ship and linger in places such as India. He studied everything and practiced everything, and he passed all this on to me, including a huge library of books, from Gurdjieff to Madame Blavatsky. Tantra, tarot, astrology—he dabbled in it all. But his whole purpose was to find out not what was different between all these beliefs but *what was the same.*

REBECCA: How did he become your guru?

FAKIR: I wanted to do graduate work in technical theater and drama, and I was encouraged by a friend to go to San Francisco. I was looking for someplace to live, and I had a list of places. I got totally lost in the fog on a street one block long that you couldn't find in broad daylight if you were looking for it! I checked the list to see if one of the houses was on this street, and it was.

I knocked on the door, and a lady answered who looked very strange. The house was weird—the walls were painted bright red and the ceiling was metallic gold. The first thing she said to me was, "I'm a reincarnate Egyptian. What are you?" I thought, "Gee, I think I'm on the right track here." (*laughter*) We got into a lively conversation. She was an avid astrologer and a Rosicrucian, and we just hit it off. There was a group of metaphysically inclined people who congregated every night in a cafeteria, and one of the people who always popped up at these gatherings was my guru, Arthur.

One night Cleo came back from work at three in the morning and brought Arthur back. He sat down and I sat down and we talked a few pleasantries, and then he said, "Oh shit! I'm stuck with you." I said, 'What do you mean?" He said, "I just got a message from your inner self that you are a *chela* [disciple] and I've got be your guru." That's how it started, and he was my guru for sixteen years.

REBECCA: How do you respond to someone who says that you're just copying, that these rituals are so ancient and so much a part of the culture that uses them that you will never really understand it, that you're always going to see it through the filter of your own culture?

FAKIR: I've heard that a lot. You can see it through the filter of your own culture, but you can still catch the fire. I could light a fire in Africa, and we could carry it somewhere else. Fire is fire, no matter where it burns.

REBECCA: Then in your view, to bring your own definitions and values to it is okay.

FAKIR: Yeah. It's still useful, and if you've found it and you can use it, you've got fire. I've had a lot of people accuse me of being hollow and of ripping off these other cultures. I find this difficult to understand. I may have been inspired by them, but much of what I've done has been quite different—I do it my way. But I thank my sources of inspiration, and I'm very appreciative that I've had a chance to be inspired to do anything at all!

REBECCA: What is the modern primitive movement a response to? What is the driving force behind it?

> *. . . the last taboo, the last hang-up, is the body.*

FAKIR: Total disenchantment with everything they see around them. It started in the sixties. I see the sixties through to the year 2000 as kind of an evolutionary revolution. I feel we're in the final phase now, and the last taboo, the last hang-up, is the body. The first was "Is what you see what you see?" When people started in mass numbers to take psychedelics and say, "Gee, maybe what we think is real isn't real," that's when the revolution started.

So then we had a whole new set of values, and we questioned everything. All institutions—religious, educational, commercial, governmental—all these things have been questioned. And more recently the evangelists, the popular spiritual guides, started to crumble and had feet of clay. General disillusionment has set in. Body modification takes you back to the beginning, to basics, to the first cave persons who started having insights and discovering things.

REBECCA: It's very easy, obviously, to put down the West and to idolize the East . . .

FAKIR: Yes, but think of the oppression that occurred in some of those other cultures. Think about the Islamic world, or India and the caste system. Wherever you go, you're going to have these same old human problems.

REBECCA: Right. So what do you think the West has to offer the rest of the world?

FAKIR: Well, I've looked at it from the perspective of an Indian who came into this culture and thought, "Man, if only I'd been back there in Lakota society and I had a flash unit. It would be like having the sun in my hand!" And when I ride in a car, to me it's a pony with fire in its belly.

As a young man I wanted to know how everything worked, and I think technology is what the West has to offer. How to manipulate things externally. Where we've lost the way here is in not learning that there are *two* kinds of technology, the mechanical and the magical. What people are looking for in the modern primitive movement is not to abandon material comfort and the technological aspects of society, but to balance it out with an understanding and an equally competent use of magic technology.

We don't have much magic technology. There are some places, in the outer limits of physics particularly, where people have got to the end of the circle and lapsed over. Some physicists are now at a point where they're into magic technology and don't know it.

> *Where we've lost the way here is in learning that there are* **two** *kinds of technology, the mechanical and the magical.*

REBECCA: Do you have people who challenge you, who come to you for a piercing, for example, but who only want to do it their way?

FAKIR: Yes, I have that happen occasionally. But I have a lot of others who come to me who have a genuine respect. They say, "You show me the way. I'll do it any way you tell me." I sometimes make people jump through a lot of hoops if I feel they're off the beam. I don't make it easy.

REBECCA: What do you think are some bad reasons to get a tattoo or a piercing?

FAKIR: If you're doing it out of social or peer pressure or haste and not your heart, you may really do something you'll regret. You're dealing with something very powerful. When you get pierced or tattooed you're not just modifying the physical body, you are doing some very strange things to the energy circuits and to the spirit that lives in the body.

In our medical science, the phantom limb phenomenon is well-known. I maintain that when a surgeon is doing surgery, the reason it works is not only because he is manipulating something in the physical body. His intent, what he's doing in the psychic, spiritual side of life, has to be there too. If the physician is very skilled in removing a limb but doesn't understand that there is an electrical counterpart also needing to be removed, you end up with a person missing a leg but who still feels the leg there.

REBECCA: So you feel that if you are connected to your inner spirit, you'll be safe?

FAKIR: Yes. In my experiments I felt that even if things went wrong somehow, I'd come out okay. I've always felt a kind of connection with something that put me here and made this heart beat. It was in charge of things in an intimate and personal way—not a remote, time-sharing god in charge of billions of people. This is part of the concept that I got from the Native Americans. To them, the Great Spirit was always a Great Spirit for each person, not one Great Spirit for everybody.

REBECCA: You've talked about the body as a tool for liberation, but it's also been used as a tool for control. We talk romantically of exotic rites of passage in other cultures, but there is also cruelty in many of these practices.

FAKIR: Yes, there can be a negative side to over-romanticism of body play, and sometimes I may be guilty of doing this. In some cultures these practices are nonconsensual. For example, the binding of young girls' feet in China was certainly an act of extreme patriarchy and a very oppressive thing.

REBECCA: So do you feel that the element of choice has to be there for these practices to be truly valid?

FAKIR: Essentially, yes. Oddly enough, I still have the feeling that even though it was nonconsensual, there was still an opportunity to rise above total body identity. You can fight and resist and suffer, or you can accept and adapt and learn. And so, even though some of these practices may have been enforced, something constructive could still come of it.

REBECCA: Why are so few people of color involved in the modern primitive movement?

FAKIR: That's an interesting question. Maybe it's because they've fought so hard to get a true hold in the mainstream, and our "rebellion" may seem like a step backward. I think it's much harder for people of color to find their way into our circle because they're conditioned to exclusion. We're trying to make it accessible with the fusion groups I'm involved with, but black people are still fighting. It's hard for many of them to get through their own barriers to inclusion, to trust that there's actually a place for them.

REBECCA: Acceptance is a theme that you discuss a lot. Was it this that attracted you to the SM community?

FAKIR: Yes. I found many people who were accepting of my queerness. I also discovered that gay people in general could be very open. In 1977 I attended the first International Tattoo Convention. These were maverick, way-out sons-of-bitches. I thought that of all places, this is where I can let it all out. I was encouraged to appear and perform as Fakir Musafar by an eccentric millionaire, Doug Malloy. So I did. I did everything that I knew how to do—and I was big hit, much to my surprise! Like on the coal-bin wall, thunder and lightning did not come down and strike me dead. (*laughter*) I found warmth, I found love, I found an opening here.

REBECCA: What kind of response have you gotten from New Age groups?

FAKIR: For a while I tried bringing my "message" to the so-called New Age audience. I did just fine getting an invitation and getting to the meeting places, but when I started talking about blood and piercing the body, they said, "Oh no! This is too much! We can think about it and contemplate it and we can smell beautiful scents, but we can't practice this!" These people were not ready to confront the last barrier to discovery—the body. So I had very little luck with the New Agers.

> *... when I started talking about blood and piercing the body,* [the New Agers] *said, "Oh no! This is too much!"*

REBECCA: The Judeo-Christian ghost . . .

FAKIR: Is still haunting them. And usually you find the parting of the ways when it touches on the body and erotic or sexual energy. "That's fine. I'll work with my crystals, but don't ask me to play with my body!" (*laughter*)

REBECCA: Based on the experiences you've had in life, what are your thoughts on death?

FAKIR: I've faced a lot of death, and I'm facing a lot of death right now. I've sat by a lot of friends who've died over the past few years. I made a connection with the gay community not realizing that, although I got the opening and the warmth, a lot of them were HIV positive, and their prognoses for long life were very grim. Now they're leaving me all the time.

Since I cultivated very close friendships with many of them, it's getting more difficult dealing with my feelings that get caught up in their dying. In some ways, it's almost been a blessing, because it's forced me again to face this issue of the ultimate change of body-state, which is called death. I've seen some beautiful deaths, and I've seen some very ugly deaths.

REBECCA: What do you think determines whether a person has a good death?

FAKIR: It's understanding and acceptance. There are people for whom I honestly feel death was a wonderful experience and transition. Death and dying is thrown into nothing but an ugly context in this culture—the whole business and commercialization of death and dying. I think it should be a conscious experience. It should be an adventure.

I sat with a woman I was very close to while she was dying. To her, life was breathing, and if she took her last breath it was like blowing out the candle. And she could not understand in any way whatsoever, or explore the possibility that there might be something beyond. And so she went way beyond the time she probably should have said good-bye. The body hung on.

REBECCA: So the more you've explored your spirituality, the more your faith in a continuity has grown?

FAKIR: Yes. How can you explore life if you don't explore death? We have so many distractions and diversions, anything and everything to keep our minds off it. This is not Tibet. We do not have a *Book of the Dead* here. We do not prepare people to die! I've sat in rooms with people who were close to death and who were in such a state of denial. The last one was just a week or so ago. He had nothing on his mind except decorating the room in which he was dying.

REBECCA: You've mentioned a guy who was trying to get together some freaks for a freak show, like they had thirty years ago, and he couldn't find any. What does that say to you?

> *This is a clean, pure society, and it goes to great pains to eliminate what it considers deformity.*

FAKIR: Physical difference is unacceptable now. This is a clean, pure society, and it goes to great pains to eliminate what it considers deformity.

REBECCA: Isn't that one of the great barriers to body modifications such as you find in the modern primitive movement—that it challenges the cultural definition of what is beautiful?

FAKIR: Exactly. That original commandment is still there for many people: "Thou shan't fuck with the body." Why not? "Because you might learn something, and then you won't come back and go to my church and bow down to my priests." That's what it's all about, to me.

> *That original commandment is still there for many people: "Thou shan't fuck with the body."*

Francis Jeffrey

———

" . . . we are separate entities with boundaries that collide . . . we
are entities with boundaries that overlap."

Plugging into ElfNet
with Francis Jeffrey

Francis Jeffrey is a pioneer and forecaster on the frontier interface between communication technologies and neuroscience. He is a consultant on ethical applications of science and technology, co-founder of civic and environmental organizations, and CEO of Alive Systems Inc., which is devoted to the application of biological principles in computer software design.

Francis devised the "Linguini code," an intercultural and human-computer communications "language." He originated the concept of "communications co-pilot," an electronic co-personality that works along with you while it learns to emulate and support your communication and computing activities. His magnum opus is a project-in-progress called ElfNet, an interactive network that will use telephones or interactive television to access global information resources in a personalized way, while building meaningful relationships and perfecting programs of action. A psychological theorist, his theory on the nature of consciousness in isolation was published in Woman & Ullman's Handbook of States of Consciousness.

In 1973, after studying computational neurophysiology at the Berkeley and San Diego campuses of the University of California, Francis began studies with John C. Lilly, M.D. (interviewed in our first volume) on sensory isolation and on human-dolphin communication research, studies which continued over the years. Recently Francis helped dolphins gain civil rights, at least in Malibu. His concept was first enacted as public policy by the Malibu city council on January 7, 1992—apparently the first legal recognition in the human world of dolphins as individuals. In 1986 Francis co-founded, with Richard B. Robertson, the Great Whales Foundation, an organization that has called upon the international community to recognize whales as "living cultural resources" rather than consumables.

Francis is the author of the well-known biography John Lilly, So Far. *His thinking has been provoked over the years by interactions with the twentieth century's best and brightest innovators and nonconformist thinkers, including Timothy Leary, Carolyn Mary Kleefeld (both of whom are in*

our first volume), Herbert Marcuse, Gregory Bateson, Lawrence Stark,
M.D., Heniz von Foerster, Roland Fischer, and Ted Turner.

In interview mode, Francis demonstrates an extremely quick mind that
is knowledgeable about an extraordinary scope of interests, free-associat-
ing surprising connections among conventional topics. Keenly perceptive
of the hidden structure of ideas and systems, he possesses a special gift for
making complex scientific concepts easy to understand in essential terms.
He is also very funny, in an off-beat sort of way. Dark, piercing eyes dart
amid birdlike features in a combination that seems to personify the arche-
type of the alchemist-wizard. I conducted this interview with Francis at his
Malibu Beach home on June 29, 1994, at sunset. As we began, just off the
deck, dolphins slid through the waves of the Pacific.

DJB

DAVID: What inspired your interest in computational neuroscience? How did you become interested in the interface between the computer and brain science?

FRANCIS: I started reading Carl Jung as a teenager and found him fascinating. By the time I was about fifteen, I had read just about everything he wrote. But it seemed to really lack any explanatory power, so I started looking for something that would help to better explain the mind. After reading Jung, I thought, "Well sure, maybe the mind does this, but how and why does the mind do this?" It became apparent that this had something to do with the brain, and I began looking into that in college.

When I was in college studying psychology, computers were just coming online in a big way. So you had the first transition from these very elite mainframe institutions that everyone had to schedule their time on and share. They were originally installed with money from the Defense Department and the Atomic Energy Commission to encourage research in physics, and virtually every university had one. Then minicomputers became available, and we had laboratories that had some of the first minicomputers in them. So your lab actually had a computer, and it was obvious that the way to do experiments in psychology was to program them, because this was much more flexible than the old fashioned way of doing experiments.

I was fascinated with what cognitive science now calls the *binding problem*. What is it that holds a perception together as a unit? Behaviorism, which is the psychology that was widely being taught at that time, contributed absolutely nothing to this question. The stimulus-response perspective didn't give you a clue as to what made a perception. A more universal spin on the question would be "What is consciousness?" There is somebody who is having an experience, and that experience seems to hold together. You're not just little bits of a picture, like an insect eye, but there's a whole thing going on that you're involved in.

DAVID: That's the Big Mystery.

FRANCIS: You can analyze it in different ways, and it's kind of like a quantum phenomenon. Depending on how you analyze it, what experiments you do, you conclude that perception is broken down into different units in different ways. Recently reputable academic scientists started saying that the binding problem—what holds a perception together—is something that they're going to start looking at. But that's just a way of getting the large question—"What creates a mind?"—in the door.

Well, there are a lot of ancient answers to that question from people who, without the benefit of any external technologies, just experimented on themselves. I think one of the best traditions of that would be *The Yoga Sutras* of Patanjali. A contemporary roughly of Plato and Buddha, back more than 2,000 years ago, Patanjali is the legendary and perhaps actual author of *The Yoga Sutras*, which is a very concise presentation of the basic ideas of yoga. Of course, that is tied to all the Hindu philosophy, and on and on. But there's something very crisp and concise about *The Yoga Sutras*, and a lot of scientifically minded people, including John Lilly, have gotten way into it.

There are a lot of scientists, such as Deepak Chopra, who have benefited from association with this yoga tradition. Now, Patanjali said—among a great many other interesting things—that artificial minds can be created by . . . how to translate it is difficult . . . "egotism." Artificial minds can be created by the drive to selfhood. Okay, so I translate this as follows. "If you want to create an artificial mind"—which sounds very modern and technological, almost like artificial intelligence [AI], but he's talking about how a yogi can project his mind into form

> *Artificial minds can be created by the drive to selfhood.*

and clone himself—"what makes it possible is that there is a universal tendency to create coherent consciousness."

DAVID: To individuate?

FRANCIS: To individuate, exactly. That's the basis of the phenomenon. So I applied this in my recent thinking, and this insight guides the communication-software development I'm currently into. What you need if you want to create an artificial mind—now in the modern technological sense— is you must somehow capture that drive toward individuation, toward consciousness. But it's not a matter of building up a bunch of rules on how some expert does things, which is how AI has turned out to be.

DAVID: How does your understanding of computer science give you insight into how the brain works?

> *. . . computer science is a completely vapid subject.*

FRANCIS: It gives an insight in a negative sense, because computer science is a completely vapid subject. As far as I can tell, there isn't any. There are departments of computer science at universities, but is it science? It's like they're studying the history of the evolution of computers or something.

DAVID: Well, it's a systems approach to a certain type of technology.

FRANCIS: That's the problem. You see, a system is like an artificial framework that you build, and then you try to fit stuff into it. To again use the quantum theory paradigm, you know what you observe depends on the kind of experiments and measurements you make. There's a certain complementarity there. You make certain measurements and observations, and you exclude others. So I think the hierarchical-systems approach is the ultimate extension and *r*eductio ad absurdum of that approach, because you end up with a created system that has no subject matter but its own constructs. It's like what Wittgenstein said, "Can it be that in mathematics what I am studying and seeking . . . is to know that which makes it possible for me to create these things."

DAVID: So then, the study of computer science can also be the study of the brain's ability to model things in a way that creates powerful computational tools and digital technology.

FRANCIS: Well, in kind of a backdoor way. But that's just psychology. The tool building is "unconscious," driven by markets. I think you wanted to ask, "What de facto, in reality, is computer science?" It's actually just studying the latest generation of personal computers, the latest generation of software, and teaching people how to use them.

DAVID: Does the understanding of computers give you any insight at all into how the brain functions?

FRANCIS: Well, experientially it gives you some insight into how your brain functions. You can go to two extremes. One of them allows you to see what happens to your brain when you interact with very sophisticated technology. Today we have very sensory computers—the hot buzzword is "multimedia interactive computers." Okay, so that's one area where you can look at it, and that's sort of what we were doing twenty to twenty-five years ago in experimental psychology—much simplified, because we didn't have the big power computers we have today.

We were using computers to throw complicated stuff at the human mind and nervous system, watching what the reaction was, and then using a computer to analyze it. But if you want to be very elegant and mathematical, you have to really go back to the original insights

the farther science progresses, the slower it goes . . .

that led to the computer as we have it today. And there hasn't been much added on in the interim. With all the work done by all the artificial intelligence people and the so-called computer scientists, there really hasn't been a bit added to that origin. And now we're talking about forty to fifty years of "progress." So it kind of contributes to the observation—which I think some historian made—that the farther science progresses, the slower it goes, because it gets bigger and more bureaucratic. So you want to go back to people like John von Neuman, Alan Turing, Kirt Godel, Warren McCullock, and Walter Pitts.

DAVID: How about vice-versa? Does the understanding of the brain give you any insight into computer science?

FRANCIS: Well sure, because it sort of sets the outer limit on what humans can achieve. I mean, humans will be doing very well if they can translate a high percentage of what they find in their brain into some kind of external technology, and so far they've translated just a little bit of that.

DAVID: I'm curious as to how you envision the future evolution of technology in regard to how it's going to interface with the brain. Do you see specific types of technologies somewhere on the horizon that will interface directly with the brain?

FRANCIS: Well, there's the good news and the bad news. Obviously there are these monitoring technologies, like SQUID, with all kinds of refinements of magnetic resonance or nuclear magnetic imaging. This allows us to start getting a very detailed view of what's going on in the brain. From the point of view of the brain, that's an output technology; from the point of view of a computer, it's an input of technology. So you can start having patterns from your brain going into the computer. The other side of it is that you can overwhelm the brain and the mind with the media technology, and of course we've already got that in a crude sort of way. Warfare and religion weren't invented in the twentieth century, they just became more efficient and industrialized. Now we've had television for a long time, and I think most of what it does is put a lot of noise into the brains of a lot of people, which causes a lot of confusion, although there are obviously certain benefits.

> *. . . you're jamming up the brains of millions and millions of people with messages that are pretty irrelevant . . .*

I watch CNN a lot because I get a lot of information that way. I find it has most of the information that's in the *L.A. Times*, only a day earlier, and just about as much depth. But it's loaded with commercial advertisements, and those are extremely irritating. So I think unless you're sitting there with a can of beer to kind of help you chill out, your impulse is to get up and turn those things off all the time. Maybe some people find them entertaining. But what's happening is you're jamming up the brains of millions and millions of people with messages that are pretty irrelevant to most of them most of the time, and are basically distorted or exploitive. So the danger and peril of this thing is that as you get more and more interactive and multimedia, you make a more compelling and more powerful medium that just basically surrounds people and drives them nuts—even more nuts than at present.

DAVID: Like interactive beer commercials.

FRANCIS: Yeah, interactive beer commercials. You'll have the spigot right on your TV, and you'll go through this elaborate set of icons and menus, click somewhere, your already overdrawn bank account will be debited five dollars, and some beer will plop out. This is progress. (*laughter*)

DAVID: When you look at the history of technology and then project into the future, what new technologies do you think will have the greatest impact on the future evolution of humanity?

FRANCIS: I think interactive technology is very big, and so is nano-technology, which covers a span from drug technology to microfabrication techniques. This stuff has extremely profound implications. On the drug technology side, where you're doing things like peptididometics or orthomolecular chemistry, you have the ability to fabricate all the molecules that are found in the human body and all those that interact with it in specific ways. So there you have the solution to all the ancient dilemmas of medicine, aging and so forth.

DAVID: How do you think it will affect the evolution of consciousness?

FRANCIS: I think it's going to create much more freedom, because the mind becomes decoupled from the usual deprivations of disease and aging. So there's a real capacity to create a new objectivity there, to create a consciousness that's less panicked and tied to immediate survival problems. Of course, again, there's the dark side, in which things can be exploited. Most science fiction is focused on giving warnings about the dark side of all these technological possibilities. For example, with nanotechnology you could create killer viruses or chemical-biological agents that can transfer ideas to people, and you can thereby control them.

> *. . . there's a real capacity to create a new objectivity there, to create a consciousness that's less panicked and tied to immediate survival problems.*

DAVID: More than the interactive beer commercials?

FRANCIS: Yeah, I think so. But there's a real competition there. To go back to the other array, interactive technology, the point is to get as much real interactivity—which means stuff relevant to the individual—and as little exploitation as possible. The problem here, again, is like the paradox of CNN—it gives a lot of information at the expense of jamming up your mind with a lot of noise, because that's what pays the bills. So you have the same problem going here—the economic engine that drives the thing is commercial advertising.

DAVID: What's your personal technique for filtering signal from noise?

FRANCIS: Well, obviously you focus on the things that are of the most interest to you, unless you've slumped into this kind of somnambulistic trance of addict television watchers, where everything goes in, probably. One thing you can say about the brain—or everything we've learned about it—is that it's driven by internal goals and expectations, and to some extent those are being shaped by external forces and interaction. But at any given moment, it's running on autopilot, and that automatically filters everything that's coming into you. In some people it does so more or less efficiently.

So if you're a real needle-nose, a real information picker, then you have a very fine filter that turns up your inputs when the stuff that's potentially interesting comes along and turns it down when its not. But at the same time, that uninteresting stuff is work that's imposed on you, if you're to filter it out. I mean, you can't go to a movie today or rent a video tape without having fifteen minutes of advertisement at the beginning. It would be much better to have a system in which you can actually zoom in on and assign your energy to new information depending on its relevance to you.

And that is the promise of interactivity. Interactivity means, for instance, if you want to buy a car, you have a system that will answer the questions you're interested in rather than pitching various things to you. First of all, that assumes that you have some questions. So if you're already completely brain-dead, that's not going to be any help. But to say that the brain is run by its own priorities and expectations is also to say, if you take that to an extreme, that we're completely paranoid, or that we're capable of being completely paranoid, because a perception is largely projection, in the psychological sense of the word. So the questions is, to what extent is it *all* just projection?

If it's complete, 100 percent projection, then you're having pure hallucinations, which you might have if you were in an isolation tank on ketamine or something, where you're completely turned out of the physical body and the physical world. Well, that mimics and extrapolates a state that all of us get into to various degrees, and that's the extreme side of the fact that the brain is run by its own priorities and expectations. So then you say, "Well maybe here is a hidden hazard of interactive technology. You can become so focused on a particular program that you lose touch with everything outside that, and it becomes a self-perpetuating and perhaps, eventually, a self-destructive pattern. There are obvious examples, such as various kinds of mental illness, various kinds of obsessions and drug addictions, that take on this character.

Historically you can see the same pattern in the rise and fall of great nations and empires. For example, take Hitler's Germany as an extreme case of paranoia, where you have a system that not only is completely wrapped up in and devoted to its own bizarre ideas, but physically harnesses the industry of an entire continent to realize them and try to spread itself.

If you have an interactive technology that does perfectly nothing but follow your expectations, projections, and interests, then you become information-tight, you don't interact with anything anymore, and you're in an increasingly descending and narrowing spiral of your own. I think you see this now in the mentality of people who spend too much time on their personal computers. It usually takes the form of some kind of game or some kind of obsessive conversation about a subject that's only interesting to a small in-group. It follows that maybe we need the journalists hawking ideas and new blips, but not the self-expanding tabloid kind.

DAVID: I'm curious about how your experience working with John Lilly and Timothy Leary influenced the development of your present belief system?

FRANCIS: Leary is a great permissionary, a term located somewhere between *missionary* and *permission*. If a missionary is someone who's out to sell you some belief systems, a permissionary is somebody's who out to sell you on doing your own thing, to give you permission. So Leary was always an upper, an excitatory stimulant, and a kind of a machine-gun blast of new information. The man is compulsively collecting the most shocking, interesting new information and blasting it at others. So it was always a challenge being exposed to him, to open up to all these new ideas and see what you could do with them. He's kind of like a great firehose, where high-pressure ideas come spurting out at you. Very stimulating guy.

> *He's kind of like a great firehose, where high-pressure ideas come spurting out at you.*

Lilly is a much more difficult case to describe. Perhaps he's almost more interesting as a specimen, and I guess that characterizes the role I ended up playing with respect to him. I wrote his biography, *John Lilly, So Far*, and that's really putting him under the microscope. I just saw him a couple of weeks ago, and he smiles a lot. He's like an example of how far somebody can go in the direction of being an extraterrestrial while living here. Very interesting. But he's also an extremely rigorous scientist, which I think people who don't know him well maybe wouldn't get, unless they went back and read some of his earlier work. So he has an enormous capacity for objectivity, for looking at things in an uncliché way, and for seeing the unobvious aspects of issues. He was, as part of his own development, maniacally committed to studying the question of consciousness and how it relates to perception, computers, and so on.

Lilly introduced me to the technology that he developed, the isolation tank, and also to cetaceans—dolphins and whales—to which I hadn't really had any prior exposure. The model operative there was that ET is already here on planet Earth. Here is this alien species that has a brain with a similar level of sensory capabilities and many other characteristics like our own. Some of them even have about the same size brain, so you have this interaction possibility with the "like-minded." Where I'm sitting right now, I literally have these guys living in the backyard.

In that ocean down there, the dolphins can't hear us on land, but they're actually hearing the whales, and together they're a global communication system. I told this to Ted Turner one night—I said that he had the *second* global news system. (*laughter*) He probably didn't like that too much, but he loves whales, so I don't think he minded. WNN, the Whale News Network, has been going on, apparently, for millions of years. It's only been in recent decades that humans have had things like transatlantic cables and global communication satellites. The whales have actually had this kind of system, through acoustic underwater communication, for millions of years.

DAVID: I'm curious about the work that you've done here in Malibu to help dolphins gain civil rights. Can you tell me how you became involved in this work and what goals you're trying to achieve?

FRANCIS: About two years ago the Malibu city council passed a resolution that I wrote up. Walt Keller, a member of our new city council and a former mayor, urged me to do this. He was one of the founders of the city of Malibu. We were able to introduce the idea that Malibu is a shared human-dolphin environment. It's a beach community, and the dolphins figure very prominently in the lives of people here. You see them every day. Just right off this porch are dolphins and whales.

So that idea caught the collective imagination. CNN carried it. I remember doing interviews with German television networks, and even *Time* and *Newsweek* ran little articles about it. Because the implication is, if a community defines itself as no longer exclusively human—it's a human-dolphin shared environment—then by implication you're making them at least honorary citizens. So then you start thinking, "Well, if the dolphins are honorary citizens, then this implies that they're individuals." I think anybody who's got any sense figures they're individuals anyway. But legally they're defined as commodities.

We have in the United States a Marine Mammal Protection Act, which is to protect the *numbers* of them. It's a resource conservation model. According to some biologist, if there are too few of a given species, then we start being extra careful to protect that species so it doesn't become extinct.

But they have no rights as individuals. In fact, just the opposite is true. Under current United States law, with a permit dolphins can be legally captured for various reasons, one of which is to put them on display in some kind of aquatic circus or something. Then they virtually become the property of the people who hold them. There's no provision for them to be liberated or eventually receive retirement pensions or anything like that, because there's no Screen Actor's Guild or Cetacean Performer's Union for dolphins. (*laughter*)

The law has worsened over the last couple months. Congress caved in to pressure from various businesses that exploit dolphins, and under the new law even the standards for making sure they're properly cared for are far more lax. They referred it to the Department of Agriculture, which administers the Animal Welfare Act. I should point out that under the Animal Welfare Act, certain mammals and birds are not defined as animals! How do you like that? The Department of Agriculture has "humane" standards, but they're pretty vapid, because they assume that the animal is being raised to be exploited or consumed in some way. That is like having "kind" ways of killing someone. The situation is a little better than that with captured cetaceans, who are considered theoretically to be held in some kind of public trust.

But when you come right down to it, they become the property of the captors. When Congress recently renewed the Marine Mammal Protection Act, they provided that the offspring of these captive dolphins actually become the property of the people who hold them. So essentially it reduced them to the status that breeding slaves had before the Civil War in this country. If you own dolphins, then their children become your slaves and property automatically. It's a pretty scurrilous situation, in my opinion. Of course, globally, the only real regulatory regime is the International Whaling Commission [IWC], which was also founded on a resource paradigm, and the original idea was to maintain enough stocks of the various species so you can continue to exploit them.

When you talk about resource conservation, basically it's about conserving now so you can exploit in the future. That's the paradigm. This year Malibu made another significant—at least ideologically significant—contribution, calling on the International Whaling Commission to recognize whales as living *cultural* resources, as opposed to *consumable* resources. That actually does coincide with the legal rubric under which the IWC was established, which was to provide for the greatest sustainable use of the whale resource. So the position we're taking now is that the greatest sustainable use of the whale resource is not to treat them as potential food, but to treat them as a nonconsumable cultural resource. Because whales are part of a global communication society, and we're all in on that today. The problem is, in addition to killing them—which is equivalent to destroying nerve cells in the "global brain"—humans have put so much noise in the sea that whales' hearing range is now down to a few hundred miles, versus the thousands they could once talk across. The big question today is whether whales are potential customers for the phone companies. (*laughter*)

DAVID: So what's the next step in what you're trying to do?

> *I'd like to see . . . the United States . . . extend individual legal recognition to dolphins and whales.*

FRANCIS: Well, I'd like to see various localities, states—and eventually the United States and other national governments—extend individual legal recognition to dolphins and whales. I think the arguments for doing that are compelling, based on their neurological parity—some would say superiority—with humans. Everything we know about the richness of their social-communication fabric supports this view.

DAVID: As a result of your experiences in the isolation tank, you developed an interesting model of consciousness, which was published several years ago in the *Handbook of States of Consciousness*. Can you briefly summarize the essence of your theory and what its implications are?

FRANCIS: Remember the isolation tank is a method of de-emphasizing your physical existence and your physical position in the universe, as well as communication and all sorts of sensory inputs and outputs. Then, by contrast, it emphasizes whatever is left. A lot of people might think, "Well there's nothing left." But that's not the case. As I said, the human mind is primarily based on projection, and so once you get over the idea that you're not supposed to be experiencing anything because nothing's happening, that ability to project becomes free, and when it's not coupled to any sensory motor input/output, it is very close to the ability to imagine. So it's basically a creative idea. But what do you find then, and what kind of world develops under these conditions? Well, the physical world has a certain logic to it that has to do with the sensory motor system, and most of the ideas that circulate among humans have to do with that kind of activity in interaction with physical objects.

Of course, there are ideas that have to do with dreams and things that are a little different. But everyday, real-world ideas, whether they're just common sense or the most sophisticated science, have to do with properties of the physical world. And there you have mores that have to do with identifying bodies and objects. Basically, there's a concept of *boundaries*, and there's a logic and a whole mind-set that comes out of this. This is the logic of the physical world, where you say that it's A or it's B. If a certain area of space and time is included in phenomenon A, then it's probably not included in phenomenon B. Because these phenomena are defined by their boundaries, it belongs to one or the other, unless they're certain kinds of weird phenomena, like waves or something, where they're allowed to overlap and intersect.

So you get the idea that most of the time what you yourself are is defined by your boundaries. You have a pretty good idea that you're somebody in a particular body in a particular place. Now, when you go far enough into the isolation mind-set, that begins to break down, and you start to see that, if you are anything, you're probably patterns of communication, which are all tangled up with other patterns of communication in the outside world. So then you have a model of what you are that isn't based on boundaries anymore, but on loops that are tied in with other loops. It's an alternative to being this physical being. You have these overlapping entities that are defined by interacting loops of communication, and everything interpenetrates everything else. Well, you know, the Buddhists said that a long time ago. I called these patterns, "Bateson loops," after a communication theorist I once knew. The "spiritual" entities, defined by boundaries that overlap rather than by inside/outside distinctions that exclude one another, are called "Booles," after the nineteenth-century logician George Booles, who instigated Boolean algebra. So you might say, "Booles rush in . . . "

DAVID: Tell me about ElfNet.

FRANCIS: ElfNet is an idea that I've been pushing on everyone since about 1980, and it's based on a Santa's workshop paradigm. See, you have

> **Imagine all the elves in some kind of benevolent organization at the North Pole.**

Santa and his elves, and all the elves are busy making toys for all the children. Imagine all the elves in some kind of benevolent organization at the North Pole. Now apply this to the information sphere. It's a collaborative model of information sharing. Everyone is contributing by providing information that might be useful to other people and taking out whatever information they can use that other people provided. This doesn't exclude that there could be some payoffs made for information within the system, but it has to be reasonable. The key thing is that the information is nonexploitive. That means the information you get is relevant to your own needs and interests. It's not someone trying to sell you something with irrational persuasion, which is what the whole commercial marketing system that dominates our media is about.

DAVID: So it would make information available to people in a more accessible format, and allow everybody to contribute and interact in a community-like way.

FRANCIS: Yeah, that's right. It's a global community based on communication rather than physical presence and physical work. So, first of all, you don't want this to be chaos. Because right now you have chaos. This is the paradox. You can pick up a phone, and theoretically you can dial anyone in the world—I mean, if you know their number or even if you just start dialing numbers at random. I don't know, maybe you should try this as an experiment. Spend the entire day doing this and see what you come up with. But there's no guarantee that by following such a procedure, or even if you have some published directory of people that are supposed to be helpful resources of information, that you're going to find anyone who either has the answer to your question, or has the capacity and willingness to help you with whatever your problem is, or even wants to hear about it.

Henry David Thoreau said that "the mass of men lead lives of quiet desperation." So there's tremendous isolation and alienation, and most people live every day in this little doggy run of their habitual activities, where they're isolated from everything else that's going on. They're mostly on the receiving end of information. So they get the news. Today we have an unparalleled ability to not only get news, but to see what's going on all over the place. O. J. Simpson is running down the highway in his white Bronco, and everybody's there with him seeing it, but it's a big "so what?" as far as everybody else is concerned.

You ought to have a two-way system that somehow breaks down the wall of isolation, so you're not just the person who is receiving what somebody else considers to be news or information, which is basically what you are now. There's somebody out there cal-

> *There's somebody out there calculating what you should consider to be news . . .*

culating what you should consider to be news or information. It's being fed to you, unless you work very hard going through libraries and computer databases. You have to work extremely hard to get a little bit of information on your own. It's a very biased, commercial-marketing, advertising system. So we thought maybe there are better solutions then this. But most of the systems that exist are fairly intractable, hard to work with. So what do you do if you want information? Where do you go? You go to your various experts—a doctor or someone—and ask them.

When you do that, you find out that most of those people are really technicians. They're experts at performing certain procedures, and if you happen to be somebody who can benefit from the particular procedure they're running, then it might be good for you to see them. You could go to a library or do the electronic equivalent—go digging through this stuff—or you could participate in one of these bulletin boards or electronic mail systems, which are really pretty chaotic. Everyone's talking about the Internet, which is terrific. I use it all the time. But try to find anything on it. It's pretty intractable, even for experts, because it's really just an agreement to forward messages. So you're back to the same basic problem as the telephone call.

You find that the really organized systems of information are primarily commercial exploitation, or noncommercial exploitation, based on irrational persuasion. I'm not saying anything that isn't obvious. But in a sense, to focus on and harp on these issues is heretical, because we're supposed to be living in an age of "markets" and so forth. And because of the way things are, that implies constant exploitation, whether it's commercial exploitation, political exploitation, or religious exploitation. So how do you set up a sys-

> *. . . how do you set up a system that's nonexploitive that gives you access to information?*

tem that's nonexploitive that gives you access to information? How do you do it technically? How do you give people access to this?

Things like CompuServe and so on, which are designed for this fragment of the population that is so-called "computer literate," are definitely growing. Your computer can log on with a modem to some network, and you can go in there and hunt for information or exchange messages. Those things are growing rapidly, but it's still a minority phenomenon, and it has some very serious limitations, as anyone who has tried to use it knows. So that medium is maturing now, but at the same time there are other media coming along, and they're eventually going to collide and converge. That would be the so-called interactive television, where you'll be online all the time. You just turn the thing on, and there you are. You're using the higher transfer rates and capacity of cable and fiber optic networks to allow a greater sensory richness of information. But still, the same basic problem is there. Even if you had that national information interstate right now, so that you could turn on your interactive television with the little remote control unit, you could only do what your son or daughter in the next room is doing right now with a PC on CompuServe.

See, you're still basically limited to what they do on CompuServe, but with a little more sensory richness. So you could see what these two things are converging into during the next few years. By the year 2000 they probably will have merged, and there won't be a lot of difference between using a utility like CompuServe and using an interactive television system. But there's really nothing new in any of that, because we've had these computer bulletin board systems and searchable libraries on a large scale for at least thirty years. What's changed is they've become a little bit easier to use, but just in a very minor way, by being sensorially richer.

DAVID: And ElfNet would do what to make the information more easily accessible to more people?

FRANCIS: First of all, ElfNet starts with what everybody has right now. That's basically telephone communications. From the beginning, I thought it has to be something that is completely accessible through acoustic communication—the telephone. By using the telephone, you don't need anything that isn't in every home in America. Everyone knows how to use it, so the technological hurdle—both in terms of personal expertise and in terms of the burden of buying equipment—is very minimal. So what else do we have today? Well, we obviously have telephone and television, and the television is verging toward what the telephone is, in the sense of being a two-way interactive medium. So everything I say about the telephone today applies to interactive television in the future.

Once the paradigm is worked out, you just have to understand that it becomes a little bit sensorially richer to do this through an interactive television. You have visual images, and you can point at things with your finger or some remote control, which is a little easier than just being on the phone. But it's the same model—interactive two-way communication—and it applies universally.

The other aspect of this communication process is how the information is organized. I put this in the broader context of how the communication is organized, because information is thought to be some kind of substance, but it really isn't. Information is really a kind of accounting that's applied to communications. If you look at any respectable academic theory of information, you find that it ultimately comes down to that, that it's not the static representation of bits and bytes, or a checkerboard with checkers on and off. That's just the physical vehicle for it. The information is really a measure of communication. If you go back to the original mathematical theory of communication that engineers use, from around 1948, it said very explicitly what information is—a measure of communication, and communication is basically between minds, and it's about questions and answers. Questions and answers implies that there's a mind that has those questions and to whom the answers are relevant. In *The Mind of the Dolphin*, John Lilly said very succinctly, "Communication is between minds."

DAVID: So ElfNet is a way of linking up more minds.

FRANCIS: Yeah. It's not really about the information, the data, or anything like that. It's about the communication patterns. So the paradigm is very different from that of an industry based on the idea that you have information, which is a commodity, a quantity that you're going to sell. CompuServe and similar services now will send you a CD-ROM that has half a gigabyte of images on it, and if you happen to have a computer that can log onto CompuServe and has a ROM reading capability, as some of them now do, you can plug this in, and you can get the same thing with more bells and whistles, much greater sensory richness. So instead of having a little Macintosh window-like icon you click on your screen, it'll give you a frog, a 747, or a door that opens up onto a magical kingdom. All that is embellishment, to the extent that it's entertaining. It's a crutch for people to interface and doesn't do anything for the basic issue, which is interaction, which-is about communication between minds. So this is where the paradigm takes off.

DAVID: Okay, so let's create a scenario. Let's say that I want to find out more about diabetes, and we have ElfNet set up. How would we go about doing that? I'd pick up the phone and dial into a central number—describe to me what would then happen.

FRANCIS: First of all, we don't want to make you put in your whole life history every time you interact with this thing. Whether you're punching buttons on a touch-tone telephone, whether you're pointing and clicking, typing away furiously at a keyboard, or blabbing, there's an enormous burden of data input, which is a context. So what you want to have is an enduring context that is represented in this system, in which you own it as your private property. We're not talking about these credit bureaus that sell information about you for potential marketing and so forth. There's an enduring context in which you own an *information action condominium.* See, you own a condo in this information sphere, and that represents you. This has very interesting extensions that are related to what I was telling you earlier about the idea of giving dolphins and whales individual civil rights and legal status. Today there are five or six billion humans on this planet, but very few of them have very much in the way of individual standing or stature. Recognizing whales raises consciousness about recognizing ourselves.

As far as the economic systems that govern the planet are concerned, they're numbers. You're a statistic. For this reason it's very hard to protect even human rights. I try to protect dolphin rights, but I also support organizations like Amnesty International, which is one of the very best at trying to protect and define human rights. It's hard to get these government bureaucracies and multinational corporations to even accept standards of human rights that are being evolved by global supergovernmental bodies, such as the United Nations. It's very difficult. So if you can give every individual public access, I think that you're going a long way toward having a global society that, in a profound sense, recognizes each individual. That raises the possibility of caring for each individual in a specific way, and all that comes from the idea of having your personal, private information condo, your cellular-awareness domain, integrated into this kind of system.

> *. . . if you can give every individual public access . . . you're going a long way toward having a global society . . .*

So to return to your first question, about what sort of interaction there is, there are two poles to this interaction. One of them is that you can take charge, direct the interaction, and anything goes. You can be completely free of your whole interactive history. The other pole is that you can let it be based on what you've built up in the system already. You can let it make for you the associations that are most likely to connect you with the new information, as well as the enduring information that's most relevant to your concerns.

> *. . . you can take charge, direct the interaction, and anything goes.*

DAVID: You were working on something years ago called Computer Co-pilot. Is that related to this in any way?

FRANCIS: It shares a common technology. There's a little revolutionary software technology at the heart of this, which I believe is a key to making it economical, at the present time, to do these sort of grandiose things I've described. This is another distinct application. The idea of a computer co-pilot, of course, relates to the idea that you have this personal entity. There's this enduring image of you, which is, again, your private property, your holding in this global communication condominium. And you could also have this

> *. . . the Computer Co-pilot . . . becomes . . . an agent that can do all kinds of work for you, because it represents you*

entity completely under your own control. You could have this cellular presence on the ElfNet, the global brain, then you could have it interacting with your personal one that's completely under your own control, which you can expand using your own equipment and facilities. That was the idea of the Computer Co-pilot. It becomes an active thing, an agent that can do all kinds of work for you, because it represents you, your priorities, expectations, and so forth.

DAVID: Almost as though it becomes your unconscious.

FRANCIS: Oh yeah, I guess you could say that, to the extent that your unconscious is this whole backload of priorities and expectations, things that go on in the background, automatic activities. You can maybe off-load or download much of your unconscious functioning to your personal computer, if it's set up

> *You can maybe offload or download much of your unconscious functioning to your personal computer . . .*

this way. That project is in the background, to be developed as a product that I'm going to call *Angel*, because we thought it's not so much like your unconscious as like your guardian angel.

It's your electronic guardian and messenger, which is the idea of an angel, if you look at classical association. It can help you manage your messaging, because as the world becomes more complicated, more communication-based, your load of messaging work becomes greater and greater, and, of course with Angel, you can handle this more efficiently. So what you can do, in the context of having this co-pilot or this agent, is you can organically automate a lot of these tasks that you have to perform, and you can achieve much greater efficiency. It gives you the ability to handle more and more information competently. You can integrate a lot of things you do now using communication devices and computers in a single model, and have it run all that stuff for you, rather than you having to master every new program that comes out. That's about it. So we're developing this now under the brand name trademark *Angel*.

There's a funny story to this. I filed this trademark protection about two years ago. As soon as it was published in the official gazette of the patent office, an objection was raised by—of all people—the Angels baseball team. (*laughter*) So we had to negotiate a stipulated demarcation of rights with the team. That was the first real outside business negotiation of this enterprise, with this huge multibillion dollar corporation that manages the Angels baseball team. And little us with our far-out ideas.

In the ElfNet, the technology base is the same. In your own private communication condominium domain in ElfNet, you have a little mini co-pilot, or guardian angel. The difference is, in that context, that it's immersed in an associative network relationship with the guardian angels of all the other participants, which obviously could be millions or billions of people participating, constantly looking for those relevant connections that will contribute to all concerned. And obviously, you're allowed to limit this so you're not exposed to all the grasping tendrils in the entire world on every one of your vulnerabilities or aspirations.

But in the other model, this is like a software product that you have on—I don't want to call it a computer anymore—your personal high-tech communicator. It's much more selective, in the sense that you're not in the public commons and it's only in touch with those parties or information sources that you privately and specifically designated. But it's the same basic technology. You can see that a lot has happened since I started blabbing about this back in 1980, and much of this has become pretty mainstream. You have these so-called personal communicators, digital assistants, organizers, which are kind of a hodgepodge of badly fitting parts right now. They don't put the most obvious things in these, such as a telephone interface. So right now it's driven by some very conflicting market pressures, and hopefully the *Angel* will be available about the time that the hardware to run it on is mature.

DAVID: The idea behind *Angel* is basically about automating activities and functions. I'm curious about whether you think it's possible to create, through a computer network, an entity composed of synthetic consciousness, or a personality with an artificial mind?

FRANCIS: I just jotted down a remark on this. I said, "We should not look for consciousness or awareness in an individual computer or program, but in a network including participants."

DAVID: Wait a minute! That's a way of skirting around the question! (*laughter*)

> *"We should not look for consciousness . . . in an individual computer or program, but in a network including participants."*

FRANCIS: Well, no, it's not, not, not. No it's not. No it's not. Remember what I said about Patanjali's words, way back 2,500 years ago. He said artificial minds have this universal tendency to individuate, to create individual coherent centers of awareness. Contemporary scientific interest in this—the *binding problem*, "What makes a perception hang together? What makes it whole"—is very close to asking who or what is having that experience. This is really the basic issue in psychology, but it has been ducked for a long time because of a lack of boldness or techniques or theoretical tools, as well as this huge prejudice from nineteenth-century materialism that still hangs around. Behaviorism is a dead-end thing that doesn't get you anywhere scientifically, but it's been proven to be very useful for exploitation, whether you're training dolphins to do things for the Navy, or you're trying to train people by repetition to smoke Brand X cigarettes.

DAVID: Do you think that this tendency toward individuation is going to lead to silicon chips having coherent centers of awareness that can interact with us?

FRANCIS: I don't know that they'd necessarily be silicon chips. See, again, there are two extreme poles to this. One of them is you say, "Well, this mind, this consciousness, is not really an individual property that is local-ized in a particular brain in a particular body. It's just somehow that it's concentrated there—it has something to do with it. Your consciousness is no more tied to your brain and body than the conversation is tied to the computer terminal, telephone, or fax machine it goes through. There's some association, but it's not dependent on a particular terminal device." So then I say, "Well, you should not look for consciousness in an individual com-puter program, no matter how it's constructed, no matter how clever the software. We should look for it in this network of relationships between communicational participants."

This ties in with your other question about this theory I published in 1986 that said essentially that, at a psychological or spiritual level, we are not separate entities with boundaries that collide; rather, we are entities with boundaries that overlap. And once you recognize that you're an entity with a boundary that overlaps, the first thing you realize is that you're both the inside *and* the outside of the boundary. The thing that distinguishes you is maybe the shape of the boundary, or something like that, but it's not even a question of inside versus outside. Second, when the boundaries of these different entities—which are not defined by physical-world logic but by this higher-dimensional logic—overlap, then the relationship is not so much a question of how much one of them encroaches into the other, because both of them own the inside and the outside.

Get yourself a couple loops of string, a red one and a blue one, and see what sort of interactive relationships you can work out with them by twist-ing them around on top of a white sheet of paper, and you'll get some idea what I'm talking about. But it's not so much how one encroaches on the other, because that is meaningless by this logic. Each boundary owns both its inside and it's outside. It's more a question of how those boundaries themselves interact, how they lie together or interrelate. Those might be relationships of common perception, common idea, which is the basis of communication. Then you ask, "Well the information itself seems to be draw-ing distinctions—yes, no, this, that, and so forth—so that in the information sphere, the boundaries that define your mind are all those binary kind of bound-aries, where you are always on both sides of them. Wittgenstein demon-strated in the 1920s that logic is totally

> *Wittgenstein demon-strated in the 1920s that logic is totally trivial . . .*

trivial, Godel that the mind is other than logical processes, and G. Spencer Brown that all the mindless consequences of mathematics can be defined by an extremely minimal system of symbols. But the mind is in the background of all this.

DAVID: Okay, so what you're describing is the process of thought, information transfer, and perception integration.

FRANCIS: Yes. Now you want to get down to the psychophysical interface. See, that's the other pole of this. You're asking now, "What is it about the brain and the whole works such that you get consciousness and self-consciousness, a sense of self, a sense of purpose, an extension in time and space beyond where you actually are, and apparently psychic communications with similarly constructed brains and minds?

DAVID: Right, that really odd sense of awareness that you're in the center of this immensely important drama.

FRANCIS: Yeah, where does all that come from? There are some *Gedenken* [German, "to think with"] experiments, as the physicists used to call them, little scientific fantasies you could run and play with, which help you dissect this problem. One of my favorites is the theme of "Beam me up, Scotty," the Star Trek teleportation paradigm. That one actually goes back quite a ways. There are ancient spiritual ideas that relate to this, but if you stick to technology and science fiction, the first I pick up is in about 1948, in A. E. van Vogt's *The World of Null A*, which incidentally has a lot to do with the rejection of Aristotelian logic, the logic of the physical world, which my model is an alternative to. What he posits there is a character who has many bodies somehow. This person was originally some real person who had been cloned, or was maybe a total fabrication by someone else. There are many physical copies of him, and they're in chronic storage somewhere in orbit around another planet. So this person finds himself one day thinking he's going about his daily activities, and then some strange events intrude. He finds out that nobody else remembers him. Although he thinks he's going about his daily activities, before that day he didn't really exist, because all the people around him don't know who he is, and his story doesn't check out. He starts finding himself in a lot of trouble, and eventually he gets blown away. He's killed, and as soon as that happens, his consciousness transfers to another clone of himself, which is instantaneously activated and carries on with the story somewhere else.

The protagonist is left realizing he really doesn't know who he is or where he came from. Even though he has detailed memories going back to childhood, he realizes that they don't agree with anybody else's memories, and as far as he knows, they're completely some kind of fabrication that was implanted in him. The next step is *Star Trek*, where you have this teleportation beam. Well, what's the premise of the teleportation idea in which you're being beamed up or down? In one location there's this device that is basically disintegrating and destroying your body.

DAVID: Breaking it into basic components, but keeping the original pattern somewhere.

FRANCIS: Keeping the pattern, because it's not transporting the material. The material is being recycled, thrown out—or we don't know what happens to the material. But all the information that is your body at that instant when you say, "Beam me up" is being recorded and transmitted like a television signal. So it's like a television or a fax machine except that it's in three dimensions and all very high resolution—it's operating at 10^{-33} centimeters resolution. So the next thing you know, you're in the teleporter room of the starship *Enterprise*, and there you are in one piece again. It reconstitutes your body, getting the material from wherever in its storage, and it puts you back together. You have perhaps just a fleeting, or maybe not even any, break of awareness or consciousness.

Various physicists have thought about this at the level of quantum theory and so on. They ask, "What would be an interface? What would be entailed?" and based on quantum theory, they usually conclude that you actually would have to destroy the original in order to make the copy exactly like it. In other words, you'd be disturbing it too much to preserve the original. So they say that you couldn't have the problem where you could still be stuck in location A while a copy of you is projected to location B and then there's two of you, one at each end of this communication link.

Of course, all this is conjectural, because no one really understands quantum theory that well anyway. But that seems to be a pretty credible position. So you don't have that dilemma because you'd actually have to physically destroy the original of you in order to make the copy in another location. Fine. What if you do that? You destroy the first copy, but you make two more copies at two different locations. Well, there doesn't seem to be anything theoretically wrong with doing that. So there's a problem. Then what's that like? Basically you've been cloned instantaneously by this process. So what happens? Are the two copies separate minds?

DAVID: Well, from that point in time on they're having different experiences, because they're not in the same space-time location.

FRANCIS: Right. Sure. They're having different experiences. So at that point the two minds diverge, and they become two people. But is there some sympathy between them? Are they inherently in contact with one another, like in Aspec's experiments in the Bell's theorem paradigm. Are those particles correlated? This is a very big, complicated thing now. We're not talking about one photon. We're talking about the whole body and the entire personality. I don't see any reason you couldn't construct two identical brains. You might have to grow them from scratch to get everything right.

But are they going to be as one, in perfect sympathy or harmonious communication? At the moment that you've got two copies of your brain, are they perfectly attuned to one another? This would seem to be the case, because it seems that we're to some degree attuned to other brains that are quite a bit different from ours. I regard this as

> *At the moment that you've got two copies of your brain, are they perfectly attuned to one another?*

such a common phenomenon, experientially and empirically, that it's like nonsense to try to refute it, even though you probably don't have a scientific theory to explain it. But that is the ubiquitous reality of so-called psychic communication, which is such a common everyday occurrence for so many people.

DAVID: What do you mean when you say "psychic communication"?

FRANCIS: For example, when you know what somebody else is thinking, or someone who is important to you has some trauma, and you immediately call up the person and say, "What happened?" Everyone has that experience. It happens all the time. This is sort of along some of the lines that Roger Penrose explores in his book. I think he's one of the most sensible theorists in this area right now. Your brain is full of quantum mechanical events, obviously. They're going on all the time. Because it's physical, it's made out of those events.

This is what I call the epistemic theory of existence. It says that the very essence of existence is knowledge, or information. I think you can come to this conclusion by taking physics down to the quantum level, where you find that real existence becomes a mathematical proposition about things observing each other. So it's an epistemic process that creates an actuality, and that actuality is the basis of all the spatial geometries that we experience in the physical world, because it's the way that these atoms bind together that creates the bonding angles and the Tinker-Toy sort of reality that builds our bodies and all this stuff around us.

DAVID: Perhaps consciousness is an inherent force in the universe, as basic as electromagnetism.

FRANCIS: I think that's closer to the ancient spiritual traditions, rather than this weird amalgam of scientific reductionism and materialism that leads to "strong" AI doctrine, which says that consciousness is an emergent phenomenon once you get a certain level of complexity, a brain of a certain size or a computer of a certain speed.

DAVID: Wasn't that the whole idea behind Marvin Minsky's book *Society of Mind*?

FRANCIS: Not exactly. But he's—at least the last I heard—an exponent of strong AI, which I think is completely wrong. I think that's a hodge-podge that derives from the history of materialistic, reductionistic, behavioristic science in the last century or so. In contrast, I think what Penrose is hitting upon is that the same principle that creates mind or consciousness creates intelligence and creative imagination. He very directly ties them together, so consciousness and intelligence are intimately related to him, inseparable, tied to creative imagination. But the same thing that creates that, the same inherent property of the universe, is the one that accounts for the true principles behind the quantum mechanics of physical objects. So although he might not be saying this, he's really in the same camp as Patanjali, Maharishi, or the ancient spiritual traditions of the West, such as the Kabbala, where you find the same principles.

DAVID: Do you see the ancient spiritual traditions and modern science eventually coming to a point of reconciliation?

FRANCIS: Well, sure. But again, there's constantly a tension here. It's being fought against by two things. The first is this whole society that's driven by the engine of commercial exploitation, based on irrational persuasion, misinformation, control of information, and the nondemocratic use of information. The second thing, which is closely tied to that, is the industrialization and bureaucratization that is pervasive in the scientific establishment today. That's what fights it, and they're tied together, because they're both based on mass production, on output-only, one-way kinds of systems.

Obviously, the brain is quantum phenomena. The question is, are those quantum phenomena expressed only through a hierarchy of larger and larger structures? In your systems view, you have molecules, and the molecules make up things like receptors and cellular organelles, and those make up neurons, and the neurons interact with one another through electrical impulses and a whole alphabet of neurotransmitters, some of which are spike-like and instantaneous like an electrical signal, and some of which are graded and continuous. So this is very complex. The old model said you only look for the interactions among the aggregates—that is to say, you look at the interactions between neurons as if the neurons were computers or transistors or something with discrete logic. I say that's nonsense. I think that what makes this nervous-system tissue so remarkably efficient, compact, and powerful is the fact that it's using interactions at all the levels of scale that define its physical existence. From the quantum-particle level on up, all those levels are interacting.

You see, that's exactly what you don't have in a computer, because you've engineered that out. You've designed the computer so that a certain minimum number of electrons—it's in the millions now, and it's heading down into the thousands—forms of quantum of information. This transistor or this logic gate is in a charged or discharged state, but you don't want that individual electron to play any role in that distinction. So you design the device so it's not allowed to. Well, now they're heading toward technology where maybe one captivated electron could be the signal. That's starting to be interesting, but it's being constrained and manipulated in such a way as to force it to be a messenger, not a player.

DAVID: But isn't that exactly what the process of biological evolution has done? Hasn't it constrained the way our brains function such that it limits unpredictability?

FRANCIS: I think on the input and output channels that's true, but I believe inside there's interaction at all levels of scale between the components of the brain, however you distinguish them. The brain works on its own principles, not only those in your philosophy, Horatio! So it means just as much to say that electron p-6 on atom 3423407 is talking to electron d-4 on that atom over here as it does to say that neuron A is talking to neuron B. The human eye is sensitive to a single photon of light. That's amazing. There are neurons in the eye, rod and

The human eye is sensitive to a single photon of light. That's amazing.

cone cells that are able to sense the incidence of a single quantum of light at the right frequency. Okay, that's a pure quantum event that's being sensed, and because of the way the neurons are hooked together, after that there's a certain amount of noise. So it turns out that the signal's not likely to get through unless there are, like, five or ten quanta impacting about the same time on adjacent cells.

Plants do the same thing. A green plant is an antenna. The chlorophyll molecule, of which there are zillions of copies in each leaf of a green plant, is a photon antenna. It picks up an individual photon, and it uses the energy of that individual photon to raise the energy of an electron. That way it can harvest the energy, and all of life on this planet—well, not all of it, now we know there are a few forms of bacteria that live in geysers and oil wells that operate on fermentation and so forth—but basically all the life on the surface of the planet is running on the energy that's collected by these individual quantum events, by individual photons hitting individual molecules of chlorophyll.

That there's a photon receptor in the eye means that the nervous system is capable of utilizing quantum events. But does it also emit quantum events? Why not? It certainly does. There are photons or quanta of all kinds of frequencies being emitted inside the brain. It can't help it— it's throwing this stuff off. But don't assume it's throwing it *away*. So you have one part of the brain that's emitting this signal and another part receiving it. These things are very specifically tuned according to the theory that goes back to Einstein's photoelectric effect. A photon antenna is a resonator that can have its energy raised or lowered a certain quantal amount by absorbing a photon at the right wavelength. Well, that defines a communication channel. So if you have two electrons that have that same bandgap—say between state N and state M—then that defines the communication channel that can be traversed only by a photon of precisely that energy.

Well, obviously the brain is full of this stuff. It's hard to imagine engineering a better sensor for the energies of nature. In spite of all the thermodynamic arguments to the contrary, which I regard as archaic nineteenth-century science, I think that this is going on all the time inside our brain. The brain is a photonic or a radio transceiver, which is communicating with itself over distance at the speed of light, in addition to everything else it's doing. And probably this phenomenon extends from one brain to another, in a much, much weaker way in relation to how in tune those brains are by virtue of their own structures.

Of course, everything I've just said could be disproven by a suitable experiment. There are other explanations you get by going in the Bell's theorem direction. If it's photonic or radio communication, then it's taking place at the speed of light. Well, maybe it's not, and there are paradoxical properties about this. Does your sympathetic communication with a significant other fall off with physical distance? Maybe it increases with distance. Well, then you have to start looking for nonlocal phenomena, which are not signal transmissions by energy, so consequently they're not limited by the speed of light. But then causality, the order of "he thought, then she thought," is lost. As Penrose elucidated the phenomenon of quasi-crystallization, coordination over distance is indistinguishable from action backward in time. The vision causes the events that lead up to it. I take this as the paradigm of metaprogramming.

There's the quantum theory. There are also subquantum theories. "Is a quark a quantum?" for instance. It takes several quarks to make each of those elementary particles, which are the subject of classical quantum theories, so where does it go from there? A physicist I used to hang out with, David Finklestien, said that there's a certain level where you stop getting smaller and smaller parts. He said that at this level it's as if you take a watch and you smash it with a hammer, and instead of a bunch of watch parts flying all over the room, you get a bunch of watches. (*laughter*) See, that's again at the level where the logic of the physical world breaks down. It breaks down in the mind in isolation, and it breaks down at the quantum level, where you have the epistemic basis of existence, because the knowledge or communication process that creates physical existence doesn't follow the logic of the physical world. A thing isn't necessarily composed of parts that are smaller than itself; rather, it might be composed of parts that are larger than itself. Same thing in the mind. So it's gone full circle. A consciousness as big as yours might be responsible for a single dot at the end of this line.

> *A thing isn't necessarily composed of parts that are smaller than itself . . . it might be composed of parts . . . larger than itself.*

Lisa Law

Ram Dass

" What is your relationship to the mystery? Are you defending
yourself from it? Are you making love to it? Are you living in it?"

Here and Now
with Ram Dass

When Ram Dass speaks, his voice contains the gentle sanctity of a Gregorian chant. His presence is filled with the warm fuzziness of that favorite stuffed animal you cherished as a child, and he nudges out of you, just by being there, a sense of your own divinity.

As Richard Alpert, he served on the psychology faculties at Stanford and the University of California, and in 1958 he began teaching at Harvard. His pioneering research with LSD and psilocybin led him into collaboration with Timothy Leary, Ralph Metzner, Aldous Huxley, and Allen Ginsberg. His mind expanded in an inverse relationship to his professional reputation, however, and in 1963, together with Leary, Richard Alpert was dismissed from Harvard in a flurry of hyperbolic publicity.

He continued his research, however, and in 1967 he made his first trip to India. There he met the man who was to become "the most important separate consciousness in my life," his guru, Neem Karoli Baba. It was Neem Karoli who gave Richard Alpert the name Ram Dass, which means "Servant of God," and baptized his spiritual path through the transmission of dharma yoga.

In 1974, Ram Dass created the Hanuman Foundation to spread spiritually directed social action in the West. The foundation birthed the Prison-Ashram Project and the Living-Dying Project, which still operate today, offering spiritual support to prison inmates, and to the dying and terminally ill. In 1978 he co-founded the Seva (Seva means "sight" in Sanskrit) Foundation, an international service organization working in public health and social justice issues, which has made major progress in combating blindness in India and Nepal. Ram Dass is the author of a number of self-help books, and in the past ten years has lectured in over 230 cities throughout the world.

He has consciously reincarnated within his own lifetime, for when his knuckles began whitening on the ladder of success, Richard Alpert took a leap into the void and, as Ram Dass, has become a bosom buddy of emptiness. He is probably the only person with a photograph of Bob Dole on his altar. It is nestled among images of his guru, Christ, and the Buddha, and at his puja, *Ram Dass attends to how his heart expands as he greets each of the first three, then flinches when he reaches Bob—an exercise that shows him where his spiritual homework lies.*

We conducted this interview in his home in San Anselmo, California on August 16, 1994. The house, of Chinese/Victorian architecture, is a fitting vessel for a man who is a living bridge for the philosophies of the East and the West. The interview was punctuated with sweet silences and bubbling laughter, and took place in a magnetic field all its own. His perspective on the bends and wiggles in life's road has elicited a humor that ensures that wherever Ram Dass goes, the cosmic giggle is not far behind.

RMN

DAVID: What was it that originally inspired your interest in the evolution of human consciousness?

RAM DASS: I'm inclined to immediately respond, "Mushrooms," which I first took in March 1961, but that was just the beginning feed-in. Once my consciousness started to move into other planes, I had to start trying to understand what was happening to me. It wasn't until after I'd been around Tim Leary, Aldous Huxley, and Alan Watts that I began to reflect about issues like the evolution of consciousness.

DAVID: Was there a common denominator between what drew you to study psychology and what drew you to spiritual transformation?

RAM DASS: I am embarrassed to admit what drew me to psychology. I didn't want to go to medical school. I was getting good grades in psychology, and I was charismatic—people in the psychology department liked me. It was as low a level as that. My whole academic career came totally out of Jewish anxiety and issues surrounding achievement and adequacy. It was totally sociopolitical—it had nothing to do with intellectual content at all.

DAVID: But wasn't that period of your life also a necessary part of your evolution?

RAM DASS: Well, that's different. I was, after all, teaching Freudian theory. Human motivation was my specialty, so I thought a lot about all that stuff. That stood me in very good stead, because it's an exquisitely articulated subsystem. If you stay in that subsystem, it's very finite and not very nourishing. But when you have a metasystem, and that subsystem is within it, then it's beautiful, it's like a jewel—just like with chemistry or physics.

But when I was *in it,* it was real. When I was a Freudian, all I saw were psychosexual stages of development. As a behaviorist, all I saw were people as empty boxes.

REBECCA: You seem to be able to incorporate and apply some of the things you learned as a psychologist into this larger understanding of the human condition.

RAM DASS: Everything I learned has validity within that relative system. If somebody comes to me with a problem, they come to me living within their psychological context. I have incredible empathy for their perception of reality, partly because of what I've been through in it myself. You've got to go into the subsystem in order to be with people within it, and then create an environment for them to come out of it if they want to. That seems to me to be a model role for a therapist.

But psychology also showed me a certain kind of arrogance in Western science. Here was Western science really ignoring the essence of what human existence is about, and presenting it as if concerns about that were some kind of bad technique. When I was in psychology, we were getting correlations of 50 on personality variables, which was very good—you are accounting for 25 percent of the variance. But that means that at least 75 percent was error. It could have been anything! So it left plenty of space. At the time, we really thought we had the theory down cold, but I realize now how hungry I was in that situation.

REBECCA: To fill in that space.

RAM DASS: Yes. But I think that everything I went into, everything I was, gives me a legitimacy with people in that field. The whole game of communicating dharma is metaphor—and in a way, I can talk the metaphor of this culture.

> *The whole game of communicating dharma is metaphor...*

DAVID: Would you say, then, that someone who has demonstrated a high degree of success at playing society's games becomes a more credible spiritual voice and gains more respect?

RAM DASS: Well, it depends on whom the respect is from. There are people who respect me because I was at Harvard and Stanford, and then there are people who respect me because I *left* Harvard and Stanford, or I was thrown out of Harvard—even better. (*laughter*)

> *The little wave is the exciting one because hardly anyone is on it, and everyone thinks you're nuts.*

What's fun is that I went from being a really good guy in the society to being a bad guy then to being a good guy again. It's fascinating to play with these kinds of energies. When you're playing on the leading edge, it's like surfing. There's a big wave that pushes a little wave in front of it. The little wave is the exciting one because hardly anyone is on it, and everyone thinks you're nuts.

The meeting at Harvard where I got thrown out was extraordinary. It was a moment when I knew I had left my supply wagon far behind. I was called into the office beforehand by the heads of the department, who said, "We can't protect Tim, but we can protect you—if you shut up." Then, in the meeting, all our colleagues got up and attacked us. They attacked our research, our design, our data—everything! They saw it as defending the department against a cult that was threatening to take them over, because out of fifteen graduate students, twelve wanted to do only psychedelic research. (*laughter*)

Tim was stunned by the attack, because he had had the feeling of everything being wonderful, of loving everybody and everybody loving him. So I got up and said, "I would like to answer on our behalf." I glanced at the chairman of the department, and he gave me a look like *Well, you've made your choice.* And I had, because I realized that I could not have lived with the hypocrisy that would have been demanded of me otherwise. The feeling I'd had through the mushroom experiences was that I'd come home. It was so familiar and so right that I couldn't leave it.

But now I've become the good guy again, and I find myself riding the bigger wave. I can make a lot of money now. People love me. It's playing with a different power—but it's not as much fun as being on the little wave.

DAVID: How has your experience with psychedelics shaped your quest for higher awareness?

RAM DASS: It had no effect on me whatsoever, and nobody should use it! (*laughter*) The predicament about history is that you keep rewriting it. I'm not sure, as I look back, whether what appeared to be critical events are really as critical as I thought they were, because a lot of people took psychedelics and didn't have the reaction I had. So the reactions had something to do with everything that went *before* that moment. In a way, I just see it as another event. But I can say that taking psychedelics and meeting my guru were the two most profound experiences in my life.

Psychedelics helped me to escape—albeit momentarily—from the prison of my mind. They overrode the habit patterns of thought, and I was able to taste innocence again. Looking at sensations freshly, without a conceptual overlay, was very profound.

REBECCA: Do you think you would have gotten to that point anyway, because of the path you were following?

RAM DASS: I don't know, but the probabilities are against it. I was being rewarded so much by the society to stay in the game I was in. I had all the keys to the kingdom—a tenured professorship at Harvard, a pension plan, et cetera. When I look at my colleagues as a control group, the ones who took acid aren't in the game, the ones who didn't are. It's as simple as that.

DAVID: How did you make the transition from Dr. Richard Alpert to Ram Dass?

RAM DASS: Well, initially it was all very confusing. I was teaching a course in human motivation. I took my first psilocybin on Friday night, and on Monday morning I was lecturing on stuff that was basically lies, as far as I was concerned. So that was weird, because my whole game started to disintegrate at that point.

I was still Mr. Psychedelic Junior in relation to Tim, and publicly my gig was turning on rich people and giving lectures on the psychedelic experience. But by 1966, I looked around and saw that everybody who was using psychedelics really wasn't going anywhere. I was around the best of them, but even if they had the Eastern models, they couldn't wear them—the suits didn't fit. I realized that we just didn't know enough. We had the maps, but we couldn't read them.

So I went to India in the hope that I would meet somebody there who knew how to read the maps. I met Neem Karoli Baba, and he gave me the name Ram Dass. My experience with him created a broader context than the drugs had. The experience wasn't any greater than the drug experience, but the social context of it had entirely changed. Neem Karoli took acid and said that chemicals like it had been known about for thousands of years in the Kulu Valley, but that nobody knew how to use them any more. I said, "Should I take it again?" He said, "It will allow you to come in and have the *darshan* of Christ, but you can only stay for two hours. It would be better to become Christ than to visit him, but your medicine won't do that."

I thought that was pretty insightful. LSD showed you an analogue *of* the thing itself, but something in the way we were using it couldn't bring us *to* the thing itself.

REBECCA: Acid seems temporarily to push the neuroses out of the way, like moving through a crowd into the space of the innocence you mentioned earlier. When the drug wears off and the crowds of neuroses swarm around us again, have we really dealt with anything?

> *I have every neurosis that I ever had. I haven't gotten rid of a single one!*

RAM DASS: But the *way* the neuroses comes back is different. The way I talk about it in my lectures is to say that they go from being these huge monsters that possess you to being these little schmoes that come by for tea. (*laughter*) I have every neurosis that I ever had. I haven't gotten rid of a single one!

REBECCA: Many people experience a kind of existential guilt because they find that they can't live up to the inner potential they've seen during the psychedelic experience.

RAM DASS: I've had *all* of that! I've had all the bad trips, all the guilt and anxiety and psychosis. In my lectures I sometimes say, "I've had hundreds of drug sessions, and a lot of people think that someone who has done that is basically psychotic. I have no idea whether I'm psychotic or not, because a psychotic would be the last to know, right? All I can say is that *you* paid to hear *me*." (*laughter*)

REBECCA: Do you see Richard Alpert and Ram Dass as two separate entities, or as more like Siamese twins?

RAM DASS: I've been through different stages. There was a stage where I had to push away Richard Alpert to become Ram Dass. For a while I saw Richard Alpert as a real drag, and then later I saw him as poignant. If Ram Dass had come into Richard Alpert's office, Richard Alpert would have hospitalized him. I would have seen myself as very pathological and very disturbed.

> *If Ram Dass had come into Richard Alpert's office, Richard Alpert would have hospitalized him.*

REBECCA: What would the diagnosis have been?

RAM DASS: Oh, schizophrenia. Psychologists don't make the distinction between vertical schizophrenia and horizontal schizophrenia, and they would see a number of different identities in me.

Once Tim and I went to New York to do an all-night radio show. We split a sugar cube of acid, but it turned out that most of the acid was on my half. (*laughter*) We got to a party at Van Wolf's house, and there was a woman doing sketches of people on the living room wall. She had already done Allen Ginsberg and Tim. She asked if she could do me, and I agreed. I stood there, and I thought, *I'm a young man looking into the future.* I had to be somebody, after all. She started to sketch me. Then I got bored with that role, and I thought, *I'm really her lover.* I didn't change any facial expressions, I just thought the thought. And she started erasing what she had done. Then I thought, *I'm actually just an old wise being*, and she erased the sketch again. That happened several times, and finally she said, "I can't do your face, it's just so liquid."

I'm not yet evolved enough so that Richard Alpert and Ram Dass are one. When somebody calls me Richard I wince a little bit, because I'm still holding onto wanting to be Ram Dass. Ram Dass represents that deep place in my being. Richard Alpert never represented that to me.

> *Ram Dass represents that deep place in my being. Richard Alpert never represented that to me.*

DAVID: What is your concept of God?

RAM DASS: [*Long pause*] I think it's a word—like a finger pointing at the moon—but I don't think that what it points to is describable. It is pointing to that which is beyond form, which manifests through form. "A God defined is a God confined." I can give you thousands of poetic little descriptions. It's everything and nothing. It's all the things that the Heart Sutra talks about. It's God at play with itself. God is the One, but the fact is that the concept of the One comes from the reference point of the two, and when you're in the One, there is no one. It's zero, which equals one at that point.

REBECCA: What is your experience of God?

RAM DASS: Presence—but not a dualistic presence. The dance goes from realizing that you're separate—which is the awakening—to then trying to find your way back into the totality, of which you are not only a part but the whole. It's like holography. You *are* the whole thing, and you go through stages of approaching that understanding.

It's like my relationship with my guru. First I had the person, and then he died. Then I had the pictures and the stories, but I got bored with that. Then there was the feeling of the qualities of his being—humor, rascality, sternness. And then there was just presence. And then, finally, there was just this feeling of being. Not even the experience of a presence any longer.

That's the quality of emptiness, emptiness of even the concept of something. The Chinese Zen patriarch says, "Even to be attached to the idea of enlightenment is to go astray." It's that moment when all the dualism just keeps falling away and falling away.

REBECCA: When you talk about God it's seen as your job, so it's okay, but when others mention the "G" word, the response is usually either pity or embarrassment.

RAM DASS: Because it's been pre-empted by third-chakra power trippers. They're using God in contexts like "my God" or "the God" or "unless you believe in God . . ." or "Do you believe in God?" It's power in both directions, and it's the reductionistic nature of the way the mind works. What the word "God" means is the mystery, really. It's the mystery that we face as humans. The mystery of existence, the mystery of suffering and of death. The question is, what is your relationship with that mystery? Are you defending yourself from it? Are you making love to it? Are you living in it? These are different stages of the process.

REBECCA: How can people speak about God without getting into these sticky areas?

RAM DASS: I think the word "God" is going to have to be put to rest for a while. I'm using it less and less. I've been trying a different thing now, and I've been saying to people in my workshops, "I challenge you all within a year

> *I think the word "God" is going to have to be put to rest for a while.*

to be living on two planes of consciousness simultaneously." They ask, "Which two?" I say, "Any two." (*laughter*) That's not talking about spirit, it's not talking about God, but it's doing exactly the same thing—it's shifting paradigm and context.

DAVID: Your guru was an extremely significant figure in your life. Could you describe what you have carried with you as a result of your relationship with him?

RAM DASS: He is the most important separate consciousness in my life, even though he died in 1973. He's more real than anybody else I deal with. It's like having an imaginary playmate who is so hip and so wise and so cool and so empty and so doesn't-give-a-fuck and so loving and so compassionate—so any-way-you-can-go. It's such fun. He is the closest I've ever come to finding unconditional love.

But it's not him—he's just the form of it. Once Maharajji was warning this girl away from this somewhat dubious guy she had met. She said, "He's only my friend," and Maharajji replied, "Your only friend is God." I really heard that. Your only friend is the reflection of the mystery in each form. And that's what you want to be friends with—not with the story line.

REBECCA: Do you feel that as time goes on you're coming even closer to him?

RAM DASS: Yeah. When I think of who he was—this giant of a being—the idea that I could *be* him is such chutzpah that I can't even entertain it in my mind. But I see that, as fast as I can, I'm *dying into him.*

REBECCA: A lot of Westerners have a hard time understanding the guru/devotee relationship. Could you describe this relationship as you understand it?

RAM DASS: Ramana Maharshi said, "God, Guru, and Self are one and the same thing." The real guru is not busy being somebody. If you asked Maharajji if he was a guru, he would say, "I don't know anything. God

> *The guru is a doorframe. You don't worship the doorframe—you're trying to go through the door.*

knows everything." The guru is a doorframe. You don't worship the doorframe—you're trying to go through the door. It's like that saying "If you meet the Buddha on the road, slay him."

You don't owe the guru anything but your own liberation, because that's the only way you come into the guru. What the guru does, as far as I can see, is to mirror for you where you aren't. The guru shows you all your neuroses writ large, because there's nothing you can project into the guru. You keep trying to make him into somebody like you, but he isn't because he doesn't want anything—and you still want something.

Understanding can come through books or on the astral plane—it doesn't have to come through a physical guru. But once you've tasted this stuff, you can get very attached to your method of getting there. For example, many people who get closest to God through sex get very addicted to sex. They get attached to the method rather than to what the method is for.

The guru is just another method, and like all methods it's a trap. But you have to get trapped for a method to work, and then you just hope it ejects. If the guru isn't pure, he won't let you eject, he won't let you go. You'll know in your intuitive heart that you're being had, but you might not want to admit it.

REBECCA: Again, there's that Western suspicion because of the history of power-tripping gurus.

RAM DASS: Right. But true gurus don't want any worldly power—it's a joke to them.

REBECCA: Did you find yourself testing your guru a lot in the beginning?

> *... the guy ... was on his face touching Maharajji's feet ... I'm thinking, "I'm not going to do that."*

RAM DASS: He so overwhelmed me with his first gambit that there wasn't any way that I could test him anymore. He just did it to me so thoroughly that there couldn't be a question. He could have gone in there with a shovel, but he went in with a bulldozer! (*laughter*)

The first time I saw him, I was coming up a hillside and I saw him sitting under a tree with eight or ten devotees around him. I was hanging back, standing at a distance, but the guy who'd accompanied me was on his face touching Maharajji's feet, while I was thinking, "I'm *not* going to do that."

Neem Karoli Baba looked up at me and said, "You came in a big car?" We had come in a friend's LandRover, which we'd borrowed. I said, "Yes." Then Maharajji said, "You will give it to me?" Now, I had been hustled before, but never like this! I was speechless. The guy I was with looked up and said, "If you want it Maharajji, it's yours." I protested and said, "You can't give David's car away!" I was aware of everybody laughing at me, but I was very serious. (*laughter*)

Then Neem Karoli said, "Take them away and feed them." So we were taken down to the temple and given lunch. Then Maharajji called me back up, and he told me to sit down. He looked at me and said, "You were out under the stars last night. You were

> *. . . he opened his eyes and looked at me, and in English he said, "Spleen."*

thinking about your mother." It was true, but I hadn't told anyone about it. My mind started to get agitated, and I started to entertain hypotheses as to how he could have known that. Then he said, "She died last year." My sense of dis-ease kept growing. Maharajji said, "She got very big in the belly before she died." My mother had died of an enlarged spleen. And then he closed his eyes, and he rocked back and forth, and he opened his eyes and looked at me, and in English he said, "Spleen."

When he said that, my mind couldn't handle it. I just gave up. Something shifted, and I started to feel a wrenching pain in my chest. I felt like a door that had long been closed was being violently forced open. I started to cry, and I cried for two days. And after that, all I wanted to do was touch his feet.

Through that encounter I had recognized that not only was Maharajji inside my head, but that everything I was, he loved. There was not a part of me that he didn't know, and still he loved me. So all my models of myself—"If they only knew that little thought, which I don't even admit to myself, they wouldn't love me"—didn't apply.

Now this wasn't an intellectual process. It was a direct experience of that quality of unconditional love. It took that long [*snaps his fingers*], and all the rest of it was basically irrelevant. I cherish everything that came after, and I got all kinds of teachings, but the thing happened at that moment. He didn't *do* anything, he just *was* it. He was an environment where my ripeness to open had a chance to express itself.

REBECCA: Did you get a lot of flack from your peers and friends when you came back from India to the United States?

RAM DASS: Well, I came back wearing a dress, I was barefoot, I had long hair, a long beard, and beads. I wouldn't have noticed flack if it had hit me in the face! (*laughter*)

DAVID: What was Timothy Leary's reaction?

RAM DASS: I don't remember precisely. Tim and I weren't very close during that period of time. He had been to India just a few years before I had, so he understood the context from which I was speaking. When we started to come back together again, we had by then gone in such different directions that there were certain topics that we kind of agreed not to deal with.

Tim is a bit of a mystery to me. He seemed fascinated by the conceptual play around the psychedelic experience, while I was much more drawn toward dying into emptiness. But then I didn't have a vested interest in being an intellectual or a scholar. Tim comes out of conceptual space, obviously—you only have to read *Psychedelic Prayers* to see that. But the venue that he wants to hang out in is the conceptual mind. That isn't my domain.

Kalu Rinpoche, who was an incredible Tibetan lama, said, "Ram Dass, you have three things to do in this life—honor your guru, deepen your emptiness, and deepen your compassion." And that's just what it feels like to me. I live a lot with mystery. Tim sees mystery as a challenge. I see it as a delightful place to play. So when somebody tells me they have just solved a mystery, I am only passingly interested.

REBECCA: That's a classic East-West dynamic.

RAM DASS: Very much so. I spent many years being very defensive about the fact that I was not schooled in Western metaphysics and philosophy, but that left a blank slate on which I could write when I went to the East. Then I came back, and I could view Western philosophy from that perspective.

I see this role of mediating between the East and West as a delicious dance. I went Western, and then I pushed West away to embrace East. I came back afraid of the West, and then slowly over the years I stuck my toe in again. I shaved the beard, put on the pants, got the credit card and the MG and a house in Marin, and—Oh my God. What happened? (*laughter*)

It's like being in the world and not of it. It has to come to a point where it's not scaring you or trapping you. It's empty form.

REBECCA: You've compared the process of persistent self-analysis to playing with one's feces. Where do you think self-analysis can take us, and what are its limitations?

RAM DASS: It depends on your intention in having fecal play. It can be done as a practice of mindfulness—in order to find a place of witnessing and seeing it for what it is. Then there is being locked in the drama, when self-analysis is just a way of exacerbating the drama and making your identity in the story line more real.

Unfortunately, this characterizes most of the dialogue between therapists and patients. Everybody is so caught in the stuff that they are just reinforcing caughtness, even as they are trying to get you out of it. It's like rearranging furniture in the prison cell rather than trying to get out of prison.

> *It's like rearranging furniture in the prison cell rather than trying to get out of prison.*

But as an exercise in mindfulness, self-analysis can be very useful. It can help you to deal with the phenomena of your life as they arise. You notice them, and the noticing gets stronger and stronger until you're not going into them so much. That's a stage, too, because you're still distant from the phenomena, so then you have to come back in until you're in them and not in them at the same moment.

I think the fallacy is that if you're standing in one place, you can't be standing somewhere else. I think that freedom is being conscious on all levels simultaneously. Freedom is not standing anywhere. You have no perspective, and then you just adopt a perspective for the functional situation. The situation brings you into perspective at that moment, but you're not resting in perspective. Is that clear?

DAVID: Yes . . . it's just difficult to do.

RAM DASS: Well, as long as you think you're doing it, that's a place. (*laughter*) That was the beauty of Trungpa Rinpoche, a wonderful Tibetan lama. He sat down with me once and said, "I want to show you a new form of meditation. Let's do it together." We sat facing one another, and after a while he said, "Ram Dass, are you trying?" I said, "Yes, I'm trying," and he said, "Don't try—just do it."

REBECCA: You speak about operating from the point of view of God's instrument, but isn't there a risk of becoming self-righteous with that perspective and thinking, "Well, I'm an instrument of God and God is never wrong, therefore I am never wrong," and losing the self-consciousness required to keep one's ego in check?

RAM DASS: I think that if your intention is freedom, then you may get caught in that, but you won't *stay* in it. You'll get caught in "I represent the Godfather, so don't screw around with me," and then you'll see that that's a horrible place to be standing. That's ego.

The mechanism that corrects you is not even the grossness of that conceptual understanding. It's almost a vibratory thing. You feel a thickness or a heaviness, and you just know that you're caught. You don't even know how you're caught. You don't know whether it's lust or anger or fear, and you don't even give a damn which one it is. You just start your mechanisms for remembering, for bringing your consciousness out of sticking in one place. You can be stuck anywhere, even in "I am God" or "I am empty."

I've lost it thousands of times, so what I've done is to surround myself as best I can with people who bust me. Because when I get caught, I can get very resistant to admitting that I'm caught.

REBECCA: What is karma?

RAM DASS: Karma is another way of saying that everything in the universe is related to everything else in the universe in a lawful way—future, past, and present. A limited interpretation of karma has to do with looking from the past to the future, but actually it's all interrelated. You just feel the unfolding of the process of interaction leading to a certain moment.

If you chart it, you can plot it somewhat and see that this came from there in a series of causes and effects. But actually it's not linear at all. You're already enlightened, so you're actually going from where you started back to where you started. You're nowhere because nothing happened, and in that moment when you realize it . . . Aaaargh! (*laughter*)

> *They say that when a being becomes free, all that is left in form is old karma running off.*

They say that when a being becomes free, all that is left in form is old karma running off. When you act with intentionality, when there is an actor with intention, it's like dropping a pebble in a pond. It creates waves. It's an action. When you are no longer identified with that which has motives—

they are there, but you're not identified with them, you're just awareness—
then you're not creating new karma. And when the old karma runs off—
you aren't. That's what a being is who's finished. You run out of karma.

In other words, in the course of things, with everything interacting
with everything else, "you" just ceases to exist as a separate thing. It's still
everything, because you were everything already. Nothing happened to *you*,
if there is a you. (*laughter*)

REBECCA: The concept of personal karma is becoming more and more
popular, but it's often seen as a justification for nonintervention in the sense
of "I have my karma and that homeless person asking me for a quarter has
his karma, and who am I to intervene with anybody else's karma?"

RAM DASS: His karma is that you have that karma. Your karma is not
intervening. He stays hungry, so that's his karma. Everybody is everybody
else's karma. The fact that you saw the homeless person is part of your
karma, and it's having an effect on you all the time. You are my karma and
I am yours at this moment.

It's so profoundly subtle, because who I see you to be is a projection of
my karma. The way karma manifests is in desire systems. If I don't have
any attachments at all, what I see is entirely different. To see symmetry, to
see familiarity, to see warmth in you—that's all stuff I'm doing with my
mind. Who you *really* are, I have no idea—until I have no karma.

DAVID: It sounds as if it's all so organized that there is little room for free
will.

RAM DASS: I've been grappling with the concept of free will for a long
time, and this is what I've come up with: to the extent that we are in form—
and that includes thought—we have no freedom, because of the nature of
karma, of everything being lawfully related to everything else. So then,
when somebody says "free choice," does that mean anything? Who has
choice?

I can *think* I have choice. I can say, "I've decided to go to the movies
tonight." But if you knew enough about me, and if you could handle a
multivariable approach, you could predict that I would say that. Or if you
knew enough about my gene structure and the shape of my hands and my
father's behavior, you could predict my position in the chair at this moment. So where, then, is the free will? The fact is, only when you aren't
anybody do you have free will.

REBECCA: So you're saying that you only really have free will when you've released the *desire* to have free will.

RAM DASS: Right. When you want something, you see only the manifestation of the outward container. God is free, or the formless is free, or nondualism is free. Awareness has no form, and so you, as awareness, are basically free. But every way awareness manifests through form is itself within law.

One of the things I got from Maharajji was a sense of his seeing the universe as law unfolding. There was nothing personal about it, it was just stuff happening. And he was offering to meet me behind the stuff, where we *are* free. I couldn't handle the fact that he understood the nature of suffering, but I learned that the line that goes, "Out of emptiness arises compassion" has the mystery right in it. You'd better be empty of intention and desire. The *Tao te Ching* says "Truth waits for eyes unclouded by longing."

DAVID: So are you saying that being embodied in form means that everything is predetermined?

RAM DASS: No, it's not predetermination. Everything is related to the future and the past. What's "pre"?

REBECCA: Be here now. (*laughter*)

> *Mostly I'm watching my life to see how it came out, rather than imagining I'm deciding what to do about it.*

RAM DASS: (*laughter*) When somebody says to me, "Don't I have free will?" I say, "It depends on who the 'I' is. Most likely if you think you're somebody who could have free will, then you don't." You *are* free will, but you don't *have* free will. So if I think, "I'm facing a choice," I always know I'm standing in the wrong place. Mostly I'm watching my life to see how it came out, rather than imagining I'm deciding what to do about it.

REBECCA: Isn't there *some* creative quality? Aren't you given a riff on which you can then improvise?

RAM DASS: Yeah, but the improvisation isn't really creative. It's creativity the way we think about it, because it's a surprise to us, but it's still lawful.

DAVID: Could you share with us the experience you had swimming with John Lilly's dolphins?

RAM DASS: I went with a friend to MarineWorld in Redwood City, because I had been invited by John and Toni Lilly to swim with Joe and Rosie, two dolphins who were living there. It was a cold, grey day. I stood on the edge of the tank and I thought, "I'm too old for this. I don't want to swim with the dolphins anyway!" (*laughter*) The problem was that everyone was standing around watching to see what Ram Dass would do with the dolphins. It was a real drag.

So I got into the water, and as the dolphins came swimming by me, I realized that they were much bigger than I'd thought they would be, and I could *feel* their power. Then one of them, Rosie, began just hovering right next to me, so I reached out to touch her. Now in my model, if it's got a tail, it's a fish, and when you touch fish, they go away. But she didn't go away. So I gently ran my hand down her back. It was the silkiest thing I had ever touched—it was like water with form. A thrill went through me. Still she didn't move.

Suddenly I realized that she had opened to the contact. The recognition that her consciousness was right there, allowing me to touch her, did the same thing to me as Maharajji's "spleen." (Of course, my mind is much more blowable by this time. I'm ready to remember.) Up until then I'd been thinking, "What am I supposed to do with the dolphins?" But while I was touching her, I gave up and my heart just opened.

When that happened, she flipped until she was upright in the water in front of me. My heart was so open that I leaned forward and kissed her on the mouth. Instead of pulling back, she started insinuating her body into mine. I was going into ecstasy. I was saying, "Oh Rosie. Oh Rosie!" (*laughter*) And I started to get an erection. Then the

> *. . . I started to get an erection. Then the thought occurred to me, "Is this legal?"*

thought occurred to me, "Is this legal?" And all the time I'm smiling, and everyone is watching to see what Ram Dass is doing with the dolphins.

Then she swam around and came in under my arm, and I thought I'd really like to swim with her. I grabbed her dorsal fin, and she went down and my hand slipped off the fin, but she came back up and I grabbed it again. I didn't want to grab it too hard because I didn't want to hurt her. She went down and my hand slipped off again. She kept coming back under my arm, so I thought, "What I really want to do is to hold her underneath the stomach." So I reached around and held her that way.

We started to go on this wild swim all through the tank. It was just incredible! But then I got to the point where my breath started to give out, and I thought, "Rosie, this is lovely, but I'm one of the those *other* creatures!" And with that thought, she immediately came to the surface while I got a breath, and then back down we went. This went on several times.

Once, we came up and people were taking photographs. I got to hamming for the camera, and I forgot to take a breath before Rosie submerged. I thought, "This is where we part company, Rosie," and she came right back up so I could get air. Finally, I started to get so cold that I was blue and shaking. She pulled away from me and went and got Joe, and they both nosed me over to the platform and out of the tank.

DAVID: That's wonderful. While we're on the subject of interspecies communication, I'm curious—have you ever had an experience that you would label an extraterrestrial contact?

RAM DASS: No. I assume there are lots of beings on every plane all around the place, but I myself have not had experiences of that kind. By extraterrestrial, do you mean beings on the physical plane? Like other beings in the solar system?

DAVID: Not necessarily. A lot of people have used the term extraterrestrial in the context of a psychedelic experience where they've encountered entities that they feel have evolved from somewhere else, either from another planet or another plane.

RAM DASS: I've met many beings on other planes, but I don't call them extraterrestrial. Maharajji is not on this plane anymore, but he's there. He's present as a separate entity, and the form I see him in is the form my mind projects into him.

> *I asked him what I should tell people about dying, and he said, "Tell them it's absolutely safe."*

I've written prefaces for two volumes of the books of Emmanuel. Emmanuel speaks through a woman named Pat Rodegast, and he is an absolutely delightful spook. I know Pat very well, and I know Emmanuel quite well now. I asked him what I should tell people about dying, and he said, "Tell them it's absolutely safe." What a superb one-liner. He also said, "Death is like taking off a tight shoe." He's just like this friendly, wise uncle.

In the preface, I say that I don't know whether this is vertical schizophrenia or whether it's a separate entity, and I don't really care. I'm *experiencing* it as a separate entity. But my criterion is whether I can use the material, not whether it's real or not.

REBECCA: How do you act or feel differently when you are in the presence of a dying person?

RAM DASS: Well, theoretically I don't act differently, because we're all dying. Basically, human relations boil down to creating an environment in which other people can manifest as they would. That's what love is. You're in love with the universe, and you want it to do what it needs to do. You're creating the environment that is least limiting.

So my job isn't to have somebody die my philosophical or metaphysical death; my job is to create a space of listening and quietness and presence, a space with no boundaries. My job is not to deny their experience out of my fear, as a way of distancing myself through being kind and helpful or whatever, because that traps them in objectivity. There is only one awareness, in which some of it is dying and some of it is visiting the part of it that's dying. To me, then, seeing the one awareness frees both of us immensely, and it frees them of being busy dying. If they're ready to let go of dying, then it's really great fun. It's *Woooooow!* It's *Ooooooooh!* (*laughter*) But if they're busy dying, it's none of my business to change them. I'm not going to say, "Come on, you know you're not really dying." I have no moral right to do that.

> *There is only one awareness, in which some of it is dying and some of it is visiting the part of it that's dying.*

REBECCA: The ability to create that space in yourself must have taken some practice.

RAM DASS: What happens is, whenever there is desire there is clinging in you. Situations that awaken the clinging are the ones that are really fruitful. Certainly dealing with death is the most clinging situation that humans have to deal with.

So I'm attached to working with dying people, because it's the closest I can get to one of my deepest clingings. I can watch my heart open and close, and I can stay mindful in it. I can also see how there is a certain cosmic giggle about the whole thing. But that's just so socially unacceptable, even to me.

DAVID: Can you describe one of the most profound experiences you've had working with a dying person?

RAM DASS: The most profound awakening I've had recently happened two years ago, while working with a woman who was dying of AIDS. I just fell into love with her, the way I've been talking about. That's what it is— it's being in love with somebody, in the sense of no boundary and no model of how they should be. I could open myself, and being that open, you experience what they experience.

I watched how I stayed open, right until she couldn't breathe any more and was dying from asphyxiation. At that moment, I watched my awareness disengage itself. I couldn't die with her. I couldn't love her *through* death, I could only love her *to* death. That's an interesting moment for me, to see where the automatic defense locks in and I get pushed back into my separateness, because that's the moment where I'm not with her.

REBECCA: How could you have gone further?

RAM DASS: If I were not caught, then whatever was catching her would have been totally in her. I wouldn't have been perpetuating it, so she could have let it go faster.

> *You're constantly saying, "Are you in there? What's it like being you this time?"*

I meet people, and they think they're real. My job is not to deny that reality, but to hold a context in which that is not the only reality. So I'm always here in case they want to let go of that one. I don't demand that they let go of it, but if they would like to, I'm here. If you're a Christian, you can speak about focusing on the soul as well as on the manifestation. You're constantly saying, "Are you in there? What's it like being you this time?"

REBECCA: How does one help a person in the dying process?

RAM DASS: By working on yourself to keep unencumbered by clingings of mind, so you stay in compassion. That's independent of whether you give them water and plump their pillows and hold them and all that stuff. The question is, where do you do it *from?* That's more interesting.

We're not dealing with the issue of *whether* you do an act—if somebody is thirsty, you give them water, naturally. The issue is *how* you do it. In order not to create suffering, you can only work on yourself. That's the gift you give. The process of working with people as they're dying is an exercise on yourself, to keep you in love and to keep you watching when you fall out of love from moment to moment.

REBECCA: It must be a challenge to maintain that kind of openness when the person dying is expressing bitterness or anger.

RAM DASS: There can be anything. There can be sweet happiness that's phony, there can be pain and struggle. But all you can do is to create the space where they can do what they need to do. They might come on with their whole trip of "This is terrible," but there's nothing they get out of you. Sometimes they come on strong, but then they see that nothing has happened in you.

I remember a woman coming to see me and telling me a sad story about being a seamstress and having a child and how her child is now forging checks. And I listened very carefully, and at the end I said, "I hear you." That didn't satisfy her, and she went through the whole story again. She was used to using that story, like the ancient mariner, to elicit sympathy. But I just said again, "I hear you." And the second time I said it, this smile crossed her face and she said, "You know, I was a bit of a rascal at that age, too." She had come up for air.

REBECCA: So you offer someone another option to the drama.

RAM DASS: Yes. You make another option available, but you don't try to get them into it. The minute you try to change somebody, you play into the unconscious paranoia that is in everybody. And when people feel manipulated, they push against you, and that isolates them even more.

> *The minute you try to change somebody, you play into the unconscious paranoia . . .*

REBECCA: What is your position on euthanasia?

RAM DASS: A human birth is an incredible vehicle for working on yourself, and you should milk it for as much as you can get out of it. But if you've had enough and you can't cut it, then you should certainly have the "choice" of ending it. Even though it's not really a choice—your karma just ran out for that round.

I have nothing against that. You just go on from that point instead of from another point. I can't see that there's any rush. It's a circle. Where's everybody going anyway? (*laughter*)

REBECCA: So you don't see some heavy karmic consequences from bailing?

RAM DASS: If somebody asks me, "Should I?" I say, "Well, I wouldn't." But I don't know. I might if I got into a certain situation.

DAVID: What do you believe happens to consciousness after the death of the body?

RAM DASS: I think it's a function of the level of evolution of the individual psychic DNA code or whatever. I think that if you have finished your work and you're just awareness that happens to be in a body, when the body ends, it's like selling your Ford. It's no big deal.

Then the question is, what of you is left after that? If you're fully enlightened, nothing of you is left, because nothing was there before. If there's something before, there will probably be something after, and it will project onward.

I can imagine beings who are so dense and so caught in life that when they die, there is no place in their awareness where they can conceive of the fact that they're dead. The word "conceive" in this context is strange, because they have no brain, so it really raises questions about who is thinking this. But I think that identifying the brain with thought is a mistake. I think that the brain is a way of manifesting thought, but I don't think it is a totally isomorphic thing. So I suspect that some beings go unconscious, go into what Christians call purgatory. They go to sleep during the process before they project into the next form.

I think others are aware of what they are going through, but are still caught. All the bardos in the *Tibetan Book of the Dead* are about how to avoid getting caught. Those beings are awake enough to be collaborators in the appreciation of the gestalt in which their incarnations are flowing. They sort of see where they're coming from and where they're going. They are part of the design of things. So when you ask yourself, "Did you choose to incarnate?" at the level at which you are free, you did choose. At the level at which you are not, you didn't.

Then there are beings who are very free though they may still have separateness. They may have taken the bodhisattva vow, which says, "I agree to not give up separateness until everybody is free," and they're left with only that thought. They don't have anything else. Then the next incarnation will be out of that intention to save all beings; that one bit of personal karma is what keeps it moving.

To me, since nothing happened anyway, it's all an illusion—reincarnation and everything. But within the relative reality, I think it's quite real.

REBECCA: It's interesting how in Buddhism you learn about the general definition of reincarnation, and then as you go up the lineage, this definition becomes increasingly relative.

RAM DASS: Right. You're the Buddha *already*—you're just in drag. And then you wake up and realize you've been had by your own mind.

> *You're the Buddha already—you're just in drag.*

REBECCA: One of the things that comes up time and time again in your writings is that when people are involved in service, they do a lot better when they can operate from a position of full acceptance of the other's condition, whether that person is a drug addict, a mass murderer, a horribly maimed patient, or whatever, and not operate from the desire to *change* the behavior or conditions. Can you elaborate on this, as many people would say that the purpose of service *is* to change certain behaviors and conditions that are perceived as harming another?

RAM DASS: The purpose of service is to relieve suffering. Now, the question is, what is the nature of suffering? Maybe if the person is thirsty, the purpose of service is to give a glass of water. God comes to the hungry in the form of food.

REBECCA: What if they're dying of thirst and they say they don't *want* a glass of water? Do you think that a person is ever justified in assuming control of another's welfare?

RAM DASS: I think that if you're dealing with very young children, where you are responsible for their biological survival, then you have some grounds for having a preference that is different from theirs. But if you're deciding what is best for somebody else when you're dealing with an adult consciousness—therein lies the tyrannical state.

DAVID: But you may still be relieving suffering, even if your efforts aren't appreciated.

RAM DASS: I had a lot of friends who were sent to mental hospitals instead of universities. Most people would think that was too bad, but I found they came out with more cylinders functioning than did many people who went to university.

I don't know how it's going to come out. I see people suffering so intensely in their dying. They've had big egos all their lives, and then the suffering and pain finally wore them down until they just gave up. And at the moment they gave up, it's like a window opened and there they were in their full spiritual splendor. Now, do I say that the suffering stank? It was terrible, and I would have taken it away from them in a minute if I could. My human heart doesn't want them to suffer, but when I look at it I say, "Boy, the game is more interesting than I thought it was." That's why I include suffering as part of the mystery.

You and I can only meet through roles. So let's say you come to me and I'm your therapist. You came to me to change you, and my job is to relieve the suffering that brought you there. Part of my job is to help you see the forms of your pathology, but the deeper suffering, as I understand it, is in your separateness, your isolation. Therefore, what I can offer you is my being and my presence. That's the *real* gift. You and I may come together through the form of therapist and client, but we can meet as two beings who are just dancing into love through the form of those roles.

Somebody might ask me if they should go to therapy, and I would say, "Yes, but try to find a therapist who doesn't think they're a therapist." If they think they're a therapist, they have an agenda, and they are caught in their mind, which treats you as an object to be manipulated for your own good.

REBECCA: You talk about how suffering can awaken us more than pleasure can. But I'm wondering about ecstasy. The ecstatic experience of God seems to be able to link up with that compassionate acknowledgment of suffering in the same way that suffering is able to lead us back to the ecstatic experience. In your view, is ecstasy as valid a path to God as suffering is?

RAM DASS: I'd much rather use the ecstatic path. I'm no fool! (*laughter*) I guess the thing is that ecstasy is easy for the ego to socialize, while suffering has an effect kind of, like, dripping water on stone. It eats your ego away.

Suffering confronts you with where you are holding. It shows you your stash, the attachments you have been hiding from yourself. If you had no attachments, you wouldn't be suffering. When you are suffering, you say, "Why am I suffering?" I'm suffering because

> *Suffering confronts you with where you are holding. It shows you your stash . . .*

I'm holding onto a model of how it should be other than the way it is. Pain is a strong stimulus, and the model you have of what pain is has a lot to do with how you cope with it and whether or not you can open to it being a part of you, rather than trying to isolate it. One of the things about pain is that you tend to try to make it separate from yourself.

The art is to be mindful of it and yet fully with it. It's the pushing against something that gets you into trouble—pushing against aging, pushing against the weather. But that doesn't mean that you shouldn't be an activist and push against things. It doesn't mean that you don't have opinions. It means that you're not *attached* to your opinions. As Don Juan said, you huff and puff and make believe it's real, even though you know it isn't.

REBECCA: How, then, do you think we can avoid the kind of polarization that we see in the abortion issue, for example, where both sides seem beyond the point of being able to communicate with one another.

RAM DASS: If I were in a position to have some say, I would bring some of the leaders from each group together for a retreat where I would invite them just to listen to each other. You not only have to hear the other people, but they have to *feel* that they have been heard. If I feel you've heard me, then you and I can start a dialogue. But if I don't feel that you've heard me, then I'm in opposition to you.

The question is, how do we create a meta-identity? We all think life is beautiful. We all think that life is sacred. It's not sacred versus profane. It's not people of ill will on either side. Everyone is trying to be as true to the light as they can.

Engaging everybody in the meta-game is a tricky one. You want to help them break their *identification* with their position. They're not giving up their position, but their primary identification can shift from being an abortionist or an anti-abortionist to being a

> *If everybody lays their cards on the table, the game is possible.*

human being who has an opinion about abortion. That's a different place. Then everyone can sit around as human beings and say, "What do we do about this?" If everybody lays their cards on the table, the game is possible.

REBECCA: So you're talking about developing a respect for the other, even if that other doesn't agree with you.

RAM DASS: Yeah. It's like in politics. Everybody is using external symbols to show they're doing that, respecting the other and trying to understand the other, but they're *not* doing it. All alignment has been pre-empted in the service of third-chakra ego power. It's inevitable, I guess.

REBECCA: You talk about learning to use all life experiences, whether good or bad, as grist for the mill and potential for spiritual growth. And I think about the people in Rwanda and what they went through, the disease and the famine and the apparent meaninglessness of it all, and I wonder what kind of spiritual growth they achieved, or had even the possibility of achieving, from that.

RAM DASS: [*Long pause*] That's the mystery. That's the mystery of suffering. If you could stand back far enough to see the whole trip, it might look quite different. Say you have freeze-frame photography and my arm is moving from pointing downward to pointing straight up in the air. If the middle frames are missing, you see one thing and then another, with no apparent connection between them. You're seeing the horror that is Rwanda, but you're missing out on witnessing the beauty.

I would sit in front of Maharajji, and I felt that he had a deck of cards of all my reincarnations. I could sense that he saw my incarnations in a context that I couldn't see. It all seemed terribly real to me. If you look back at the events of your life, you'll notice that when you were in them you didn't see the context. I look back at my miserable times and realize how profoundly they helped me in where I am now.

REBECCA: So if you see suffering in the context of a continuum, then it becomes easier to understand.

RAM DASS: It all has to do with your time frame. For the people in Rwanda, it's hell. None of this means that you don't do what you can to relieve suffering. You do what your heart calls you to do. Saying that it's all karma isn't a justification for nonaction. That is a confusion of levels of consciousness. On the level of the human heart, you do what you can to relieve another's suffering. But on another level, it's all karma.

REBECCA: How do you move within your meditation space so that you stop getting trapped in the now-I'm-meditating-now-I'm-not syndrome, so the high can keep leaking into your life?

RAM DASS: You give up *not* meditating. It's called meditation in action. There's no way out of that. Meditation means to be constantly extricating yourself from the clinging of mind.

REBECCA: So it becomes part of the fabric of your life, rather than another thing on your list to do, like the laundry or something?

RAM DASS: That's right. People ask me, "How much meditation practice do you do?" Sometimes I say none, and they give me a worried look. (*laughter*) But the other answer is, all the time! I don't do anything else *but* meditate.

DAVID: What are some of the current projects that you are working on?

RAM DASS: There are several on the burner. I've just accepted a contract to do a book on aging, which will allow me to take about two years off to write. I'm hoping to understand the dysfunctional mythology around aging—aesthetically, cross-culturally, and spiritually.

I'm also on the board of a group called Social Venture Network. Out of that core group, we've started three organizations in the past year. We've started Businesses for Social Responsibility, we've started Students for Responsible Business, and we've started a European SVN. We have two conferences a year, and there are some five hundred people involved, including Ben and Jerry's and the Body Shop. It's about exploring the relationship between spirit and business. Working with dying people is dealing with my issues about death, and working with business people is dealing with my issues about money and power.

For fifteen years I've been doing major fundraising work for SEVA, which has been involved in relieving blindness in India and Nepal. I have one project I work with in South India. The hospital there has been given 1.25 million dollars by Lions International to set up an international community ophthalmology institute to train people to carry ophthalmology programs into Indonesia and Africa. But I'm phasing down a lot of the service stuff, because I really don't think I can carry it all at once.

I have to listen—we all have to—to hear how we honor all the different levels of the games we are in. I'm a member of a family, I'm a member of a nation-state, I'm a member of a community. I have a sexual identity, I have an age identity, I have a religious identity. It's important to feel how your incarnation takes form through these identities and to ask yourself, "What does it mean to live with integrity within each of those systems?" That's something I have had to learn, because I used to be busy seeing the spiritual journey as something that you did by yourself.

REBECCA: You've said that everyone should try to work from the edges of their experience. What did you mean by that?

RAM DASS: As chaos increases—and there's a lot of inertia in the system that seems to suggest that chaos is the direction in which we're going—it behooves us to prepare ourselves to ride with the changes. If, in the face of uncertainty, people are busy holding onto something, the fear increases, then the contraction increases, and prejudice increases. The question is, what are you adding to the system to shift the balance? What you're adding is yourself, and what yourself has to be is somebody who can handle uncertainty and chaos without contracting.

> *I've gotten over the feeling of being somebody special.*

I've gotten over the feeling of being somebody special. You've come with a camera and tape recorders, but that's your trip, not mine. I really experience the web of interconnectedness of all beings. It's like C. S. Lewis's line, "You don't see the center because it's all center."

REBECCA: There are so many people who spend all their time dreaming about being somebody special.

RAM DASS: And the horror is to see people who thought that that would be something, and then got it. Then you see them trying to hold onto it, and they know it's empty. I've been in a hall with thousands of people applauding and bringing flowers and loving me, and then gone to the hotel alone, feeling the absolute wretchedness of all of that.

DAVID: Could you sum up the basic message of your life?

RAM DASS: [*Long pause*] I would say that the thrust of my life was initially to get free, and that I then came to realize that my freedom is not independent of everybody else. So now I see it as a circle in which I help people as I work on myself, and I work on myself to help people.

> *. . . I help people as I work on myself, and I work on myself to help people.*

I've been perfecting that circle for thirty years now. It's karma yoga. It's the bodhisattva vow. My life is about applied dharma. Once the faith and connection and emptiness are strong enough, then I experience looking around for the fields I can play in.

I work with AIDS, with business, with government, with teenagers, with people dying of cancer, with blindness. It doesn't matter, because your agenda is always the same. Do what you can on this plane to relieve suffering by constantly working on yourself to be an instrument for the cessation of suffering. To me, that's what the emerging game is all about.

Bibliography

Marija Gimbutas

Die Bestattung in Litauen in der vor eschichtlichen Zeit, J. C. B. Mohr Verlag (Tubingen), 1946.

The Prehistory of Eastern Europe, Harvard University, 1956.

Ancient Symbolism in Lithuanian Folk Art, American Folklore Society, 1958.

Rytprusiu ir Vakaru Lietuvos priesistorines kulturos apavalga (A Survey of Prehistory in Prussia and Western Lithuania), New York: Studia Lithuanica, 1958.

The Bats, Praeger, 1963.

Bronze Age Cultures in Central and Eastern Europe, Mouton, 1965.

I Baltici, II Saggiatore, 1967.

The Slavs, Praeger, 1971.

The Goddesses and Gods of Old Europe, 6500-3500 BC, University of California Press, 1974.

Obre, Neolithic Sites in Bosnia (editor), Heft. A. Archaeologie, 1974.

Neolithic Macedonia: As Reflected by Excavation at Anza, Southeast Yugoslavia (editor), UCLA Institute of Archaeology, 1976.

Die Balten. Volk in Ostseeraum, Herbig (Munich), 1983.

Baltai priesistoriniais laikais. Etnogeneze, materialine kultura ir mitologija, Mokslas (Vilnius), 1985.

Excavations at Sitagroi: A Prehistoric Village in Northeast Greece, vol. I (editor with C. Renfrew and E. Eister), UCLA Institute of Archaeology, 1986.

The Language of the Goddess, Harper San Francisco, 1989.

Civilizatie si cultura. Vestigii prehistorice in sudestul European, Editura Meridiane (Bucharest), 1989.

Achilleion. A Neolithic Settlement in Thessaly, Greece: 6400-5600 BC, UCLA Institute of Archaeology, 1989.

The Civilization of the Goddess: The World of Old Europe, Harper SF, 1991.

Die Balten. Urgeschichte eines Volkes im Ostseeraum, Ulistein Verlag (Frankfurt), 1991.

Os Baltas, Frederich A. Praeger (Rio de Janeiro), 1991.

Dios y Dioses de la Veija Europa 7000-3500 AC: Mitos, leyendas e imagineria, Colegio Universitario de Ediciones lstmo (Madrid), 1992.

Annie Sprinkle

Annie Sprinkle: Post Porn Modernist, Art Unlimited, NYC, 1991.

Films

Deep Inside Annie Sprinkle, Dispripix, 1982.

Consenting Adults, Dispripix, 1984.

My Father Is Coming (by Monika Treut), Hyena Films, 1991.

Female Misbehavior, (by Monika Treut), Hyena Films, 1992.

Sacred Sex, Triple Image Film, 1992.

Real Sex 2 (workshop) and *Real Sex 3* (performance), HBO specials, 1992-3.

Video

Rites of Passage, Passion Rltes, 1987.
Portrait of a Porno Star—Inmost Inside Annie Sprinkle, Michelle Auder, 1984.
Deep Deconstruction, Steven Kolpan, 1989.
Current Flow, GMHC, 1989.
Linda/Les & Annie: The First Female to Male Transexual Love Story, Sprinkle Productions, 1991.
The Sluts and Goddesses Video Workshop, or How to Be a Goddess in 101 Easy Steps, Beatty-Sprinkle, 1992.
Temple of Fetus, Kathy High, 1993.

Audio

Sound Suck, Radio Art Foundation, 1979.
Masturbatorium (CD), Touch Music (London), 1990.
Annie Sprinkle in my Dreams (by Steve Rathe and Leslie Peters), New Wilderness Foundation, 1993.
Cyborgasm (CD), Algorythm, 1993.

Jerry Garcia

J. Garcia: Paintings, Drawings, and Prints, Celestial Arts, 1992.

Albums with the Grateful Dead

The Grateful Dead, Warner Brothers, 1967.
Workingman's Dead, Warner Brothers, 1967.
Live/Dead, Warner Brothers, 1969.
America Beauty, Warner Brothers, 1970.
Aoxomoxos, Warner Brothers, 1971.
Vintage Dead, Sunflower, 1971.
Anthem of the Sun, Warner Brothers, 1972.
Wake of the Flood, Grateful Dead, 1973.
Blues for Allah, United Artists, 1975.
Steal Your Face, United Artists, 1976.
Terrapin Station, Arista, 1977.
Shakedown Street, Arista, 1979.
Go to Heaven, Arista, 1980.
Dead Set, Arista, 1981.
In the Dark, Arista, 1987.
Dylan and the Dead, Columbia, 1989.
Built to Last, Arista, 1989.
Without a Net, Arists, 1990.

Solo Albums

Hotteroll?, Douglas, 1971.
Garcia, Warner Brothers, 1972

Live at Keystone, Fantasy, 1973.
Dead Set, Arista, 1981.
Cats Under the Stars, Arista, 1978.
Run for the Roses, Arista, 1982.
Compliments of Garcia, Round, 1974.
Old & in the Way, Round, 1975.
Reflections, Round, 1976.

<u>With the Jerry Garcia Acoustic Band:</u>

Almost Acoustic (Live), G.D.M., 1988.
Jerry Garcia Band (Live), Arista, 1991.
Jerry Garcia/David Grisman, Acoustic Disc, 1991.
Jerry Garcia/David Grismari: Not for Kids Only, Acoustic Disc, 1993.

Jaron Lanier
Instruments of Change, PolyGram, 1994.

Alexander Shulgin
Controlled Substances! Chemical and Legal Guide to the Federal Drug Laws,
    Ronin Pub., 1992.
PIHKAL (with Ann Shulgin), Transform Press, 1991.
TIHKAL (with Ann Shulgin), Transform Press, 1995.

Mathew Fox
BreakThrough: Meister Eckhart's Creation Spirituality in New Translation,
    Doubleday, 1980.
Hildegard of Bingen's Book of Divine Works (editor), Bear & Co., 1987
Illuminations of Hildegard of Bingen (editor), Bear & Co., 1985.
Manifests for a Global Civilization (with Brian Swimme), Bear & Co., 1981.
Meditations with Meister Eckhart, Bear & Co., 1983.
On Becoming a Musical, Mystical Bear: Spirituality American Style, Paulist Pr.,
    1976.
A Spirituality Named Compassion, Harper and Row, 1979.
Western Spirituality: Historical Roots, Ecumenical Routes (editor), Bear & Co.,
    1981.
Whee! We, Wee All the Way Home: A Guide to Sensual, Prophetic Spirituality,
    Bear & Co., 1981.
Original Blessing: A Primer in Creation Spirituality, Bear & Co, 1983.
The Coming of the Cosmic Christ, Harper and Row, 1988.
Creation Spirituality: Liberating Gifts for the Peoples of the Earth, Harper SF,
    1991.
Sheer Joy: Conversations with Thomas Aquinas on Creation Spirituality, Harper
    SF, 1992.
Spirituality of Work, Harper and Row, 1993.

John Allen/Johnny Dolphin

The Collected Works of the Caravan of Dreams, Vol. 1: Gilgamesh, Marouf the Cobbler, Faust: Part One, Synergetic Press, 1983.

The Collected Works of the Caravan of Dreams, Vol. 2: Billy the Kid, Metal Woman, Tin Can Man, Synergetic Press, 1984.

Kabuki Blues (with Corinna MacNeice), Synergetic Press, 1984.

The Biosphere Catalogue (edited with Tango Parrish Snyder), Synergetic Press, 1985.

Thirty-Nine Blows on a Gone Trumpet, Synergetic Press, 1987.

Succeed: A Handbook on Structuring Managerial Thought, Synergetic Press, 1988.

The Dream and Drink of Freedom, Synergetic Press, 1988.

Journeys Around an Extraordinary Planet, Synergetic Press, 1990.

Biosphere 2: The Human Experiment, Viking/Penguin Books, 1991; Wild, Synergetic Press, 1992.

Films

Dark Planet, Caravan of Dreams Productions, 1986.

Ornette: Made in America, Caravan of Dreams Productions, 1987.

Journeys into Other Worlds, Caravan of Dreams Productions, 1987.

Biosphere 2: Life, Earth, Space, and Technology, CD-Rom, IBM's Multi-Media Publishing Group, 1993.

John Robbins

Diet for a New America, Stillpoint Publishing, 1987.

In Search of Balance: Discovering Harmony in a Changing World (with A.Mortifee), HJ Kramer Inc., 1991.

May All Be Fed: Diet for a Now World, Morrow, 1992.

Jean Houston

The Varieties of Psychedelic Experience (with Robert Masters), Holt, Rhinehart & Winston, 1966.

Psychedlic Art (with Robert Masters), Grove Press, 1968.

Mind Games (with Robert Masters), Delacorte, 1973.

Listening to the Body (with Robert Masters), Delacorte, 1979.

The Possible Human, J.P. Tarcher, 1982.

The Search for the Beloved, J.P. Tarcher, 1987.

God Seed, Amity House Inc., 1987.

Soulcycle: The Journey of Odysseus, Amity House Inc., 1988.

Grailquest. The Joumey of Percival, Amity House Inc., 1988.

Godseed: The Journey of Christ, Theos Publishing House, 1992.

The Hero & the Goddess: The Odyssey *as Mystery & Initiation*, Ballantine, 1992.

Life Force: The Psycho-Historical Recovery of the Self, Theos Publishing House, 1993.

Public Like a Frog, Theos Publishing House, 1993.

Elizabeth Gips
Scrapbook of a Haight-Ashbury Pilgrim, Changes Press, 1991.

William Irwin Thompson
The Time Failing Bodies Take to Light, St. Martin's Press, 1981.
Blue Jade from the Morning Star: An Essay & a Cycle of Poems on Quetzalcoati LC 82-84052, Lindisfarne Press, 1983.
Selected Poems, Lindisfarne Press, 1989.
At the Edge of History & Passages about Earth, Morningtown, 1989.
Islands Out of Time: A Memoir of the Last Days of Atlantis, Bear & Co., 1990.
Imaginary Landscape: Making Worlds of Myth & Science, St. Martin, 1990.
Gaia Two: Emergence: The New Science of Becoming (editor), Lindisfarne Press, 1991
American Replacement of Nature, Doubleday, 1991.

Francis Jeffrey
"Working in Isolation: States that Alter Consensu," *Handbook for States of Consciousness* (anthology edited by B. Wolman & M. Ullman), Von Nostrand Reinhold, 1986.
John Lilly, So Far, J.P. Tarcher, 1990.

Ram Dass/Richard Alpert
Identification and Child Rearing (with R. Sears and L. Rau), Stanford University Press, 1962.
The Psychedelic Experience: A Manual Based on the Tibetan Book of the Dead, (with T. Leary & R. Metzner), University Books, 1964.
LSD (with S. Cohen and L. Shiller), New American Library, 1966.
Be Here Now, Lama Foundation, 1971.
The Only Dance There Is, Anchor-Doubleday, 1974.
Grist for the Mill (with S. Levine), Celestial Arts, 1977.
Journey Of Awakening, Bantam Books, 1978.
Miracle of Love: Stories about Neem Karoli Baba, E.P. Dutton, 1979.
How Can I Help? (with P. Gorman), Alfred A. Knopf, New York, 1985.
Compassion in Action (with Mirabai Bush), Bell Tower, New York, 1992.

Addresses

Marija Gimbutas's archives are located at:
The Pacifica Graduate Institute
249 Lambert Road
Carpinteria, CA 93013
(805) 969-3626 ext. 118

For more information regarding *John Robbins'* organization to "help society's transition toward a substainable plant-based diet" write:
EarthSave Foundation
706 Frederick Street
Santa Cruz, CA 95062
(408) 423-4069

To find out more about *John Allen's* biospheres write:
Cyberspheres, Inc.
32038 Caminito Quieto
Bonsal, CA 92003

Publications by *Alexander and Ann Shulgin* are available through:
Transform Press
P.O. Box 13675
Berkeley, CA 94701

For *Ram Dass's* teaching schedule and a catalog of his books and tapes write:
The Hanuman Foundation
524 San Anselmo Avenue, Suite 203
San Anselmo, CA 94960
(415) 453-5111

Annie Sprinkle is managed by:
Carrellas & Cooper
240 West 44th Street
NY, NY 10036
Phone: (212) 768-2866

Ms. Sprinkle's art work is represented by:
Torch Gallery Amsterdam
Lauriergracht 94
1016RN Amsterdam, Holland
31-20-6260284

Tapes and books by *Elizabeth Gips* can be obtained through:
Changes
P.O. Box 7305
Santa Cruz, CA 95061-7305

To find out more about *Francis Jeffrey's* organization to help dolphins and whales write:
Great Whales Foundation
111 Hancock Street
San Francisco, CA 94114

BodyPlay magazine and *Fakir Musafar's* School of Professional Body Piercing can be reached through:
Insight Books
P.O. Box 2575
Menlo Park, CA 94026-2575
(415) 324-0543

Videotapes of events hosted by *David Brown* and *Rebecca McClen Novick* are available through:
Sound Photosynthesis
P.O. Box 2111
Mill Valley, CA 94942-2111
(415) 383-6712

David Jay Brown and
Rebecca McClen Novick
can be reached through:
Brainchild Productions
P.O. Box 1082
Ben Lomond, CA 95005
E-mail: dajabr@well.sf.ca.us

David Jay Brown is the author of the science fiction novel Brainchild *(New Falcon Publications, 1988) and co-author with Rebecca McClen Novick of* Mavericks of the Mind *(Crossing Press, 1993). David holds an M.A. degree from New York University in psychology (1986) and completed a year of post-degree work in the University of Southern California's behavioral neuroscience doctoral program (1990). He has worked as a psychiatric counselor, a neuroscience researcher, and he writes regularly for many national magazines on the interface between high technology and the mind. David lives high in the Santa Cruz Mountains of California, where he is currently at work on three books:* Uses of Adversity, *a book with Oscar Janiger about how a large number of culturally innovative people have gained inspiration from chronic illness;* Storming Eden, *a book with Abigail Alling on the Biosphere 2 project; and* Virus, *a science fiction novel about someone with multiple personality disorder who becomes infected with an alien virus. He can be reached via E-mail at: dajabr@well.sf.ca.us.*

Ronny Novick

Rebecca McClen Novick is a writer and poet. Born in England, she now lives in the foothills of the Santa Monica Mountains with her husband and other animals.

The Crossing Press
publishes a full selection of titles of
general interest. To receive our current
catalog, please call toll-free,
800-777-1048